CSWE EPAS 2008 Core Competencies

Professional Identity

2.1.1 Identify as a professional social worker and conduct oneself accordingly.

Necessary Knowledge, Values, Skills

- Social workers serve as representatives of the profession, its mission, and its core values.
- Social workers know the profession's history.
- Social workers commit themselves to the profession's enhancement and to their own professional conduct and growth.

Operational Practice Behaviors

- Social workers advocate for client access to the services of social work;
- Social workers practice personal reflection and self-correction to assure continual professional development;
- Social workers attend to professional roles and boundaries;
- Social workers demonstrate professional demeanor in behavior, appearance, and communication;
- Social workers engage in career-long learning; and
- Social workers use supervision and consultation.

Ethical Practice

2.1.2 Apply social work ethical principles to guide professional practice.

Necessary Knowledge, Values, Skills

- Social workers have an obligation to conduct themselves ethically and engage in ethical decision-making.
- Social workers are knowledgeable about the value base of the profession, its ethical standards, and relevant law.

Operational Practice Behaviors

- Social workers recognize and manage personal values in a way that allows professional values to guide practice;
- Social workers make ethical decisions by applying standards of the National Association of Social Workers Code of Ethics and, as applicable, of the International Federation of Social Workers/International Association of Schools of Social Work Ethics in Social Work, Statement of Principles;
- Social workers tolerate ambiguity in resolving ethical conflicts; and
- Social workers apply strategies of ethical reasoning to arrive at principled decisions.

Critical Thinking

2.1.3 Apply critical thinking to inform and communicate professional judgments.

Necessary Knowledge, Values, Skills

- Social workers are knowledgeable about the principles of logic, scientific inquiry, and reasoned discernment.
- They use critical thinking augmented by creativity and curiosity.
- Critical thinking also requires the synthesis and communication of relevant information.

Operational Practice Behaviors

- Social workers distinguish, appraise, and integrate multiple sources of knowledge, including research-based knowledge, and practice wisdom;
- Social workers analyze models of assessment, prevention, intervention, and evaluation; and
- Social workers demonstrate effective oral and written communication in working with individuals, families, groups, organizations, communities, and colleagues.

Adapted with the permission of Council on Social Work Education

Diversity in Practice

2.1.4 Engage diversity and difference in practice.

Necessary Knowledge, Values, Skills

- Social workers understand how diversity characterizes and shapes the human experience and is critical to the formation of identity.
- The dimensions of diversity are understood as the intersectionality of multiple factors including age, class, color, culture, disability, ethnicity, gender, gender identity and expression, immigration status, political ideology, race, religion, sex, and sexual orientation.
- Social workers appreciate that, as a consequence of difference, a person's life experiences may include oppression, poverty, marginalization, and alienation as well as privilege, power, and acclaim.

Operational Practice Behaviors

- Social workers recognize the extent to which a culture's structures and values may oppress, marginalize, alienate, or create or enhance privilege and power;
- Social workers gain sufficient self-awareness to eliminate the influence of personal biases and values in working with diverse groups;
- Social workers recognize and communicate their understanding of the importance of difference in shaping life experiences; and
- Social workers view themselves as learners and engage those with whom they work as informants.

Human Rights & Justice

2.1.5 Advance human rights and social and economic justice.

Necessary Knowledge, Values, Skills

- Each person, regardless of position in society, has basic human rights, such as freedom, safety, privacy, an adequate standard of living, health care, and education.
- Social workers recognize the global interconnections of oppression and are knowledgeable about theories of justice and strategies to promote human and civil rights.
- Social work incorporates social justice practices in organizations, institutions, and society to ensure that these basic human rights are distributed equitably and without prejudice.

Operational Practice Behaviors

- Social workers understand the forms and mechanisms of oppression and discrimination;
- Social workers advocate for human rights and social and economic justice; and
- Social workers engage in practices that advance social and economic justice.

Research Based Practice

2.1.6 Engage in research-informed practice and practice-informed research.

Necessary Knowledge, Values, Skills

- Social workers use practice experience to inform research, employ evidence-based interventions, evaluate their own practice, and use research findings to improve practice, policy, and social service delivery.
- Social workers comprehend quantitative and qualitative research and understand scientific and ethical approaches to building knowledge.

Operational Practice Behaviors

- Social workers use practice experience to inform scientific inquiry; and
- Social workers use research evidence to inform practice.

Human Behavior

2.1.7 Apply knowledge of human behavior and the social environment.

Necessary Knowledge, Values, Skills

- Social workers are knowledgeable about human behavior across the life course; the range of social systems in which people live; and the ways social systems promote or deter people in maintaining or achieving health and well-being.
- Social workers apply theories and knowledge from the liberal arts to understand biological, social, cultural, psychological, and spiritual development.

Operational Practice Behaviors

- Social workers utilize conceptual frameworks to guide the processes of assessment, intervention, and evaluation; and
- Social workers critique and apply knowledge to understand person and environment.

Policy Practice   2.1.8 Engage in policy practice to advance social and economic well-being and to deliver effective social work services.

Necessary Knowledge, Values, Skills

- Social work practitioners understand that policy affects service delivery and they actively engage in policy practice.
- Social workers know the history and current structures of social policies and services; the role of policy in service delivery; and the role of practice in policy development.

Operational Practice Behaviors

- Social workers analyze, formulate, and advocate for policies that advance social well-being; and
- Social workers collaborate with colleagues and clients for effective policy action.

Practice Contexts

2.1.9 Respond to contexts that shape practice.

Necessary Knowledge, Values, Skills

- Social workers are informed, resourceful, and proactive in responding to evolving organizational, community, and societal contexts at all levels of practice.
- Social workers recognize that the context of practice is dynamic, and use knowledge and skill to respond proactively.

Operational Practice Behaviors

- Social workers continuously discover, appraise, and attend to changing locales, populations, scientific and technological developments, and emerging societal trends to provide relevant services; and
- Social workers provide leadership in promoting sustainable changes in service delivery and practice to improve the quality of social services.

Engage, Assess, Intervene, Evaluate   2.1.10 Engage, assess, intervene, and evaluate with individuals, families, groups, organizations, and communities.

Necessary Knowledge, Values, Skills

- Professional practice involves the dynamic and interactive processes of engagement, assessment, intervention, and evaluation at multiple levels.
- Social workers have the knowledge and skills to practice with individuals, families, groups, organizations, and communities.
- Practice knowledge includes
  - identifying, analyzing, and implementing evidence-based interventions designed to achieve client goals;
  - using research and technological advances;
  - evaluating program outcomes and practice effectiveness;
  - developing, analyzing, advocating, and providing leadership for policies and services; and
  - promoting social and economic justice.

Operational Practice Behaviors

(a) Engagement

- Social workers substantively and affectively prepare for action with individuals, families, groups, organizations, and communities;
- Social workers use empathy and other interpersonal skills; and
- Social workers develop a mutually agreed-on focus of work and desired outcomes.

(b) Assessment

- Social workers collect, organize, and interpret client data;
- Social workers assess client strengths and limitations;
- Social workers develop mutually agreed-on intervention goals and objectives; and
- Social workers select appropriate intervention strategies.

(c) Intervention

- Social workers initiate actions to achieve organizational goals;
- Social workers implement prevention interventions that enhance client capacities;
- Social workers help clients resolve problems;
- Social workers negotiate, mediate, and advocate for clients; and
- Social workers facilitate transitions and endings.

(d) Evaluation

- Social workers critically analyze, monitor, and evaluate interventions.

Practice Behavior	Chapter
Professional Identity (2.1.1)	
Social workers advocate for client access to the services of social work;	8
Social workers practice personal reflection and self-correction to assure continual professional development;	10
Social workers attend to professional roles and boundaries;	7
Social workers demonstrate professional demeanor in behavior, appearance, and communication;	
Social workers engage in career-long learning;	
Social workers use supervision and consultation.	7
Ethical Practice (2.1.2)	
Social workers recognize and manage personal values in a way that allows professional values to guide practice	1, 8
Social workers make ethical decisions by applying standards of the National Association of Social Workers Code of Ethics and, as applicable, of the International Federation of Social Workers/International Association of Schools of Social Work Ethics in Social Work, Statement of Principles	9
Social workers tolerate ambiguity in resolving ethical conflicts	3
Social workers apply strategies of ethical reasoning to arrive at principled decisions	
Critical Thinking (2.1.3)	
Social workers distinguish, appraise, and integrate multiple sources of knowledge, including research-based knowledge, and practice wisdom	4
Social workers analyze models of assessment, prevention, intervention, and evaluation	4, 9
Social workers demonstrate effective oral and written communication in working with individuals, families, groups, organizations, communities, and colleagues	
Diversity in Practice (2.1.4)	
Social workers recognize the extent to which a culture's structures and values may oppress, marginalize, alienate, or create or enhance privilege and power	1, 2, 4, 6, 7, 8
Social workers gain sufficient self-awareness to eliminate the influence of personal biases and values in working with diverse groups	1
Social workers recognize and communicate their understanding of the importance of difference in shaping life experiences	2, 4, 6
Social workers view themselves as learners and engage those with whom they work as informants	1, 7
Human Rights & Justice (2.1.5)	
Social workers understand the forms and mechanisms of oppression and discrimination	1, 2, 5, 9
Social workers advocate for human rights and social and economic justice	6
Social workers engage in practices that advance social and economic justice	1, 10

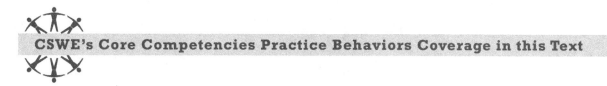

Practice Behavior	Chapter
Research Based Practice (2.1.6)	
Social workers use practice experience to inform scientific inquiry	2
Social workers use research evidence to inform practice	2
Human Behavior (2.1.7)	
Social workers utilize conceptual frameworks to guide the processes of assessment, intervention, and evaluation	1, 3, 5, 7
Social workers critique and apply knowledge to understand person and environment.	1, 3, 5, 6
Policy Practice (2.1.8)	
Social workers analyze, formulate, and advocate for policies that advance social well-being	5, 6, 8, 9
Social workers collaborate with colleagues and clients for effective policy action	9
Practice Contexts (2.1.9)	
Social workers continuously discover, appraise, and attend to changing locales, populations, scientific and technological developments, and emerging societal trends to provide relevant services	1, 5, 7
Social workers provide leadership in promoting sustainable changes in service delivery and practice to improve the quality of social services	7
Engage, Assess Intervene, Evaluate (2.1.10 (a)–(d))	
A) ENGAGEMENT	
Social workers substantively and effectively prepare for action with individuals, families, groups, organizations, and communities	1, 3, 5, 6
Social workers use empathy and other interpersonal skills	
Social workers develop a mutually agreed-on focus of work and desired outcomes	7
B) ASSESSMENT	
Social workers collect, organize, and interpret client data	1, 4
Social workers assess client strengths and limitations	1, 2, 4, 5, 6
Social workers develop mutually agreed-on intervention goals and objectives	
Social workers select appropriate intervention strategies	
C) INTERVENTION	
Social workers initiate actions to achieve organizational goals	
Social workers implement prevention interventions that enhance client capacities	
Social workers help clients resolve problems	
Social workers negotiate, mediate, and advocate for clients	
Social workers facilitate transitions and endings	
D) EVALUATION	
Social workers critically analyze, monitor, and evaluate interventions	

CONNECTING CORE COMPETENCIES **Chapter-by-Chapter Matrix**

Chapter	Professional Identity	Ethical Practice	Critical Thinking	Diversity in Practice	Human Rights & Justice	Research Based Practice	Human Behavior	Policy Practice	Practice Contexts	Engage Assess Intervene Evaluate
1			✔	✔		✔				✔
2	✔	✔		✔		✔				
3		✔	✔	✔		✔				
4			✔	✔		✔				✔
5			✔			✔				✔
6		✔	✔	✔		✔				
7		✔	✔			✔				✔
8		✔		✔	✔	✔				
9		✔	✔	✔		✔				
10		✔		✔		✔				✔
11		✔		✔		✔				✔
12		✔	✔			✔				✔
13			✔			✔		✔		✔
14	✔	✔				✔				✔
Total Chapters	2	10	9	9	1	14	0	1	0	9

Research Methods for Social Workers

Bonnie L. Yegidis
University of South Florida

Robert W. Weinbach
University of South Carolina

Laura L. Myers
Florida A&M University

Allyn & Bacon

Boston   Columbus   Indianapolis   New York   San Francisco   Upper Saddle River
Amsterdam   Cape Town   Dubai   London   Madrid   Milan   Munich   Paris   Montreal   Toronto
Delhi   Mexico City   Sao Paulo   Sydney   Hong Kong   Seoul   Singapore   Taipei   Tokyo

Editor in Chief: Dickson Musslewhite
Executive Editor: Ashley Dodge
Editorial Product Manager: Carly Czech
Executive Marketing Director: Jeanette Koskinas
Senior Marketing Manager: Wendy Albert
Marketing Assistant: Craig Deming
Production Manager: Pat Brown
Interior Design: Joyce Weston Design

Media Editor: Thomas Scalzo
Cover Art Director: Jayne Conte
Cover Designer: Karen Salzbach
Cover Photo: Don Farrall/Getty Images, Inc.
Full-Service Project Management/Composition:
  Paul Smith/PreMediaGlobal
Printer/Binder: RR Donnelley
Cover printer: RR Donnelley

Credits appear on Page 329, which constitutes an extension of the copyright page.

Library of Congress Cataloging-in-Publication Data

Yegidis, Bonnie L.
  Research methods for social workers / Bonnie L. Yegidis, Robert W. Weinbach, Laura L. Myers.—7th ed.
    p. cm.
  Includes bibliographical references and index.
  ISBN-13: 978-0-205-82011-5 (alk. paper)
  ISBN-10: 0-205-82011-5 (alk. paper)
  1. Social service—Research—Methodology.   I. Weinbach, Robert W.   II. Myers, Laura L.   III. Title.
  HV11.Y43 2011
  361.3'2072—dc22

                                                                              2010054453

8 9 10 11 12 VOUD 20 19 18 17 16

                                                        Student Edition:
                                                        ISBN-10: 0-205-82011-5
                                                        ISBN-13: 978-0-205-82011-5

                                                        Instructor Edition:
                                                        ISBN-10: 0-205-02254-5
                                                        ISBN-13: 978-0-205-02254-0

**Allyn & Bacon
is an imprint of**

www.pearsonhighered.com

                                                        à la Carte Edition:
                                                        ISBN-10: 0-205-02276-6
                                                        ISBN-13: 978-0-205-02276-2

Contents

Preface

Social work practice continues to evolve. Research, now an integral part of practice, is changing along with it. In this edition of *Research Methods for Social Workers,* we have attempted to retain those features that faculty and students told us they liked. At the same time, we have added new material to address the needs of today's students of research and of those conscientious practitioners who aspire to be critical consumers of research reports.

What Can the Reader Expect to Find?

Like the previous editions, this book is designed for a one-semester or one-quarter course on research methods. It is well suited to either undergraduate or foundation-level graduate social work courses. Its content is consistent with both current Council on Social Work Education (CSWE) accreditation standards and curriculum policy guidelines. This book offers a brief conceptual overview of such specialized topics as statistical analysis and evaluation research, and encourages its readers to seek a more in-depth coverage of them.

The book is written for both current and future social work practitioners to assist them in becoming evidence-based practitioners. It presents research as a logical, nonintimidating activity that is inextricably linked to social work practice.

This book contains no unnecessary research terminology or references to obscure, rarely used methods of knowledge building. Necessary terminology is italicized and explained. Students, even those with no prior research background, should find the text interesting and easy to understand. It is written in a crisp, straightforward style and refers to contemporary social work practice on virtually every page. Examples are real—the kind of situations that social workers encounter every day.

Our belief that the knowledge, values, and skills of the social worker are much more of an asset than a liability in conducting research permeates the book. We do not take the approach that research is a "necessary evil" to be grudgingly studied and conducted. It is a logical extension of good practice and absolutely essential to it. Thus, the areas that are given a disproportional amount of attention (relative to other texts) reflect this orientation. For example, tasks such as problem identification and formulation, question selection, and use of existing knowledge receive extensive coverage. Are these not also important tasks in good social work practice intervention? Research design—the rich array of alternatives available to do the job of acquiring knowledge to inform our practice decision making—is also discussed in detail.

Over the years, we have come to believe that many research texts create a false dichotomy by describing research as either quantitative or qualitative. We have tried to emphasize that, while some research methods are clearly predominantly one type of research or the other, most research studies today have elements of both. Researchers conducting predominantly qualitative research now attempt to quantify their research data to the degree possible; those conducting more quantitative studies often attempt to verify and expand on their findings using qualitative methods. We have divided research methods into three chapters in this new edition. Chapter 6 covers the group research methods generally associated with more quantitative research studies. Chapter 7 looks at the single-system evaluation method used by social work practitioners to evaluate their practice with individuals, families, schools, communities, and so forth. We decided to devote a separate chapter to qualitative research methods in this edition. Chapter 8 looks at several research methodologies that are most often used to conduct more qualitative studies. We continue to believe that qualitative and quantitative research methodologies are mutually supportive and of equal importance in knowledge building for our profession. This belief is reflected in every chapter of this book.

Connecting Core Competencies Series

The new edition of this text is now a part of Pearson Education's new *Connecting Core Competencies* series, which consists of foundation-level texts that make it easier than ever to ensure students' success in learning the ten core competencies as stated in 2008 by the Council on Social Worker Education. This text contains the following:

- ▶ **Core competency icons** throughout the chapters, directly linking the CSWE core competencies to the content of the text.
- ▶ **Critical thinking questions** are also included to further students' mastery of the CSWE's standards. Page vi displays, for easy reference, which icons are used in each chapter, in a chapter-by-chapter matrix.
- ▶ **End-of-chapter practice tests**, with multiple-choice questions that test students' knowledge of the chapter content and mastery of the competencies.
- ▶ **Additional questions pertaining to the videos and case studies found on the new MySocialWorkLab** at the end of each chapter to encourage students to access the site and explore the wealth of available materials. If this text did not come with an access code for MySocialWorkLab, you can purchase access at www.mysocialworklab.com.

Acknowledgments

Sherry Edwards, University of North Carolina at Pembroke; Roselle Scaggs, Edinboro University of Pennsylvania; and Makeba Green, Bowie State University, reviewed this edition and recommended changes. We are also indebted to a number of colleagues who critiqued the earlier editions of this book and made many valuable suggestions. They are Gordon Casebolt, Felix Rivera, Murray Newman, Ram Cnann, Miriam Johnson, James Stafford, Gail Leedy, Stephen M. Marson, Donald S. Pierson, Freddie Avant, John D. Clapp, Sophie Dziegielewski, Gary Widrick, and Bruce Thyer. We greatly appreciate their input and have responded to their helpful suggestions whenever possible. Students who used the previous edition and faculty who adopted it for classroom use also were generous with their comments and suggestions.

A colleague and new coauthor, Dr. Laura Myers, has joined us for this edition of the book. Dr. Myers is currently the BSW Program Director and teaches undergraduate social work students at Florida A&M University. She has brought new energy and new perspectives to the book based on a great deal of teaching and research experience. Her many contributions to the seventh edition of *Research Methods for Social Workers* enrich every chapter.

BONNIE L. YEGIDIS
University of South Florida

ROBERT W. WEINBACH
University of South Carolina

LAURA L. MYERS
Florida A&M University

Toward Evidence-Based Practice

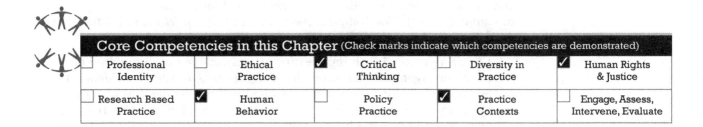

Core Competencies in this Chapter (Check marks indicate which competencies are demonstrated)				
Professional Identity	Ethical Practice	✓ Critical Thinking	Diversity in Practice	✓ Human Rights & Justice
Research Based Practice	✓ Human Behavior	Policy Practice	✓ Practice Contexts	Engage, Assess, Intervene, Evaluate

Social workers must make many decisions every day. Good, informed decisions require knowledge.

What are the sources of our knowledge? Some of it is acquired through formal education in bachelors' and masters' programs in social work, or from attending continuing education programs. It may come from reading articles in professional journals, textbooks, or through online searches. It may also come from senior-level practitioners who have been successful social workers for many years. Historically, much of the knowledge derived from these sources has had one characteristic in common—it may *not* have been derived from research! However, this is changing.

The Council on Social Work Education (CSWE), the organization responsible for the accreditation of BSW and MSW programs, recognizes the importance of research content in social work curricula. The Educational Policy and Accreditation Standards (EPAS) (Council on Social Work Education, 2008) specify that research content and skills must be taught in both undergraduate and graduate social work education programs. Standard 2.1.6 maintains that social workers

- use practice experience to inform research,
- employ evidence-based interventions,
- evaluate their own practice,
- use research findings to improve practice, policy, and social service delivery,
- comprehend quantitative and qualitative research, and
- understand scientific and ethical approaches to building knowledge.

These standards form the basis for what we have chosen to include in this book. By teaching students the best ways to conduct research, we hope that they will be equipped to acquire the knowledge needed for making good, informed decisions in whatever social system level they may work. However, understanding how research should be conducted has a second benefit—it allows social workers to critically and knowledgeably evaluate the research methods of others and, thus, assess the credibility of the findings and recommendations that they generate.

Knowledge of research makes possible a methodology that has been widely discussed and advocated: evidence-based practice (EBP). EBP is a process designed to help social workers make important decisions regarding the care they provide their clients. This model originated in the field of medicine in the early 1990s and has since been adopted in a wide array of health and human service disciplines. The primary source document for learning about EBP is a slim volume by Strauss, Richardson, Glasziou, and Haynes (2005), and it defines EBP as "the integration of the best research evidence with our clinical expertise, and our patient's unique values and circumstances" (p. 1). A related definition is found in Guyatt and Rennie (2002): "The conscientious, explicit, and judicious use of current best evidence in making decisions about the care of individual patients. The practice of EBP requires integration of individual clinical expertise and patient preferences with the best available clinical evidence from systematic research" (p. 412). The National Association of Social Workers (2010) offers a definition of EBT as it relates to the broad field of social work:

> EBT is a process involving creating an answerable question based on a client or organizational need, locating the best available evidence to answer the question, evaluating the quality of the evidence as well as its applicability, applying the evidence, and evaluating the effectiveness and efficiency of the solution. EBP is a process in which the practitioner

combines well-researched interventions with clinical experience, ethics, client preferences, and culture to guide and inform the delivery of treatments and services.

EBT practices often relate to the services that social workers offer, for example, the choice of a method of intervention or the design of a social program. However, EBP is also applicable to other types of decisions that social workers make, for example, selecting the best diagnostic tool for defining a client problem, making management decisions, or making decisions relating to the design of a needs assessment or an outcome evaluation of a social program.

EBP is not just reliance on reports of research studies for decision making, although it is an important feature of EBP. If decision making were based entirely on EBP, it would result in problems. For one thing, such decision making practices would not take into consideration our own uniqueness as practitioners, who we are, and what we do well and not so well. It would also not factor in professional ethics or professional values, for example, the right of clients to be involved in decision making that affects them. Thus, EBP entails a careful consideration of (1) what the best research on the question has suggested; (2) our own practice experience and expertise; and (3) the values and preferences of the clients we serve.

How might this work? Suppose a medical social worker is assigned to work with the parents of a 9-year-old boy who has a diagnosis of acute leukemia. She knows (from medical knowledge acquired through research and the knowledge of the boy's specific situation) that he has a very small probability of surviving more than a few weeks without a bone marrow transplant. She also knows (from the same sources) that the likelihood of a successful transplant is quite low. Her practice experience reminds her that if the transplant is unsuccessful, his suffering is likely to be worse than if he never had the transplant. She has seen it happen before and it has been stressful for all concerned. Ethically, she recognizes the need for the parents and the child, to the degree possible, to be involved in the decision to have or not have the transplant. She feels an ethical responsibility to inform the parents of how the transplant could result in worse suffering and death for their child. As a caring and concerned social worker, she feels compassion for the child and his parents. This will influence her behavior as well. She cannot and should not make the decision for them, but she understands that they will look to her for help in making it (and probably seek her advice) and require her support for whatever decision they make. In EBP, how she ultimately presents the options to them (her intervention) will be determined by the combination of all of these factors.

EBP entails a careful consideration of (1) what the best research on the question has suggested; (2) our own practice experience and expertise; and (3) the values and preferences of the clients we serve.

HISTORICAL ANTECEDENTS

Historically, social workers have not always emphasized the importance of research knowledge for practice decision making as much as have other professionals. In 1979, a sociologist, Simpson, shared his perceptions of social work practitioners and their relationship with research. He noted that practitioners tend to shun abstract knowledge and to rely instead on (1) humanitarian impulse, (2) occupational folklore, and (3) common sense. He also observed that most of the knowledge that is used for practice decision making is drawn from the work of researchers in other fields. He went on to describe social work literature as permeated with faddism and lacking an empirical base.

Human Behavior

Critical Thinking Question: What are three factors the social worker might consider when deciding how to discuss the treatment options with the patient and his parents?

At the same time, leaders in the social work profession expressed concern over practitioners' reluctance to rely on scientific research knowledge for practice decision making. During the late 1970s, both the Council on Social Work Education and the National Association of Social Workers (NASW) devoted considerable effort to examining the problem of research utilization. They convened groups of leading practitioners and researchers to study it. They tried to determine, for example, why social work practitioners rarely read reports of research in their professional literature, and why they tended to ignore those research findings that reflected unfavorably on their current practice methods. They concluded that responsibility for the gap between practice and research must be shared by both practitioners and researchers, and that both groups must work toward closing the gap.

Practitioners in the groups convened described their distrust of researchers and much of the knowledge that they generated. They viewed researchers, most of whom historically have been academicians, as people who did not really understand the realities of social work practice. Researchers were perceived as more interested in conducting esoteric research to enhance their careers than in producing knowledge that might inform practice. In addition, they tended to present their research findings in a form that few practitioners could understand and apply to their work.

In response, the researchers described their frustration with many practitioners' lack of research knowledge and general lack of interest in research. They cited a tendency of practitioners to reject those research findings that did not agree with what they "knew" to be true, and to assume falsely that research knowledge was too abstract to be of value to them.

In an effort to resolve some of the tension between practice and research and to increase research utilization, Kirk (1979) proposed four objectives for research in social work:

1. **Research findings should be practice relevant.** The goal of research should be to inform practice.

2. **Specific applications to practice should be contained in research reports.** In the past, many researchers neglected this condition, allowing findings to speak for themselves. But the reality is that research findings often speak less than eloquently, if at all, to social work practitioners if the practitioners lack skill in interpreting the findings. Researchers need to describe their findings in simple, straightforward terms.

3. **Research findings should be disseminated effectively.** A practitioner cannot use information that he or she has never seen or heard. Although professional journals continue to be a primary vehicle for knowledge dissemination, they are certainly not the only one. Other ways to share research findings include seminars and workshops, staff newsletters, audio- and videotapes or CD-ROMs of research presentations, and the Internet.

4. **Practitioners should possess both the skill and the incentive to assess and to change their practice behaviors based on research knowledge.** In order to achieve this, social workers must possess a knowledge of scientific concepts and procedures that will allow them to evaluate critically the research methods and findings of others. This implies a capacity to read between the lines in order to determine whether research findings were obtained using those methods that

give the researcher's conclusions credibility. Social workers should be able to recognize the difference between sound, ethical research and that which contains findings and recommendations that are suspect because the research was methodologically flawed. (p. 12)

Of course, it was pointed out, the incentive to change social workers' practice on the basis of emerging research knowledge must evolve from several sources. First, practitioners must have the knowledge and understanding of scientific methods required to gain an appreciation of them. If they learn to appreciate the rigor that is built into well-designed research, practitioners are more likely to believe in and value the findings that are produced. They also will be more likely to distrust the conclusions and recommendations of the researcher whose methods are flawed.

In addition, it was suggested, practitioners will rely more heavily on research only if there is an expectation of reward for this behavior. For example, they may ask, "Is there more reward for practice based upon research findings or for doing things the way they have always been done? Will there be support for conscientiously evaluating our practice effectiveness, or will it be viewed by others as time that could be better spent in other ways? Will we be encouraged to attend professional conferences where research knowledge is disseminated or to read and discuss professional journal articles with colleagues, or will this be viewed as more time wasted?" Therefore, we may conclude that practitioners require support at all levels of human service organizations to effectively use research findings for decision making.

Practitioners require support at all levels of human service organizations to effectively use research findings for decision making.

Over the years, the need to bring social work practice and research closer together has produced a wide variety of conceptual models. One was proposed by Scott Briar (1979); he called it "the clinical scientist." In this model, social workers have many similarities to that of the professionals social workers have often tried to emulate, physicians. Briar's model reflects a realistic understanding that social workers are unlikely to have at their disposal the amount of cause-effect knowledge that may be available to physicians. Clinical scientists, as conceptualized by Briar, would

Practice Contexts

Critical Thinking Question: What are three things that administrators could do to encourage social work practitioners to use research findings in making their practice decisions?

- ▶ use with clients the practice methods and techniques that are known empirically to be most effective.
- ▶ continuously and rigorously evaluate their own practice.
- ▶ participate in the discovery, testing, and reporting of more effective ways of helping.
- ▶ use untested, unvalidated practice methods and techniques cautiously and only with adequate control, evaluation, and attention to client rights.
- ▶ communicate the results of evaluations of practice to others.
  (pp. 132–133)

In 1981, Garvin conceptualized three overlapping research roles that the social work practitioner can play: (1) consumer of research, (2) creator and disseminator of knowledge, and (3) contributing partner. In performing the first role, the practitioner has a professional obligation to seek, evaluate, and use, when appropriate, the research knowledge that is generated by others. The second role implies an obligation to be directly involved in doing research and to share the results of one's own research with others. This role is recognition that there is a wealth of untapped knowledge that exists within the practice milieu, which can be systematically collected, organized, and shared for the benefit of other practitioners. The third role, that of contributing partner, recognizes that not all social workers may have the knowledge or interest necessary to under-take large-scale research projects. But this does not preclude their making contributions to the research efforts of others. Specifically, they can participate in some of the necessary tasks of the research process, such as identifying researchable problems or providing data for evaluation of social programs.

The 1990s saw important refinements in our understanding of what should constitute the relationship between research and practice and thus moved us closer to our current understanding of EBP. The arrival of two professional journals—*Social Work Research* and *Research on Social Work Practice*—emphasized the publication of outcome research and encouraged social work's move to a more accountable era. The creation of the Institute for the Advancement of Social Work Research (IASWR) and the Society for Social Work Research (SSWR) was yet another indication that the gap between practice and research was narrowing. SSWR hosts a well-attended annual conference in which a wide variety of research findings have been disseminated.

At about the same time, a dramatic increase in the number of social work doctoral programs occurred. This meant that, at least potentially, more social workers would be educated and trained in advanced social work research methods. They, in turn, could assume teaching roles, replacing educators who, all too frequently, had not received much education in research methods or who had received it in fields such as sociology or behavioral psychology and sometimes struggled to adapt it to the realities of social work practice.

Also during this time, the *scientist-practitioner model* gained acceptance and became a major influence on social work education and practice. The model, developed as a training program for psychologists, trained and encouraged practitioners to adhere to scientific methods, procedures, and research to guide their practice. Gelso and Lent (2000) offer a synopsis of the scientist-practitioner model, stating that "ultimately, our science and practice will be enhanced by helping our student learn how scholarly work can be done in the context of practice and practice settings" (p. 135). A central premise of the model is that social work practice should closely resemble scientific research. However, in 1996, Wakefield and Kirk cast doubt upon the model's value, suggesting that social work practitioners have not been (and probably cannot be) simultaneously both practitioners and researchers, regularly conducting research to make their practice more effective. The authors contend that there should continue to be a division of labor, with researchers continuing to take the major responsibility for determining which practice methods are most effective and practitioners conscientiously using the findings of research in making informed practice decisions—EBP.

Later in the 1990s, a number of events and developments combined to move us to where we are today—to recognition of the importance of EBP. On a broad level, the demands for accountability that began several decades earlier continued to increase. Funding organizations, the general public, and individual stakeholders increased demands for accountability, specifically for proof that social programs and services demonstrate both their effectiveness and efficiency. More studies were conducted, and their findings (viewed collectively) began to suggest which interventions work and, just as important, which do not.

Clearly the most effective way for practitioners and researchers to work together to identify evidence-based treatments and services is still a debated issue in the field of social work. One type of researcher-practitioner relationship that has emerged is the university-community research partnership. These partnerships encourage research collaboration between the university researchers and the community practitioners and help both to achieve their goals. A recent article (Begun, Berger, Otto-Salaj, & Rose, 2010) looks at the development of these partnerships and offers "a set of strategies for building and sustaining research collaborations between university and community-based social work professionals" (p. 54).

EVIDENCE-BASED PRACTICE

We have looked at the current definitions of EBP; now let us turn to a more detailed discussion of the process of evidence-based practice. EBP consists of a five-step process (Strauss et al., 2005, pp. 3–4):

Clearly the most effective way for practitioners and researchers to work together to identify evidence-based treatments and services is still a debated issue in the field of social work.

1. **Step 1.** Convert our need for information about the causes of the problem, and for possible interventions, into an answerable question.
2. **Step 2.** Track down the best evidence with which to answer that question.
3. **Step 3.** Critically appraise that evidence for its validity, impact, and applicability.
4. **Step 4.** Integrate the critical appraisal with our clinical expertise and the client's unique values and circumstances.
5. **Step 5.** Evaluate our effectiveness and efficiency in carrying out steps 1–4 and seek ways to improve our practice.

A considerable literature, both within and outside the field of social work, is available that focuses on each of these steps. An excellent resource for understanding EBP is the *Social Worker's Desk Reference* (Roberts, 2009). Gambrill and Gibbs (2009) describe effective ways to develop well-structured questions (related to step 1 of EBP). These questions typically contain four parts, the *population* of clients (P), the *intervention* of concern (I), what the intervention may be *compared* to (C), and hoped for *outcomes* (O). Some examples of PICO questions include "How do persons with obsessive-compulsive disorder fare after being treated with exposure therapy and response prevention, compared to similar clients who are not treated at all?" or "How do clients receiving TANF benefits who also receive a job-finding club intervention fare compared to TANF recipients who did receive this intervention?" or "Are alcoholics who regularly attend AA meetings more abstinent than similar alcoholics who do not attend AA?" The idea is when a social worker meets a client with a problem, one of the outcomes of the assessment process will be to formulate one or more such answerable questions, which might have a bearing on what options are presented to that particular client. Not all answerable questions bear on the topic of choosing interventions. Similar questions may be created for various methods of assessment, as in "Do children who are assessed for potential sexual abuse through the use of anatomically correct dolls more accurately report actual episodes of abuse compared to similar children who are assessed without the use of such dolls?" or "Does the use of the genogram to assess clients result in a more accurate understanding of the client's background than standard clinical interviews?" Other questions may be focused on issues such as the etiology of certain conditions, the cost-benefits of certain interventions, or questions related to the potentially harmful effects of a possible treatment (e.g., rebirthing therapy or facilitated communication). Chapter 3 will provide a more thorough discussion on creating research questions.

Once one has formulated one or more answerable questions, the next step is to track down credible information that may help answer it (Chapter 4). This process is addressed in Rubin and Parrish (2009) and may involve searching electronic databases, locating credible practice guidelines, or finding systematic reviews bearing on one's topic. Among the higher or more credible forms of evidence that EBP particularly seeks to locate are randomized controlled trials (see Montgomery & Mayo-Wilson, 2009), meta-analyses (Corcoran & Littell, 2009), systematic reviews (Littell & Corcoran, 2009), and practice guidelines (Howard, Perron, & Vaughn, 2009). The third step, critically appraising studies for evidence-based practice, is the focus of Bronson's (2009) study. Here, the social worker brings to bear his or her skills in reading and appraising research, paying attention to issues of internal and external validity, relevance, sampling, statistical analysis, and so forth.

The fourth step in EBP is integrating the information found from diverse sources with one's clinical expertise and the client's unique values and preferences. Of course, one's professional ethical standards are also a crucial consideration, as are available resources. This important topic is discussed by Gambrill (2009). The fifth step involves self-evaluating one's effectiveness and efficiency. This requires one's ability to not only conduct EBP but also evaluate the outcomes with one's client, which is actually the point of the entire exercise. Thyer and Myers's works (2007, 2009) are good resources to use in this regard. Portions of the preceding description of EBP are based on Thyer and Myers (2010).

In the twenty-first century, there still remain obstacles to the use of and objections to EBP (Rosen, 2003). However, most of the obstacles can be overcome and many of the objections reflect a misunderstanding of EBP. EBP is not intended to dictate to social workers what decisions they should make, only to get them to use all available data (including their practice expertise, professional values, and their knowledge of individual clients and their values and preferences) in making them. While EBP can result in cost saving for health insurance providers and other third parties, that is not its purpose—it is to offer services and programs with the greatest potential for success. Besides, what is wrong with cost cutting, as long as our clients are the ultimate beneficiaries?

While there are still problems for which effective interventions have not been identified through research, these gaps do not negate the need for social work practitioners to know how to conduct research, locate and evaluate critically the research of others, and, when available, to use the findings of researchers as an important component of their practice decision making.

RESEARCH AND PRACTICE: MORE SIMILAR THAN DIFFERENT

Although there is now a fair consensus that research and practice cannot be totally merged, they are not all that different. In fact, many of the attributes that are associated with good practitioners are the same ones that make for a good researcher. Even the tasks of practice and research are quite similar. We mention them here to emphasize that research is not some mysterious activity. It entails a logical process not too unlike the steps involved in successful practice intervention.

An early practice model (which was actually a variation of the scientist-practitioner model) described by Grinnell and Siegel (1988) highlights the many

Box 1.1 Research and Practice as Problem-Solving Methods: Related Activities	
Research Tasks	**Related Practice Tasks**
1. Identify needed knowledge.	1. Identify broad problem.
2. Identify focus of the study.	2. Partialize the problem.
3. Specify question(s) for study.	3. Specify problem(s) for intervention.
4. Develop research design.	4. Develop action plan.
5. Collect data.	5. Implement action plan.
6. Organize, analyze, and interpret data.	6. Evaluate, summarize.
7. Disseminate knowledge, identify areas for more research.	7. Terminate intervention, identify other client needs.

ways in which research methods and the social work problem-solving process are alike. The authors note that, in its ideal form, practice problem solving follows a sequence of activities that is virtually identical to the traditional research process. Even the same kind of problems—for example, biased assessment in practice and faulty measurement in research—are likely to be present.

Box 1.1 illustrates some parallels that can be drawn when one conceptualizes research and practice intervention as problem-solving processes.

The various models for research utilization (including more that we have not mentioned) all suggest that research should not be an activity that is foreign to social work practice or that necessarily draws precious resources away from it. On the contrary, social workers who wish to provide the best possible services to their clients can hardly afford not to be evidence-based practitioners. The models underline the fact that a research-oriented and research-involved practitioner is likely to be a better informed and a more effective and efficient practitioner than one who is not. In turn, a practice-oriented and practice-informed researcher is likely to produce research findings that will have value and be of benefit to those who deliver services to clients.

ALTERNATIVE KNOWLEDGE SOURCES

Social workers have always recognized the need for knowledge that would inform their practice with and on behalf of client groups. Often, they have had to rely on less "scientific" sources of information, such as the opinions of supervisors or peers, when stuck with a particularly difficult client problem or decision. These sources have limited utility and can be misleading.

Is there still a need to use these sources of knowledge? Yes. When research-based knowledge is lacking or is not trustworthy, we still must turn to these alternative sources of knowledge. However, when we do so, we must use extreme caution.

Logic

Often, we assume that some things are self-evident and logical. They just "make sense." Unfortunately, logic can lead to beliefs that are just plain wrong in some circumstances. For example, membership in a white supremacist group is generally a good indication of the presence of racist or anti-Semitic attitudes. But this logical assumption may break down in the case of an FBI infiltrator or a reporter seeking to understand the group firsthand. Similarly, we cannot depend on the self-evident truth that an individual who attends graduate school values an education, even if most graduate students probably do. He or she may have enrolled to appease a parent, to avoid having to work in the family business, or even to pursue a future partner.

Overreliance on logic has led to some costly errors among helping professionals. In the 1970s, a program called Scared Straight was promoted as a logical approach to reducing crime. It involved taking young people who had committed minor crimes, such as shoplifting, on a tour of prisons to see what might happen to them if they did not abide by the law. They experienced the booking procedure firsthand and talked with inmates who were serving long sentences. Logically, the experience should have turned the youths into model citizens. But it didn't. Petrosino, Turpin-Petrosino, and Buehler (2005) conducted a meta-analysis, a research method discussed in Chapter 4, and concluded that not only did the Scared Straight program not deter participants from future delinquency, participants were actually more likely to commit crimes than young people not participating in the program. The authors state, "despite the gloomy findings reported here and elsewhere, Scared Straight and its derivatives continue in use . . . when the negative results from the California SQUIRES study came out, the response was to end the evaluation, not the program" (p. 52).

Logic and common sense have produced other costly errors among helping professionals over the years. For example, many communities have implemented the Drug Abuse Resistance Education (DARE) program. Its curriculum, designed to prevent young students from abusing legal and illegal substances, has been taught widely in public schools in the United States. It links local law enforcement agencies with middle school students and teaches students a range of refusal skills that they could put to use when confronted with offers of drugs and alcohol. DARE was initially presumed to be an effective program. However, Van Burgh, Redner, and Moon (1995) conducted a study of over 100 eighth graders that showed that the program was not effective in changing students' knowledge or their skills in refusing drugs and alcohol. Subsequently, other researchers reported similar findings (Lyman et al., 1999). Nevertheless, probably because it is so logical and is now so well established, many communities continue to use and support DARE. Following is a quote from Salt Lake City mayor, Rocky Anderson (2000), who questioned the efficacy of Project DARE:

After I was elected Mayor, I examined Salt Lake City's participation in DARE, a substance-abuse prevention program with great popular appeal, but which has been demonstrated by study after study as being completely ineffective in reducing drug abuse over the long-term. Once my intent to terminate the DARE program in Salt Lake City became known, I was beseiged by police officers, parents, and school officials who demanded that I retain DARE in our schools.

> Notwithstanding all the parents who have yelled at me during parades, I know it is my obligation to honestly and conscientiously examine the data and insist that our School Board put in place drug-prevention programs that have proven to be effective.

Tradition

Another dubious source of knowledge is tradition. We may believe something to be true simply because it has never really been challenged, at least not within our culture. This kind of knowledge is particularly dangerous. As social workers, we may confront it on a daily basis. It can take the form of relatively innocuous misconceptions (e.g., that all retired military people are good bureaucrats). But it is more likely to result in destructive, negative stereotyping. Traditional beliefs may promote the continued oppression of some members of our society. The persistence of erroneous stereotypes, such as that gay men and lesbians choose their sexual orientation and wish to convert others, that all older people suffer from intellectual deterioration, or that single-parent families are necessarily dysfunctional, have all helped to foster discrimination against members of specific groups.

People have a tendency to hold tenaciously to traditional beliefs, sometimes even in the face of scientific evidence to the contrary. Human beings seem to have a need for some knowledge that represents a universal truth. We crave certainty in our lives, perhaps because so much of life is uncertain. Unfortunately, once we are convinced that something is correct, occasional selective observations are all that we seem to require to confirm its correctness. This is problematic enough for us in our social transactions, but in our professional roles, tenacious reliance on traditional beliefs can seriously affect our ability to provide competent services. The social work practitioner cannot afford to make practice decisions and undertake interventions on the basis of traditional beliefs.

Authority

Still another way we sometimes get our "knowledge" is through deference to authority. Social workers employed in medical and psychiatric settings are especially vulnerable to assuming that the physician always has a scientific basis for what, in actuality, may be little more than an opinion. We sometimes mistakenly conclude that "if she said it, it must be true" or "he ought to know, or he wouldn't be where he is today." Unfortunately, people in authority (e.g., our bosses), just like all of us, are subject to bias, limited experience, and perhaps the tendency to confuse reality with wishful thinking. Or they may simply be relying on logic or tradition!

FAULTY KNOWLEDGE CAN PROMOTE STEREOTYPES

Logic, tradition, and authority can mislead us in many ways. They can affect our practice judgment, cause us to draw erroneous conclusions, or waste our time and energies looking for problems that don't exist. As mentioned earlier, they can promote unhealthy stereotypes and generalizations about people who may become our clients. What are some of them?

Welfare Recipients

Who is a welfare recipient? There never has been any shortage of "knowledge" about welfare recipients in our society. We rarely encounter people who admit that they really do not understand their situation or do not have a solution—often, a punitive one—for it. Families receiving Aid to Families of Dependent Children (AFDC) benefits and, more recently, Temporary Assistance to Needy Families (TANF) have been especially the subject of erroneous

Critical Thinking

Critical Thinking Question: Give an example from your own life when you used knowledge on the basis of (1) logic, (2) tradition, and (3) authority to make a decision. In each case, did the knowledge lead you to a good or a faulty decision?

beliefs. The mother in such families was often described as a "welfare queen." According to this stereotype, she had five or seven children, lived well on the benefit level, had no intention of finding work, and had more children to increase benefits.

How accurate was this "knowledge" of welfare recipients? In 1994, Rank, a social work professor, published the results of an eight-year study of 3,000 AFDC recipients. He noted the following:

- Most welfare recipients had no more than two children.
- During the previous twenty years, the value of welfare benefit levels had sharply declined when adjusted for inflation.
- States with the highest out-of-wedlock birthrates tended to have the lowest welfare benefit levels.
- Benefits to teenage mothers were lower in the United States than in European nations. (p. 6)

These findings clearly pointed out that AFDC was hardly a good deal in the United States. It would have been illogical, for example, for an AFDC mother to become pregnant just to receive a small increase in benefits.

People Who Are Homeless

Many people in our society, including some helping professionals, may feel comfortable with their "knowledge" of homelessness. What are some common beliefs about people who are homeless? They are older men. They are likely to suffer from mental illness and problems with alcohol and drugs. They are dropouts from mainstream society, prone to violence and public drunkenness. But what does research tell us about homeless people in the United States? There are some similarities to these common stereotypes but also some important differences. For example, in 2005, data compiled by The United States Conference of Mayors revealed that

- a greater percentage of homeless men have served in the military than the general population;
- approximately one-third of the homeless were families with children, the fastest growing homeless population;
- about 30 percent of the adult homeless population has an addiction to alcohol or other substances;
- while about 22 percent of the adult homeless population suffers from some severe, chronic mental illness, only a small percentage (5–7 percent) requires institutionalization.

We have offered just two examples of the wide disparity between what is generally believed to be true and what research has revealed. Reliance on knowledge from dubious sources can create problems for the social worker. For example, social workers or other helping professionals who make diagnostic or treatment decisions on the basis of false preconceptions about people who are financially dependent on government assistance or homeless would be likely to assume that certain attitudes and problems exist among their clients when they really may not be present at all. They might be misled into misdiagnosis, bad treatment planning, and/or ineffective intervention methods. This is exactly the opposite of what knowledge is supposed to do. Knowledge should inform our practice, not mislead it.

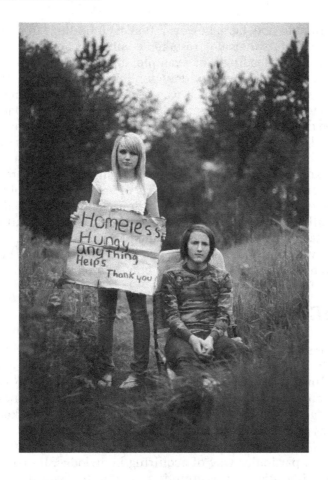

MISUSE OF RESEARCH DATA

Research studies, such as those cited here, have the potential to dispel myths and stereotypes derived from less trustworthy sources. But research, especially when reported in the popular media, can also lend credence to myths and stereotypes. We would be remiss if we did not point out that one cannot always trust research findings, especially when they are selectively reported for "shock value" or to boost circulation or Neilson ratings. For example, during the 1980s, there was great concern about the use of crack cocaine by pregnant women and its long-term health effects on their babies. Logic, common sense, and early research studies suggested that the children can suffer major physical and psychological damage from their mothers' chemical addiction. The newspapers and television channels picked up on it. The selective use of research findings made this "knowledge" more believable. However, a meta-analysis conducted by the Drug Policy Alliance (2004) of most studies conducted on the topic in the 1980s revealed serious methodological flaws that had led to numerous erroneous conclusions about the extent and severity of the potential problem. Research has shown that problems among babies of crack-addicted mothers could be attributed to other factors, such as poverty, violence, and demoralization (Day & Richardson, 1993). Unfortunately, the early, flawed studies have been used in at least one state, South Carolina, to assist in the successful prosecution of addicted women for child abuse, thus adding to their problems.

Human Rights & Justice

Critical Thinking Question: Can you think of three examples when you have seen faulty knowledge promote stereotypes or prejudice?

It is important to note here, however, that even findings from well-designed research studies, unless they are presented completely and in an unbiased way, can sometimes be misleading. For example, a Vietnam-era veteran (Burkett & Whitley, 1998), whose data were widely publicized, was seeking to present veterans in the best possible light as a way of compensating for the usual media portrayal of veterans. Did he perhaps neglect to mention a few facts that might give us a more complete understanding of what he offered? For example, would it be helpful to know that a large number of Vietnam-era veterans (including one of the authors of this text) "volunteered" for service as he reported, but only because they knew that they would be drafted anyway and were hoping for a better assignment? Or that a high percentage of veterans were college graduates but that many of them had a college education made possible only by benefits from the GI Bill? Or that although a large percentage of those killed were officers (not enlisted men), they were also pilots? Our message to the reader is this: Even facts derived from sound research can be used to present a biased picture. That is where research ethics (Chapter 2) enter the picture.

THE SCIENTIFIC ALTERNATIVE

Social work practitioners need many types of knowledge. Given the shortcomings of the alternative sources of knowledge we have just discussed, aren't research findings still the best alternative? Yes. Knowledge derived from research, although certainly imperfect and still subject to unethical distortion, is the knowledge most likely to help us do our jobs as social workers effectively. Research relies on the use of the scientific method.

The *scientific method* (alternately referred to as *scientific thinking* or simply *science*) is a particular way of acquiring knowledge. It is a way of thinking about and investigating assumptions about the world. It differs from *scientific knowledge*, which is really only a collection of facts that were acquired through use of the scientific method. We could theoretically use scientific knowledge even if we did not know how to practice the scientific method. But that would be dangerous. Unless we engage in scientific thinking and understand and use the scientific method, we might have blind faith in scientific knowledge. That would be almost as bad as uncritically depending on logic, tradition, or authority because, as has been suggested, scientific knowledge, when selectively reported, can be misleading. To correctly use the products of the scientific method (scientific knowledge), we must understand it. That is why we study it.

Certain characteristics of the scientific method set it apart from other ways of acquiring knowledge and, we believe, make it more likely to yield knowledge on which the social worker can depend.

▶ **Science is empirical.** *Empirical* is a word that is widely used but not always understood. It means that knowledge derived from scientific methods is based on direct observations of the real world, not on someone's beliefs or theories. Scientific knowledge has undergone a rigorous evaluation and verification process to determine whether what was assumed to be true or what was believed to be true really is true. Because science is empirical, it is not appropriate for validating a phenomenon that cannot be directly observed, such as the existence of God. However, many phenomena that on the surface would seem inappropriate for study through science (e.g., how people experienced some event from their perspective) can nevertheless be studied by the imaginative researcher using the scientific method.

▸ **Science strives for objectivity.** No conscientious and ethical scientist would deliberately introduce biases into research findings. Scientists take deliberate actions to avoid the possibility of their own preferences or beliefs influencing the results of their research. At the same time, there is recognition that total objectivity may be impossible and that a certain amount of subjectivity is inevitable, and these factors influence findings in all research to a greater or lesser degree. But the scientist attempts to assess how much subjectivity may have played a role and to evaluate its effects to arrive at the truth.

▸ **Science produces provisional knowledge.** As noted earlier, the possibility that research findings and conclusions may be wrong is always present. Science speaks, in effect, on the basis of what we know right now, what we think to be the case now. It leaves open the possibility that subsequent scientific inquiry may lead to modified or even to totally contradictory conclusions. In this way, scientific knowledge is always regarded as tentative. Even the conclusions drawn from statistical tests of inference are based on a premise of *reasonable certainty*, usually greater than 95 percent.

▸ **Science employs a public way of knowing.** In science, it is not enough for a researcher to share findings with other scientists and the public. It also is expected that the methods used to produce the findings will be made available for critique so that other researchers can try to achieve similar results, which is called *replication*. In this way, a researcher's findings can be checked, and, once verified, they tend to have greater credibility.

▸ **Science employs certain rules, procedures, and techniques.** Although creativity and innovation are also characteristics of science, there are definitely acceptable and unacceptable ways to conduct scientific research. There are also correct and incorrect sequences in which to perform research tasks, depending on the type of research that is undertaken. Even research that ventures into problem areas where we have very little knowledge attempts to go by the rules.

TYPES OF SCIENTIFIC KNOWLEDGE

If we are to become evidence-based practitioners, at least to the degree possible, we need access to different types of scientific knowledge. They are acquired in different ways using different research methods, a topic we will address in considerable detail in Chapters 6 through 8. While there is overlap among them, scientific knowledge tends to come in one of three forms.

Descriptive Knowledge

Descriptive knowledge is knowledge that helps us understand. It gives us a reasonably accurate picture of the way things are, or to be more precise, of how they were at the time that the research took place. It does not allow us to go much beyond having a better and more accurate perception of a problem or situation at some point in time, or even what certain individuals perceive to be the situation at the time. Descriptive knowledge is limited, but this does not mean that it is inferior to other types of knowledge. It is not any less valuable or (acquired correctly) any easier to achieve. In fact, descriptive knowledge often requires many months or even years of work and ingenious research methods. For example, Israel and Jozefowicz-Simbeni (2009) studied the strengths of homeless elementary-aged children as perceived by their mothers. Another study (Hamilton, Nelson Goff, Crow, & Reisbig, 2009) looked at the primary trauma and relationship satisfaction experienced by the wives of Army soldiers who had recently returned from Iraq. Learning how people experience an event or situation can be of great assistance to social workers and other human service workers who work with people in similar circumstances.

Descriptive knowledge, as we shall discuss in the context of research design in later chapters, may be exactly what the social work practitioner needs. It also frequently forms the basis for desirable changes within our society. The accurate description of a problem—for example, the statistical documentation of discriminatory employment practices or identification of the amount of sexual harassment in the workplace—has been the basis both for bringing these problems into public awareness and for subsequent social change.

Predictive Knowledge

Predictive knowledge is knowledge that helps us anticipate. It allows us to go a step beyond describing what is or was. It allows us to project into the future and predict with reasonable accuracy what will be. Predictive knowledge evolves from the accumulation of descriptive knowledge, which reveals consistent reoccurring patterns. For example, suppose that several descriptive studies of gay adolescents reveal that a large percentage of them are victims of bullying. From this, we might evolve the predictive knowledge that a gay teenager is likely to experience bullying behavior. We can increase the likelihood of success in predicting a problem that he may face when we observe what has tended to happen to others like him in the past.

Predictive knowledge can tell a social worker what is likely to occur. For example, one study (Prentky et al., 2010) looked at the ability of an instrument to assess the risk of future sexually abusive behaviors among a group of juvenile sexual offenders. A great deal of research has been conducted to determine if individuals who were victims of child sexual abuse are at a greater risk of later becoming perpetrators of such abuse (see Glasser et al., 2001). If we understand who is most at risk for experiencing a problem in the future, we can better identify who might require careful monitoring and/or intervention. But predictive knowledge stops short of telling a social worker exactly how to intervene to prevent a problem from occurring or how to treat one that already exists.

Prescriptive Knowledge

Prescriptive knowledge is knowledge that suggests the method of intervention that is most likely to be effective. In EBP, social workers use prescriptive knowledge, along with their experience, client preferences, and so forth, to decide what intervention should be used to address an existing problem or to prevent one that they can predict. Prescriptive knowledge is most frequently based on the findings of carefully designed research studies in which the researcher had considerable control over the ways in which the research was conducted.

When prescriptive knowledge exists, we know not only what is and what probably will be but also what needs to be done to avoid something undesirable or to cause something desirable to occur. In fields such as sociology or anthropology, descriptive knowledge and, to a lesser degree, predictive knowledge are often the end product of research. In EBP, however, our goal is to identify interventions with a high likelihood of success. For example, one recent study (Rotheram-Borus, Desmond, Comulada, Arnold, & Johnson, 2009) examined the efficacy of the Healthy Living Program, a program designed to reduce risky sexual behavior and substance use among marginally housed adults with HIV infection. The authors reported that program participants showed significantly greater reductions than the control group members in unprotected risky sexual acts, the number of HIV negative sexual partners, alcohol and marijuana use, and hard drug use. Another study (Parish, Rose, & Andrews, 2010) assessed the success of TANF to reach its goals to increase employment, enhance family stability through marriage promotion, and reduce welfare reliance. The researchers looked at different categories of mothers and concluded that the program had not led to an overall reduction in welfare reliance among low-income women raising children with disabilities. Mears, Yaffe, and Harris (2009) compared the outcomes of severely emotionally disturbed youth receiving wraparound services to youth receiving more traditional child welfare case management services and concluded that the youth receiving the wraparound services exhibited a higher level of functioning and experienced significantly fewer placements than the comparison group.

In terms of its value for decision making, it is clear how these and other prescriptive studies offer the social worker invaluable knowledge when developing interventions, as well as promoting policy changes that will help clients. Purely prescriptive knowledge is still relatively rare in social work, but it is becoming increasingly available as more and more carefully designed research studies are conducted. The more widespread use of meta-analyses has also added more prescriptive knowledge to the social worker's professional knowledge base.

It should be emphasized again that prescriptive knowledge alone should not dictate the choice of a method of intervention. That would not be consistent with EBP. There is, of course, no guarantee that you or I will find an intervention that will be effective with a given client or a given client group. That is where our own experience, knowledge of ourselves and our client or client group, ethical practice issues, and client wishes and preferences must be factored into the decision as to how best to intervene.

It would also be inaccurate to say that prescriptive knowledge is the only type of knowledge that suggests how we might best intervene in a problem situation. Virtually all research findings can have some prescriptive potential. With thought, predictive and even descriptive knowledge can help to inform our practice decision making and thus increase the likelihood of successful intervention. For example, a descriptive study of youth gang activities and the social needs that gang membership appears to meet may suggest what other activities and programs might provide an attractive alternative to gang membership. Or, the findings of several studies of youth gangs might allow us to predict at what age pressure for membership is most likely to occur. This predictive knowledge can then help us to decide what age group an activity or program should target and thus how to structure it.

In reality, most research studies generate a variety of knowledge, including some that does not fit cleanly into one of the three categories discussed. The knowledge typology (like most typologies) is not perfect and clean. However, we discuss it primarily because it emphasizes the benefits that research can offer to the social work practitioner. Also, this discussion will prove useful in later chapters, when we examine different types of research and, especially, how they differ in their purpose.

BASIC AND APPLIED RESEARCH

A research study is sometimes described as *basic* or *applied*. The labels are assigned on the basis of a study's general goal or purpose, specifically, when and how any knowledge derived from it is intended to be used.

Basic Research

Basic research (sometimes called *pure research*) is research that is designed to contribute to our general professional body of knowledge. Social workers conduct basic research but also rely heavily on researchers from other fields to conduct basic research. For example, they benefit from the research of sociologists, anthropologists, economists, and psychologists to help them understand and predict human behavior. As social workers, we sometimes immediately apply findings from basic research in our practice. The knowledge from basic research is often tucked away, available for us to tap into at some future time for some as yet unknown purpose. We might not use it at all until a new social problem is identified or we conclude that we have misunderstood an old one. Then we might revisit the findings of basic research conducted years or even decades earlier to provide some insight into the problem. For example, some of the basic research conducted in the 1971 Stanford studies (Zimbardo, 2010), on the behaviors of college students when given power over others in a prison setting, have been used to help us to better understand the abusive treatment of prisoners in Iraq and Afghanistan by their American guards over forty years later.

Applied Research

In contrast to basic research, applied research is designed to produce knowledge that has immediate, and often narrower, applicability. Its findings are often used for answering a burning question or for making a decision that cannot wait, for example, whether an intervention should be terminated or whether a social program should be continued. Social workers identify the potential beneficiaries of applied research before it is conducted and design the research in a way that yields the data that will help to answer the questions that must be answered.

Applied research is not inherently more valuable or more useful than basic research. Although its findings may appear to be more practical and more relevant to successful evidence-based practice, we could not be successful evidence-based practitioners without also having access to knowledge acquired through basic research. Sometimes, the practice benefits of basic research are quite indirect; we may even be unaware of their contribution to our current practice. As Proctor (2003) pointed out, "some research will have impact only over the long haul, shaping theory that in turn informs hypotheses for further study" (p. 195).

As we might suspect, not all research falls neatly into one of the two categories (basic or applied). In fact, some basic research studies produce findings that are of immediate use for practice decision making. Conversely, some applied research studies (often along with the findings of other, similar studies) produce knowledge that represents a major contribution to our professional knowledge base. While some research studies have elements of both basic and applied research, the two terms are still widely used to communicate the broad characteristics of a research study.

QUANTITATIVE AND QUALITATIVE RESEARCH

Another way to broadly categorize research, based partly on the purpose of the research, is to describe it as *quantitative* or *qualitative*. This categorization is also based on other factors, such as the methods of data collection most frequently used, sources of data, the place of hypotheses, and even the methods of data analysis employed. As we shall see, as in the case of the basic and applied labels, the labels *quantitative* and *qualitative* can easily suggest a false dichotomy, since many research studies contain elements of both.

Quantitative Research

Quantitative research often has been thought of (erroneously) as being synonymous with the scientific method. It is sometimes even called *empirical research*, yet it has no monopoly on either the scientific method or empiricism. Quantitative research emphasizes the building of knowledge through what is referred to as *logical positivism*. It stresses the use of deductive (linear) logic to arrive at conclusions.

Studies that employ quantitative methods are characterized by, or attempt to employ, the following:

1. Careful measurement of variables
2. Relatively large, randomly selected case samples
3. Control of other variables through random assignment of cases to groups
4. Standardized data collection methods
5. Statistical analyses of data

Each of these concepts will be defined and discussed more fully in later chapters.

Quantitative methods are often employed in research studies that seek to describe a problem or phenomenon. They are used to provide an accurate measurement of the distribution of variables of interest and to identify possible relationships among them. The sequence of activities that occurs in quantitative research reflects the deductive logic of this approach to knowledge building. In broad terms, this entails

1. specification of a theory;
2. statement of a hypothesis to test the theory;
3. observation (data collection);
4. confirmation (or disconfirmation) of the theory.

This deductive logic is reflected in the sequence of activities that occurs. It is how many of us in years past were taught "the correct way" for research to be conducted. The steps generally used in quantitative methods are as follows:

1. **Problem identification.** The problem—that is, the condition or phenomenon that is unsatisfactory—must be clearly understood to the point that it can be specified precisely, along with its magnitude and consequences.

2. **Research question formulation.** After developing a number of broad questions, the answer to any one of which would have potential to partially alleviate the problem (or at least to understand it better), the researcher selects one or more of these questions that will constitute the focus of inquiry for the research.

3. **Literature review.** The state of existing knowledge is assessed and assembled into a logical order to determine what is already known concerning answers to the research questions, or at least to enable the researcher to specify the questions more precisely. The literature review is also used to formulate an appropriate research methodology for the current research.

4. **Construction of hypotheses and/or refinement of research questions.** Based on the literature review and the type of knowledge sought, the researcher formulates hypotheses and/or specific research questions that will provide the focus for research activities that follow.

5. **Design and planning.** A series of decisions are made as to how the research hypotheses are to be tested and/or answers to questions are to be sought. Tasks involved in this activity include the following:

   a. Selecting or formulating operational definitions of key terms
   b. Specification of what people or objects will be studied
   c. Development of a method for sampling (if the entire population of people or objects is not to be studied)
   d. Identification and definition of variables to be measured (conceptualization)
   e. Specification of exactly how variables will be measured (operationalization)
   f. Identification and/or development of instruments for measurement (including their pretesting)
   g. Specification and pretesting of methods for data collection
   h. Specification of methods for analysis of data

6. **Data collection.** Data are collected according to predetermined methods.

7. **Sorting and analysis of data.** The data are examined, summarized, and analyzed using appropriate statistical methods. If hypotheses have been formulated, tests of statistical significance are used to determine if support for them can be claimed.

8. **Specification of research findings.** Results of data analysis are displayed in tables, graphs, or other standard formats.

9. **Interpretation of research findings.** Results of data analysis are examined in order to draw conclusions relative to the research hypotheses and/or questions. The findings are examined in relation to the findings of other similar studies.

10. **Dissemination of research findings.** The researcher uses one or more vehicles to report the methods and findings of the research.

11. **Use of findings by the social worker.** Practitioners who have access to the research report critically evaluate both the findings and the methods that produced them and adapt their practice methods accordingly.

This traditional sequence of tasks for performing research is described in most research methods texts. However, steps 1 and 11 are not universally included. By including them, we have emphasized our concern for the importance of research utilization by the social work practitioner as an integral part of evidence-based practice.

The knowledge generated by quantitative research that is supportive of EBP can take many forms. For example, quantitative research can provide evidence of a relationship between the incidence of child abuse and substance abuse or compare the effectiveness of two approaches to treatment of the problem of child abuse. The knowledge generated by quantitative research can be the results of an evaluation that measures how well a program to treat perpetrators of child abuse achieved its objectives or a social worker's systematic ongoing evaluation of his or her own practice effectiveness with an abusive parent or a treatment group of abusive parents.

For many years, quantitative methods were considered the best (if not the only) way to conduct research. They are still described as such in many high school science classes and in research courses in other disciplines. Indeed, the principles of quantitative research are ideal for obtaining certain types of knowledge. However, quantitative methods have their limitations. They are not well suited to studying certain subjective phenomena. We cannot always separate knowledge and values; they are hopelessly intertwined in human thought and behavior. For example, quantitative methods can provide reasonably accurate data about the incidence of date rape on college campuses or even which individuals are most at risk. However, it cannot provide much insight into how individuals perceive their experience or what the experience means to them. The limitations of quantitative research, along with the evolution of feminist research (discussed later), have taught us the importance of other, complementary approaches to knowledge building.

Qualitative Research

Qualitative research seeks to understand human experiences from the perspective of those who experience them. Qualitative research emphasizes words like *subjective, relative,* or *contextual*—words that might have a connotation of failure within quantitative studies. Qualitative research relies on inductive logic instead of deduction. Often, vast amounts of data are collected, sorted, and interpreted. A helpful definition of qualitative research is offered by Denzin and Lincoln (1994):

> Qualitative research is multimethod in focus, involving an interpretive, naturalistic approach to its subject matter. That means that qualitative researchers study things in their natural settings, attempting to make sense of or interpret phenomena in terms of the meanings people bring to them. Qualitative research involves the studied use and collection of a variety of empirical materials—case study, personal experience, introspective, life story, interview, observational, historical, interactional, and visual texts—that describe routine and problematic moments and meaning in individuals' lives. (p. 2)

Data collection often occurs through in-depth interviewing, conducting groups, or by participant observation (Chapter 8). In-person interviews, an important component of most qualitative studies, generally tend to be less structured and less standardized in qualitative research than in quantitative research. Often, what the researcher learns in conducting one interview results in adaptations for the next. Sample representativeness (Chapter 9) often is not a major concern.

In qualitative research, the researcher is really the primary instrument for data collection and analysis. The data are processed as they are received. There is no pretense that the researcher can collect data in an objective, value-free manner. In fact, when interviews are used, the relationships between the researcher and those being interviewed may be openly supportive and even therapeutic at times.

When using qualitative approaches to knowledge building, many of the same activities seen in quantitative studies take place. However, they often receive greater or lesser emphasis or may occur in a different sequence. There are two important differences that are especially common. First, hypotheses are unlikely to be formulated prior to data collection and then tested in qualitative studies, as in quantitative studies. Instead, they may evolve from and be the final product of the research process. Thus, they generally appear late in the report of a qualitative study (if at all), as tentative conclusions drawn from the research study. Second, in qualitative studies, an extensive review of the literature generally does not occur prior to data collection. Vast amounts of data may be collected quite early in the research process. Some will be useful; others may be discarded. During and after data collection, the professional literature is used to either verify or question what the data seem to be suggesting, that is, to help in conceptualizing what is being and has been observed.

The sequence of activities that occurs in qualitative research reflects the inductive logic of this approach to knowledge building. In broad terms, this entails

1. collection of a wide range of data;
2. observation of patterns in the data;
3. formulation of tentative explanations;
4. development of theories (and sometimes, hypotheses).

Qualitative research also differs more widely from study to study in adherence to rules and procedures when compared to quantitative research. Some studies are quite rigorous and adhere strictly to a specific sequence of activities; others are more flexible. However, below is one fairly common sequence:

1. Problem identification.
2. Research question formulation.
3. Limited literature review.
4. Initial data collection and analysis.
5. Continued data collection and analysis.
6. Data interpretation.
7. Formulation of theories or hypotheses.
8. Dissemination of findings.
9. Use of findings by the social worker.

Results of quantitative studies are often reported using tables and graphs. Reports also contain the results of statistical tests and conclusions about support or nonsupport for research hypotheses. In reports of qualitative studies, these tools may not be used. Findings are more likely to be presented in narrative form or as case scenarios. There may be long descriptions of the researcher's interaction with individuals who provided data for the research, including direct quotations from them and speculation by the researcher on what their choice of words may suggest or imply. Increasingly, computer software is being used to perform a content analysis (see Chapter 4) of transcripts of interviews to attempt to quantify, for example, the presence of emotions in the subjects such as anger, despair, or anxiety. Results of such content analysis, if performed, are included in the findings.

The Quantitative versus Qualitative Debate

In the late twentieth century, the merits of qualitative versus quantitative research were the topic of lively debates among social work researchers. However, it is now generally agreed that both quantitative and qualitative methods are necessary to truly understand many problems or phenomena. For example, how could we have a complete understanding of an experience such as post-traumatic stress disorder among returning war veterans if we focused only on, for example, its incidence, the forms it takes, and what experiences may be associated with it, and did not also explore such topics as how it is perceived by its victims or how they experience it emotionally?

It is now generally agreed that both quantitative and qualitative methods are necessary to truly understand many problems or phenomena.

Neither type of research is inherently superior to the other. Both quantitative and qualitative studies make valuable contributions to our knowledge base and help us to make better decisions as evidence-based practice social workers. Of course, there is good and not-so-good qualitative research, even as there is good and not-so-good quantitative research. Simply running a focus group and writing up a summary of what transpired is not good qualitative research, any more than mailing out a hastily constructed survey is good quantitative research. Conducting good quantitative or qualitative research is not a haphazard process.

The findings of qualitative research and quantitative research often complement each other. It is not surprising, then, that research studies often are hybrids—they contain features of both. Qualitative methods may be used to collect and analyze one type of data, while quantitative methods may be used to collect and analyze some other type. Or both methods may be used to attempt to answer the same question so that the results can be compared to help in finding the correct answer. For example, to try to gain an accurate perception of the merit, worth, or value of a social program, we might rely on quantitative data about changes in the social functioning of its clients and in-depth interviews with some of its clients, group meetings with program staff, and so forth.

It is probably more accurate to describe many studies as *predominantly quantitative* or *predominantly qualitative*, rather than simply *quantitative* or *qualitative.* In the chapters that follow, when references are made to quantitative or qualitative research, it should be remembered that "pure" examples of either type of research are now probably more the exception than the rule. We will look more in depth at quantitative research designs (Chapter 6) and qualitative research methods (Chapter 8) later in this book.

THE CURRENT CLIMATE FOR SOCIAL WORK RESEARCH

The demand for research in the human services has never been greater, largely due to an emphasis on EBP. A high percentage of the research conducted by social workers is now some form of mandated evaluation research. Human service organizations contain many excellent potential sources of research data, for example, surveys of and interviews with clients or organization staff, and agency data (such as number and characteristics of clients served), which are routinely collected and compiled. Recent changes in laws have made client record data off limits to researchers in many settings. These data can provide evidence of the effectiveness of services and programs to program managers, administrators, and organizations that provide funding for programs and to other stakeholders. However, analysis of program data may also have the potential to identify areas where individuals and programs have not met their responsibilities or have failed to achieve their objectives. Thus, a researcher conducting a mandated program evaluation may either receive excellent cooperation and assistance from organizational staff or encounter resistance and efforts to obstruct research activities that might reveal program deficiencies.

Is it any wonder that administrators (and board members) are often fearful of research? On the surface, it would seem that they may have more to lose than to gain from it. Still another concern relates to the protection of client and staff rights, especially their privacy rights. Fears about the possibility of litigation (a major concern of administrators today) are likely to surface when a researcher, even an employee of the organization, asks to collect data from staff or clients. Sometimes, permission to conduct research requires a series of compromises and accommodations that result in research methods that the researcher knows are less than ideal. This is an unfortunate reality. But, if done thoughtfully, these adjustments can be made in a way that will maintain the integrity of the research and its findings. As we shall discuss, no research design is ever perfect, but there are ways to make less-than-perfect research acceptable if social workers understand and apply the principles of scientific inquiry.

The professionalization of social work over the past few decades has influenced the ways in which social workers are able to conduct research. Leaders of organizations such as NASW have worked hard to ensure high-quality services to clients and acquire greater public recognition for the contributions that social workers make to society. Professionalization has also been enhanced by the passing of state licensing bills that protect both social workers and their clients and has been accompanied by the codification of certain values, ethical standards, and traditions. Overall, these developments undoubtedly have produced better services and served to protect clients from unqualified or incompetent service.

Generally, as we shall see in Chapter 2, professional values are highly consistent with research ethics. On occasion, however, a researcher will (and should) be constrained from using methods and designs that represent sound research but that are unacceptable to social workers and the values that guide their behavior. For example, professional values are likely to go against such practices as random assignment of clients to two different types of treatment, direct observation of treatment, denial of services to some to see if treatment really makes a difference, or certain forms of deception. If allowed to occur, these practices might produce research findings that are more definitive and possess greater credibility. But, of course, research should serve practice; it should never be the other way around. Professional values and ethics must be adhered to, even if the quality of research suffers a little.

Professional values, such as a client's right to services, confidentiality, and the sanctity of a treatment relationship, will and should continue to present impediments to conducting scientific research. The welfare of individual clients cannot be sacrificed in the interest of knowledge building, sometimes even that which has the potential to produce better future services to clients. However, the knowledgeable researcher knows that many apparent conflicts that pit professional values against research imperatives actually result from misunderstandings that can be cleared up. Conflicts that are real can often be resolved through compromise and trade-off. Frequently, an almost-as-good alternative exists and can be employed. The influence of professional values may make research in the social work practice milieu a little more difficult, or it may require special creativity on the part of the researcher. But fortunately, it rarely precludes conducting good research altogether.

Despite some of the obstacles and concerns that we have mentioned, the environment for social work research continues to improve in the twenty-first century. Social workers are becoming more aware that well-designed, credible research studies are essential if they are to provide the best possible services to their clients. They are also more aware that sound research is a necessity if they are to demonstrate that their efforts are worth their cost to governments and employers, who must make decisions about which services will be supported and who should offer them (O'Neill, 2000). Without good research evidence of benefits, the profession faces the threats of financial cuts and elimination of valuable and needed programs. Other disciplines and professions, which have a longer history of conducting research that demonstrates their effectiveness, could move in to fill roles that social workers historically have filled. Whether out of choice or out of necessity, the market for social work research, especially research that evaluates social work interventions, is now very favorable.

SUMMARY

In this chapter, we looked at the history of the relationship between research and social work practice. Many of the steps in the research process are quite similar to those of good practice intervention. Yet, in the past, social workers have tended to rely primarily on such unreliable sources as supervisors' opinions, logic and common sense, tradition, and authority to provide the knowledge they required for making practice decisions. They relied less frequently on the findings of research that employed scientific methods. However, this has gradually changed. Social workers now advocate and acknowledge the value of EBP, with its emphasis on the use of research findings as an important component of practice decision making. We need to understand the best ways to conduct research to (1) design and implement our own research findings and (2) evaluate critically the research methods and findings of others so that we can make informed practice decisions on the basis of their findings.

We looked at several broad descriptions of different types of research. Different research methods focus on the production of different types of knowledge, which were classified as descriptive, predictive, and prescriptive. Some studies can be described as basic research, whose primary purpose is to provide broad, generalized knowledge for future use. Other research, which is described as applied research, has as its purpose to provide knowledge for immediate use in decision making. The major differences between research that is primarily quantitative and research that is primarily qualitative also were described. They will be discussed in more detail in the chapters that follow.

Finally, we looked at the current environment for social work research, its sources of support, and the obstacles it faces. Some of the obstacles result from misunderstandings that can be corrected, while others are likely to continue or even become more substantial. Such challenges will require social work researchers to be sensitive and diplomatic and also willing to learn new and creative ways to evaluate and improve social work interventions.

Log onto **www.mysocialworklab.com** and answer the following questions. (If you did not receive an access code to **MySocialWorkLab** with this text and wish to purchase access online, please visit www.mysocialworklab.com.)

1. **Watch the Connecting Core Competency Video: Engaging in Research-Informed Practice.** What client strengths did the social worker discover through his interview? How did he use this knowledge to guide him toward a specific intervention?

2. **Read the Case Study: Crisis and Kinship in Foster Care.** After gathering the psychosocial history of Blanche and her family, what are two topics the social worker might look for in the social work research literature? After the death of the child, what are two more topics the social worker might need to review in the literature?

PRACTICE TEST

1. The following is an example of using tradition as a source of knowledge:
   a. The social worker assumed that the DARE program would help the high-risk adolescents at his school.
   b. The counselor based his intervention on a theory he had been taught in class.
   c. The style of parenting used by the house parent was the same style used by every house parent for the past 100 years.
   d. The school counselor selected the topics he discussed with students on the basis of his intuitive feelings about the student.

2. The following is an example of using logic as a source of knowledge:
   a. The social worker assumed that the DARE program would help the high-risk adolescents at his school.
   b. The counselor based his intervention on a theory he had been taught in class.
   c. The style of parenting used by the house parent was the same style used by every house parent for the past 100 years.
   d. The school counselor selected the topics he discussed with students on the basis of his intuitive feelings about the student.

3. The following is an example of using authority as a source of knowledge:
   a. The social worker assumed that the DARE program would help the high-risk adolescents at his school.
   b. The counselor based his intervention on a theory he had been taught in class.
   c. The style of parenting used by the house parent was the same style used by every house parent for the past 100 years.
   d. The school counselor selected the topics he discussed with students on the basis of his intuitive feelings about the student.

4. Qualitative research is characterized by all of the following features except one:
   a. Relies on inductive rather than deductive logic
   b. Control of other variables through random assignment of cases to groups
   c. Often, vast amounts of data are collected, sorted, and interpreted
   d. Hypotheses are unlikely to be formulated prior to data collection

5. How might you use qualitative research methods to study the homeless population in your city? How could you use quantitative methods to study the same population? What is one strength of each type of research?

ASSESS YOUR COMPETENCE   Use the scale below to rate your current level of achievement on the following concepts or skills associated with each competency presented in the chapter:

1	2	3
I can accurately describe the concept or skill	I can consistently identify the concept or skill when observing and analyzing practice activities	I can competently implement the concept or skill in my own practice

_____ Recognizing knowledge from logic, authority, and tradition

_____ Understanding scientific knowledge and how it differs from other types of knowledge

_____ Understanding the difference between descriptive, predictive, and prescriptive knowledge

_____ Understanding the differences and similarities between quantitative and qualitative research

2

Ethical Issues in Research

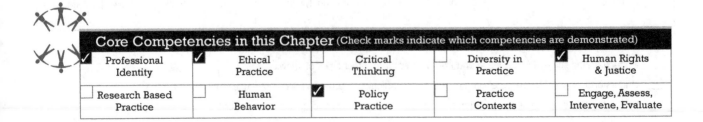

Core Competencies in this Chapter (Check marks indicate which competencies are demonstrated)									
✓	Professional Identity	✓	Ethical Practice		Critical Thinking		Diversity in Practice	✓	Human Rights & Justice
	Research Based Practice		Human Behavior	✓	Policy Practice		Practice Contexts		Engage, Assess, Intervene, Evaluate

In the previous chapter, we described many similarities between research and social work practice. There is at least one other similarity, and a very important one: both research and practice are shaped by ethical constraints.

In this chapter, we will examine (1) what is meant by research ethics; (2) some well-known research studies in which abuses of research participants contributed to the establishment of current ethical standards to ensure that individuals who allow social workers to collect research data from them are protected; (3) contemporary issues, such as research with vulnerable people who may volunteer to become research participants and the rights of individuals to participate in research even if it has the potential to harm them; and (4) the researcher's ethical obligations to others, such as the sponsors of research, other researchers, colleagues, and the general public.

In some areas, research ethical standards have been clearly delineated. However, in others, there is often a lack of clear-cut guidelines to assist decision making. In social work practice, ethical dilemmas and constraints are always with us. And that is good, because they cause us to regularly question whether what we are doing is both justifiable and fair to others.

We have chosen to devote an entire chapter to the topic of research ethical issues because they play such an important part in the design and implementation of research studies. However, our intention is not to simply cover the topic and then dismiss it. Ethical issues impact all aspects of research; they can and do occur at any point in the research process. Thus, the reader will see reference to ethical issues in the later chapters of this book as well.

WHAT ARE ETHICS?

In some areas of both practice and research, ethics clearly dictate what is forbidden or required under certain circumstances. For example, in social work practice, sexual contact with current and former clients is universally regarded as unethical. Similarly, research that is likely to cause permanent harm to its research participants is unethical. More frequently, however, ethics fall into the category of *issues*. An issue is debatable—individuals can hold two opposing positions on it, and a good argument can be made for either of them. In practice, an issue might be whether it is unethical to discontinue needed counseling with a client after her medical coverage has been exhausted. In research, an ethical issue might arise over whether deception is necessary to acquire certain types of knowledge, or whether it might actually be harmful to research participants.

The term *ethics*, derived from the Greek word *ethos* (which comes closest to the English word *character*), refers to principles within a society that reflect what the society generally views as right or wrong behavior. Ethics are a little different from laws—they often fall into what is commonly called the *gray area*. Thus, we sometimes find ourselves asking the question, "It is not illegal, but is it ethical?" In the context of research, ethical issues generally revolve around three related questions: (1) Who should benefit or suffer from the actions of the researcher? (2) Whose rights should take priority over those of others? and (3) Does the end (increased knowledge) justify the means (the methods used to acquire it and their potential for harm). In the ideal world, all individuals and groups should benefit from the development of new knowledge. Beneficiaries might include the researcher, those who provide research data, the institution sponsoring the research, the community, and other researchers whose efforts can build on the researcher's findings. But we know that, in the real world, the needs of one group sometimes are met at the expense of another. The Tuskegee Public Health Studies described later in this chapter is an example where the methods used by researchers to acquire valuable knowledge was extremely harmful to the individuals who provided the data.

WHO PROVIDES DATA FOR OUR RESEARCH?

As social workers, most of our research depends on our fellow human beings to provide the data that we need to conduct research. They may be our clients, family members of clients, fellow professionals, or anyone else who can help us to better understand some problem and/or to intervene more effectively in solving it. Whoever they are, they generally have one characteristic in common—they are asked to give much more than they will ever receive from their participation. For this reason and others, we have an ethical obligation to safeguard their health and well-being.

People who provide data for research purposes are referred to by various terms within the professional literature. Three of the most common are *research subjects*, *research partners*, and *research participants*. All three refer to the same individuals, but the terms have different connotations. Some people use the most traditional term, *subjects*, because it is universally understood within research circles. Others contend that the term is condescending or dehumanizing and that it is not consistent with the way those who provide data relate to the researcher, especially in studies that use primarily qualitative research methods. They also suggest that it implies that these individuals are somehow subservient, and thus susceptible to exploitation by the researcher. For a combination of these reasons, this term is being used less frequently now.

Researchers who conduct certain types of qualitative research prefer the term *research partner*. It suggests a different perception of the respective roles of research participant and researcher. They contend that the word *partner* most accurately reflects the relationship between those who provide research data and the researcher. They point out that those who agree to share so much of themselves (which often includes very personal information) to assist the researcher in building knowledge are as important as the researcher and that the relationship is thus one of equality.

We, however, have chosen to use the third term, *participant*, throughout this book. This choice is not simply a compromise. *Participant* seems to recognize the importance of those who provide data for research purposes, while also recognizing that their objectives and degree of involvement in knowledge building generally differ from those of the researcher. The term is consistent with both the quantitative and qualitative approaches and conveys the awareness that these individuals are entitled to both respect and attention to their rights. It acknowledges that although they may sometimes choose to be involved in research that results in their discomfort, they should never be tricked or forced into doing so.

EARLY ABUSES OF RESEARCH PARTICIPANTS

Researchers and those who sponsor or permit research have an ethical obligation to ensure that research participants are protected from harm. Unfortunately, this is a relatively new idea. Many of the ethical issues that must be addressed by today's researchers simply were nonissues for researchers in the nineteenth and early twentieth centuries. The history of humanity is replete with examples of research that valued knowledge building more than the rights of research participants. It reflects a lack of concern for how research might negatively affect the physical and emotional health of those who provide data for scientific analysis. Research participants often were individuals who were either powerless or defenseless (e.g., the poor, minorities, children, the mentally ill, prisoners of war). Others, it was believed, had essentially abdicated their right to protection under the law or under principles of common decency because of their behavior (e.g., those incarcerated for a serious crime).

The belated emergence of guidelines for conducting research with human participants occurred during the second half of the twentieth century. It came about because of a gradual recognition that, in a quest for scientific knowledge, the end cannot always justify the means. Our society has come to acknowledge that in some research studies done in the past, the cost to research participants was not justifiable, no matter how much knowledge was generated.

Some widely publicized research studies are considered "milestones" in the development of today's research ethical standards. They are better known for their contribution to an increased concern for the protection of research participants than for the scientific knowledge that they produced. They employed methods that ranged from those that are now universally condemned to those that still continue to be defended by some people within the scientific community. Many examples of unethical treatment of human participants could be cited. We have chosen to describe a few of the better-known ones and have noted how each has contributed to one or more standards that are used to protect research participants today.

The Nazi and Japanese Medical Experiments

Following World War II, it was revealed that concentration camps in Europe and prisoner-of-war compounds in Asia had been the scenes of heinous and repugnant medical experiments conducted in the name of science (Annas, 1992). During the Nuremberg war crime trials in 1945 and 1946, many shocking stories were recounted that detailed how Jews, Gypsies, and other "undesirables" detained in German concentration camps were deliberately exposed to life-threatening diseases in order to study the course of the diseases. They were exposed to severe cold, injuries were deliberately inflicted upon them to study the effects of new antibiotic treatments, and they were subjected to unnecessary surgery or placed in decompression chambers to study their tolerance for lack of oxygen and other effects of high altitude. Of course, viewed in retrospect, these experiments were little more than sadistic atrocities committed in the name of science.

Prior to the Nuremberg trials, little attention had been paid to the rights of prisoners and other vulnerable groups. All too often, they were regarded as convenient targets for experimentation. The shocking revelations that emerged at Nuremberg set about a process of questioning whether incarceration for any reason, even for conviction for illegal activity, can ever justify the nonvoluntary participation of prisoners in medical and other research. A consensus emerged that it cannot. Research participation must be voluntary.

Interestingly, one ethical issue related to the medical experiments conducted on American prisoners in Japanese prison camps did not surface until the 1980s. Access to previously classified documents revealed that American authorities had apparently suppressed information about the experiments after the war, in exchange for access to the medical knowledge acquired through them. As the news of the research became widely disseminated, current medical researchers sought access to data obtained in the prisoner-of-war camps. Newer and broader ethical questions were debated. Should research findings obtained through unethical methods be publicized or made available to other researchers for their use? Can suppression of valuable knowledge that has the potential to save lives be justified on the basis that the researchers' methods cannot be condoned? Who owns the data? Should the survivors of the experiments (who did not participate voluntarily) or the relatives of those who did not survive have the right to decide whether data from the experiments can be released or under what conditions it can be used? Like most research ethical issues, these are difficult questions with no easy answers.

The Tuskegee Public Health Studies

A second group of research studies that addressed some of the same ethical issues took place in the United States. In 1932, the American Public Health Service began its studies of the long-term effects of syphilis on men in the Tuskegee, Alabama, area (Jones, 1982). Ethical questions relate to whether these men were truly voluntary participants, because of their vulnerability (health status, socioecono-mic class, and race). The studies were influential in the development of today's ethical principle of *no unnecessary pain and suffering*.

The Tuskegee research was conducted on 625 African-American males. Most (425) had been diagnosed as having syphilis; the others were followed for comparison purposes. In 1937, penicillin was discovered and was shown to be an effective cure for syphilis. It became available to the general public several years later. Yet, for purposes of research, participants in the Tuskegee experiment, who were mostly poor and illiterate, were not told about penicillin, and it was not given to them unless they somehow learned about it and requested it. Participants unaware of penicillin continued to be given painful regular medical examinations, including spinal taps, to chart the course of their disease. They received only a placebo, an inert substance that had no potential to cure their disease or alleviate their pain and suffering. In the interim, they experienced the long-term effects of syphilis, including skin disorders, insanity, heart disease, and even death. The study continued until 1957, at which time it was halted following public outcry.

Unlike many of the experiments conducted within Nazi concentration camps during World War II, the Tuskegee experiments probably were not the product of depraved minds. They were designed to gather data that would be accurate and would have the potential to benefit humanity. Prior to the availability of penicillin, there may have been a legitimate reason to study syphilis to learn more about the course of a then essentially incurable disease. But when the drug became available, there was no logical justification to continue the research, and there was a very good ethical reason to discontinue it immediately and treat participants with the effective drug. Looking back now, those who made the decision not to treat these men with penicillin appear no less insensitive in their lack of regard for the protection of research participants than the medical "researchers" of Dachau or Auschwitz. Some of the researchers later rationalized that the participants were fortunate in that they were given free regular medical examinations and did not have to pay for their burial expenses. Not until 1997 did the U.S. government offer a public apology for their treatment, and the participants and their families were awarded limited financial compensation for their suffering.

The Milgram Studies of Obedience to Authority

In 1963, Stanley Milgram conducted a series of ingeniously designed studies that sought to learn more about the phenomenon of human obedience to authority figures. His research evolved in part from the defenses of Nazi war criminals, who contended that they were just following orders and therefore could not be held responsible for their actions. (Similar defenses were subsequently used by American soldiers in Vietnam and by many others in military conflicts in Bosnia and Iraq, where atrocities were committed.) Milgram hoped to learn what ordinary, civilized people are likely to do when ordered by a more powerful individual to do something that they would otherwise never do. He hoped to learn how far they would go in their obedience to authority figures.

The research used adult males as participants. They were told that they would participate in research on learning and would be assigned a partner for the research. In fact, the partner was a person working with the researcher; he was not another research participant. Through the use of a rigged drawing, the true participants always drew the role of the person assigned to reinforce learning through the administration of what they believed to be painful electric shocks to their research partner. The participants sat in a room where they could hear but not see the alleged learner who was supposedly wired to receive electrical shocks. The participants read off pairs of words and asked their partner to match them. When the learner made a mistake, the participant was told to throw a switch placed in front of him to give a shock to the errant learner. The switches were labeled with phrases such as "Extreme-intensity shock" and "Danger—severe shock." As more mistakes were made, the participant was told to throw switches indicating increasingly severe electrical shocks. As higher and higher voltage switches were thrown, the learner began to beg for the experiment to end. When the switches continued to be thrown, he began to kick the wall and scream. Finally, as the highest voltage switches were thrown, the learner became silent, indicating that he might have lapsed into unconsciousness or perhaps died.

Many participants became emotionally upset by what they were doing and asked and even begged to be allowed to stop. However, when ordered to continue, most did not stop. Only a third of the participants refused to complete the experiment; nearly two-thirds continued to throw the switches as ordered, despite the fact that they had reason to believe that they might be administering disabling, if not fatal, shocks to another human being.

Of course, as was later explained to the research participants, they were made to *think* that they were causing pain to their partner. In reality, no electrical shock was ever administered. Following the conclusion of research, participants were told that their partners were only acting to their throwing the switches. So why did some researchers and even the general public (subsequent to the showing of a made-for-TV movie on the research) object so strenuously to Milgram's methods? How did the Milgram studies come to be almost synonymous with unethical treatment of research participants? For one thing, people questioned whether the physical discomfort and anguish experienced by the research participants (unnecessary pain and suffering) could be justified in light of the knowledge acquired through the research. They experienced a great amount of stress. Critics asked if another method could not have been used to get the same results without causing so much duress for the participants. This question had already been asked about earlier research, for example, the Tuskegee studies.

A second ethical issue raised by the Milgram research is a relatively new one. People asked if some research should not take place because its effects on participants could not be undone. Had permanent harm been done to the research participants in the Milgram research? Apparently so. As a result of participating in the research, many of the men tended to view themselves in a different way than they had before. They now knew that, under the right circumstances, they were capable of causing severe physical harm to another person who represented no threat whatsoever to them. As we might anticipate, this was a disturbing revelation. No amount of debriefing to assure them that they had harmed no one while following orders could undo its effects.

The Milgram research helped us to formulate an ethical question: Does the researcher ever have a right to leave research participants in worse physical or emotional condition than that in which they were found?

The Milgram research helped us to formulate an ethical question: Does the researcher ever have a right to leave research participants in worse physical or emotional condition than that in which they were found? A consensus emerged that such a consequence is not justified if the researcher should have been able to anticipate it. Certainly, this had been the case in the Milgram research.

It is interesting to add that, despite the ethical questions raised by Milgram's original research, similar experiments have been carried out repeatedly since the original study results were released. At least some of these experiments were fashioned very closely after the original study. Most have added the use of female participants. The outcomes of these more recent experiments seem to be similar to the outcome of the original study, with a majority of the participants willing to inflict the highest level of shock to their partner. You can view portions of the documentaries created from these new studies on www.youtube.com, by entering "Milgram's obedience to authority experiment in 2009" and "Milgram re-enactment 2002."

The Laud Humphreys Studies of Homosexual Behavior

Laud Humphreys's studies (1970) of homosexual behavior in public restrooms sound quite dated today, but they were an important milestone in the development of ethical standards for the treatment of research participants. They also remain one of the most controversial research efforts in the human science professional literature. They have been defended and touted by some people as innovative, while being denounced by others as simply unethical snooping.

Professional Identity

As a social worker, how do you feel about the fact that the Milgram experiment has been replicated several times since the original experiments? Do you feel social workers should be involved in this type of research? Why or why not?

The special focus of Humphreys's research was casual homosexual sex acts between strangers who led otherwise heterosexual lives. He conducted observations of homosexual encounters between men in parks. Humphreys knew that the people he wished to study would be unlikely to agree to let him observe their behavior for research purposes. Even if they did, the data thus obtained would be of questionable value. So he engaged in a series of deceptions. He first gained the confidence of his intended research participants. He frequented the public restrooms and implied through his regular presence that he shared in their activities. He began to assume the role of watch queen, which entailed being a lookout for the police or other potentially threatening people. The payoff for being a watch queen was the opportunity to watch sexual acts being performed—exactly what he needed for his research. But the deception did not end there.

Because he believed that he needed to know more about his research participants, especially about their public lives, Humphreys conducted follow-up interviews. When possible, he recorded the license plate numbers of his participants' vehicles and obtained their addresses through access to police records. Disguising himself so that he would not be recognized as their watch queen, he interviewed them under the pretense of conducting a survey and obtained additional descriptive data.

Many ethical questions were raised by the Humphreys study. Some of them continue to be debated. Had he violated the participants' right to privacy? Had their participation in the research been voluntary? They had granted permission for the researcher to watch, but he had misrepresented his real purpose for being there. Was there any other way that he could have obtained the same knowledge without this elaborate deception? If he had informed the men of his real purpose, would he have been able to acquire accurate knowledge? How much would he have had to tell them about his research for them to be true voluntary participants? Some defenders of the research study contend that his deception caused no one any harm. After all, he conscientiously concealed the identities of his participants in his book that described the research.

The way in which Humphreys learned the identities of his participants and conducted his follow-up interviews was especially infuriating to some of his critics. They charged that the men's permission to be interviewed in their homes was not valid because he had been dishonest about the real reasons why he wished to interview them. He misrepresented both the real focus and the scope of his research. He also put participants at risk of someone making a connection between his survey in their homes and their activities in public restrooms. Although highly unlikely, a research participant's secret behavior could have come to light as a result of Humphreys pursuing them for a follow-up interview at home.

TODAY'S STANDARDS FOR PROTECTION OF RESEARCH PARTICIPANTS

Fortunately, today we need not operate in a vacuum in wrestling with ethical issues. As a result of public responses to abuse of research participants in earlier research studies such as those we have just described, there now exists a list of generally agreed-on standards that govern the conduct of research.

Institutional Review Boards

Ethical standards have been developed for research that uses human beings as participants. Many organizations now require review and approval of proposed research studies by a team of researchers and other concerned individuals. These groups are labeled an institutional review board (IRB), a human subjects review team, an ethics committee, or some similar title. Any project that involves a systematic investigation with the intent to develop or contribute to generalizable knowledge is considered *research*. One helpful question to determine if a project is research is whether the investigators plan to publish the results of the project or present the results at an academic meeting. If the project is deemed research, the next step is to determine if human subjects are involved. Federal regulations define *research with human subjects* as research that either obtains data through intervention or interaction with a living person or obtains identifiable private information (Florida State University, 2010).

Research involving human subjects is reviewed and approved by an IRB before the subjects are recruited and data is collected. Federal regulations have defined three categories into which human subject research can be divided. These categories are based on the level of risk posed to the research subjects:

Exempt. Research in this category poses the least amount of risk to potential subjects. They generally involve either the collection of anonymous or publically available data or research that is deemed least harmful, such as research on normal educational practices.

Expedited review. Research in this category involves the collection of data that is not anonymous, but involves no more than minimal risks to the potential subjects.

Full committee review. Research in this category involves greater than minimal risk or vulnerable populations, such as pregnant women or prisoners.

Individual IRBs define the policies and procedures they follow with regard to review of research proposals. For example, Florida State University (FSU) requires that all research proposals involving human subjects be submitted to its IRB. The researcher cannot make the decision whether his or her proposal meets the federal criteria for the exempt category. Therefore, FSU uses the expedited review process for research that meets the criteria for exempt. Another policy defined by the FSU IRB is that all research involving vulnerable populations, such as children, prisoners, or pregnant women, must be reviewed by the full committee. Expedited reviews are completed by two members of the committee and the chairman of the committee and take approximately three weeks. The full committee review takes approximately six weeks. The members carefully review proposals for research to ensure that the rights of participants will not be threatened or violated and that protection measures are in place. Until the review team is convinced that this is the case, the research is not allowed to be initiated. We will look more closely at four of the major standards the IRB considers when reviewing a research proposal: voluntary informed consent, no unnecessary pain and suffering, anonymity/confidentiality, and the need to conduct the research.

Voluntary Informed Consent

We already know what is meant by the word *voluntary*. It refers to "by choice, not because of coercion or intimidation or because of promises of rewards." As we will discuss later in this chapter, it is often difficult to determine if this condition has been met.

When used in the context of research, *informed* relates to the following question: will the potential participants know what they need to know (at least in general terms) to determine if they wish to participate in the research? Prior to agreeing to participate, a person should have a fairly clear idea of what that participation will entail. This is designed to protect participants from unknowingly getting themselves into a situation that they never would have chosen had they been more fully informed from the outset. It also limits the researcher's ability to deceive research participants by grossly misrepresenting the purposes of their research or the nature and limits of the demands that will be made on research participants.

Consent refers to the fact that there is a clear, generally written, agreement to participate. A consent form, signed by the participant, provides a potential research participant with a description of what to expect. It also provides legal protection for the researcher, who may later need proof that participants willingly took part in the research. This principle is consistent with the social work practice value of self-determination, which upholds an individual's right to make decisions about matters that affect his or her life and well-being. Box 2.1 shows examples of a research participant request letter and an informed consent form that could be used to acquire the voluntary informed consent of potential research participants. Note that it allows a participant to withdraw from the research at any time if he or she no longer wishes to participate for any reason.

In obtaining voluntary informed consent, special care needs to be taken in the case of persons from groups that are linguistically or culturally different from the majority population. Consent forms should be provided in the research respondent's native language, and clarifying comments and responses to questions should be addressed in the language most familiar to the respondent. Sometimes, such persons may simply not have understood the subtleties of the wording in the consent form. Such situations may require using bilingual or native-speaking research assistants to help obtain voluntary informed consent.

Researchers also need to be sensitive to culturally determined patterns of deference to authority, which may cause respondents to feel that they cannot or do not have the right to refuse participation in the study. This may be a relevant issue when the researcher is from a dominant group and the respondent is from a historically less powerful group where there is a shared history. The issue may also exist with cultures that emphasize deference to age or social status, as in some Asian cultures. If a researcher is unfamiliar with the culture of the target population in a cross-cultural research situation, someone familiar with the culture should be consulted regarding issues in obtaining voluntary

Human Rights & Justice

What are some reasons why special care needs to be taken when obtaining consent from minority populations?

Box 2.1 Research Participation Request and an Informed Consent Form

Dear Mr. or Ms. _____

During October and November of 2008, students from the University of XYZ, School of Social Work, will be conducting a study to learn more about how support groups may be helpful to women who are HIV positive. Specifically, the study will identify the characteristics of these groups that have been found to be most helpful over time, as described by the group facilitators.

You have been selected to participate in this study because you facilitate such a support group in our state. Your participation would require that you complete a brief survey instrument that will be mailed to you, and also participate in a follow-up phone interview with a student researcher. Some biographic and demographic information about you (gender, age, religious affiliation, academic preparation, and work experience) will also be gathered. Any data that you provide would only be published or made public in the aggregate form.

Participation in this study is completely voluntary. Those who elect to take part in it may discontinue their participation at any time without prejudice, or loss of benefits of any sort.

I hope you will agree to participate in this research. It has the potential to provide valuable knowledge to those in the helping professions who work closely with this population. If you agree to participate, please sign and date two copies of the attached consent form, keeping one copy for your records, and mail the other one back to me in the postage-paid envelope. After we receive your signed consent form, you will be contacted by a student to confirm a mailing address where we may send your survey form.

If you have any questions about the study, please contact me at 806-555-1234 or e-mail address: acharles@hotnet.com. Thank you.

Sincerely,

Alfred B. Charles

Professor, School of Social Work
Att.: Informed Consent Form

Informed Consent Form

I agree to participate voluntarily in a study from the University of XYZ, School of Social Work, examining support groups for women who are HIV positive. I understand that my participation in this study involves completing a survey form and participating in a phone interview with a social work research student. I may withdraw my participation in this study at any time without any prejudice or penalties of any sort.

Signature:

Printed Name:

Date:

---

informed consent and protection of human participants within the specific cultural context. A perception of a power differential or an emphasis within the participants' culture on deference to people with more social status or educational credentials may lead participants to believe that they had little choice but to volunteer.

The principle of voluntary informed consent recognizes that some vulnerable people—for example, very young children or people with a mental disability—may not be able to understand a description of their proposed participation in research and make an informed decision as to whether they wish to participate. In research that proposes to use people who may be considered incapable of giving voluntary informed consent, another responsible person may serve as an *advocate* to protect them and decide for them what should be permitted in the interest of scientific knowledge building. A parent, guardian, or, in some cases, a social worker or other helping professional, are logical choices to assume the advocate role.

Children, as they get older, should be allowed a greater role in deciding if they wish to participate in research. This is the ethical principle of *assent,* which entails involving older children in decision making, to the extent possible, based upon their developing capacity for rational thinking and their need for autonomy. The ultimate decision should result from an interactive process between the researcher, the child or adolescent, and the advocate.

No Unnecessary Pain and Suffering

Medical research and many research studies that social workers conduct have the potential to cause pain and suffering. In social work research, the pain is more likely to be emotional than physical, although physical discomfort (symptoms of emotional distress) may occur as well. For example, studies that entail interviewing adult victims of child abuse are likely to require research participants to think about and react to events that they would prefer to repress. This can be very painful (or it may provide a healthy catharsis if the interviewer is sensitive and uses his or her social work skills appropriately).

It is impossible to know all of the potential risks to participants posed by a proposed research study. By definition, science always works in areas of inquiry, where cause-effect knowledge is fragmentary, if not totally absent. However, the realities of science do not absolve the ethical researcher from protecting participants from *unnecessary* risk. Certain questions are appropriate. Can the knowledge be derived in a way that has less potential to cause physical or emotional harm to the participant? Have protections been built into the research design that will minimize the risk of causing pain and suffering? If the research absolutely must cause some physical or emotional discomfort, will its severity and duration be the absolute minimum that is necessary to acquire data?

The realities of science do not absolve the ethical researcher from protecting participants from unnecessary risk.

One study conducted by the University of California at Los Angeles (UCLA) during the 1980s and 1990s (Health and Medicine, 1994) illustrates the difficulty of balancing the need for knowledge and the principle of no unnecessary pain and suffering. It also shows how this principle can be related to the principle that we discussed earlier: voluntary informed consent. The researchers were attempting to learn if some people were unnecessarily taking antipsychotic drugs that may produce involuntary tremors. Fifty young patients being treated for schizophrenia had their medication abruptly discontinued. Of these fifty participants, twenty-three experienced severe relapses (including one suicide). Although their parents had signed consent forms for their children, they alleged that they were never told how severe the relapses might be or that it would be safer if the medication were continued.

The UCLA research was designed with good intentions. It sought to acquire knowledge that might help to alleviate a problem experienced by schizophrenic patients—unnecessary medication and its side effects. But in attempting to address the problem, some of the patients were harmed. Many ethical questions can be raised. Did the ends justify the means? Was the pain and suffering experienced by some of the participants in the research (and their families) necessary? Was there another way besides stopping their medication (perhaps gradually reducing it) to learn if the medication was necessary, while causing the patients less pain and suffering?

An important subissue that relates to pain and suffering is the presence of any negative aftereffects that people might experience from their roles as research participants. (Remember, this was a major issue in the Milgram studies.) A researcher is ethically obligated to leave research participants preferably in better condition than they were found, but at least in no worse condition. In recognition of the fact that virtually all research involving human participants has the potential to harm or change people in some way, human subject review teams generally pay careful attention to a researcher's plans for debriefing and restoration of participants' well-being after data have been collected. They may wish to ensure that, for example, counseling or other indicated follow-up will be provided, if needed.

Anonymity/Confidentiality

As social workers, we need not be reminded of the importance of safeguarding the privacy and identity of our clients. The ethical principles of anonymity and confidentiality exist to safeguard research participants from the harm that can come to them if their identities are intentionally or inadvertently associated with any data that are collected. The two terms are used in research much as they are used in other areas of social work practice. The ideal condition under which participants provide data is anonymity. When it exists, even the researcher does not know the participants' names and cannot attribute to them any data that were provided. An example of anonymity might be a mailed questionnaire survey that does not use case numbers or other identification on the questionnaire or on the return envelope. The researcher cannot know who returned one and who did not or who said what in their replies. This protects the participants' anonymity, but it can have real logistical disadvantages for researchers. For example, what if researchers wish to send a follow-up questionnaire to those who did not respond or to acquire clarification about some data provided by those who did respond?

A more realistic and generally acceptable alternative involves protection of confidentiality. Especially when data are collected by in-person interviews, researchers are likely to know and recall who revealed what about themselves. Under principles of confidentiality, the researcher is ethically obligated not to reveal the participants' identities or in any way let others be able to associate any of the data provided with any one participant. However, even if nothing is ever revealed, sometimes the data themselves can disclose the identity of the participant. Anastas (2010) warns that inferred identification is a particular hazard in qualitative research. She states, "When case data are given in detail or verbatim quotations are used in the text, it is possible that certain readers of a research report will be able to identify a specific research participant even when no identifying data are given" (p. 60). Identification in quantitative research can also be inferred when there are very few participants in a particular minority category. For example, if a sample includes 240 Caucasians, 60 African Americans, 12 Asian Americans, and 1 Native American, all data reported for the Native-American category could be easily traced back to the one Native-American participant. Upholding confidentiality requires careful editing of the data before disseminating study findings to minimize the risk of participant identification. This may require that some potentially valuable data be excluded, unless it can be aggregated along with that of other participants in some way. Because these issues can be more complicated in qualitative research, Anastas (2010) calls for "a fuller discussion and articulation of consent, disguise, boundary issues, and other normative practices to protect participants in qualitative evaluation" (p. 61).

The principle of confidentiality often governs how social workers handle data about their clients. As researchers, it seems familiar and natural to protect participants from harm. However, people outside the social work academic and practice communities may attempt to convince a researcher to compromise the principle. What if, for example, a research report reveals that a participant is guilty of a crime such as fraud or has threatened the well-being of others? Does the public have the right to know the identity of that participant and to take appropriate legal action? It is a good idea to check out relevant laws and statutes when such issues arise or, better yet, before they do.

In the role of researchers, social workers may not enjoy the protection of privileged communication, as this varies from state to state. Research data can and have been subpoenaed and will continue to be subject to public scrutiny. For this reason, some researchers have chosen to destroy the names and other identifiable data from files about their research participants once the data have been coded and case numbers assigned.

For some actions that we may learn about in the process of conducting research, such as child abuse, we may have no clear-cut solutions. We have an ethical and a legal obligation to notify the proper authorities that transcends our role as researchers. However, the appropriate course of action is not always that clear. Delva (2007) points out that researchers who conduct research on illicit behaviors, such as substance abuse or unsafe sexual practices among adolescents, often face an ethical dilemma. Should they respect the confidentiality of the research participants who have shared knowledge of their behaviors, or should they share the information with the participants' parents or other helping professionals since the behaviors are putting the participants at *risk?* What is the researcher's primary responsibility to participants—to protect confidentiality or to protect their health and welfare? Is the risk to participants less important than the knowledge that can be acquired (that can potentially help others in a similar situation) by adhering to promises of confidentiality? Such issues are not easily resolved. Whatever decisions are made, they can leave the researcher feeling a little uneasy.

Need to Conduct the Research

Although sometimes not mentioned specifically among the criteria by which review panels evaluate a research proposal, there is a fourth ethical concern that should always be considered. Even if the proposed research represents no physical or emotional threat to them, research participants have a right to assume that whatever demands are made on them (e.g., their time or other costs) are necessary for the advancement of knowledge. Ethically, research cannot be justified when it merely provides a research learning experience for the researcher, does not promise to significantly advance knowledge, or might provide knowledge that simply is not worth knowing. Thus, IRBs may question whether a proposed research is justifiable, given the nature of the products that it promises to yield, or whether it represents an unnecessary imposition on its participants.

Research may not be approved if it seems designed only to advance a political or economic agenda. The issue of conducting research for purposes other than the advancement of knowledge came to the fore during the late 1980s as a result of people active in the antivivisection movement. A frequent argument against the use of animals for experimentation by the American cosmetics industry was that research on chimpanzees, rabbits, guinea pigs, dogs, and other laboratory animals was not conducted to learn anything new. Its primary purpose was to provide legal protection for manufacturers against charges that products had not undergone sufficient testing prior to their release in the market.

Ethically, research cannot be justified when it merely provides a research learning experience for the researcher, does not promise to significantly advance knowledge, or might provide knowledge that simply is not worth knowing.

Is there a danger that social work researchers might conduct unnecessary research for purposes other than the advancement of knowledge? Yes. Even ethical researchers may inadvertently conduct unnecessary research. For example, a researcher may not conduct a thorough review of the literature to determine what knowledge is already available. Thus, researchers repeat the work of others and waste the time and energies of their research participants, as well as their own.

Research may also be conducted for purely educational purposes, that is, to give social workers supervised practice in conducting research. This can occur within colleges and universities, and even within human service organizations. Deriving new knowledge may not be a high priority—the same research questions may be studied year after year, and nothing productive is ever done with the acquired data.

Ethical Practice

Do you feel it is justified to require social work students to conduct research on their clients during their field placement experience? Why or why not?

Learning to conduct research by actually designing and implementing it can be a very effective way to become a good researcher. So what's wrong with this practice? Conducting research over and over on research questions whose answers are already available is ethically questionable, even if it does not represent a major imposition for research participants. It is a waste of scarce research resources and, what's more, it does not "model" good research. With a little extra effort, new questions (those begging answers) can always be found.

Concern over the ethics of unnecessary research is recognition that scientific inquiry involving human participants almost always represents an unequal trade. It offers less to the research participants than it takes from them. This "bad deal" can be justified only if some greater good can come out of the research, specifically, the advancement of knowledge that can help others.

CONTEMPORARY ISSUES RELATED TO RESEARCH "VOLUNTEERS"

By the latter part of the twentieth century, the standards for ethical protection of research participants had been developed. They have changed little since then. However, ethical issues are still with us and always will be.

Are Research Volunteers Truly Voluntary?

One important question relates to the standards of voluntary informed consent and no unnecessary pain and suffering. Some people choose to become research participants even if they know that the research might result in some discomfort or suffering to them. If the researcher knows that the participant would probably choose not to participate if his or her situation were different, can the participant ethically be considered a volunteer?

What are some of the situations that cause us to question whether it is ethical to allow people to participate in research, even when they wish to do it? Perhaps they have little to lose (they may have a terminal illness and wish to make some contribution to knowledge before they die). Others find themselves in a situation (they may be homeless and/or struggling financially) where even small rewards for research participation (a few dollars, a meal, or the opportunity to get out of the heat or the cold) can provide a strong incentive to become research participants. Prisoners within correctional settings may volunteer to participate in research studies. However, we must ask, would they have agreed to be research participants had they not been incarcerated? Can we be absolutely certain that they are not being coerced by something or someone, or influenced by some implied promise of reward, such as more privileges or time off their sentences? How can we know if they are agreeing to do something that they would not do under other circumstances? And, what if they are? Is it not their right to do so?

There is a similar ethical issue in research that involves new or experimental drugs or other interventions. For example, efforts to find a cure for or to delay the course of AIDS and other serious illnesses such as cancer, Parkinson's syndrome, and Alzheimer's disease have resulted in the experimental use of many unproven drugs. Some of them have painful and even potentially lethal side effects. Yet many people have willingly agreed to become research participants in medical research designed to test the efficacy of various medications and treatment regimens. Their "willing" participation, perhaps as a result of desperation or an inability to afford more proven medication (the cost is usually borne by the researchers), has caused us to ask a number of questions. Would they undergo the risks and discomfort if they had any alternative? Are researchers who conduct the research taking unfair advantage of their unfortunate situations? Or are they merely trying to make something good happen? Similarly, people who have been convicted of the crime of pedophilia have agreed to undergo aversive therapy to attempt to cure a problem that many currently regard as incurable. Has their desperation (and, perhaps some pressure from prison authorities) caused them to undergo the considerable physical discomfort that they would otherwise have not selected? Probably. Is that necessarily unethical?

There are many other groups that are vulnerable to being unethically used as research participants. Their rights must be protected. However, that entails a difficult balancing act between (1) their right to not be exploited as a result of their vulnerability and (2) their right to participate in research that may be of benefit to them. Sieber (1992) lists different categories of people who are vulnerable:

Policy Practice

Do you think people should be allowed to try unproven experimental treatments? Why or why not?

People who lack resources or autonomy

People who are stigmatized by society

People who are in a weakened position, perhaps in an institutional setting

People who cannot speak for themselves and their best interests

People whose illegal activities might become known to law enforcement authorities

People associated with research participants who may be damaged by data revealed by the participants (p. 147)

Medical research provides some of the clearest and most dramatic examples of ethical issues relating to the vulnerability of people who might "volunteer" to become research participants. These issues are just as prevalent in social work research. Naturally, most social work research focuses on people and the problems they experience. Although these problems are not always life threatening, they can be serious obstacles to life quality. People, often current or prospective clients, may "volunteer" to participate in a study of a new method of intervention or one designed to evaluate the merit or value of a social program. Perhaps, to complicate matters further, the intervention being tested is offered at no cost to them, while the "usual" intervention is offered for a fee. Is the research exploiting their vulnerability and is thus unethical? This is not an easy question to answer.

Dual-Role Relationships

Is it ethical to use our own clients or former clients as research participants? What about a colleague's clients, where the colleague serves as what researchers refer to as a *broker,* a person who asks potential participants if they would be willing to participate in research? Either group may readily agree to volunteer to participate in our research. Or what about the use of potential research participants who are not our clients but who share a problem or condition with us who we may have met through a support group or in a social situation? Would any of these individuals be considered volunteers in the purest sense of the word? We might ask, would they agree to serve as research participants if a previous relationship between us and them did not already exist? Can we be certain that obligation, gratitude, or even fear of offending us is not influencing their decision?

What we have just described can be referred to as *dual-role relationships.* When researchers have a preexisting relationship with potential participants, it is sometimes difficult to know if they are volunteer participants in the strictest sense and, if not, whether research can still be conducted without a violation of research ethics.

The presence of a dual-role relationship has often prevented good research from being conducted. However, IRBs have sometimes approved research studies despite the presence of a dual-role relationship. Why? This occurs most frequently when access to data would not have been possible had there not been a preexisting relationship with the participants. Anyone else attempting the same research would have had much greater difficulty in establishing trust and may not have been able to get potential participants to agree to participate. For example, one social work researcher (Taylor, 1998) conducted in-depth interviews with parents who had lost an adult child to AIDS to better understand how different people cope with such a loss. She had gotten to know her research participants while providing social work services to their sons or daughters. Another researcher (Pryce, 1995) interviewed children whose parent had suffered a massive traumatic head injury and had survived, but at a much lower level of functioning. She had experienced the problem in her own family and was able to locate her participants because she was a member of an organization that consisted of persons in similar circumstances.

Was research participation in these two studies truly voluntary? Probably not. The IRB members who approved them also acknowledged that the interviews with participants were likely to be stressful for them. However, no one was likely to be seriously harmed. In fact, the researchers later concluded, it was probably psychologically beneficial to the participants to express some of their feelings about their losses to a caring professional who they already trusted. The fact that the potential benefits of the research for others in similar situations probably outweighed any discomfort to participants was another factor in the decision to allow the studies to be conducted.

When dual-role relationships exist, certain special precautions are required to protect research participants. Special effort must be made to assure potential participants that they will suffer no loss or disadvantage (including the respect of the researcher) if they decide not to participate. The preexisting relationship should also not be damaged in any way. A third, neutral person—not the researcher—should be provided to offer counseling, if needed, and to help at any time in deciding whether or not it is in the participant's best interest to continue participation. Finally, if feasible, participation should be anonymous, so the researcher cannot know exactly who participated and who did not. Of course, in studies where the researchers themselves must gather data using in-person interviews with participants who they already know (such as the two examples previously described), anonymous participation is impossible.

There is still another issue related to voluntary informed consent that we as social workers sometimes encounter when we attempt to conduct research. Because of the nature of our work and the trust often placed in us by clients, we may have access to sensitive or private data not readily available to outside researchers. Clients often tend to become quite candid in what they say and do around social workers because they trust that the social worker is concerned primarily with helping them.

Should data (in the form of case records) gathered for the purpose of providing treatment assistance to clients be used for a purpose for which they never were intended—research? In such cases, did clients and patients really give voluntary consent to be research participants? Sometimes, but not usually. Federal legislation, the 1996 Hospital Insurance Portability and Accountability Act (HIPAA), made access to medical records data difficult, if not impossible, for use for research in many medical and psychiatric settings. However, in some settings, such as teaching hospitals, patients can still agree from the outset that data collected relative to their treatment can be used for research and teaching purposes. Even in other settings, records data sometimes are still used for research if clients or patients agree to their use. However, is this really voluntary informed consent, since it could be argued that consent may be granted under some duress? Undoubtedly, some participants want to provide information that might help others with the same problem. However, others may fear that not agreeing to participate may antagonize their social worker and thus affect their treatment.

Using Deception in Research

The social work researcher is perhaps less likely than researchers in other disciplines to conduct research that could result in irreparable physical or psychological damage to participants. We are sensitized to recognize the ways in which life experiences can negatively affect people's self-esteem or their ability to function. For example, we would not conduct or condone research that would involve telling clients that they should get out of a healthy marriage in order to study their emotional responses, or lying to medical patients that they have a fatal disease in order to observe what changes they might make in their lives. We know the potentially negative consequences of any behavior designed to alter how we think of ourselves or others. Our training in human sensitivity combined with our professional values mostly precludes research that could negatively and permanently alter the self-concept or mental or emotional health of our clients or others. However, does this mean that all research designs that entail deception of any kind are unethical? Not necessarily.

In some instances, deception may be necessary to study behavior or emotional responses that would be easily influenced if the participant had a complete understanding of the researcher's objective. In these cases, if the deception is deemed to be relatively harmless to the participant, it may be accepted as an ethical research technique. But deception can be an unnecessary and dangerous shortcut. It has been used when other, less potentially harmful methods, such as simulations, would have been equally effective. Before considering the use of deception, the ethical researcher should ask, Is deception absolutely the only way that I can get the knowledge that I need? And if so, what will

I do to be certain that I will not leave my research participants in worse phys-ical or emotional condition than when the research began? Pittenger (2002) offers three recommendations to the researcher considering the use of deception: (1) A researcher who uses deception should provide, in their research report, a detailed account of the procedure used to minimize the harm created by the deception; (2) The American Psychological Association should develop a definition of deception that describes the techniques com-monly used in research; and (3) The informed consent procedure should be revised to indicate that the researcher may use deception as part of the study (p. 117).

Withholding Treatment and Use of Placebos

Another old ethical dilemma is still with us, and probably always will be. It is most often discussed in relation to recent medical research but is equally relevant for many forms of social work research. It relates to whether it is ever ethical to deny some research participants access to an intervention method that may prove helpful for them. For example, what is the best way to exam-ine the effectiveness of one of the many experimental drugs being developed for the treatment of persons who are HIV positive or have other serious or life-threatening illnesses? Or, how do we learn most definitively if a social program is really effective? Traditionally, the most rigorous research designs have used a control group, a group of people who are identified as having the problem of interest but are merely followed and not offered the intervention. In medical research, members of the control group might instead be given a placebo (such as a sugar pill), but they would not know whether they received the experimental drug. The use of a control group may be methodologically sound, but is it ethically defensible? Either method might generate more pre-cise and more definitive findings than another research design that would simply provide the intervention to all participants and then monitor the course of their illness. But what about the people in the control groups? What if the intervention is subsequently found to be effective? Their quality of life might have been higher or their lives even saved if they had received the inter-vention that they were denied.

The notorious Tuskegee experiments are sometimes still mentioned in crit-icisms of current research, especially in studies that rely on research partici-pants who are vulnerable. For example, research in Third World countries has attempted to determine if HIV-infected mothers in a control group who were given a placebo or low dosages of drugs known to be effective for delaying the onset of HIV symptoms had a comparable or higher rate of passing the disease on to their babies than those given the full dosage of the drug (Associated Press Report, 1997). Critics have questioned whether such research, like the Tuskegee experiments, is unethical and exploitive of participants, in part because less vulnerable people may not have opted to participate in such research. Ellenberg (2009) presents the debate of the ethics involved in using placebos in research, stating that "the scientific considerations for using place-bos in trials are complex and often poorly understood, thereby complicating the dialogue around the ethical issues" (p. 259). She summarizes the debate into two distinct issues: (1) Is it ethical to assign participants to a placebo when effective agents are available, as long as no irreversible harm will result from remaining untreated for the duration of the study? (2) Is it ethical to assign participants to a placebo when effective agents have been identified and are available in some regions but not where the study is taking place, even if the known effective agents have been shown to prevent irreversible harm in the regions where they have been evaluated?

Availability of Experimental Interventions

The pressure to find a way to prevent or cure serious chronic illnesses has spotlighted other common research ethical issues that are relevant to social work research. One of these might be described as *the right to be a research participant*. We have already discussed the issue of people of certain vulnerable groups opting to participate in experimental interventions only because of their circumstances. A closely related issue is whether such experimental interventions should be made available at all. For example, what about society's responsibility to people in a control group, who are denied access to what may prove to be life-saving experimental drugs? These drugs are not available to many who might benefit from them because they have not yet been cleared for use in the United States by the Food and Drug Administration (FDA). Most likely, some of these drugs remain in a warehouse awaiting further research into their efficacy and possible side effects. Should the usual seven- to ten-year testing process be waived on the basis of the urgency of a situation? Similarly, for example, how many studies of a program designed to prevent adolescents from experimenting with methamphetamines should we require before we include the program as part of our "best practices" and seek funding for its widespread use? If one well-designed program evaluation concludes that its intervention has been effective, should that be enough for us to factor the results into our decision making (EBP)? Do we need two such studies? More?

Falit and Gross (2008) discuss this important ethical issue in light of a recent case, *Abigail Alliance v. Von Eschenbach*, in which the U.S. Court of Appeals ruled that the Fifth Amendment's due process does not include the fundamental right to access experimental treatments. Therefore, Congress and the FDA will continue to regulate access to such treatments as they see fit. Nevertheless, this will continue to be an ethical debate in social work and other research. Falit and Gross outline key themes for policy makers, advocates, and potential research participants to consider.

OTHER ETHICAL OBLIGATIONS OF RESEARCHERS

The ethical positions adopted by the National Association of Social Workers (NASW) provide guidelines for both professional practice and research. They limit one's behavior with clients and research participants. In the National Association of Social Workers' (1999) *Code of Ethics*, it is evident that the unethical use of human participants for knowledge building is never condoned. However, the *Code of Ethics* and the professional literature suggest that the researcher has ethical obligations not only to the participants but also to the sponsors of research, other researchers, colleagues, and the general public. Most obligations relate to broad issues, such as the scientific integrity of researchers, the requirement that they adhere to certain standards in conducting research, and that they honestly report and interpret findings.

What do these position statements tell us about the general characteristics of ethical researchers? For one thing, they recognize the seriousness of scientific inquiry and the potential of research findings to influence the work and lives of others. Policy makers are aware that any research finding, no matter how unexpected or contrary to what they believe to be true, is potentially valuable. In addition, any misrepresentation of what is learned is potentially dangerous because, in an era of EBP, social workers rely more heavily than ever on research findings for their decision making. Thus, for example, ethical researchers will honestly report null findings. In other words, they will report findings that demonstrate the ineffectiveness of a social program or the failure of an intervention as well as those that support the effectiveness of an intervention. They will place truth above the personal gain that can be attained through the manipulation of data to achieve desired results.

Ethical researchers function with neutrality and, to the degree possible, objectivity. They strive to keep an open mind to let empirical knowledge, not their own preferences, form the basis for any conclusions drawn from their research. When this is not totally possible—as it generally isn't—they candidly describe the amount and types of bias that they may have introduced.

Ethical researchers resist outside influences, such as political or economic pressures, that might influence either the results of the research or its dissemination. They give proper credit to funding organizations that provided support for their research, and, at the same time, do not allow these organizations to distort or suppress their findings.

Ethical researchers avoid research with which they have a conflict of interest. This includes any situation in which the researcher has the potential to benefit or lose depending on the outcome of the research. If research is going to provide social workers with scientific knowledge on which to base practice and policy decisions, they must be able to trust that the outcomes have been presented in a truthful and nonbiased way. If researchers have a personal investment in the findings of their research, the validity of the research findings may be compromised. Ethical researchers are aware of the tentative nature of scientific knowledge and remain open to reinterpretation and even contradiction of their findings. They do not claim to have more definitive answers to research questions than are justifiable on the basis of their findings. They value constructive confrontation and debate with their fellow researchers. They take responsibility for their research methods and findings, and they welcome legitimate critique.

Ethical researchers never attempt to take credit for work that they did not perform and always share the credit for collaborative efforts. They openly acknowledge the support and contributions of others to their research. They insist that appropriate credit be given to students and/or research assistants and consultants who contributed to the research effort. They will not allow their own names to appear as coresearchers on efforts where their own contributions were only minimal or as the primary researcher when others did most of the work.

Ethical researchers are aware of the tentative nature of scientific knowledge and remain open to reinterpretation and even contradiction of their findings.

While recognizing the importance of building knowledge to promote better client services, ethical social work researchers resist any use of research that appears to represent a breach of professional ethics. Their activities are shaped by both research ethical standards and their professional ethics as social workers. They are social workers first, then researchers. When using clients as research participants, they acknowledge that their clients' best interests must take precedence over knowledge building. They will not allow confidentiality to be violated without permission, even if it requires them to suppress potentially valuable findings. They discontinue any research if it begins to threaten their participants' welfare.

Ethical researchers are also concerned about the ways that research findings are disseminated and used. They want the findings of research to help rather than degrade or contribute to the harassment of the people they serve. They will attempt to halt the use of their research data by others when it is taken out of context to embarrass others, support erroneous stereotypes, or otherwise create or contribute to a false public impression about them. They may insist that their findings be presented only in their entirety. They may seek to discredit interpretations of their research findings that they perceive to be self-serving or that otherwise misrepresent them.

Much of what we have been describing falls under the heading of research integrity. It was discussed at a symposium devoted to the responsible conduct of research at CSWE's annual program meeting in Chicago in 2006. Subsequently, a subgroup of those in attendance began to meet to develop a statement that would continue and summarize the discussions. The members, with support from CSWE, produced a document, the National Statement on Research Integrity in Social Work (Council on Social Work Education, 2007), which is an excellent reference for social workers who wish to meet their ethical responsibilities to all parties likely to be impacted by their research efforts. Excerpts are included in Box 2.2.

Box 2.2 Excerpts from the CSWE's National Statement on Research Integrity in Social Work

To ensure the responsible conduct of research, social work researchers need to: (1) work to protect the people and communities whom they study; (2) ethically and effectively participate in mentoring relationships that are crucial to scientific activity; (3) manage apparent and implicit conflicts of interest and commitment; (4) collaborate ethically with researchers from other professions and disciplines; (5) ensure that research data issues are managed properly; (6) employ responsible publication and authorship practices; (7) responsibly conduct and contribute to the peer-review process; and (8) understand and prevent research misconduct (Office of Research Integrity, 2006). In the sections below we discuss each of these areas of concern and briefly discuss particular issues facing social work researchers.

1. Human Subjects and Communities

Social work researchers must strive not to harm the people or communities that they are studying. Research protocols should first ensure the protection of study participants, including consideration for the Basic Ethical Principles described in the Belmont

Report. Respect for persons "incorporates at least two ethical convictions: first, that individuals should be treated as autonomous agents, and second, that persons with diminished autonomy are entitled to protection" (p. 4). Beneficence assures that persons are "treated in an ethical manner not only by respecting their decisions and protecting them from harm, but also by making efforts to secure their well-being" (pp. 4–5). Justice requires that the "selection of research subjects needs to be scrutinized in order to determine whether some classes (e.g., patients receiving government assistance, vulnerable racial and ethnic minorities, and institutionalized persons) are being systematically selected simply because of their easy availability, their compromised position, or their manipulability, rather than for reasons directly related to the problem being studied" (p. 6) (National Commission for the Protection of Human Subjects of Biomedical and Behavioral Research, 1979).

Research involving vulnerable populations needs to assure that risk of harm is minimized and benefits from the research are equitably distributed. While designing protocols to protect vulnerable people and

(continued)

Box 2.2 *(continued)*

communities can be extremely challenging, total or arbitrary exclusion of vulnerable populations from research is detrimental to the people the profession serves and can sometimes constitute research misconduct. Social work research in developing countries poses additional and specialized ethical problems in human protection that deserve special consideration. Rather than avoiding these difficulties, researchers should work with their colleagues and the appropriate IRBs to develop ways to ethically include vulnerable populations in research. Participation in research should be predicated on the potential participant's understanding of the project, including obtaining informed consent. Finally, social work researchers should keep in mind that students involved as research participants are to be afforded the same protections as any other population.

Before beginning any research investigation, researchers should receive all necessary approval from the organizational regulatory bodies. The organizational regulatory bodies, such as the researcher's Institutional Review Board, will provide another layer of protection for the participants and communities in research, by ensuring that pertinent laws and guidelines have been met by the protocol and that the research is ethical. Researchers should consult with colleagues and the Office of Research Integrity/IRB staffs in their institutions and universities if they have questions regarding regulatory bodies.

2. Mentor/Trainee Responsibility

Social work researchers have a responsibility to mentor trainees in a manner that enhances the professional development of the latter and advances the general progress of the profession. Mentoring junior researchers and trainees in social work research serves to instill the mentee with the ethics, techniques, and community of the profession (Vasgird & Hyman-Browne, n.d.). Social work's commitment to advancing the careers of traditionally underrepresented and marginalized groups indicates a special commitment to mentoring trainees who often experience isolation and exaggerated expectations in academic and research settings. Senior researchers and mentors have a special responsibility to act ethically toward junior researchers and trainees by avoiding implicit and explicit exploitation. Mentoring relationships are complex; collaborative agreements that are developed early in the working relationship and that clearly

delineate the rights and responsibilities of all parties can be very helpful in ensuring fair and just outcomes.

3. Conflicts of Interest and Commitment

Social work researchers are encouraged to develop relationships with public and private institutions. However, social work researchers should scrutinize their research endeavors and seek to avoid and eliminate any improper conflicts of interest that might result from their activities. These can involve tangible conflicts, such as untoward financial gain, but may also involve other and intangible forms of improper personal enhancement or advancement. Despite institutional pressures to attract high levels of external funding and to lead multiple projects, social work researchers should judiciously commit only to those projects and positions which they can reasonably undertake. The number and complexity of contemporary researchers' roles make this a challenging domain of responsible conduct.

4. Collaborative Science

Contemporary social work research is rarely an individual enterprise. Multidisciplinary and community-based research are often required, especially for significant research investigations. Social work researchers should engage in collaborative enterprises with other professions and disciplines to advance scientific knowledge. These efforts will require special attention and sensitivity to the ethos and cultures of those research partners. Social work researchers also should seek to clarify, and in many cases commit to a written agreement, issues pertaining to data ownership, authorship, project roles, and financial management.

As the growth of translational science continues, social work researchers will increasingly collaborate with communities. It is important that researchers work hard to understand and reasonably respond to local needs and expectations as research projects are designed, implemented, and published. This is especially challenging as social work researchers often collaborate with community members who come from very different backgrounds and have goals that are divergent from the researchers.

5. Data Acquisition, Management, Sharing, and Ownership

The rapid development of exciting technologies for data acquisition, analysis, and sharing create complex ethical challenges for social work researchers. Researchers need to consult and understand the regulations and obligations involved as they conduct research. The federal government and most other sponsors stipulate what these obligations shall be when a researcher is awarded a grant or contract. Universities also have policies and regulations in this domain which create obligations for researchers who are, in effect, agents of these academic institutions. The best strategy is to discuss the particular approaches the researcher will take with sponsors and their academic colleagues early in the life of the research project. It is important that the entire research team understands these issues as well, as they often intersect with more mundane personnel issues, for example, changing jobs or moving to a new institution.

6. Publication Practices and Responsible Authorship

An important part of social work research is the reporting of study results. Publication of research findings should include appropriate attribution of authorship. Authors and co-authors should be determined on the basis of the type and amount of work completed. There can be controversy over who should be included as an author, especially since being identified as an author or first author on a publication can have implications for tenure, funding, and other professional opportunities; beginning discussions of authorship earlier in the research process can reduce confusion. Many universities, departments, peer-reviewed journals, and professional organizations have specific policies outlining the criteria for who qualifies as an "author" for a publication (Eisner, Vasgird, & Hyman-Browne, n.d.).

Social work researchers must never fabricate data or publish data that are known to be fabricated or otherwise compromised in nature or engage in plagiarism. All ideas and phrasing not originating with the author or co-author should be appropriately acknowledged in publication of results. Researchers should respect ethical obligations, regulations, and laws pertaining to intellectual property, copyright, and patents. Complex developments in technologies and regulations regarding data acquisition, management, sharing, and ownership demand special consideration. The emergent quality of these areas requires social work researchers to regularly study pertinent issues, problems, and solutions as they develop.

7. Peer Review

Peer review is critical for the advancement of science. Journals and federal- and private-granting organizations are reliant upon reviewers to ensure the quality of their publications and awards. Social work researchers should participate in the peer-review process in a fair, constructive, and rigorous manner. Additionally, peer-review processes should be timely and protect the confidentiality of all participants. Social work researchers should identify all potential conflicts of interest and also strive to subordinate their personal preferences and biases to the higher purposes of advancing the profession, scientific activity, and the public welfare.

8. Research Misconduct

Consequences for engaging in research misconduct are varied but may include ineligibility for future grants, termination of positions, monetary penalties, or other penalties. Findings of research misconduct result in negative publicity for the researcher/research team and for the university. If the university is also implicated in misconduct (e.g., chronic nonresponsiveness of the IRB) sanctions may include the withdrawal of federal authorizations and funding for selected or for all federally-sponsored research. It is also important to note that local or state jurisdictions might impose criminal or civil penalties if such investigations reveal criminal misconduct or tortious behavior. Loss of personal integrity, moral authority, and community trust transcend the particular events associated with misconduct cases by destroying the relationships enjoyed by researchers and the wider community for years. In sum, research misconduct can be extraordinarily costly to all persons and organizations concerned. Consequences extend beyond issues of liability and damage to reputation, to include damage to: (1) relationships with the participating communities; (2) individuals involved in the work; and (3) professional integrity.

Undetected research misconduct can have even graver consequences, including the dissemination of practice technologies, programs, and social policies that have relied on unfounded or distorted scientific work. The result might be the waste of limited social resources, loss of life, or reduced personal well-being for clients and significant harm to the public welfare. Therefore, social work researchers have an obligation to work hard to prevent research misconduct, to report such misconduct when it occurs, and to support colleagues who attempt to do both despite the personal and professional risks involved.

Source: Reprinted with permission from the Council on Social Work Education © 2007. *National Statement on Research Integrity in Social Work.*

SUMMARY

In this chapter, we examined some of the major ethical issues that social workers face when they conduct research. Past research has helped to produce current ethical standards that are designed as general guidelines to protect the physical and psychological well-being of human research participants. However, as we discussed, there are many situations where even highly ethical researchers and members of IRBs struggle with the specific meaning and application of these standards.

We looked at today's standards for the protection of the research participant, and some of the other major ethical responsibilities that researchers have toward the sponsors of research, other researchers, colleagues, and the general public. These standards are designed to ensure that, in the process of knowledge building, researchers respect the needs of others who may stand to benefit or lose from their activities.

Log onto **www.mysocialworklab.com** and answer the following questions. (If you did not receive an access code to **MySocialWorkLab** with this text and wish to purchase access online, please visit www. mysocialworklab.com.)

1. **Watch the Connecting Core Competencies Video: Research-Based Practice: Contracting with the Client to Select an Evidence-Based Therapy.** At the beginning of the next session, the therapist may ask the client to sign a voluntary consent form. What are five things that the therapist would want to include in this consent form?

2. **Read the Case Study: Crisis and Kinship in Foster Care.** We talk about voluntary informed consent a great deal in social work. What are some adjustments that need to be made when we are working with involuntary clients?

PRACTICE TEST

1. The Tuskegee public health studies helped to develop what ethical principle?
   a. No unnecessary pain and suffering
   b. Confidentiality
   c. Dual-role relationships
   d. Anonymity

2. All of the following ethical questions were raised by the Laud Humphreys studies of homosexual behavior except one:
   a. Had the researcher validated the clients' right to privacy?
   b. Had participation in the study been voluntary?
   c. Could the researchers have obtained this data without the use of deception?
   d. Was this research necessary since so much was already known about this population?

3. All of the following are possible examples of voluntary clients not really being voluntary, except one:
   a. Business owners will share information about their companies in order to improve service delivery.
   b. Poor single mothers will get free child care for participating.
   c. Students will get extra credit for volunteering.
   d. Drug addicts will receive monetary payment for participating.

4. Deception may be considered ethical if
   a. the information acquired in the end is known to be very valuable.
   b. the researcher can be reasonably confident that the participants will not suffer long-term damage.
   c. the deception is deemed relatively harmless and there is no alternative nondeception method that can be used.
   d. the clients never know they are being deceived.

5. What are five questions the researcher might ask to help ensure that the research participants are truly voluntary?

ASSESS YOUR COMPETENCE
Use the scale below to rate your current level of achievement on the following concepts or skills associated with each competency presented in the chapter:

1	2	3
I can accurately describe the concept or skill.	I can consistently identify the concept or skill when observing and analyzing practice activities.	I can competently implement the concept or skill in my own practice.

_____Being familiar with some of the historical events that led to the creation of ethics in our field

_____Understanding the concepts of voluntary informed consent, no unnecessary pain and suffering, and anonymity and confidentiality

_____Understanding the problems involved in ensuring that research participants are truly voluntary

_____Being able to identify dual-role relationships and understand the problems involved in these relationships

3

Research Problems and Questions

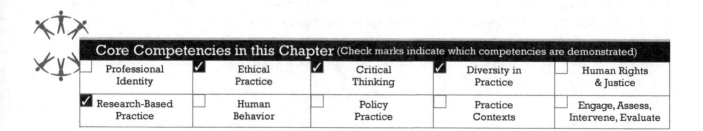
Core Competencies in this Chapter (Check marks indicate which competencies are demonstrated)				
☐ Professional Identity	☑ Ethical Practice	☑ Critical Thinking	☑ Diversity in Practice	☐ Human Rights & Justice
☑ Research-Based Practice	☐ Human Behavior	☐ Policy Practice	☐ Practice Contexts	☐ Engage, Assess, Intervene, Evaluate

Research should begin with the identification of a research problem and then move on to selecting research questions that relate to that problem. While this may seem self-evident, social workers are sometimes tempted to begin conducting research with insufficient articulation of the problem or the research questions that emanate from it.

In their discussion of research problem selection in social work research, Rubin and Babbie (2008) note that "the impetus for selecting a topic should come from decisions that confront social service agencies or the information needed to solve practical problems in social welfare. . . . A study is more likely to have value for the social work field [and to be considered social work research] . . . if the topic is selected because it addresses information needed to guide policy, planning, or practice decisions in social welfare" (p. 129).

Frankfort-Nachmias and Nachmias (1992) define a research problem as "an intellectual stimulus calling for an answer in the form of a scientific inquiry" (p. 51). Rothery (1993) describes research problems as "situations that are characterized by doubt and ignorance and that represent felt difficulties. There is something in the situation that is unknown, and there is a reason for wanting to reduce this doubtfulness" (p. 17). Definitions (and those within other texts) differ slightly, but they also have a considerable amount in common. For one thing, they suggest that a research problem ought to be stated as a declarative, descriptive statement of a condition—never as a question.

What makes all research problems similar, yet different, from other kinds of problems? How are social work research problems different from personal problems, social problems, or even research problems in general? A social work research problem is a specific type of problem. It is an undesirable condition attributable (at least in part) to the nonexistence of some potentially useful knowledge. Not only is this knowledge gap felt by social workers, but there is a desire to fill it. For example, for some social work practitioners, a research problem may be the absence of knowledge that is needed to effectively influence pending legislation. For a social work manager, it may be the absence of evidence that a social program is effective, which makes the decision about whether to continue it more difficult. For the social work educator or trainer, it may be the absence of knowledge that could indicate which methods are most effective for inculcating certain values or teaching certain skills that students need. Note that the preceding examples describe problems faced by individuals and not caused by their own deficiencies. The knowledge that they require does not exist. It has not yet been generated.

WHY WE BEGIN WITH RESEARCH PROBLEMS

When designing and conducting research, it is important to not get ahead of ourselves. In both qualitative and quantitative research, there is a logical sequence of events; in both types, articulating a clear problem statement must precede all other tasks. Stating the research hypothesis, identifying the design for conducting the research, selecting an appropriate data collection instrument, and developing a plan for statistical analysis of data are all important tasks in research, but to perform these tasks without formulating the research problem is to ask for trouble later. Social workers would inevitably waste time and resources trying to fit a research problem to the hypothesis, the research design, the data collection instrument, or the statistical analysis instead of (correctly) allowing the research problem to guide all subsequent decisions about how the research should be conducted. Thus, the research problem that is ultimately selected and specified should set the stage for and heavily influence all later steps in the research process. It should never be the other way around, that is, all or part of a research methodology developed first and then an appropriate problem specified. A properly conducted project is an integrated whole from start to finish (Shontz, 1986). The start should always be research problem identification and specification, with all subsequent activities flowing from and clearly relating to the problem that is selected.

Identifying and then specifying research problems might seem like tasks that can be easily and quickly accomplished. Unfortunately, this is not always the case. Often, we know of research problems that we would like to study but have difficulty articulating them in a researchable form. This is true primarily because problems, by their very nature, seem to be perceived in different ways by different people. If there were perfect consensus on exactly what the problems are, why they exist, and what should be done about them, most problems would have ceased to exist a long time ago!

IDENTIFYING POTENTIAL RESEARCH PROBLEMS

For the social work practitioner, the identification and specification of a problem is the first stage involved in developing intervention strategies. Thus, beginning the research process with a problem would seem to be a pretty natural thing for us to do. However, in social work research, *a problem* is a little different. It is not a problem of our client or a client system, such as a group, organization, or community, as it is in other areas of social work practice. A research problem is *our* problem, a problem that *we* experience in our professional practice, specifically a knowledge gap that leaves us unsure about how best to intervene to address a problem of a client or a client system. We sometimes find ourselves thinking, "If only I knew if . . ." or "I wish I had more knowledge about . . . ." If the missing knowledge existed, we believe that we would be able to intervene more effectively and with greater likelihood of success. Examples of such knowledge gaps follow:

> ▸ A social work therapist might think, "If only I knew how others have experienced this loss and what it meant to them."
> ▸ A family counselor might think, "If only I knew if it would promote or decrease candid discussion of the family's problems if I were to include the mother's boyfriend in treatment sessions."
> ▸ A social worker running a support group might think, "If only I knew if providing name tags for members will result in better group participation."
> ▸ A social work administrator might think, "If only I knew if my staff would appreciate my reviewing some of their correspondence before it goes out or whether they would resent it as 'micro-managing.' "
> ▸ A social worker engaged in community organization might think, "If only I knew whether it would be better for me to personally chair a 'get-out the vote' campaign or attempt to encourage leadership from within the community."

Often, research problems are identified through interaction with others. Sometimes, clients tell us about some phenomenon or behavior that is relatively new (at least to us) or that has not been studied for various reasons. It may be

A research problem is our problem, a problem that we experience in our professional practice, specifically a knowledge gap that leaves us unsure about how best to intervene to address a problem of a client or a client system.

something we need to understand better if we are to intervene effectively with certain client groups. For example, as norms and practices continually change, our understanding of youth gangs and how to work with them is often hampered by our inability to understand their behaviors and the importance of gang membership to its members. A client who describes the behavior can cause us to want to learn more about it (who is most likely to engage in it, how it started, what police have done to prevent it, and so forth). We may identify one or several areas where knowledge is incomplete or missing altogether—potential research problems.

Other potential research problems emerge in case supervision. For example, a social worker, seeking assistance, may ask her supervisor a question about a client problem, its incidence (descriptive knowledge), what is most likely to happen if some intervention is attempted (predictive knowledge), or what intervention will produce the desired results (prescriptive knowledge). The supervisor, being candid, admits that she doesn't know, but will try to find out. She reports a week later that the answer to the social worker's question does not appear to be available within the professional body of knowledge. A potential research problem has just been identified.

Sometimes, just in casual conversation, two or more coworkers may recognize that they share the same sense of frustration because the knowledge that would help them be more effective in their practice seems unavailable. For example, a group of hospice social workers may feel frustrated in being unable to be as helpful to stressed-out family caregivers as they would like. So they first try to determine if the knowledge needed to assist them is already available. An Internet search and/or a brainstorming session may be used to articulate the problem better. It is possible that they will discover that the knowledge they lack is available, and they were just not aware of it. However, it is also possible that they will conclude that there exists little knowledge about the need for certain types of self-care among caregivers and which type of caregiver support groups have been found to be most effective in addressing them. If so, they may have identified a potential research problem.

Setting Problem Priorities

Not all knowledge gaps can be regarded as either equally important or equally well suited to social work research. In determining whether they can justify their attention and limited research resources on a particular problem, social workers must address certain issues and questions.

In the ideal world of unlimited research resources, any knowledge gap that might be hindering social workers' capacity to help others would be a problem suitable for study. But in the real world, certain knowledge gaps must be regarded as higher priorities than others. Social workers must ask the basic question: Among those potential research problems that exist and that are of current concern, which are most in need of a solution?

Identifying a gap in knowledge as a higher or lower research priority can be a complicated process. It is not a task that comes naturally or comfortably to many social workers, because to conclude that some knowledge gaps—although a source of frustration for some people—currently do not justify the limited research resources seems to go against social work practice values. However, we do not say that research problems of lower priority are unimportant or should be ignored by social workers once and for all. As in any decision that employs EBP principles, social workers combine their knowledge of the

Critical Thinking

Identify three specific social or psychological problems about which you would like to increase your knowledge by either studying the available literature or conducting your own research.

problem (e.g., who is most affected by it, how severe it is) with factors such as practice experience, social work values and ethics, and even a little compassion, and decide, based on objective standards, whether the research should be conducted.

In attempting to set priorities, we acknowledge that in a world of limited research resources, we sometimes must opt to get the greatest possible benefit out of our time and efforts. What questions can we ask to help us objectively assess the research priority of a potential research problem?

Is the problem really an important one? Sometime early in the research process, we need to demonstrate that the research problem selected for study ranks high in priority. This is especially important if a formal proposal must be written and submitted to a potential research sponsor or for review by an IRB (see Chapter 2). After the research has been conducted, we also would like to be able to demonstrate to potential critics, as well as to those favorable to the research, that the problem studied was important, more important than others that might have been studied.

The question of what makes one research problem more important than another relates to a wide array of factors, such as the scope of the problem, which people are most affected by it, how badly knowledge is needed, and the potential value of the variety of products that can evolve from the research process.

Sometimes, the real importance of a research problem and the research that examined it cannot be fully appreciated until years after the research has been completed. The fact that the findings of research are widely publicized, widely cited, or widely used seems to add importance retroactively to a research study. Other times, a study's importance may relate less to its findings than to some other product of the research. For example, a standardized data collection instrument (see Chapter 12) developed to study a research problem may later gain widespread usage and may ultimately be considered that research project's greatest contribution to knowledge. The instrument may help to legitimize the researcher's efforts, even if the research findings themselves prove to be of limited value.

It is difficult to assess the ultimate importance of a proposed research problem. How can one envision all possible difficulties that could depreciate the value of the research? How can one accurately predict the final judgment of others as to whether the research effort was truly worthwhile? Fortunately, we can use certain guidelines to help us in wrestling with the issue of research priority. There are certain characteristics of research problems that seem to suggest that they are of higher priority than others. For example, problems may be considered high priority if they (1) reflect a widely felt and critical knowledge gap; (2) relate to a difficulty that affects many people; (3) have the potential to generate specific recommendations rather than highly abstract knowledge; or (4) are likely to produce by-products that will benefit other researchers conducting scientific inquiry on a wide variety of topics.

Do we already have enough knowledge about the problem? Some human conditions have been thoroughly studied, often by people other than social workers, through major funding from government agencies or private foundations. Many knowledge gaps have already been filled. For example, we know a great deal about the eating disorders, bulimia nervosa and anorexia nervosa. Studies have looked at diagnosis, prognosis, prevalence, risk factors, protective factors, group versus individual interventions, and inpatient versus outpatient interventions for these disorders. That does not mean, however, that some aspect of the problem does not have potential for social work research. For example, Vrabel, Ro, Martinsen, Hoffart, and Rosenvinge (2010) conducted a five-year study of adults with eating disorders to determine the prevalence of personality disorders in this population. In addition to prevalence rates, they found that people who recovered from their eating disorder were less likely to have a comorbid personality disorder. Fennig and Hadas (2010) examined depression and suicidal behaviors in adolescents with eating disorders to identify risk factors associated with suicidal ideations and suicide attempts. Research studies like these generate new knowledge that will be of immediate use to social work practitioners working with people with eating disorders.

Are people in other disciplines better suited to conduct research on the problem? There may be a need for research on a potential research problem, but it might be better to let others, on account of their specialized expertise, conduct it. For example, although social workers counseling children with attention deficit hyperactivity disorder (ADHD) could benefit from knowing the long-term physical effects of a child taking certain prescription medications designed to treat it, pharmacology or physiology professionals might be better suited to conduct research on the problem. However, social workers are better suited to conduct research designed to fill gaps in our knowledge, for example, about how use of medications may affect the need for certain types of parenting behaviors, or what patterns can be expected in a child's behavior in the evening hours after a medication's influence on behavior begins to wear off. Additional knowledge in either of these areas would be helpful to social workers in deciding how to work with children diagnosed with ADHD and their parents.

What is the potential for use of any findings and recommendations that would be generated by the research? Who will care, and what is the likelihood that anyone with the power to use the acquired knowledge will be inspired to take the recommended action? A study of a potential social work research problem that is not likely to result in needed change is of little value.

The lack of any positive result from research frequently results from financial and political obstacles to research use. People who might be able to use the findings may lack either the necessary resources or the value commitment necessary to do what research indicates is needed. Sometimes, both obstacles are present. For example, a community might have a problem of dangerous apathy among adolescents regarding the possibility of their contracting a sexually transmittable disease. A lack of understanding of the apathy and the lack of knowledge of how best to address it could be the impetus for good, worthwhile, methodologically sound research that would both identify the source of the apathy and generate recommendations as to how social workers could be effective in heightening adolescent awareness of the dangers involved. But because of certain conditions present within the community, research on the problem might be a waste of time. The research might recommend that school social workers provide education on sexuality or at least run needed information groups. However, it might already be known that a school board operating with a deficit budget might be unable to purchase the educational materials needed to successfully offer this service. Or it might be common knowledge that the powerful fundamentalist minister who chairs the school board would almost certainly intimidate other board members into blocking what he has already publicly described as "instruction in sinning." Therefore, the probability of implementation of research recommendations might be very small, even zero. Despite the need for research, it may have lower priority because research findings and recommendations would have little hope of being used. *Am I sufficiently interested in studying the problem?*

Ethical Practice

Can you think of an ethical reason why a research study may be conducted even though the researcher knows the findings will not be used immediately?

The development of knowledge to benefit social workers and their clients can be an exciting activity. But research is hard work. Certain tasks can become very tedious at times. Even a general interest in a research problem may not be sufficient to carry a researcher through times when necessary but less-than-exciting tasks must be performed. For example, entering research data collected from hundreds of participants into a computer, even when we are curious about the findings of our research, can be pretty boring.

Is there a temptation for social workers to choose to study problems about which they have little interest? Unfortunately, yes. Pressures from supervisors and higher-level managers sometimes make it difficult to say no. On other occasions, the lure of grant money can help to convince social workers that they might be more interested in studying a research problem than they really are.

A social worker conducting research without any real interest in it may be making a big mistake because it may negatively affect the quality of the research. It also can have a negative effect on the attitudes of the researcher about future scientific inquiry. All other factors being equal, a problem about which a researcher is interested and concerned should have higher priority than one in which the researcher's interest results primarily from political or financial motives.

What logistical obstacles are present? Some potential social work research problems may face major logistical obstacles. Although it is probably correct to state that any problem can be studied, some problems, by their very nature, are so complicated, would require so many resources, or would require so many methodological compromises that it would be virtually impossible to do the job right. In determining if a problem is researchable on a practical and logistical basis, the following questions are worth asking:

- **Is the problem just too large?** Some problems are so widespread and pervasive that they would be totally unmanageable as the focus for a single research study. However, it might be possible to break off some small piece of the problem for study. For example, to attempt to understand the origin and extent of ageism within North American human service organizations would require a research study of such large scope that most social work researchers would lack the budget and other resources necessary to undertake it. (Research almost invariably ends up costing more than anticipated.) However, social work researchers with limited resources might be able to design research to study some aspect of the phenomenon, such as the discriminatory methods used for advertising supervisory job openings in not-for-profit organizations within their own state.
- **Can the needed measurement be accomplished?** As we shall discuss in more detail later, good measurement is absolutely essential to sound research. But some things are more easily measured than others. For example, behaviors, generally speaking, are more easily measured than attitudes or values. Although researchers have made great progress in the development of measurement of the latter in recent years, in many cases, measuring attitudes that might be of interest to us remains an imprecise art.

Which treatment interventions are effective and which ones are not provides special measurement difficulties. The success or failure rate in a job-training program can be fairly easily determined by counting how many people complete the program and successfully find and keep related jobs. However, the success or failure rate associated with a particular approach to marriage counseling can be much more difficult to ascertain. Was divorce indicative of success or failure? How should we interpret the fact that a couple voluntarily terminated counseling? They could have stopped seeing the social worker because most of their difficulties had disappeared, or because they perceived that they were getting no help! Indicators of successful or unsuccessful treatment in such instances may be limited to notations in a case record or follow-up phone calls.

If studying a research problem would require the measurement of certain phenomena that seem to defy measurement, the entire problem may be regarded as not researchable, and no amount of research can provide needed answers. A classic example of a nonresearchable problem is the debate that preoccupied some theologians several centuries ago. The problem of not knowing how many angels can dance on the head of a pin was not a candidate for scientific research then, and it would not be now either. Some contemporary social work problems—for example, a lack of understanding of why some physicians seem to undervalue the professional education of social workers—may be only slightly more researchable than medieval philosophical questions. Physicians' respect for social workers' education might be so difficult to measure that the problem, if it is indeed a real one, may not be able to be studied. Besides, it may not be a high research priority, given the other criteria that we suggested earlier.

Do I have the necessary skills and expertise to conduct research on the problem? Specialization is characteristic of people who conduct scientific inquiry. Some researchers are especially adept at certain specialized research tasks, such as use of the Internet, interviewing, questionnaire construction, or statistical analysis of data, and less competent to perform other tasks. Although it is possible to learn to do what is required or to hire a consultant to do it, this can represent a costly use of limited research resources. If studying a research problem would require skill and expertise not currently possessed by a potential researcher—for example, the use of statistical analysis—the problem may as well be considered unresearchable. Similarly, if the researcher's knowledge and skills lie in quantitative research methods, and studying the research problem would require a more qualitative approach, it might be best to let a researcher competent in the qualitative approach study it.

Will I have access to needed data? Some research problems that would seem like excellent candidates for study by social workers may not be researchable because the data needed to study them are not accessible. For example, sealed court records and patients' medical records are safeguarded by law. Thus, it is generally impossible to access them for use in research. Knowledge that could be acquired only with access to data that is beyond reach should be regarded as unattainable. Unless other ways of addressing the research problem can be found that will produce findings of comparable credibility, it might be better to find another research problem to study.

In the past, some promising research studies have reached a costly dead end when researchers found out too late that they would not be allowed to, for example, conduct interviews with clients or staff, or review and record data from records that were assumed to be readily available. Similarly, some social workers have just assumed that it would be acceptable to record interviews with research participants, but found out belatedly that permission was denied. Today, most researchers understand the importance of inquiring into the availability of needed data prior to the selection of a problem for study

Research-Based Practice

Identify two questions that are interesting to you but would probably be inappropriate for a scientific research study.

and submission of a research proposal to an IRB. The IRB members will want to be assured that permission to access the data has been received prior to their granting approval to conduct the research.

Identifying and Specifying the Research Problem

As noted earlier, a careful identification and specification of a researchable problem has a way of keeping all the other steps in the research process on track. But any vagueness or ambiguity about the problem can haunt the researcher at many junctures in the research process and can result in a considerable amount of wasted effort. In this way, research is similar to social work intervention with individuals, families, groups, organizations, or communities. Much valuable time has been wasted because social work practitioners failed to obtain a clear understanding of the problem or accepted at face value the presenting complaint of a client or client group. For a researcher, this barking-up-the-wrong-tree phenomenon can be especially costly.

Years ago, one of the authors of this text was involved in an extended discussion that attempted to specify the research problem for a proposed project (Bellomy et al., 1989). The process that took place still provides a good example of the effort involved in identifying and specifying a research problem. It took several hours and produced a considerable amount of frustration. But the time was well spent. The process was absolutely essential prior to beginning other steps in the research process.

The director of a county agency had proposed that the researchers (a group of social work graduate students) might conduct research on a problem that he had identified in his organization as their research practicum assignment. He had noticed that during the past year, child protection workers were receiving many more reports of possible child abuse by local professionals than in previous years. A large percentage of the cases were never opened for services because the worker assigned to investigate quickly determined that they were unfounded. From the director's perspective, this was an inefficient use of workers' time. They were spending much of their day dealing with reports where no abuse had taken place, while not having enough time to devote to those cases where abuse was probable. Simply stated, from his perspective, there were too many unfounded cases. He didn't know why this was occurring, and thus did not know how to act to address it.

Further discussion with the administrator allowed the students to compile a list of five possible explanations for what was happening:

1. Social workers in the community were making too many inappropriate referrals.
2. Inappropriate referrals were the result of inadequate training of social workers.
3. Child protection workers were erroneously declaring cases to be unfounded because they were overworked.
4. Cases were being declared unfounded for fear that a determination of founded would result in more work for child protection workers.
5. Certain workers were contributing to the large number of unfounded cases by determining that all or most of their cases were unfounded.

Note that each of these statements reflects what *might* have been occurring and, in some cases, even a possible reason for it. Each also suggests a different gap in knowledge that needed to be filled. Once the researchers could identify what was happening, they could understand better why it was happening and what could be done to address it (the best intervention).

Through additional discussion and further investigation of existing knowledge and available data, it is often possible to eliminate bogus explanations of a phenomenon and identify the real one that needs to be studied. That is exactly what happened in our example. Following more inquiries and another meeting with the director, all but one of the preceding statements were eliminated. With respect to the first two explanations, it was decided that the great majority of the referrals were apparently quite appropriate, given what the literature suggested at the time about possible indicators of abuse. Their increased number was probably related to recent training that had emphasized recognition of conditions that suggest that abuse may have taken place and that a referral was in order.

As for the third explanation, although some instances of child abuse might have been missed, there was no evidence to suggest that this was the case, at least not any more so than in previous years. On the basis of recent data in the professional literature, it was impossible to know whether the current rate of founded versus unfounded cases among child protection workers was high, low, or about normal. It also would be difficult to measure accurately whether a case determination had been correct or incorrect, a measurement obstacle (see previous discussion) that was sufficient to preclude giving serious consideration to the third statement as the impetus for a research study. It was possible that the ratio of founded versus unfounded cases was about average, but that the cases were being categorized incorrectly; there was simply no way to know.

The fourth explanation was also unlikely, because a policy existed whereby a case with a determination of founded was referred for follow-up services by another worker in another division of the organization. Thus, it resulted in no additional work for the worker who made the determination.

On the basis of the director's observations and a quick count of records, the students found that some workers seemed to have a much higher rate of unfounded determinations than others over the previous three years. Given the random assignment of cases and the large number of cases seen, such a disparity should not have existed. The director speculated that the identity of the worker assigned to a referral might have more to do with the determination of founded or unfounded than the facts of the case. Consequently, a variation of the fifth explanation was seen as the most plausible explanation for what was occurring.

To have used precipitously any of the first four explanations proposed by the research group as the research problem would have produced difficulties later on in the research. Much effort would have been wasted. The time spent in clarifying the exact nature of what was occurring was a productive and necessary exercise. It improved the overall efficiency of the scientific inquiry by saving much more time than it consumed.

Through additional discussion and further investigation of existing knowledge and available data, it is often possible to eliminate bogus explanations of a phenomenon and identify the real one that needs to be studied.

SELECTING RESEARCH QUESTIONS

A concise, well-articulated problem statement is a good beginning. However, it is too broad to provide the needed focus for a research study and so the process of narrowing continues. Next, researchers generally select a group of broad research questions that relate to the problem, more than they could ever hope to address in a single study. In predominantly quantitative studies, one or more of the questions may get answered during the extensive literature review that generally follows. The answers were there; the researcher just was not aware of them. Other questions may be eliminated as "unresearchable" or of relatively low priority. One or a few will be revised, usually made more specific, by what is learned from the literature review process (Chapters 4 and 5). A research design (Chapters 6–8) is then selected to attempt to arrive at tentative answers. After that, the questions (and the plan for answering them) are essentially "set." Changes are unlikely to occur.

In predominantly qualitative studies, the process of data collection often begins quite early, following a less extensive literature review. While some research questions may be answered or others revised by what is learned from the literature, the process of eliminating, revising, and even adding research questions is ongoing. It is not limited to and does not end with the literature review. It continues throughout the data collection process. New questions are often added as the data suggest other important areas of inquiry. Others may be dropped along the way if they prove unproductive for knowledge building. Creswell (1998) argues, however, that qualitative research should be guided by a clearly stated question that provides "a single focus" for the research study (p. 21).

Box 3.1 provides examples of some research problem statements and broad research questions that might relate to them. They are just examples; many other questions could be developed for each problem statement.

The broad research questions that ultimately are selected help to keep a researcher on track. For example, whether one is deciding what data must be collected, how to collect them, what statistical analysis to perform, or which research findings are most important to disseminate, the same question can be asked: How does that bear on the research question and contribute to its answer? Answers that can pass this test suggest an appropriate use of researchers' time.

What is the connection between a research problem statement and a research question? How do they differ? Researchers choose to focus on certain research questions because they believe that, if answers to them can be found, those answers will help to alleviate the research problem. Even if answers cannot be found, the knowledge obtained through the process of seeking them generally provides increased insight into the problem itself. Unlike a research problem statement, a research question always is followed by a question mark.

There are many gaps in knowledge related to a research problem that could serve as the focus for the research. But they cannot all be studied. How many questions should a researcher attempt to study? What are the characteristics of a good research question? What makes one potential research question a better choice as the focus of research than another one? Selection of research questions, like the selection of a research problem, is often a matter of priorities.

We observed in Chapter 1 that all scientific knowledge is tentative by definition. But the researcher still hopes to generate knowledge that is as definitive as possible. Therefore, as a general rule, it is better to do a good, thorough job of studying just a few research questions than do a more superficial job of inquiring into the answers to many.

Many of the criteria that are applied in selecting broad research questions are the same ones that we examined in selecting a research problem. The following questions are often helpful, both for limiting the number of

As a general rule, it is better to do a good, thorough job of studying just a few research questions than do a more superficial job of inquiring into the answers to many.

Box 3.1 Some Research Problem Statements and Related Questions

Problem: The parents of children who die while committing violent crimes are also victims. However, we know little about how the parents experience this tragedy.

Q1. How do these parents perceive potential sources of support in their time of loss?

Q2. What obstacles to their own grief process do they experience?

Q3. What feelings do they have toward the families of the victims of the violence?

Q4. How have their relationships with friends and relatives been affected?

Problem: Homicide by children 8 to 12 is increasing. Social workers working with children this age often hear them talk about wanting to kill someone. There is little available knowledge to help them decide how to respond.

Q1. What behaviors of children immediately prior to homicidal acts might have indicated that the acts might occur?

Q2. What common experiences exist in the social histories of homicidal children?

Q3. What common experiences exist in the current life situations of homicidal children?

Q4. What have been the experiences of social workers who notified authorities when their young clients talked about homicide?

Problem: Welfare reform has dramatically reduced the number of families receiving public financial assistance. However, we have little knowledge about the impact of welfare reform on those people who are no longer on welfare rolls.

Q1. Have those no longer receiving welfare assistance found good jobs, or are they now relying on other institutions for financial assistance?

Q2. What has been the effect on children of former AFDC recipients who went to work after their benefits ran out?

Q3. Have day care facilities increased to adequately meet the needs of an increased number of working mothers?

Q4. How has a weaker economy and higher unemployment rates affected the numbers of welfare recipients?

Problem: High unemployment has resulted in a recent reduction in charitable giving. We don't know how this has affected not-for-profit agencies and their clients and what we can do about it.

Q1. Has the funding led to the deletion of some valuable programs?

Q2. What are agencies doing to try to replace reduced funding?

Q3. Have the United Way's new priorities for allocating funding caused some agencies to redefine their mission?

Q4. Have agencies become more competitive and less cooperative with each other?

Problem: Social workers are encountering an increasing number of middle and high school–age students who claim to be in "friends with benefits" relationships. The workers are uncertain how to address it in their counseling, or even whether to treat it as a problem.

Q1. Are these relationships really as widespread as some adolescents say they are?

Q2. If an adolescent is in such a relationship, how does he or she perceive it?

Q3. Do these relationships seem to occur most frequently among adolescents with certain problems or characteristics?

Q4. What long-term effects are these relationships likely to have on adult sexual relationships?

---

questions and producing a clearer understanding of just why the research is being conducted:

1. Which potential research questions would be most likely to contribute
   - new knowledge?
   - knowledge for more effective practice intervention?
   - knowledge that can be disseminated?
   - knowledge that will make a difference?
   - knowledge that other researchers will find useful?

2. Which potential research questions are most likely to have an answer that
   ◆ is attainable?
   ◆ would contribute the most to alleviation of the problem (the knowledge gap)?
3. Which potential research questions would require
   ◆ measurement of phenomena that can be easily measured?
   ◆ access to information that is likely to be available?
   ◆ the use of research methods that are considered ethical?
   ◆ the knowledge and expertise possessed by the researcher?

Each of the preceding questions reflects an important issue in the selection of a research question. To see how social workers can select a research question, we will return to the example used in our discussion of how the students handled problem specification. Having settled on what apparently was happening (i.e., some child protection workers had a much higher rate of unfounded cases than others), they began to identify possible research questions, the answers to which might help to explain and/or alleviate the problem. Some of the many possible ones that were seriously considered included the following:

1. What laws and regulations govern child protection workers' decisions about whether a case is determined to be founded? Could ambiguity contained in them be producing different reporting rates (founded versus unfounded) among workers? Could recent changes in reporting procedures somehow be affecting whether a case is regarded as founded?
2. Could different working conditions in some way help to explain the different rates?
3. Could differences in education and training of workers somehow relate to the different rates?
4. Do coworkers perceive that some workers are more conscientious in their investigations than others?
5. How great an influence does supervision have in worker determinations regarding reports of suspected abuse?
6. Are community professionals somehow influencing the decisions of some workers more than others? If so, how is this occurring?
7. Do some workers perceive rewards for either founded or unfounded cases that other workers do not perceive?
8. How might the work experience of the child protection worker affect the way that a case is perceived?
9. Does burnout somehow contribute to the different rates of founded cases among workers?
10. Are the different demographic characteristics of workers (e.g., age, race, sex, parenthood) related to their determinations?

What can we observe about the preceding questions? First, they all relate to the research problem in the same way. Each, if answered, could contribute to its alleviation. All the questions also relate to factors that may influence the decision making of child protection workers. However, each suggests a very different focus of inquiry. Note, too, that all of them are stated in a way that suggests that the cause for the different rates is unknown. This kind of noncommittal wording is appropriate for this stage of the research process. It suggests that the researchers were keeping an open mind and not beginning the research with any preexisting biases.

All of the questions are quite broad. As we shall discuss later, the tasks of refining broad research questions to make them more specific, and, when possible, even proposing tentative answers to them, all come later in the process. In predominantly qualitative studies, this step often occurs much later.

Because researchers hope to acquire as much relevant knowledge as possible in a research study, they select questions that can be combined with other possible questions. As long as the research does not become unmanageable or lose focus, combining questions can be an efficient use of time. It is exactly what occurred in the research that we have been describing.

Most of the original questions (including many that are not in the preceding list) were rejected for reasons related to the issues discussed earlier. For example, question 4 could not be examined because it was concluded that obtaining the required data would be difficult without damaging working relationships among staff members. All the caseworkers were found to share the same supervisor and work under virtually identical working conditions, so questions 2 and 5 were discarded. Question 8 was summarily answered without the need for further study: it was learned that another study had just examined this question and found no evidence of any such influence.

Question 1 was concluded to be just a little too complex to study within the time available and with available resources. To study it would have required extensive interviews with the workers and the development of methods to test their job knowledge. The director stated that he could not permit his staff to take enough time off from their regular duties to participate in a series of extended interviews or other similar forms of data collection processes. Question 6 presented logistical obstacles. To answer it would have entailed collecting data from more than 100 individuals in the community who frequently make referrals, a formidable and costly endeavor. In light of the small amount of knowledge related to the problem that would be generated, the effort involved did not seem justified.

A variation of question 10 appeared to be the best choice. The answer to it seemed obtainable. No one in the group had ever seen it discussed within current professional literature. What's more, questions 3, 7, and 9 could easily be answered along with question 10 by adding a short personal interview designed to collect some of the needed data. The research question was restated as follows: Are characteristics of workers related to their determinations of whether a case is judged to be founded?

In quantitative research, it is particularly important to develop research questions to guide the research process. Let us look at a couple of examples of quantitative research questions in the current research literature. Ramos-Lira, Gonzalez-Forteza, and Wagner (2006) defined their research study using the following research questions: (1) Is there an association between violence victimization and exposure to opportunities to use marijuana, inhalants, and cocaine? (2) Is there an association between violence victimization and actual drug use among youth with drug-using opportunities (p. 850). Another study (Shields, Broome, Delaney, Fletcher & Flynn, 2007) attempted to answer the following research questions: (1) What is the relationship between an individual's religiosity and retention in treatment and commitment to treatment? (2) How does the ecological context of treatment programs shape the individual-level relationships? (3) To what extent are program practices and characteristics directly linked to outcome level (p. 355). Clearly, these research questions guided the researchers in defining their literature review, research design, data collection methods, data analysis techniques, and all other aspects of the research process.

QUALITATIVE VERSUS QUANTITATIVE QUESTIONS

It is during the step of formulating and selecting potential research questions that the researcher will generally identify whether the research design will be predominantly quantitative or qualitative in nature.

It is during the step of formulating and selecting potential research questions that the researcher will generally identify whether the research design will be predominantly quantitative or qualitative in nature. Let us look at another example research problem and broad research questions. One of the authors is currently interested in an area where there seems to be a knowledge gap. Since African-American women have, in the past, had a lower prevalence of both anorexia nervosa and bulimia nervosa than Caucasian women, there seems to be little available research to explain, describe, and understand eating disorders among African-American women. Research has in the same way neglected studies on men and older women, instead focusing on young Caucasian women, the group most affected by eating disorders. When looking at this potential gap in the knowledge, there are many broad research questions that could be researched. The author came up with the following list of questions in which she was interested:

Diversity in Practice

Think of at least one other problem area in which a population has been understudied because they were less likely to suffer from the problem than another population.

1. What is the current prevalence of anorexia nervosa and bulimia nervosa among African-American women? *quan*
2. How does the prevalence among African-American women compare to the prevalence among Caucasian women? *quan*
3. How do African-American women view their own bodies? *qual*
4. What societal pressures do African-American women experience to be thin? *qual*
5. For those African-American women who are suffering from disordered eating behaviors, what types of behaviors (i.e., binging, vomiting, diuretic use, laxative use) are they more likely to exhibit? *quan*
6. How do African-American women respond to various treatments for bulimia nervosa and anorexia nervosa? *qual*
7. What are the risk factors among African-American women for developing an eating disorder? *quan*
8. How is weight reflected in the African-American woman's concept of beauty? *qual*

Looking at these questions, it is fairly straightforward to assume that a research study looking at questions 1, 2, 5, 6, or 7 would be predominantly quantitative. If one were to select question 8, the resulting study would probably be predominantly qualitative. Questions 3 and 4 could be studied using quantitative, qualitative, or a mixed research method. It would depend on the specific research question developed and the measurement instruments and data collection methods the researcher selects. Therefore, in addition to the many factors we discussed earlier, the researcher will also be led by the type of research he or she is interested in conducting and in which area he or she feels most capable.

DEVELOPING QUALITATIVE RESEARCH QUESTIONS

Agee (2009) offers a process for developing effective qualitative research questions. She states that "the ongoing process of questioning is an integral part of understanding the unfolding lives and perspectives of others," and in her article addresses "both the developing of initial research questions and how the processes of generating and refining questions are critical to the shaping of a qualitative study" (p. 431). She describes the qualitative research question as a navigational tool that not only helps guide the researcher through the research process but also encourages the exploration into unexpected directions the research may take.

Agee (2009) further points out that some qualitative researchers prefer to begin the research process without a research question. However, this is often impractical in today's research arena. Since dissertations and most funded research must have a research question and a plan before the research begins, she has developed some suggestions for developing qualitative research questions. In qualitative research, we as social workers are often interested in how an individual is experiencing an event or condition. We try to understand what is happening in a particular situation with a particular person or group of people. A good example of a qualitative research question is from a study by Rortveit, Astrom, and Severinsson (2009). They asked, "How do women who suffer from eating disorders experience the bodily aspects related to their condition" (p. 91)? A research question that led to a mixed research method is presented by Smith (2007): "What are the needs of students with Asperger's Syndrome, and what are the services and accommodations available to them at the post-secondary level" (p. 515)?

Agee (2009) lists the following guidelines for developing good qualitative research questions: (1) The question should be clear enough to provide focus for the study. This allows the researcher to gather specific data that can add knowledge and potentially make a difference to the field of study; (2) The question should be framed in a way that either implicitly or explicitly makes a link with the theory being used by the researcher; (3) The question should be answerable. Will it be possible to answer the question with the time and resources available? (4) It is important not to phrase the question in such a way that it leads to presuppositions about the participants and events involved in the study; and (5) The question should be worded so that it is clear and avoids multiple subquestions being included within the question.

Qualitative researchers, as we have already stated, do not necessarily start out with a clearly stated research question. Walsh and Tzelepis (2007), for example, developed a qualitative study to look at tobacco use among adolescents with an emphasis on three areas of interest: peer influences, access/sales issues, and dependence/addiction. There were no specific research questions developed at the beginning of their study. Other qualitative research studies may develop one or more research questions as part of the conclusions of the study. For example, Kartalova-O'Doherty and Doherty (2008) examined the experiences and needs of family caregivers for people with enduring mental illness. They suggest that the findings of their study raise the following research questions: In what ways and to what extent do contextual factors shape personal coping strategies? Are contextual factors more powerful predictors of coping styles than personal or developmental ones? To what extent and in what way are personal, developmental, and contextual factors related to individual coping (p. 26)? The hope is that these questions will lead to further research studies.

In quantitative research, once the research question and hypothesis (when used) are defined, they are not altered or augmented in any way. On the contrary, research questions in qualitative research can change throughout the research process. Research questions are viewed as tools for giving a research study a primary focus, but it should be remembered the question will generally evolve throughout the research process. Creswell (2007) states, "Our questions change during the process of research to reflect an increased understanding of the problem" (p. 47).

If the research question selected lends itself to a predominantly quantitative design, the next step in the process is a thorough review of the literature to find out if the knowledge gap perceived by the researcher is real or if there is indeed information available to answer the question. In addition, the research may answer part of the question leading the researcher to another aspect of the problem, or research may be found that supports the need for research in this area and may give the researcher ideas about how to proceed.

In qualitative research, the step following formulation of the research question is not as clearly defined. Some qualitative researchers believe that completing a thorough literature review early in the process may bias the researcher as she begins to collect the data. Still others do not even emphasize the formulation of the research question early in the research process. Denzin (1989) offers a list of steps for conducting qualitative research, which starts out with "learn to prepare oneself, read the literature, and focus." There is, however, a school of thought among many qualitative researchers who believe the researcher should develop a research question, and then complete a literature review to become familiar with the current research on the topic. For example, Anastas (2010) states, "Qualitative or not, evaluation research should be informed by prior work—the theory that explains the nature of the problems to be addressed and the intervention to be used as well as prior research examining what has and has not worked in the past" (p. 59). Clearly the qualitative research process is more flexible than the quantitative process and depends to a large extent on the qualitative method and techniques chosen by the researcher.

SUMMARY

In this chapter, we examined the earliest tasks in the research process: problem identification and selection of broad research questions. We devoted an entire chapter to these tasks because we regard them as critical to a thoughtful, organized approach to knowledge building. They are the first steps in all quantitative research and in much qualitative research.

A distinction was made between problems in general (such as social problems or the problems of an individual social worker, client, or client system) and potential social work research problems. A research problem can be thought of as a gap in our knowledge that interferes with our practice functioning and makes decision making more difficult. Potential research problems are sometimes identified when we find ourselves thinking, "I wish I knew something that I don't know." Other times, our interaction with clients uncovers some phenomenon that we don't understand or, perhaps, didn't even know existed. A potential research problem may also emerge from discussion with our colleagues or with our supervisors. However, not all gaps in knowledge that are identified are necessarily good candidates for research. The needed knowledge may already exist, and, with a little effort (like an Internet search), can be easily acquired. Even if there really is an important knowledge gap, it may not be a good candidate for social work research because of priority issues, political or financial reasons, or its suitability for the application of scientific methods.

Broad research questions evolve from and are closely related to a social work research problem. If answers can be found, they will help reduce the knowledge gap that constitutes the research problem and thus have potential to alleviate the problem. We offered guidelines to assist in selecting the best research questions to study from among those that might be studied. Examples illustrated the importance of identifying and articulating the *real problem* and how a long list of possible research questions can be reduced to a manageable number.

Log onto **www.mysocialworklab.com** and answer the following questions. (If you did not receive an access code to **MySocialWorkLab** with this text and wish to purchase access online, please visit www. mysocialworklab.com.)

1. **Watch the Core Competencies Video: Diversity in Practice: Engaging client to share his or her experiences of alienation and marginalization.** Identify one potential research problem you might want to study with this client. Develop two broad research questions that would add to your understanding of

the identified problem. Would these questions be studied better through qualitative or quantitative research methods?

2. **Read the Case Study: Domestic Violence: Betty and Charlie Bristol.** After reading pages 1–8 of the case study, identify one potential research problem you would want to study with regard to Charlie. Develop two broad research questions related to this problem. Would these questions be studied better through qualitative or quantitative research methods?

PRACTICE TEST

1. All of the following are logistical obstacles to research except one:
   a. Research requires more resources than are available.
   b. The researcher does not have the expertise to conduct the research.
   c. Very little research has been conducted in this area.
   d. The researcher does not have access to the needed data.

2. One of the following research questions would probably lead to a predominantly quantitative study:
   a. How do men and women differ in the meaning they ascribe to physical beauty?
   b. How do Native Americans feel about the way their ancestors were treated by Europeans?
   c. Are IQ scores and income levels positively correlated among adult males in the United States?
   d. How do men and women differ in the way they view the aging process?

3. Which of the following research questions would probably lead to a predominantly qualitative study:
   a. Has the number of students entering college been affected by the economic recession?
   b. What is the trend in the number of men staying home to care for young children over the past twenty years?
   c. How do men and women differ in the meaning they give to staying at home to care for children?
   d. Has the total number of cases of anorexia reported in college health centers increased or decreased over the past decade?

4. The following statements are true regarding qualitative and quantitative research except one:
   a. Both identify a research problem.
   b. Both almost always identify a research hypothesis.
   c. Both usually conduct a literature review at some point in the process.
   d. Both often develop a research question.

5. Identify one problem area in which you are interested. Create a list of five research questions that relate to the problem.

ASSESS YOUR COMPETENCE   Use the scale below to rate your current level of achievement on the following concepts or skills associated with each competency presented in the chapter:

1	2	3
I can accurately describe the concept or skill.	I can consistently identify the concept or skill when observing and analyzing practice activities.	I can competently implement the concept or skill in my own practice.

_____ Understanding the process and importance of identifying a research problem

_____ Creating broad research questions that relate to the problem

_____ Identifying potential problems in studying each of the research questions

_____ Distinguishing between research questions that lead to predominantly quantitative or qualitative research methods

4

Finding and Using Existing Knowledge

Core Competencies in this Chapter (Check marks indicate which competencies are demonstrated)				
☐ Professional Identity	☐ Ethical Practice	☐ Critical Thinking	☑ Diversity in Practice	☐ Human Rights & Justice
☑ Research-Based Practice	☑ Human Behavior	☐ Policy Practice	☐ Practice Contexts	☑ Engage, Assess, Intervene, Evaluate

Reference to existing knowledge can occur at many points in the research process. Researchers often use it to select and specify a social work research problem, and they use it again to narrow their list of possible research questions (Chapter 3). Answering questions about, for example, how widespread a problem is or whether a phenomenon is easily measurable may require a quick trip to the library or an Internet search. However, the use of existing knowledge does not stop there. We use it to see if there are already partial answers to our research questions and, at least in predominantly quantitative studies, formulate hypotheses about what we expect to learn. It also helps us to make important decisions about how best to conduct our research. After data have been collected, the literature can help us to interpret our research findings in light of the knowledge accumulated by others.

WHAT IS A REVIEW OF LITERATURE?

In research, the term *review of literature* is used in two ways. It refers to both an activity and a written product. As we already noted, the activity of reviewing relevant literature occupies the attention of the researcher to a greater or lesser degree at many points in the research process. However, there is generally one time period when the researcher focuses intensely on the accumulated work of others who have studied and written about the research problem or some related topic. In studies that are predominantly qualitative, this is most likely to occur after some or all data have been collected—when the researcher is attempting to interpret them in relation to existing knowledge. In more traditional, quantitative studies, it generally occurs prior to data collection and is used to help plan for the rest of the research process that is to follow. As we shall see, *literature* is also a somewhat generic term in research. It includes sources of knowledge that go far beyond the printed word, such as Internet Web sites, personal interviews, movies, and television programs.

Eventually, what is learned from reviewing the literature is organized and written in summary form as a separate section of a research report or chapter of a book. This is the product known as the *review of literature, relevant literature*, or something similar. It is written for the reader of the report and describes the existing knowledge that was considered relevant to the current study, what the researcher learned from it, and how it influenced both the way the research was conducted and, ultimately, any conclusions drawn from its findings.

Even new problems or ones that for one reason or another have received little or no attention in the past always bear some similarity to other problems that already have been studied. Knowledge drawn from research on related topics can be productively brought to bear on current proposed research. For example, during the late 1980s and early 1990s, the problem of date rape belatedly received widespread attention in the media. There were conflicting opinions expressed about its incidence, the reasons for it, and how it should be addressed. This was a potential social work research problem because without a clear understanding of the dynamics surrounding date rape and how it was perceived by both perpetrators and victims, we could not know how best to provide successful intervention. When research on the problem began, there initially was limited knowledge about the problem. Yet, a review of the literature was extremely useful for acquiring both insight into date rape and how best to design research to study the problem. Research on this newly identified problem was greatly facilitated by an examination of previous studies on literally hundreds of diverse topics. Each made a valuable contribution that helped researchers focus their attention on the best ways to advance knowledge about date rape. Among the major topics examined were the following:

- History of violence against women
- Violence against women within different cultures
- Legal parameters defining *rape*
- Substance abuse and physical violence
- Law enforcement and judicial handling of rape accusations
- Sexual violence
- Anger expression and management

Another "new" problem, our lack of understanding of the unwillingness of sexually active teenagers at risk for teen pregnancy to use free contraceptive injections, was identified in the late 1990s. Because such injections (and contraceptive implants) were not even available until the mid-1990s, it would seem on the surface that a researcher wishing to study the problem would be in the dark. But there is plenty of literature on related topics that would address the problem and questions that relate to it, some of which are listed here:

- History of contraception
- Emerging pregnancy prevention methods
- Outcome studies of various methods of contraception
- Attitudes about contraception among adolescents
- Attitudes about pregnancy among adolescents
- Distrust of health care providers
- Obstacles to use of public health services

In the first decade of the twenty-first century, problems such as cyber-bullying and cyber-exhibitionism emerged related to the increasing availability of the Internet. As in the previous two examples, social workers could find related knowledge that would be helpful to clients in need. For every research problem and for its related research questions, there is an existing body of knowledge that can guide a researcher. Whenever researchers report that little or nothing is known about the problem or that no relevant literature exists on the topic, it is an indication that (1) they probably do not understand the nature and purpose of the literature review or (2) they probably did not invest sufficient energy and time in this important step in the research process. There are no research problems and no research questions for which there is no existing relevant knowledge. Although it is conceivable that no one may have previously studied the exact questions selected, there is always knowledge available that could help to enlighten and inform the researcher.

Human Behavior

Suppose you want to learn more about attention deficit disorder among adults. What are five major topics you might explore?

PURPOSES OF A REVIEW OF LITERATURE

Sowers, Ellis, and Dessel (2010) point out that a literature review can serve three important and distinct purposes: (1) It constitutes a reservoir of knowledge for understanding previous research and planning for future research. This allows the researcher to identify gaps in knowledge that may be addressed. (2) It affords a tool for conceptualization and operationalization. (3) It provides an atlas of potential error, facilitating the identification of potential problems in the research process (p. 504). In addition, citing relevant literature fulfills three functions for the reader of the research report: (1) It helps

---

Box 4.1 How Researchers Make Use of the Literature

When a problem is first identified, to

- specify the problem;
- determine its suitability for study;
- select broad research questions related to it.

Prior to data collection, to

- learn more about the history, origin, and scope of the research problem;
- learn what methodologies have been applied successfully (and unsuccessfully) to study related research problems;
- learn what answers already exist for their broad research questions;
- decide what is the best way to acquire needed data, who or what might best provide them, and how best to analyze them;
- refine and better specify their research questions;

- identify variables that will need to be measured and learn what methods already are available to measure them (quantitative studies);
- construct operational definitions of key variables (quantitative studies);
- propose answers to their research questions in the form of hypotheses (quantitative studies).

After data collection, to

- attempt to explain differences between current findings and existing knowledge;
- identify ways in which current findings are consistent with and support existing knowledge;
- interpret the data in light of existing knowledge;
- specify how current findings advance knowledge;
- develop additional theories and formulate hypotheses for future research studies to test.

---

to establish the credibility of the researcher and his or her background work. (2) It helps the reader to gain a basic understanding of the findings of other researchers as a foundation for evaluating the results of the current study. (3) It may form a source for additional information if the reader desires to learn more about the research (p. 505). Whenever it is conducted, a literature review is a recognition that knowledge building is a cumulative process that goes on over long periods of time and that each study has (or should have) a unique contribution to make to that process. The literature review has several complementary objectives that occur at different times in the research process. These are summarized in Box 4.1.

POTENTIAL SOURCES

Several important steps are involved in conducting a literature review. The first step is identifying what sources of literature will be included in the review. There are many potential sources, such as books, journals, the Internet, electronic databases, and governmental reports. For researchers, the term *literature* really means relevant knowledge. This knowledge can be found in many places and forms.

What qualifies a source of information for inclusion in what we have called the product known as the *review of literature*? It should enlighten and inform the researcher and the reader of the research report. It also should be credible. The issue of credibility is often debatable. Even the best of sources are sometimes vulnerable to political or economic influences.

The most common sources (some of them clearly more credible than others) for a review of the literature include the following:

- Professional journal articles
- Trustworthy Web sites

- Books
- Personal interviews with authorities
- Research reports and monographs
- Research presentations at conferences
- Newspaper articles
- Standard reference materials

Professional Journal Articles

Articles in social work professional journals, such as *Social Work Research*, *Social Work*, *Research on Social Work Practice*, and *Journal of Social Work Education*, usually represent a sizable and important portion of the knowledge available on a social work research question. Generally, they undergo an anonymous peer review process that, although it gives no guarantee of scholarliness, at least suggests that others believe that they are worthy of publication.

Journals in social work and related fields have proliferated in recent years. Some publications that purport to be professional journals are not refereed; that is, their publishers do not use a blind review process, which ensures that a friendship, the name of the author, or the author's prestigious affiliation will not influence publication decisions. Also, some of those that do use a blind review process receive so few submissions that they publish the majority of all submissions that are received. A reference book published by National Association of Social Workers (2009) reports on the percentage of article submissions that were accepted for publication among nearly 200 social work and social work–related journals. The high rate of acceptance (a rate of over 50 percent) of some refereed journals was enlightening. Are they simply receiving mostly good, publishable submissions? Or are they "taking what they can get" in order to have enough articles to publish an issue?

If being refereed is no guarantee that a journal's content reflects the highest levels of scholarship, how can we tell the difference between a scholarly journal and one that is not so scholarly? Box 4.2 offers guidelines for evaluating professional journals as a potential source of trustworthy literature.

Libraries have limited budgets for purchasing journal subscriptions, either in print or online. Since journals are expensive (many journals actually charge libraries more for subscriptions than they do individual subscribers), difficult choices must be made. Not surprisingly, librarians have shown a special interest in the scholarliness of professional journals and devoted whole reference books to the evaluation of the quality of these journals (see LaGuardia, 2003). Such books are frequently available in the reference section of university and public libraries.

It sometimes seems as if the topic of a journal article (maybe it was a hot topic at the time of publication) or its use of a particular research method or statistical procedure may have had more to do with its publication than the quality of the study. Sometimes, the findings of research may be a major factor in the decision to publish. Undoubtedly, some findings are more popular than others, especially if they are consistent with popular opinion or seem to be supportive of the social work profession rather than critical of it. A question we might ask ourselves is, "Is it possible that the topic of the article, the research methods used, or research findings, rather than the quality of the research, resulted in publication of the article?"

Relevant literature can be found in professional journals in many other fields besides social work (e.g., psychology, nursing, sociology, criminal justice,

Box 4.2 Evaluating Professional Journals as a Literature Source

▶ Does the journal disseminate important knowledge that social workers can use to help them be better practitioners?

▶ Are any research methods described in sufficient detail that the reader is able to judge whether they were methodologically sound and ethical?

▶ Is the journal published by a professional organization, respected university, or teaching institution? Is it widely cited in the professional literature?

▶ Is the journal more *serious looking* than other, less scholarly publications? Does it contain tables, graphs, and the results of statistical analyses rather than pictures or colorful graphics?

▶ Do articles consist of mostly reports of primary research (original research conducted for the first time) and far fewer compilations of research results previously published elsewhere? If the journal contains any replications of previous studies, is the justification for the replication clearly articulated and convincing?

▶ Do articles contain technical terminology that is specific to the discipline for which it was written, since there is the assumption that anyone interested enough to read them has some scholarly background in the area?

▶ Do the authors of articles have credentials (advanced degrees, but also work experience, reputations and/or previous publications in the topic area) that qualify them as scholars or authorities? (An Internet search by the author's name can help to confirm this.)

▶ Does the style of the writing of articles reflect objectivity, rather than an effort to try to win over the reader to the author's position?

▶ Do the articles contain footnotes and bibliographies, which would suggest that the authors did not just present their own beliefs or theories but tied it to the work of others?

education, health, anthropology, public administration, public health). The journal may have been published anywhere in the world. If an article has been written in a foreign language and is considered critical to understanding the problem being investigated, English translations will need to be found or undertaken. Bilingual and bicultural students in the helping professions at nearby universities may be a good resource for both identifying relevant literature and translation.

Additional effort may be required to locate journal articles written by either indigenous social scientists or social work researchers and practitioners who possess special expertise in conducting research within a specific culture.

Especially when conducting certain forms of research, social work researchers must take special care so that the literature that they cite informs rather than misleads other researchers and the readers of their reports. When a researcher is conducting a study with a different ethnic or cultural group or within a cross-cultural context, literature that helps the researcher to better understand the manifestation of the target problem or research issue within that particular cultural framework is especially useful. Additional effort may be required to locate journal articles written by either indigenous social scientists or social work researchers and practitioners who possess special expertise in conducting research within a specific culture.

Trustworthy Web Sites

The Internet is a popular source for existing knowledge. For many people, it is now the first place to look when they want information about most anything. Its easy accessibility and the breadth of information available on it can greatly expedite a literature search. Unlike books, journal articles, or other commonly used reference materials, which often are out of date before they are available in print, data on the Internet can be updated as frequently as is necessary. The ease with which knowledge can be put on the Internet is, at the same time, its greatest weakness. Individuals can put anything they want on it—no verification is required. Freedom of speech also permits individuals to play loosely with facts or just plain fabricate information.

If the Internet is so vulnerable to misinformation, why do we include it as a source of literature? Along with Web sites that we would never want to quote from in a review of literature, there are also some useful ones for the social work researcher. The latter group is sometimes referred to as *reliable Web sites*. The adjective *reliable*, as used in this context, comes closest in meaning to *trustworthy*, which is the term we prefer to use, since the term *reliability* has a different connotation, as we will see while discussing measurement (Chapter 10).

Many of the sources of literature described throughout this chapter (including journal articles) are now accessible via the Internet; more undoubtedly will follow. Web sites come and go, addresses are subject to change, and even the content and credibility of specific sites tend to vary based upon the preferences and biases of their current webmaster. Therefore, it is important that we learn to distinguish trustworthy information obtained from the Internet from that which cannot be trusted and should not be cited in a review of literature. The question of what constitutes a trustworthy Web site is itself widely discussed on the Internet. Box 4.3 contains some of the more commonly mentioned indicators that reflect on a Web site's credibility.

Box 4.3 Evaluating Web sites as a Literature Source

▶ What does the URL tell you? Does it contain a personal name, often an indicator that it is a personal Web page, rather than the name of an institution or organization? If it does not appear to be a personal Web page, what is the domain? Is it where you would expect to find the knowledge that you are seeking, for example, .gov or .us for data collected by governmental organizations; .org for information relating to problems addressed by not-for-profit organizations; .edu for research conducted in colleges or universities; and so forth.

▶ Are there links that would allow you to verify the credibility of the site and the author of the material it contains? More reputable sites will contain links that, for example, take us to a description of the organization that sponsors it and its mission, goals, and philosophy or the author's professional vitae or biography. If there are links to other Web sites, such as "additional sites," they should not just be those that reflect the same positions as those of the current one. Their credibility should also be examined. The links should work. When was the site last updated?

▶ What are the author's (or the organization's) claims to expertise in the area? Credentials are important, but look at the content of the Web page. Is it what we should expect from a true scholar? Does the content seem to be little more than an opinion, a diatribe, or an attempt to sound off about some issue? A rambling discourse is not characteristic of scholarly writing. Scholars are well organized and concise; they rarely repeat themselves, unless it is for emphasis.

▶ Does the page seem to have been put there as a service to the scientific community or to other professionals? Or does it seem like it was put there to try to influence others to adopt the author's ideas or sell them on his or her way of viewing things? Is it possible that it contains deliberate exaggerations and misstatements or was just meant to be funny or outrageous or to shock others in order to get some reaction?

▶ How well documented were statements that were made? How credible are they? Could citations have been taken out of context or the position of articles cited otherwise distorted or altered in order to make a point?

Books

Books remain a popular source for literature reviews. The reports of some major research studies are published in book form. Other books contain scholarly presentations of carefully researched theories, research designs, and statistical methods. Of course, books also may contain material that falls far short of the standard of scholarliness that is expected for citation in a literature review. Just because something is in print is no guarantee of its trustworthiness. Much of what is published in book form has not undergone rigorous review and scrutiny. Some textbook publishers consider potential sales along with quality issues and other factors when they make the decision to publish (or not to publish) a book. Checks on the accuracy of the content often are delegated to a few academicians who receive only minimal compensation for their reviews and who may be less than thorough in their efforts. There are also vanity publishers, who will publish virtually any material in book form (including a professor's course notes and other writings) if the author is willing to pay enough to become a published author.

In deciding whether to use what is in a book to influence one's own research or include a citation from it in the literature review section of a report, it is desirable to ask certain "credibility" questions. Many of them are similar to those we would ask in evaluating any source's credibility. We have listed them in Box 4.4.

Personal Interviews with Authorities

Some of the other usual sources should be approached with even more caution. Unless they are examined critically, researchers can be misled by assertions that are questionable, while simultaneously damaging the credibility of their own research efforts. Often, the following questions must be asked: Where do I draw the line? What constitutes usable knowledge and what does not?

The reader will recall that authority is one of the nonscientific sources of knowledge that we described as untrustworthy in Chapter 1. So why would we include it here as a possible source of knowledge? Because sometimes people in authority do know something important! The principal problem surrounding content drawn from interviews with authorities is lack

---

Box 4.4 Evaluating Books as a Literature Source

- Does the author have a reputation for scholarly integrity? What are his or her credentials? With what professional institution is he or she affiliated? Is it considered reputable? Does it have any unusual beliefs, values, or commitments? Is the author frequently cited by others as an expert on the topic?

- Does the author's position in the book seem to be based on well-designed research, either original or a scholarly review of the work of others?

- Does the author seem intent on the advancement of knowledge, not on pursuing some personal or political agenda?

- Was the book published by a reputable, well-established publisher with a reputation for quality and selectivity, such as a major university press or widely used publisher of textbooks in the field?

- Is the book a recently revised edition? If it was published some years ago, is it considered a classic in its field that contains material of historical significance?

- Are reviews of the book generally positive? What strengths do reviewers identify, and do they relate to those parts of the book that you plan to cite?

of consensus regarding who is an authority. Unfortunately, in some parts of Western society, authority frequently has been assumed to reside in all individuals with certain academic credentials or job titles. For the social work researcher, an authority whose comments are worth quoting in a literature review is someone who has in-depth knowledge of some aspect of the research problem or who has arrived at answers (or at least partial answers) to certain research questions, preferably through the use of scientific methods. This greatly limits the number of authorities who should be quoted in a review of literature.

A researcher in colonial America might have had some justification for quoting a community leader or member of the clergy on virtually any topic, because the limited amount of available knowledge was concentrated within just a few people. But today's researcher should not make any assumptions about an individual's claims to knowledge based solely on academic or other formal credentials. There are no Renaissance men or women alive today who have knowledge in virtually every area. It would be erroneous to assume that, for example, a quotation from any physician is appropriate on a medical question or one from a lawyer will provide needed knowledge on a legal topic. The physician may see primarily older patients; thus, her position on a problem related to child rearing may have no basis other than her experiences as a child or as a mother and may even be distorted through interaction with a biased sample of patients. The lawyer may specialize in contract law and may speak more out of personal opinion than out of knowledge in discussing needed changes in child abuse reporting laws. This is not an indictment of these or other professions; it is only a recognition that the base of knowledge within most professional fields (including social work) and even their subspecialties has grown dramatically during the past century, to the point where no one can possibly know it all.

Use of a few, carefully chosen quotations from interviews with authorities in the literature review section of a research report usually will not harm the credibility of the researcher's efforts. On the contrary, it may suggest balance and thoroughness in the final product. However, it might be wise to prevent any possible challenges to the credibility of authorities by including brief descriptions of the source of their expertise in the narrative. For example, a descriptive statement such as "one medical researcher, who has conducted research funded by the National Institute of Mental Health on the possible relationship between the use of party drugs and suicide among young men, has concluded that . . . " would help to justify why that particular physician was cited in the literature review section of a research report.

Research Reports and Monographs

Research reports and monographs generally are intended to be honest communications of a researcher's methods and findings. Although the findings are only as good as the methods used to produce them, the fact that a researcher's methods are open to public critique and to replication increases the likelihood that a report or monograph will be credible. Of course, if the research was funded by an organization or special interest group that may have exerted undue influence over what was reported, the findings may not be trustworthy. For example, the credibility of findings about the benefits to society of payday loans or title loans by research sponsored by companies that have much to gain by their continued legality would be highly suspect. They would not be suitable to cite.

Research Presentations at Conferences

While there is a great amount of knowledge disseminated at conferences and symposia, there is also a good amount of unsubstantiated opinion and misinformation shared. A presentation may not be selected using a blind review process. Often, the reputation of the presenter or the topic (if it is a popular one) is a major factor in its selection. Frequently, a conference presentation may have no basis in research at all. It may be little more than a show-and-tell description of what the presenter has done and why he or she thinks it was good.

Most presentations at annual conferences, such as those sponsored by the NASW, the SSWR, the CSWE, or the Child Welfare League of America, have undergone a fairly rigorous screening procedure. Only a small percentage of proposals submitted are accepted for presentation. These gatherings also give program space to invited speakers whose past expertise in a subject area has been recognized by one or more members of their planning committee but who may not have been active in the field for years. Personal friendships, quid pro quos, or other political concerns sometimes influence the decision to invite these individuals.

Many other professional gatherings that call themselves national and international conferences and symposia have far less credibility. (After all, any group can describe its conference as "national" or "international" if it chooses.) Some of the most suspect of these consist of a small group of individuals who share some specialized interest. They get together annually to present to each other (sometimes even on the same topic as the previous year) at geographically desirable locations. Participants take turns hosting the annual gathering and inviting each other to present their work. Although some knowledge is undoubtedly shared, there also is a liberal amount of networking, rest and recreation, and sight-seeing. The conference is viewed as more of a "perk" than the fulfillment of a professional responsibility to remain knowledgeable in one's field of specialization.

Presenting at such conferences does not always require prior involvement in social or professional networks. Some national and especially international conferences that may sound highly prestigious welcome new participants and will accept nearly any program proposal submitted if the person submitting it agrees to show up and pay the registration fee. Conference registration fees represent a major source of revenue for some organizations; they could not exist without well-attended conferences at which high registration fees are required.

Information acquired at regional, state, and local conferences also varies widely in its credibility. Before placing too much credence in what is presented, inquiries should be made as to the selection process for presentations and the credentials of the presenters. Of course, a critical assessment of the research methods used also should be made.

Newspaper Articles

Newspapers, either in print or online, can be a valuable source of knowledge. Some of the better ones (e.g., the *Christian Science Monitor, New York Times*) are frequently cited in a literature review. They provide news of general interest and are written for educated readers. However, it should be remembered that even the better newspapers depend on commercial success for their continued existence. Newspaper sales and a large number of Internet hits at their Web sites are good for newspapers. Utilization data can be used to help sell print advertisements and online links, which can generate the needed cash to survive. Thus, what will *sell* sometimes has higher priority than carefully researched contributions to knowledge.

Newspapers acquire some of what they publish from generally credible sources, such as reports of government-sponsored research. But they also publish findings (sometimes selectively) from research of questionable quality. They regularly publish guest editorials written by invited "experts" who may have more name recognition than expertise. When a topic is believed to be of widespread interest, it sometimes seems that getting the facts is less important than producing a timely piece that will be widely read.

Unless an article can be determined to possess a carefully researched origin and contains only firsthand information, it probably is best to use it with extreme caution. Often, newspapers are best used to learn about the existence of the knowledge-building work of others. It is then possible to seek out the original source, obtain a full report, and evaluate its merits on the basis of the description of the researcher's methods.

Standard Reference Materials

For relevant knowledge that is available in written form, publications of abstracts (e.g., *Social Work Abstracts*, *Sociological Abstracts*, *Psychological Abstracts*, *Dissertation Abstracts International*, *SAGE Urban Studies Abstracts*) are always a good place to start a literature search. Listed by topic area as well as by author, they provide a good overview of where recent publications on various topics can be found. However, quotations from abstracts publications should not be used in the report of a review. They are not meant to be a substitute for the original source, just a convenient way to learn about the existence of a publication that may (or may not) prove to be helpful.

Historically, standard reference materials, such as almanacs, encyclopedias, atlases, statistical abstracts, directories, annuals, and yearbooks, have contained verified facts that can be cited in a review of literature. They have tended to possess higher credibility than, for example, data obtained from unverified sources on the Internet, because they have undergone a more thorough review and verification process. However, the publishers of many standard reference materials are increasingly replacing printed material with material available electronically, where they can be kept up to date much better than in print. There is no need for a periodic new edition or supplement—just make the needed changes as they are required and they are immediately available to the researcher.

The Internet has also produced another phenomenon related to standard reference materials. In the past, volumes such as encyclopedias and almanacs were compiled and published by specialists who worked full time, year after year, carefully verifying and reverifying the content that went into them. In recent years, Web sites have emerged that also claim to be standard reference materials and are regarded as such by many people. Yet they lack the quality controls that we expect in a standard reference. Whether or not they possess the knowledge or expertise, anyone can contribute to them and can even edit the contributions of others. Currently Wikipedia, "the people's encyclopedia," is the best known example of this trend. It is now one of the first links that appears when we do almost any Web search. Can it be trusted? Like most of the other sources of knowledge described in this chapter, it undoubtedly contains many useful facts, submitted by knowledgeable people. However, it also undoubtedly contains misinformation and falsehoods, at least until a more knowledgeable contributor comes along and corrects them. At some point in time, it may become a trusted resource. However, that time has not come yet. For now, its primary usefulness is to locate links to other, more trustworthy sources, such as research monographs or high-quality professional journal articles, that can be used in a literature review.

One standard reference commonly used by social workers to get their literature search underway is the National Association of Social Workers' (2008) *Encyclopedia of Social Work*. It is a good place to begin a search of the literature, but because of the breadth of topics covered and there are generally several years between publication of editions and supplements, it is not too useful beyond that function. While some topics remain pretty much unchanged, others (including best practices for intervention with certain types of problems) do not. To accomplish the objectives of a literature review, it often is necessary to venture into other areas of the literature that are more current or detailed, such as journal articles and trusted Web sites.

Reference materials such as public documents and records of public gatherings also can be useful resources. For example, a researcher wishing to understand the values and thinking underlying current or pending legislation can learn a great deal by studying testimony of various individuals and interest groups that appears within the Congressional Record. Of course, because they are open to the public, these documents sometimes contain more posturing and efforts to appear politically correct to a legislator's constituents than knowledge. In fact, much of what gets entered into the Congressional Record is never verbalized in debates and discussions; it is entered, just so it will be there. Other public documents and records of public gatherings may also have undergone a certain creative revision that often leaves their credibility as a source of knowledge somewhat suspect.

OTHER, MORE QUESTIONABLE SOURCES

What we have just described are those sources that, if used selectively, tend to be among the most credible sources of literature. However, there are others that, while they possess less credibility, appear in literature reviews from time to time. We mention them here not to encourage their use but to caution why they should be used only when better sources are unavailable or cannot be found, and then only after a careful check of their credibility.

Content of Workshops

Workshop content may be based on empirical findings; often it is not. Frequently, workshop leaders have been contracted with and paid to deliver content in a way consistent with the wishes of the individual or organization paying for it. This leaves the knowledge contained in the workshop vulnerable to influence and distortion. The researcher may need to explore whether the material was based on the best knowledge available or simply reflective of what the workshop's sponsoring organization wanted its participants to hear. If it is the former, workshop content may be appropriate for inclusion in a research literature review. However, it would still be better to go to the original sources that the presenter may have relied on in putting together the presentation.

Radio and Television Broadcasts

There is a great amount of knowledge and advice shared gratuitously by network radio and television talk show hosts and their "authority" guests. Very few, if any, of such sources would enlighten the researcher or convince others of the scholarliness of a literature review citing them.

Occasionally, news specials and documentaries on major networks and public radio and television are well researched and present excellent sources of information. However, the proliferation of certain types of television journalism and pseudo–news specials in recent years, along with the revelation that some of what was reported on documentaries was falsified or staged, have cast increasing doubt on the credibility of television news broadcasts. Frequently, they appear to be designed to entertain and appeal to the lower interests of viewers and listeners. Special care and discretion should be used in separating knowledge from content that, if cited, would only weaken the researcher's scientific credibility.

Magazines and Periodicals

Magazines and periodicals vary widely in how much credible knowledge they publish, as opposed to how much pure fiction they include to sell subscriptions and single copies in supermarkets and other outlets. They run the gamut from informative and generally trustworthy (e.g., the *Scientific American, Economist, National Geographic*) to popular but unscientific (e.g., *Reader's Digest, Parents, Cosmopolitan*) to sensational (e.g., *Star, Globe,* or *National Enquirer*). Only the first group is occasionally cited in a scholarly literature review without jeopardizing the researcher's credibility. Some newsmagazines and pop science seem to walk a thin line, attempting to appear scholarly and scientific while selecting topics and presentation formats (e.g., short, topical articles featuring provocative pictures) that clearly reflect an eye on sales figures rather than the knowledge needs of their readers. They may even reflect a pragmatic mixture within a single issue; for example, a fairly scholarly article written by a respected researcher juxtaposed with another bit of fluff that would be an intellectual insult to anyone with more than a superficial knowledge of the topic. The message to the social work researcher should be obvious—think very carefully before you rely on such publications for knowledge. You may subscribe to it, read it religiously, learn some things that are helpful to you in your work, and even display it on your coffee table without embarrassment. But that does not mean it is a potential source of knowledge that can be cited with confidence.

Is there ever a place for acknowledging within a social work researcher's review of literature such unscholarly publications that occur at the extreme end of the credibility continuum? Not in the usual way. However, these publications have one thing in common: high sales. Their owners and editors maintain high sales by maintaining a finger on the pulse of what is of interest to the general public. A social problem that is in some form the topic of virtually every magazine at the supermarket checkout stand during a certain period (e.g., spousal battery or the activities of the press) can be assumed to have reached a certain level of public consciousness. The observation that, during the week of August 8, 2008, nine of the ten most popular magazines in America carried at least one article on the use of medication to increase libido among post-menopausal women might be a useful contribution to a literature review, even though the sources cited might make some scholars cringe. The researcher would certainly not be saying that everything (or even anything) within the text of the articles can be construed as knowledge, only that the fact of its publication in popular magazines attests to the topic's popular interest.

We have chosen an extreme example of how far the researcher occasionally may go in seeking and using information for the review of literature. Obviously, even a single use of some of the more suspect sources of information that abound could seriously harm the researcher's credibility and others' assessment of the findings and recommendations generated by the researcher's methods. They should be used rarely, if ever, and only for the limited purposes described. If more scholarly sources would accomplish the same purposes, they should be used instead. Our example makes an important point, however. Any source that relates to the research problem and a research question may have the potential to inform the researcher in some way, even if the knowledge it contains may have no credibility whatsoever.

USING INTERNET SEARCHES TO LOCATE INFORMATION SOURCES

Even a single use of some of the more suspect sources of information that abound could seriously harm the researcher's credibility and others' assessment of the findings and recommendations generated by the researcher's methods.

Regardless of what sources of information the researcher is looking for, he will eventually turn to Internet searches to locate information. Internet search engines have made the task of finding relevant data for literature reviews much easier than it was in years past. But there is a certain finesse involved in performing an effective search, regardless of the type of search engine you are using. Once you have learned some of these skills, they can be transferred (with slight variations) to many search engines, electronic databases, and virtual library systems.

For example, returning to the example used in the preceding chapter, suppose a researcher is interested in studying the disordered eating behaviors among African-American women. The researcher could start with one of the many electronic library systems available through universities and state governments. One such system is the University System of Georgia's virtual library called Galileo (Georgia Library Learning Online). Once you have logged onto Galileo, you can search through a long list of licensed commercial databases as well as other free Internet resources. These resources offer access to thousands of full textbooks, journals, magazines, and encyclopedias. There are many electronic databases that may be relevant to research completed in the social work

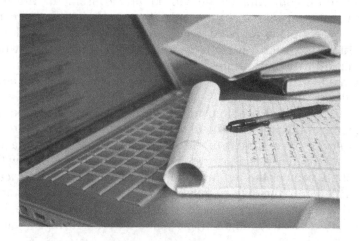

field. It is wise to select the database(s) that most closely matches the general topic area of the literature review. In the case of eating disorders, for example, it is likely that psychological databases will include the most relevant research. Some psychology databases that are available through Galileo and other virtual library systems include PsychINFO, PsycARTICLES, and Psychology and Behavioral Sciences Collection.

Once the database has been selected, the researcher is ready to enter the search parameters to locate research studies in the area of interest. To continue with the eating disorders example, the researcher might enter "eating disorders and African American women." Using the connector *and* in the search parameter returns only those publications that include both phrases; using *or* returns publications that include either phrase. Most search engines will automatically search for the phrase or phrases entered anywhere in the title, abstract, body, or reference list of the publications included in the selected database. If you want only those documents that include these phrases in their title or abstract, you can complete what is often called an *advanced search*, in which more specific search criteria are entered. In an advanced search, other parameters can be used to further delineate the search, including type of research (i.e., quantitative, qualitative, meta-analysis), year of publication, author's name, type of publication.

Suppose this search returns several thousand articles. After looking at the titles of the first several, the researcher may find that the majority of the articles are looking at African-American women and obesity, and, while an interesting topic, is not what the researcher is interested in. He can then return to the search parameters and narrow the search somewhat by entering "bulimia nervosa and African American women" and subsequently "anorexia nervosa and African American women." The search will now return publications that are more closely related to the problem selected by the researcher.

Once the researcher has narrowed the search to his area of interest, he can then begin to look at each publication listed. You can often tell by the publication's title and abstract if the material might be helpful. If you are lucky, the full text of the article will be immediately available. If not, you can search further on the Internet. Journal articles can sometimes be found on other Web sites, such as the journal's Web site or publisher's site. If you still fail to locate the full text, you can visit your university's library and find a hard copy of the journal or book. If the library does not have the needed publication, there is usually an inter-library loan system in place, which allows the researcher to get a copy of an article or book from another library that does have the needed publication.

Research-Based Practice

What are three ways you could limit an Internet search that has returned too many journal articles?

ORGANIZING THE PRODUCT OF A LITERATURE REVIEW

After a search of existing knowledge, researchers usually find themselves with a great deal of information. It may consist of a stack of file cards (or some computer-assisted variation) with useful quotations on one side and the full citation (including all page numbers, volume numbers, and other necessary specifics) on the back. A good first step in making sense out of all this knowledge is to sort it into several broad topic areas. These may have been identified prior to embarking on the literature review, or they may simply suggest themselves during the sorting process. An example will help to illustrate how this can be done.

Suppose that a researcher has conducted a literature review on the question, How has the increasingly chronic nature of HIV affected the role of caregivers and the demands made upon them? The variety of relevant knowledge that she has collected could be sorted and organized using an outline format like the following:

I. Terminal and chronic illnesses
   A. Definitions and examples
   B. Interventions
   C. Caregiver roles
      1. Terminal illness
      2. Chronic illnesses

II. HIV/AIDS: The early years
   A. Confusion, fear, and misunderstanding
   B. Beginning insights
      1. Diagnosis
      2. Symptoms
      3. Course of the disease
      4. Methods of transmission
      5. Those most at risk
      6. Prevention options
      7. Treatment options
      8. Role of the caregiver
   C. Judgments and accusations
   D. Social and political responses

III. Changes and developments
   A. Increased social acceptance
   B. Pharmacological advances
      1. Ethical issues
      2. Economic issues
   C. Incidence
      1. Traditional populations
      2. Third world
      3. Nontraditional groups
   D. Longevity

IV. HIV as a chronic disease
   A. Perceptions of those who are HIV-positive
      1. Self
      2. The community
      3. Friends and relatives
   B. Current services
      1. Hospital
      2. Outpatient
      3. Hospice
   C. Caregiver requirements
      1. New stressors
      2. Relationship issues
      3. Economic impact

Organizing the products of a literature review into an outline containing broad topic areas can serve a number of useful purposes. Some knowledge that has been collected may not seem to fit perfectly within any of the areas. It may be concluded that it is not as relevant to the research problem or questions as had originally been assumed. Thus, it may be discarded. Or, if it seems to stand alone but clearly does enlighten some aspect of the research problem or questions, new topics may be added to incorporate it, and the new topic may have to be expanded with some additional literature. It may be necessary to go back to the sources of literature to seek out additional references.

If it appears that there is no logical sequence to the topics (note the logical progression of the preceding topics) when a broad outline is constructed, additional topics may be required to link those already identified. When all topic areas and their subtopics have been developed, they should reflect a logical flow, often from the more general to those most closely related to the current research question or questions. The topics frequently are used as headings and subheadings when the report of the literature review is written.

WRITING THE LITERATURE REVIEW

What are the characteristics of a good literature review section of a research report? How can the researcher's compilation of existing knowledge be organized and presented so that it will be of maximum benefit to the reader? Entire books have been written on this topic (see Galvin, 2006; Hart, 1998). We will address only the major issues here.

Direction and Flow

In the literature review of a research study that is primarily quantitative, the reader should expect to find topics (identified by subheadings) of general relevance to the research questions near its beginning. For example, in a research study seeking an answer to the broad research question, "Is there a relationship between use of party drugs such as ecstasy and adolescent suicide?" early sections of the literature review might be devoted to a historical overview of substance abuse, a summary of what is known about adolescent drug usage, and a description of statistical trends in the incidence of adolescent suicide in North America. Knowledge that is more directly related to the research question—for example, a summary of the results of suicide autopsies conducted on recent cases of adolescent suicide, or results of other studies that examined the relationship between other substance abuse and adolescent suicide—should appear later. Reports of research that studied the same questions or similar ones should be summarized and discussed near the end of the review, so that the current research will appear to be a logical extension of previous scientific inquiries.

Thus, the flow of the literature review is reflective of deductive logic, a characteristic of quantitative studies in general. It reflects both direction and a logical progression from the general to the specific. It demonstrates how the quantitative researcher used existing knowledge to refine his or her thinking about research problems and questions, and how more specific questions and, often hypotheses, evolved from it.

In reports of qualitative research studies, there is also a review of literature section in which the researcher describes how existing knowledge relates to the current study. By convention (since that is the way it is done in quantitative studies), this section is often found early in the report, just before the methodology section. However, it may be more appropriate in some cases to place it after a description of the data, or to have two literature reviews, a brief one before the methodology section and another after the presentation of the data. This would be more consistent with the ways that the literature is used—often to learn just enough to move forward with the data collection and then later to attempt to interpret the data in light of existing knowledge.

Use of Quotations and Citations

Direct quotations should be used sparingly in a literature review. It is the substance of what others have to say rather than their specific words that are important to the researcher. Excessive use of quotations may mislead the reader because quotations are always taken out of context. In addition, because all writers have their own style, quotations can make the flow of the text uneven while providing more detail than the reader requires (Pyrczak & Bruce, 2005).

If factual reports, such as statistical results, are included, it is always appropriate to provide citations. They allow the reader to verify the accuracy of what was included. But, like quotations, they should be included only if the work cited contributes a unique perspective to the literature review, not simply as evidence that the researcher was thorough.

There may be a natural tendency to want to include every bit of knowledge that has been discovered. After all, finding it took a considerable amount of effort! But, if ten articles present essentially the same position, there is no reason to cite them all—that would be overkill. One or two will make the point and be less likely to disrupt the flow of the text.

How relevant should knowledge be in order to be cited? How much detail of others' work is needed or desirable? Daryl Bem (2002) has provided some useful guidelines:

- Only cite articles that are pertinent to your specific research question
- Emphasize major findings and conclusions, avoiding unnecessary detail
- If another review article surveys the literature relevant to your research question, simply refer the reader to the review
- When you do want to describe an entire research study, condense it as much as possible while still communicating the relevant details

Are some types of citations better than others? Yes. But a good mix often is desirable. The best citations to use (all other factors being equal) are those that refer to recent, well-designed research, as opposed to those that may be dated or methodologically flawed. But it is perfectly acceptable to include some older citations, especially if the contribution was a major influence on subsequent thought on a topic or issue. Older citations can also be useful for providing a historical perspective on a problem or event. They reflect the state of the art of knowledge, beliefs, and attitudes at a point in history.

It should be clear to the reader by now that the quotations and citations included in a report of a literature review are there to help explain how the researcher went from point A to point B. They are not there to impress others with how much relevant information was examined. If anything will impress the reader of a good research report, it is the researcher's objectivity and open-mindedness.

Objectivity can be demonstrated in a number of ways. For example, it can be seen in a willingness to include the conflicting opinions and conclusions of other researchers, which almost invariably exist. It is not unusual for two scholars to express beliefs and conclusions that are diametrically opposite. The inclusion of references that reflect both sides of an argument suggests that the researcher has been both thorough and objective in the literature review. Similarly, open-mindedness can be demonstrated by including the ideas and opinions of others that are controversial or generally not consistent with mainstream beliefs and the reasoning behind them.

Role of the Researcher

We do not mean to suggest that the researcher should always remain behind the scenes in a literature review or express no opinions or conclusions. In fact, the opposite is true. Although biases should not be evident in a good literature review, the researcher's thought processes should be both obvious and open to critique. The reader should be able to sense the presence of the researcher in the text. A good literature review is a carefully woven mixture of knowledge and how it has been used by the researcher.

The inclusion of references that reflect both sides of an argument suggests that the researcher has been both thorough and objective in the literature review.

The role of the researcher in a review of the literature section of a research report has some similarities to that of a travel guide. Suppose you are visiting a city like San Francisco for the first time and you only have one full day to take in the sights. You could spend hours or days surfing the Internet before your travel, plan an itinerary on the basis of what interests you, and then rent a car to get around when you arrive. Or, you could simply sign up for a city tour in a van or bus with a travel guide to drive and take you to the most commonly visited tourist attractions, while giving you some background on them. The latter choice might cost a little more and some of what you see may not interest you too much, but the savings in time and effort will be well worth it. Like a travel guide, researchers have identified and organized what they believe is of interest and relevant to the research problems and questions related to it. This is a real time and effort saver for readers—relevant knowledge has been distilled down into an organized, well-written narrative. But there is more to the analogy. A travel guide would not tell you that you must be very impressed by the Golden Gate Bridge or that Coit Tower is really disappointing. He or she would simply provide access to a number of potentially interesting sights and let you decide for yourself if you share his or her opinion of them. Similarly, researchers do not tell the readers of a review of literature what to conclude or how to interpret it—they merely summarize what they derived from it (perhaps a hypothesis or a design for answering their research questions), and readers are free to agree or disagree with their conclusions.

In a well-written literature review, the researcher helps the reader navigate through existing, relevant knowledge, stopping along the way to pull together conclusions and evaluate where—in the researcher's opinion—the literature seems to be leading. The researcher tries not to exert too much influence on the reader, whenever possible letting the literature speak for itself. In a well-written literature review, the reader generally will come to the same or similar conclusions as the researcher and will agree about what the literature has to say about the research questions and how best to study them. The researcher's conclusions should contain no surprises. They will have been anticipated by the reader on the basis of the evidence (the literature) that has been presented.

If the researcher perceives his or her role as similar to that of a travel guide, neither of the two problems that frequently characterize literature reviews is likely to occur. One fairly common problem is one that occurs when the researcher's own thinking dominates the literature review and appears to be invulnerable to influence by it. The reader is left with the suspicion that existing knowledge had little influence on the conclusions that were drawn. Even if a fair number of citations are present, they do not reflect balance. It appears that the researcher selectively used only literature that would support existing biases and did not grow in an understanding of the research problem or questions. The researcher emerged from the literature review with unchanged beliefs. The reader, sensing this, is likely to doubt whether other stages of the research process were conducted in an unbiased manner.

The second problem occurs when the development of the researcher's thinking is barely evident in the literature review. The literature review seems to be little more than a long series of quotations, included in the research report because they are expected. They lend a scholarly appearance, but have no other apparent purpose. There is no way for the reader to evaluate the researcher's thought processes. There is not enough evidence that the knowledge assembled by the researcher was even assimilated.

In the preceding scenarios, we can see that the researcher has not made productive use of the accumulated literature. Doing so may hopelessly damage the credibility of a research report. But if the author assumes the role of guide, the proper mix of quotations reflecting relevant knowledge and the use of that knowledge to refine thinking about the research topic will be evident. The literature review will be a unified whole that seems to take the reader somewhere.

RESEARCH METHODS USING LITERATURE REVIEW AS FOCUS

Some types of research methods use the literature review as the object of the research study. Three of these methods are systematic review, meta-analysis, and content analysis. Since the research designs and data collection methods used for these types of research studies directly involves the literature review, we will include a description of these methods here.

Systematic Reviews

In looking at articles published in professional journals, researchers (and clinicians) are encouraged to seek out and pay greater attention to the findings of higher quality studies rather than lower quality studies. There are a number of simple guidelines on how to evaluate outcome studies in terms of their credibility, which explain why stronger designs are capable of producing more credible knowledge (Pignotti & Thyer, 2009; Thyer, 1989, 1991). Most social workers get some training on this topic in their graduate research coursework. A newer form of evidence that provides a more comprehensive look at research evidence is the systematic review. Littell and Corcoran (2010) offer the following definition:

> Systematic reviews are carefully organized, comprehensive, and transparent studies of previous research on a particular topic. They follow written protocols (detailed plans) that specify their central objectives, concepts, and methods in advance. Systematic review methods include procedures for identifying, critically appraising, synthesizing, and presenting results of previous studies. (p. 313)

The authors further point out that rigorous reviews always include precautions to minimize error and bias at every step in the process. In addition, each step in the process is documented so the readers can follow and evaluate the research methods being used.

There are two international and interdisciplinary organizations dedicated to commissioning, approving, and publishing systematic reviews, and these are known as the Cochrane Collaboration and the Campbell Collaboration. The former focuses on the preparation of systematic reviews in the general field of health care and the latter in the areas of social welfare, criminal justice, and education. Their end products are open-access and Web-based systematic reviews, which can be found in the Cochrane (www.cochrane.org) and Campbell (www.campbellcollaboration.org) libraries. In addition, systematic reviews are sometimes published as independent journal articles, by governmental organizations or private groups, and are not a formal part of either of these collaborations. However, such standalone systematic reviews are not usually held to the exemplary research standards maintained by either the Cochrane or Campbell groups. Standards and guidelines for systematic reviews have been developed by both the Cochrane and Campbell collaborations.

Following are examples of completed systematic reviews that can be found on the Cochrane Collaboration Web site that summarize the effectiveness of various psychosocial interventions:

- Advocacy interventions to reduce or eliminate violence and promote the physical and psychosocial well-being of women who experience intimate partner violence
- Culture-specific programs for children and adults from minority groups who have asthma
- Culturally appropriate health education for type 2 diabetes mellitus in ethnic minority groups
- Behavioral interventions for decreasing HIV infection in racial and ethnic minorities in high-income economies
- Day care for preschool children
- Indigenous health care worker involvement for indigenous adults and children with asthma
- Morita therapy for schizophrenia

The federal Substance Abuse and Mental Health Services Administration maintains a constantly updated searchable Web site called the National Registry of Evidence-Based Programs and Practices (www.nrepp.samhsa.gov). This site contains descriptive information about a wide array of interventions and their outcomes, along with an appraisal of the quality of research, the intervention's readiness for use in community settings, and sources of contact information for social work researchers to learn more about providing the intervention. Of particular importance is an indication of what study populations the intervention has been used with. It is obvious how helpful such a site could be during the initial phase of a research study, when the researcher is searching for other research that looked at similar problems, interventions, and/or populations (Thyer & Myers, 2010).

Littell and Corcoran (2010) emphasize the importance of using a systematic approach when reviewing research. Traditional reviews, sometimes referred to as haphazard reviews, use convenience samples of published studies. A systematic approach informs the reader how the studies included were selected and evaluated. One of the main steps in conducting a systematic review is formulating the eligibility criteria that specify which studies will be included and excluded from the review. The Cochrane Collaboration offers a PICO framework for delineating these criteria. PICO stands for *participants* (or *populations* or *patients*), *intervention*, *comparison or control group*, and *outcomes*. These are the four eligibility criteria that should be defined in detail before beginning the literature search. See Littell and Corcoran (2010) for a detailed discussion of the steps involved in conducting a systematic review.

Meta-Analysis

Another type of research study that uses the literature as the focus of the research is the meta-analysis. Corcoran and Littell (2010) define *meta-analysis* as "a set of statistical methods for combining quantitative results from multiple studies to produce an overall summary of empirical knowledge on a given topic" (p. 299). Meta-analyses can be particularly helpful when completing a review of literature on a certain topic, as they examine the reports from various research studies that focused on the same questions or tested the same hypotheses. These reports may be found in professional journals, research monographs, program evaluation documents, theses, dissertations, or any document in which research designs and findings are described in sufficient detail to be analyzed critically.

Most meta-analysis is cross-sectional and is regarded as explanatory research. Thus, designs generally include hypothesis specification and testing, and statistical analysis of data, characteristics of research studies that are more quantitative than qualitative. Designs can be highly rigorous and may contain various methods to control for problems of design bias and confounding variables, some that are unique to this type of research and some that are common to other forms of secondary analysis.

Meta-analysis has made major contributions to evidence-based practice. A common use of meta-analysis is to try to ascertain if a method or model of intervention is effective for addressing a problem or condition. For example, suppose you are completing a literature review prior to evaluating the effectiveness of a specific school social work practice. Early in your review, you could describe the meta-analysis by Franklin, Kim, and Tripodi (2009), in which they analyzed the overall effectiveness of school social work interventions. Or suppose you are conducting a literature review for a study in which you are analyzing the effectiveness of a specific treatment for children diagnosed with conduct disorder. You might want to describe Litschge, Vaughn, and McCrea's (2010) meta-analysis, in which they identified and summarized treatment effects for children and adolescents with conduct disorders on the basis of 2,000 studies! This could provide the researcher not only a potentially excellent study directly related to the researcher's area of interest but also a reference list of many other pertinent research studies.

Because findings of meta-analyses are based on the reports of studies conducted by many researchers in different settings, they are often based on data collected from very large numbers of research participants. This has certain advantages. Although a particular design bias may have been in operation in one or two studies, it is unlikely to exist in all of them. Also, the large number of cases on which the findings are based should make the likelihood of sampling error quite low. Thus, meta-analysis studies have the potential to possess a high level of both internal and external validity.

A common use of meta-analysis is to try to ascertain if a method or model of intervention is effective for addressing a problem or condition.

Engage, Assess, Intervene, Evaluate

How can a meta-analysis assist the social work practitioner in the selection of the most effective intervention as well as a useful measurement instrument for use with a client?

There are also several problems associated with the use of meta-analysis. Like all forms of secondary data analysis, meta-analysis studies are limited by the quality of the data that are available. The report of one study may be comprehensive; the report of another may be sketchy. This can cause problems in drawing conclusions about the credibility of their respective findings. Also, it is rare that two or more research studies that examined the same research questions used exactly the same research methods. Because of this, the researcher inevitably ends up asking, "How comparable must research methods be for me to include the report of a research study in a meta-analysis?"

Another potential problem relates to the selection processes that sometimes influence what gets into print. Some people have suggested that professional journals may be more likely to publish articles that support their research hypotheses than studies where the variables of interest were found to be unrelated. If this is true, when program evaluations are used in meta-analysis, they may be biased to show programs in a good light. Certain statistical corrections and design features (beyond the scope of this book) have been developed to attempt to address the problem of bias in the meta-analysis.

Meta-analysis is growing in popularity among social work researchers. It is becoming more feasible as we begin to accumulate reports of research that are either replications of earlier research or are reports of research that are similar enough that they lend themselves to this type of analysis.

Content Analysis

The final research method that we will consider here is *content analysis*. Content analysis uses both qualitative and quantitative methods to analyze the content included in literature as well as other types of information on a selected topic. Rubin and Babbie (2007) state that

> content analysis can be a quantitative or qualitative technique. As a qualitative technique, it is a way of discovering patterns and meanings from communications. As a quantitative technique, it involves transforming qualitative material into quantitative data. (p. 262)

Content analysis is a systematic method for analyzing some form of human communication. It is (see Chapter 8) versatile form of secondary analysis, analyzing various types of preexisting data sets. It has features that are typical of quantitative research, such as an emphasis on the use of representative samples and the accurate measurement of variables. It can be used to test for associations and correlations between and among variables. It can be used in predominantly qualitative studies, for example, in analyzing CD or DVD recordings of interviews in studies that use grounded theory methods. Content analysis is cross-sectional, since the data are examined at one point in time. Yet, if those data were accumulated over a long period of time, they can be used to identify changes that occurred during the time that they were being accumulated, a feature usually associated with pretest-posttest or longitudinal research.

Content analysis can be used for analyzing the original data from a research study or, more frequently, for attempting to answer research questions using secondary data, such as journal articles, that are a form of communication. When secondary or preexisting data sets are analyzed, the method is called secondary analysis. Communication can take many different forms, such as

- ▶ DVD or CD recordings of in-person interviews;
- ▶ oral histories;
- ▶ documents such as newspaper articles, professional journals, or congressional records;
- ▶ movies or television programs;
- ▶ minutes of meetings;
- ▶ films or DVD recordings of social gatherings;
- ▶ photographs;
- ▶ recorded phone conversations;
- ▶ e-mail or text messages.

Content analysis generally entails a categorization and counting process. Questions that might be answered using content analysis might include the following:

- ▶ Has the media's representation of women changed over the past ten years?
- ▶ How many articles about people with disabilities does a journal publish?
- ▶ Are males more likely to be published than females?

A single type of communication can answer different research questions using content analysis. For example, a researcher could use the previous five years of a university's student evaluations of instructors to answer any of these questions:

- ▶ Do students seem to be getting more critical of instructors?
- ▶ What are the most common strengths and weaknesses of instructors that are listed?
- ▶ Do part-time students make fewer negative comments about instructors than full-time students?

Content analysis used to be a tedious process. The development of computer programs that can quickly scan various forms of human communication and, for example, count how often certain words or phrases appear, has made it much easier. As the technology for doing this continues to expand so that more and more types of communication can be examined by a computer, content analysis is likely to continue to gain in popularity.

Let's look at some examples of current research that demonstrate the diverse use of content analysis. Ryan and Sheehan (2009) conducted a content analysis of all the articles published in the journal *Australian Social Work* from 1998 to 2007. In this study, the researchers were interested in research studies that examined the efficacy of specific social work interventions. Out of 313 articles published during this time, 138 or 45 percent reported research findings. However, only six articles involved evaluation of practice or testing of an instrument. The researchers concluded that if social workers are going to adopt an evidence-based approach to practice, more research studies must focus on evaluation of social work interventions. Content analysis was used by Scherrer (2009) to examine the portrayals of aging and sexuality in articles published in twenty-one gerontological journals over a twenty-year span from 1988 to 2007.

As we mentioned earlier, content analysis is not limited to the analysis of journal articles or other printed material. Suppose you are interested in how gay men are portrayed in television and movies and how this has changed over the past twenty years. Content analysis could be used to analyze the various gay and lesbian characters that have been created for movies and television since 1990. Of course, this would be a time-consuming technique. The researcher would have to determine how the television shows and movies would be selected, how the gay characters would be located, how the characters would be classified and recorded for analysis, and so forth.

Content analysis is often used in qualitative research to analyze the content of data collected in a variety of ways, such as interviews, personal journals, and meeting minutes. The variety of data sources that can be used as the focus of a content analysis is clear from the following examples. One recent study (Dauz Williams et al., 2010) considered the experiences of siblings of children with developmental disabilities. Interviews were completed with 151 parents of children with developmental disabilities, in which they were asked their perceptions of how other siblings in the home were affected by living with their brother or sister with a developmental disability. Researchers identified 363 themes, and found that over 60 percent of the parents felt that their children who were not suffering from the developmental disability nevertheless experienced increased risks because of their home environment. The researchers were thus able to recommend additional intervention with this vulnerable population. Another content analysis (Bengtsson-Tops, Saveman, & Tops, 2009) examined interviews with thirteen staff members working with abused women suffering from mental illness. The aim of the qualitative study was to attempt to describe how these workers experience and understand their work with this vulnerable population. Findings suggest that workers experience their work as ambiguous and painful and as a result tend to act pragmatically to achieve concrete results through their interventions. Still another study (Timmerman, 2006) used content analysis to examine food journals to compare the restaurant-eating behaviors of women diagnosed as binge eaters to women who were dieting but did not report a history of binge eating.

The need for another type of content analysis has emerged during a time in which many people turn to the Internet for information on everything from recipes and movie reviews to medical diagnoses and medication choices. New studies are using content analysis to examine information found on the Internet to both learn from this information as well as evaluate its validity. For example, Moncrieff, Cohen, and Mason (2009) conducted a content analysis on a database of comments made by people about prescribed medications. They analyzed over 400 comments on five antipsychotic medications to understand the subjective experiences of people taking these prescribed medications. The researchers were able to learn a great deal about the desired benefits as well as the undesirable side effects of taking these drugs.

For a more detailed description of the techniques used in content analysis, the reader can turn to thorough discussions provided by Krippendorf (2004), Neuendorf (2002), and Rubin and Babbie (2007).

Diversity in Practice

Suppose you want to study the representations of gay characters in television shows. Identify one qualitative question and one quantitative question that could be studied using content analysis.

SUMMARY

The term *literature review* refers to both a process of referring to existing knowledge at different points in the research process and to a product, namely, a section of a report or chapter of a book. A body of knowledge exists for any research question. The process of reviewing existing knowledge about a research question can shape our thinking about the question and its possible answer. We discussed the purposes and objectives of completing a literature review.

The pros and cons of including various potential sources of knowledge in the review of literature section of a research report were discussed, with special focus on how the selection of a source can affect the credibility of the researcher and the research findings. Practical suggestions also were given for organizing a wide array of knowledge into a logical and coherent report of what is known relative to the research problem and the questions chosen for study. We proposed the analogy that the writer of a research report functions much like a tour guide. The writer compiles relevant knowledge and presents it to the reader along with his or her interpretations and conclusions drawn from it. The writer encourages the reader to critique these conclusions and the thought processes that produced them and agree or disagree with them.

Finally, we looked at various types of research in which the focus of the research is the literature: systematic reviews, meta-analysis, and content analysis. Systematic reviews follow a systematic strategy for compiling the research on a selected topic. Meta-analyses use statistics to convert the results of collected studies into standardized numbers that can be used for making comparisons, and to generate an overall estimate of the effect of the interventions across the combined studies. Finally, content analyses review all types of communications for the presence of certain topics and ideas and sometimes follow the development of an idea over time. These types of research studies can be particularly useful when completing a literature review on a topic.

Log onto **www.mysocialworklab.com** and answer the following questions. (If you did not receive an access code to **MySocialWorkLab** with this text and wish to purchase access online, please visit www. mysocialworklab.com.)

1. **Watch the Core Competencies Video: Diversity in practice: Learning from the client to cocreate an action plan:** If you want to turn to journal articles for assistance in selecting an intervention for this client, what are three words or phrases you could use to begin your search?

2. **Read the Case Study: Domestic violence: Betty and Charlie Bristol.** If you want to look for possible interventions to help in your work with Charlie, what word or phrase would you use to begin your search? If this search returns too broad an array of articles, what are two ways you could limit the search? What word or phrase would you use if you were looking for possible interventions to use with Charlie's mother, Betty?

PRACTICE TEST

1. Why are articles in professional journals considered one of the most trustworthy knowledge sources?
   a. Because journals are very expensive to publish and purchase
   b. Because journal articles undergo an anonymous peer review process before being published
   c. Because only professors can publish articles in professional journals
   d. Because editors of journals select the articles based solely on their extensive knowledge of the field

2. What is probably the greatest strength of information found on the Internet?
   a. The information can be updated easily and so may be more up to date than books or journal articles.
   b. The information on the Internet is always checked for accuracy before being placed on a Web site.
   c. Once information is put on a Web site, it will always stay the same.
   d. Only experts put information on social work Web sites.

3. In a literature review on depression among children following divorce of their parents, which of the following would you probably see first?
   a. Studies that have looked at the effects of divorce on children
   b. Discussion of depression among children
   c. Specific hypotheses for the research study
   d. Overview of depression

4. Which of the following research questions would not be answered using content analysis?
   a. How have a group of clients responded to cognitive-behavioral therapy for their depression?
   b. How has television's portrayal of men staying at home with children changed during the last twenty years?
   c. How has the number of comedy versus dramatic television shows changed since 1960?
   d. What types of books have made it to the New York bestseller list over the past ten years?

5. Suppose you are writing a literature review on stress experienced by African-American college students. Create a possible outline for your literature review.

ASSESS YOUR COMPETENCE
Use the scale below to rate your current level of achievement on the following concepts or skills associated with each competency presented in the chapter:

1	2	3
I can accurately describe the concept or skill.	I can consistently identify the concept or skill when observing and analyzing practice activities.	I can competently implement the concept or skill in my own practice.

_____ Understanding the purpose of the literature review

_____ Being able to recognize reliable and unreliable sources for knowledge

_____ Understanding the best way to organize a literature review

_____ Being familiar with the systematic review, meta-analysis, and content analysis

5

Focused Research Questions
and Research Hypotheses

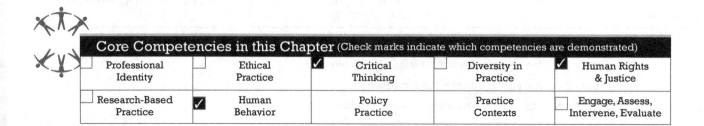

Core Competencies in this Chapter (Check marks indicate which competencies are demonstrated)				
☐ Professional Identity	☐ Ethical Practice	☑ Critical Thinking	☐ Diversity in Practice	☑ Human Rights & Justice
☐ Research-Based Practice	☑ Human Behavior	☐ Policy Practice	☐ Practice Contexts	☐ Engage, Assess, Intervene, Evaluate

As we noted in the previous chapter, researchers rely heavily on existing knowledge (the literature) to assist them. When they consult it prior to data collection, it helps them in selecting the most appropriate design for their research (see Chapters 6–8). It also helps them to specify more clearly the research questions that will be examined in their research. Depending on the amount of knowledge available and what is learned, they may even be able to predict what answers will be found. These two latter products of literature reviews, focused research questions and hypotheses, are so important to research that we devote this chapter to them.

FOCUSED RESEARCH QUESTIONS

Selecting broad research questions (Chapter 3) is a useful exercise. It reduces the study of a research problem to a manageable size. As we suggested, no one study can possibly do a thorough job of examining all questions that might relate to a research problem; some choices must be made. However, broad questions, such as those in the examples in Chapter 3, do not provide a specific-enough focus to guide the researcher in performing such necessary tasks as identifying the most appropriate people or objects to study, determining what needs to be observed and/or measured, or determining how best to do it. Broad questions also provide little or no guidance for selecting the methods to sort and analyze data. Before these tasks can be undertaken, further refinement and specification of the research questions are required.

What is the difference between a broad research question such as those discussed in Chapter 3 and the more specific questions that are likely to be formulated following a literature review? How does a review of existing knowledge help the researcher to move from the former to the latter?

To illustrate the difference between broad and focused research questions, we will return to the example used in Chapter 3 (Bellomy et al., 1989). The reader will recall that after eliminating other options, the student researchers, looking into the problem of large numbers of unfounded child abuse determinations, settled on one broad question, "Are the different demographic characteristics of workers (e.g., age, race, sex, or parenthood) related to their determinations?" This was a good start. The question provided a beginning focus for the study and helped to narrow the literature review to a manageable number of topics. It committed the researchers to gaining a better understanding of the decision (founded versus unfounded) that child protection workers must make when they receive a referral for possible child abuse or neglect. It provided a research focus—exploration of a possible relationship between various social worker characteristics and those decisions. But the question was still too general to provide any real direction to the researchers as to the best way to go about seeking an answer.

Before the literature review was completed, the researchers did not know to what degree answers to the question already existed, what methods had been used to study it, or what other researchers had learned in the process of conducting their research. For example, without reviewing the literature, it was not possible to know which worker characteristics would or would not be promising to examine.

Before conducting their literature review, the researchers had only vague ideas as to how to proceed with their research. When they began to search the literature, the researchers soon confirmed what they had suspected—they were not attempting to build knowledge in a vacuum. For example, it was learned that other researchers had been studying professionals' decision making for many years; some had even used human service workers as research participants. Other literature confirmed their hunch that there was a lack of consistent, clear federal procedural guidelines, and that the definitions of what constitutes child abuse were vague. A review of state policy manuals suggested that state guidelines were no less ambiguous.

The researchers found one article that was especially helpful in suggesting how to study their research question. It described the relative merits of different research methods that were used to identify factors that seem to influence social workers' decision making in a variety of settings other than child protection.

As they continued to search the literature and speak with child welfare administrators, group members began to compile a list of personal characteristics that, on the basis of past research, might be related to the decisions that the workers make. Several especially good prospects included level of educational achievement, discipline methods used in the workers' homes of origin, feelings about their jobs, and whether they were parents themselves. Each of these characteristics was found to be related to social workers' decision making. The researchers decided to collect data on each of these characteristics. Just as importantly, they decided not to gather data on certain other worker characteristics (e.g., age, health status, or gender) that, on the basis of past research, probably would not be related to decision making about cases referred for possible child abuse or neglect.

Some of what the researchers learned from their literature review could be described as inconclusive or even conflicting. For example, the human behavior literature suggested that parenting practices in the home of origin of the child protection workers would likely have some effect on their adult attitudes toward the ways that clients treated their children. But personnel data also indicated that the child protection workers had undergone both formal education and special training for their jobs. Wasn't it logical to conclude that parenting practices in their homes of origin might no longer influence their decision making to any significant degree? Maybe. But remember, logic is pretty untrustworthy as a source of knowledge (see Chapter 1).

The literature review produced focused research questions that would have been impossible to formulate without the knowledge obtained—finding out what was already known about the problem, what related questions had been studied, and what answers had been found.

The literature review produced focused research questions that would have been impossible to formulate without the knowledge obtained—finding out what was already known about the problem, what related questions had been studied, and what answers had been found. Because of the review, the researchers were able to take their broad research question and reformulate it into two more focused or specific questions:

▸ Is there a relationship between disciplinary practices in child protection workers' families of origin and their decision making about cases referred for suspected child abuse or neglect?

▸ To what degree do workers perceive that their formal education and training in child protection services has influenced their decision making about cases referred for suspected child abuse or neglect?

With these more focused questions to work with, the research took on a clearer focus. As a result of conducting the literature review, it was now possible to know what data about workers and their decisions should be gathered, and, by learning from the experiences of other researchers, the best ways to go about gathering it. Box 5.1 provides additional examples of broad research questions and corresponding focused research questions that might be produced through reviewing relevant scientific literature.

Box 5.1 **Examples of Broad Research Questions and Focused Research Questions**	
Broad Research Questions	**Focused Research Questions**
A. Are people with developmental disabilities unhappy working in sheltered workshops?	A. What working conditions contribute most to dissatisfaction of workers in sheltered workshops?
B. How do value conflicts affect client services when social workers are supervised by nurses?	B. When nurses supervise social workers, why are patients less likely to refuse painful life-extending treatment?
C. Have day care facilities increased to meet the needs of families denied extended benefits since welfare reform?	C. Is there a correlation between the increase in day care facilities and reports of abuse or neglect?
D. Why do social work students dislike courses in research and statistics?	D. Is the rate of math phobia higher among social work students than in the general population?
E. What obstacles to the grief process do parents of children who die while committing violent crimes perceive?	E. Why do parents of children who die while committing violent crimes often withdraw from contact with their communities

RESEARCH HYPOTHESES

A *research hypothesis* is a tentative answer to a research question. It is based on existing knowledge (and sometimes, to a lesser degree, on practice experience) and is a prediction of what the researcher will find. It generally takes the form of a statement of a relationship between certain variables. As previously noted, in predominantly qualitative studies, researchers usually do not formulate research hypotheses. Relevant variables often are not even identified when data collection begins, so it would be impossible to predict a relationship between them. However, the final product of a qualitative study may be one or more theories or *hypothesis statements*. Other researchers may subsequently adopt them as their research hypotheses and then attempt to learn if there is support for them, often using predominantly quantitative methods.

In most qualitative research, a brief search of available literature prior to data collection helps to formulate a plan or design for conducting the research and to narrow and refine the research question or questions. But it goes no further. The literature does not suggest answers to the questions. Thus, data collection begins without the researcher being able to predict what will be found, just with a little clearer idea of the questions to be examined.

In predominantly quantitative studies, the research problem or a similar one may have been studied for some time, and a considerable amount of related knowledge may have accumulated. Data that have been collected are examined using statistical tests to determine whether support for the research hypotheses exists. The literature review may suggest what will be found after data are collected and analyzed. In this case, it is possible to formulate one or more research hypotheses.

Research hypotheses generally are stated in either the present or the future tense. In rare instances, such as in the case of historical research (Chapter 8), the past tense is used. They are stated in the form of declarative statements, never as questions, because they are tentative answers to research questions.

Related Definitions

To understand fully just what research hypotheses are and how a literature review can help in formulating them, we will first need to define certain key research terms.

Variable and Constant

We have already used the term *variable* several times, because the study of variables is essential to research. A variable is an attribute or characteristic that differs in quantity or quality among different persons, objects, times, places, and so on. In our earlier example, the different parenting experiences of child protection workers within their homes of origin would be a variable. If all the workers had been parented in the same way, parenting experience would not be considered a variable; it would be a *constant*. A constant is a characteristic or attribute that does not differ either in quantity or in quality among the cases involved in the research study. For example, the employment position of all the subjects in this study did not differ—they were all child protection workers. Therefore, employment position is a constant in this study. In research, constants usually are of less interest than variables.

Demographic Variable

A demographic variable is a type of variable. The term *demographic variable* is a generic term that refers to those commonly measured variables that give researchers (and, when reported, readers of research reports) a clearer understanding of the general characteristics of research participants. Some of the variables generally referred to as demographic are age, gender, income, religious affiliation, education, and marital status. Demographic variables sometimes are collectively referred to as bio-data.

Although certain demographic variables frequently are included in questionnaires and other research data collection instruments, there is no rule that says that they must be. Unless researchers have reason to believe that a demographic variable is related to the research question in some way (as determined through the literature review) or that the readers of their research report will require information about it (e.g., to determine if their clients are similar to researchers' participants), there is really no justification to measure it. In fact, unless one of these justifications exists, there may be ethical and practical reasons not to measure it. Some demographic variables (e.g., age, religious affiliation, marital status, or income) may be considered sensitive and personal. Collecting data about them when the researcher has no practical use for them is an unnecessary invasion of the participants' right to privacy. Besides, requesting unnecessary data from participants who are less than eager to provide them can jeopardize the collection of other data that are really needed from them.

Value Label or Value

The terms *value label* and *value* (as used in research) mean essentially the same thing. They are the name (value label) or number (value) assigned to a specific measurement of a variable.

A value label (some people prefer the term *attribute*) is a word or words used to denote a form that a variable can assume. For example, for the variable Parenting Style in Home of Origin, different value labels might be "autocratic," "democratic," "laissez-faire," or some other group of words that reflect the differences in parenting style that existed within child protection workers' homes of origin. Note that the differences reflect different kinds or qualities (rather than quantities) of the variable. A value is a specific measurement of a variable and is expressed as a number reflecting the quantity of the variable. For the variable "number of siblings," for example, possible values would include 0, 1, 2, 3, 4, and so on, indicating the number of siblings present in the home.

Whether we use the term value label or value is a function of how precisely a variable can be measured (see Chapter 10) and whether its different measurements reflect a difference in kind or quality or a difference in quantity. Thus, a variable "children" might use the value labels Yes or No to denote whether each worker is a parent. However, if we were to ask how many children under age 18 reside with the worker, the same variable "children" could indicate the number of children in the home, taking on values such as 0, 1, 2, 3, and so forth.

Human Rights & Justice

What are some possible problems with creating the attributes for such variables as "race" and "sexual orientation?"

Frequency

Frequency refers to the number of times a given value label or value was found to exist among the persons, objects, and the like that were studied (referred to as cases in a given research study). If five workers were found to have been reared in homes that used autocratic parenting styles, we would say that the value label "autocratic" had a frequency of 5. If democratic styles existed in the homes of nine workers, the value label "democratic" would have a frequency of 9, and so forth.

Dependent Variable and Independent Variable or Outcome Variable and Predictor Variable

Researchers often use one of two pairs of terms while communicating their predictions within a hypothesis. The terms *dependent variable* and *independent variable* form one such pair. *Dependent variable* refers to the variable whose variation the researcher is most interested in understanding and explaining. In social work research, the degree of treatment success that occurs among clients is a common dependent variable, but a dependent variable can be any variable that the researcher has declared to be the one whose variations are of primary interest.

The label dependent variable is not applied to a variable unless at least one other variable, an independent variable, has been hypothesized to be at least a contributor to its variations. The term *independent variable* is applied to the variable or variables that the researcher believes may produce at least some of the variation that exists within the dependent variable. If, for example, the variable degree of treatment success among clients in a hypothesis is labeled the dependent variable, the independent variable might be method of treatment, degree of family involvement, or fee paid by the client. It also could be some other variable that the literature and practice experience has indicated as likely to contribute to the variations in the degree of treatment success that clients experience.

Ideally, an independent variable is introduced and/or manipulated in some way by the researcher so that its effects on the dependent variable can be monitored and recorded. As long as the researcher is asserting that one variable is believed to influence the values of a second variable (and not vice versa), it is appropriate to refer to the first variable as the independent variable and to the second as the dependent variable. The terms dependent variable and independent variable are used together or not at all.

The terms *predictor variable* (in place of independent variable) and *outcome variable* (in place of dependent variable) are sometimes used when the researchers feel they more accurately describe what is believed to be the relationship between variables. Like the dependent variable, the outcome variable generally refers to the variable of primary interest to the researcher. The terms predictor variable and outcome variable are used when the researcher has no control over the variables. Instead, the research has hypothesized that the variables are either associated or correlated (discussed later in this chapter) and that one variable (the predictor variable) can be used to predict the value of the second variable (the outcome variable). For example, Townsend, Floersch, and Findling (2009) conducted a study to determine to what extent scores on the Drug Attitudes Inventory (DAI) (Hogan, Awad, & Eastwood, 1983) would predict the rate of adherence to psychotropic medication among adolescents. They concluded that there was a low but significant correlation between DAI scores (the predictor variable) and adherence rate (outcome variable). To use the terms *independent variable* and *dependent variable* to refer to the variables in this study would be misleading, since the researchers did not manipulate either of the variables. While they cannot assume or hope to demonstrate conclusively that the DAI scores cause or even contribute to variations in the adherence rate, they can conclude that the two variables are correlated and that DAI scores can be used to predict the adherence rate.

The terms *dependent variable* (or outcome variable) and *independent variable* (or predictor variable) are specific to a given piece of research. That is, they describe the focus of one researcher's investigation and the nature of a relationship between variables believed to exist within it. Another researcher is likely to have a different focus and suggest a different relationship. Thus, a variable may be defined as the independent or predictor variable in one research study and the dependent or outcome variable in another study. For example, one study may use scores on the Beck Depression Inventory (Beck, Steer, Ball, & Ranier, 1996) as the dependent variable to determine the effectiveness of a cognitive intervention. In another study that looks at the influence of depression level on the severity of disordered eating behaviors (such as binging or purging), scores on the same depression inventory may be defined as the predictor variable.

The terms *dependent variable*, *independent variable*, outcome variable, and predictor variable should be regarded simply as convenient labels. They help the reader of a research report understand the focus of the researcher's area of inquiry and better understand exactly what the researcher believes to be the nature of the relationship between or among variables. They also suggest the type of research methods used and the type of statistical analysis most likely to have been applied.

Sometimes, neither pair of labels is appropriate. In some research that predicts the existence of a relationship between variables, it may not be possible or appropriate to identify one variable in a hypothesis as clearly dependent (or outcome) and another as independent (or predictor). For example, the literature may suggest that alcoholism and unemployment are related, but in a study of the relationship between the two social problems, it may not be possible to make a case for applying the label *outcome* (or *dependent*) to one variable any more than to the other. The researcher may be more interested in studying their interaction than in examining to what degree (if any) one may influence or predict the other. Or the research goal may be simply to learn the extent to which one problem tends to be found *with* the other. If either is the primary research focus, the terms *dependent* (or *outcome*) variable and *independent* (or *predictor*) variable would not be used. In this case, the hypothesis should be stated so that it is clear that the researcher is not communicating that one variable is of any greater interest than the other or that one variable is contributing to the different values of the other; the hypothesis should be stated to indicate that they covary, that is, they vary together in a certain pattern. For example, Bonewell (2009) compared intrinsic and extrinsic religious beliefs to the extent of sexual compulsivity among Christian males and found no relevant association between these two variables.

Confounding Variable

We know from our knowledge of human behavior that the relationship between two variables is rarely a simple one. For example, the decision to join or not join a youth gang is not solely a function of whether or not there is a father figure in the home. Many other variables come into play that can easily confuse researchers about the true relationship between these two variables. Researchers have labels to describe these other variables as well.

The terms *confounding variable* or *extraneous variable* refer to any variable that can mislead the researcher about the true relationship between the dependent and independent variables. The term *intervening variable* has a more specific usage, relating to the time when the variable's influence on the relationship between an independent variable and a dependent variable was believed to occur. A variable can be considered potentially intervening only if it may have influenced the dependent variable after the effects of the independent variable have been experienced. For example, sexual experiences during adolescence might be considered an intervening variable if a researcher wished to study the relationship between the presence or absence of sexual abuse as a child (independent variable) and current sexual satisfaction of adults (dependent variable). The independent variable (the presence or absence of sexual abuse as a child) may have influenced the intervening variable (sexual experiences during adolescence), which in turn influenced the dependent variable (current sexual satisfaction).

Other terms more precisely describe the specific way in which one or more other variables might have the potential to mislead the researcher about the true relationship between the dependent and independent variables. For example, the term *antecedent variable* describes a third variable that preceded both the dependent and the independent variables and influenced variations of both. Leung (2007) studied how peer relations and perceived social self-worth affect the level of shyness among a group of young adults. She identified two variables, temperament and parental characteristics, as antecedent variables that had an effect on all three of the variables of interest in her study: peer relations, perceived social self-worth, and the level of shyness. Another term, *obscuring variable*, describes a variable that interacts with the dependent and independent variables in such a way as to make them appear less closely related than they really are.

In an introductory book like this one, these distinctions are not too important. We will use the term confounding variable to refer to any variable that has the potential to distort or misrepresent the true relationship between the dependent (or outcome) and independent (or predictor) variables, no matter how (specifically) it does this or in which direction it may potentially mislead the researcher.

Social work practitioners are aware of and work with confounding variables all the time, although the label may be an unfamiliar one. In practice, as in

The terms confounding variable or extraneous variable refer to any variable that can mislead the researcher about the true relationship between the dependent and independent variables.

research, we hope to control confounding variables and minimize or eliminate their influence, but this often is not possible. For example, as practitioners, we might wish to know to what degree our treatment is influencing a client's social functioning. But we may be concerned about how the attitude or behavior of a spouse or an employer (potentially confounding variables) might influence the level of treatment success that our client may achieve. We sometimes must acknowledge that the treatment may be less a factor in the client's social functioning level than either of these other variables. Either may have a major influence on what appears on the surface to be the relationship between our treatment and our client's social functioning. The spouse's and the employer's behaviors and attitudes and any number of other possible confounding variables can muddy the water as we attempt to determine the relationship between our treatment and the client's level of social functioning.

Fortunately, researchers have devised ways to minimize or at least help sort out the influence of variables potentially confounding their understanding the relationship between dependent and independent variables. In such cases, we no longer refer to a variable as confounding or extraneous or by any of the other terms that denote the specific way the variable may be affecting the relationship between independent and dependent variables. We instead refer to it as a *control variable* (sometimes called a *moderating variable*), a potentially confounding variable whose influence has been recognized and controlled. This can be done using one of several statistical tests that employ mathematical formulas designed for this purpose. If the apparent relationship between the independent and the dependent variables disappears following introduction of the measurements of the control variable into the formula, researchers describe the original relationship as *spurious*. In research, a spurious relationship is one in which there is actually no relationship between two variables, but a relationship has been inferred because of the influence of a confounding variable, (that has not been identified and controlled for). Of course, the introduction of the control variable can also have the opposite effect—it can reveal an apparent relationship between the independent and dependent variables that was not previously in evidence. This suggests that the control variable was really an obscuring variable.

Types of Relationships between Variables

A research hypothesis, as we noted, states that researchers believe (on the basis of existing knowledge as revealed by the literature and their experience) that certain variables are related. The research hypothesis sends notice that researchers are seeking additional evidence for this presumed relationship. In addition, a research hypothesis generally goes a little further, stating the nature of the relationship between the variables. Certain types of relationships are commonly stated in hypotheses (see Box 5.2). Some reflect a very subtle distinction; others are more dramatic. We will describe the three most commonly used relationships.

Human Behavior

In evaluating the improvement in a client's functioning after completing a treatment for depression, identify some potential confounding variables that could also have affected the client's depression level.

Box 5.2 **Relationships between Variables Expressed in Hypotheses**	
Association	Certain value categories of X are found with certain value categories of Y.
Correlation	Higher values of X are found with higher values of Y and vice versa, or, higher values of X are found with lower values of Y and vice versa.
Causation	Values or value categories of X cause values or value categories of Y.

Association

A research hypothesis that states a belief in an association between variables asserts that certain value categories of one variable (usually one that cannot be measured with much precision) tend to be found with certain value categories of another variable.

To describe a relationship between variables as an association is to acknowledge that the influence of one or more confounding variables is likely and that they probably have not been adequately controlled. It also acknowledges both the limits of measurement of the variables (see Chapter 10) and the limits of the statistical analysis (see Chapter 13) used to determine the likelihood of a true relationship between the variables. A research hypothesis is likely to be stated so as to reflect only an association between variables (and nothing more) if

- the variables can be measured so that their values reflect only qualitative differences (differences of kind) and not the precise quantity of the variable present;
- the statistical analysis produces only an indication of degree of association; and
- the researcher was unable to introduce or manipulate the predictor variable in any way or to exert control over potentially confounding variables.

An example of a research hypothesis that suggests a relationship of only association is as follows: "Among adolescent patients, those who receive group treatment are more likely to be rehospitalized than those who receive individual treatment." Note that, in this hypothesis, all three of the preceding conditions are present.

Research hypotheses that state beliefs about association between or among variables are quite common in social work research. Although an association between variables gives researchers less information about the relationship than they might like to have, knowledge of an association between variables still can be useful to the social worker. For example, Donate-Lopez et al. (2010) looked at the association of age, gender, and helmet use with the risk of death for occupants of two-wheeled motor vehicles involved in crashes. In another study, Marmorstein (2010) examined the longitudinal associations between depression and alcohol problems, while accounting for the potential interaction effects of delinquent behaviors during adolescence.

Correlation

A correlation might be regarded as a special type of association. If a research hypothesis predicts a correlation between variables, it implies a little more about their relationship than just a simple association. A prediction that variables will be found to be correlated predicts that the values of the variables covary. It does not predict that the values of one variable will be shown to have caused the values of the other to occur. As in the case of association, inadequately controlled confounding variables (or some other cause) may be producing any apparent relationship between the variables. A hypothesis is likely to be stated so as to reflect a correlation between or among variables if

- the variables can be measured so that their values reflect different, precise, and measurable quantities of the variables;
- certain statistical analyses designed to determine the strength and direction of the relationship will be used; and
- the researcher was unable to introduce or manipulate the predictor variable in any way or exert control over potentially confounding variables.

Unless specifically stated otherwise, when a correlation between variables is predicted in a research hypothesis, it refers to a linear correlation (see Weinbach & Grinnell [2007] for a description of other types of correlation). A linear correlation between two variables is a relationship in which one of two patterns exists: (1) high values (indicating large, quantitative measurements) of one variable are found (disproportionately) with high values of the other variable and low values of the first are found with low values of the second (described as a positive correlation); (2) high values of one variable are found with low values of the other variable and vice versa (described as a negative or an inverse correlation). These patterns of a relationship can be seen in a graph called a scattergram, which portrays simultaneously the measurements for both variables for every case. In a scattergram, strong correlations will be reflected in a pattern of dots that approximate a straight line, hence the term *linear correlation*.

An example of a research hypothesis that predicts a linear correlation between two variables is as follows: "Among adolescent psychiatric patients, there is a negative correlation between number of group treatment sessions attended per week and length of time the patient was hospitalized." Note that the hypothesis predicts a negative correlation. It predicts that patients who attended the most group sessions per week will have spent less time hospitalized than those who rarely attended, and vice versa. A hypothesis that predicts a positive correlation between the predictor and outcome variables, predicting that the more group sessions attended per week the more time hospitalized, would have been illogical, assuming that the group sessions were believed to be making a positive contribution to patients' recovery.

In the most common usage of the term, a correlation is just a little more precise statement of a relationship between variables (based on their measurement and the type of statistical analysis used) than an association. Like association, correlation does not prove causation. Many variables are highly correlated, yet the different values of one variable do not cause the different values of the other. In a research hypothesis that predicts a relationship of correlation, researchers generally use the labels predictor variable and outcome variable (rather than *independent variable* and *dependent variable*) to describe the relationship between variables. Such a hypothesis is used when it is believed that values of one variable (the predictor variable) are a better predictor of values of the other (the outcome variable) than the other way around, or when the values of one (the predictor variable) occur before the values of the other (the outcome variable). If neither variable is seen as predicting the other, only that the variables covary, these terms would not be used.

One example of a correlational study, by Smith (2009), explored the relationships between levels of job burnout, intrinsic spirituality, and social support among perinatal social workers. Another correlational study (Acker, 2010) explored the relationships between the level of conflict that social workers experience when interfacing with managed care organizations and the worker's job satisfaction, organizational commitment, emotional exhaustion, and turnover intentions.

Causation

A research hypothesis that states a belief in causation goes out on a limb. It states that the values or value categories of the independent variable produce different values or value categories of the dependent variable. It leaves no room for the possibility that one or more confounding variables or any other phenomenon (such as a biased sample or chance) may have produced this apparent relationship within cases that are studied. An example of a hypothesis that states a relationship of causation between variables is as follows: "Among adolescent psychiatric patients, group treatment produces lower rates of rehospitalization than individual treatment." To demonstrate support for this relationship, three conditions would have to be present:

- ◗ The treatment must have occurred before the rehospitalization/non-rehospitalization.
- ◗ There must be an association between the independent and dependent variables.
- ◗ All other explanations for rehospitalization or non-rehospitalization (besides the type of treatment given) must have been ruled out.

The first two conditions can be easily computed with statistical methods (discussed in Chapter 13). The third condition is more problematic. To rule out all other explanations for an outcome requires a research design that can be logistically difficult and may, perhaps, be unethical. The requirements of such a design will be discussed in Chapter 6.

Research hypotheses suggesting a relationship of causation between variables (also known as a cause-effect relationship) have historically been relatively rare in social work research. If the dependent variable is a behavior or human condition (which often is the case), it is difficult to conclude that it is caused by the influence of any one other variable, since social systems theory maintains that behavior or conditions have many interrelated causes. Because of ethical (see Chapter 2) and logistical reasons, it is difficult to identify, let alone control, potentially confounding variables that are likely to influence the relationship between the dependent and the independent variables.

However, with the use of rigorous research designs, researchers are learning methods to control for not only those confounding variables that have been identified but also those that may never be recognized or fully understood. In

Critical Thinking

If two variables are found to have a strong positive correlation, can we assume that one variable causes the other variable?

these designs, techniques are used to ensure the comparability of the experimental and control groups. One interesting study (Fernandez-Aranda et al., 2009) examined the effectiveness of an Internet-based therapy for clients diagnosed with bulimia nervosa. Clients were randomly assigned to either the experimental group or the control group (actually a wait list who received the treatment after the posttest for the study was completed). The researchers made sure the two groups were equivalent on variables that they identified as potentially confounding, such as age, duration of the disorder, number of previous treatments, and severity of the disorder. Because the clients were randomly assigned to the two groups, we can assume that the two groups would be equivalent on other potentially confounding variables that had not been identified. The researchers concluded that the Internet-based therapy appeared to be a valid treatment option for clients with bulimia nervosa, particularly those clients who present with a lower severity of symptomatology.

However, many studies with a less rigorous research design sometimes point to a specific cause-effect relationship. In these cases, researchers may still arrive at the conclusion that such a relationship truly does exist. For example, let us consider the cause-effect relationship between cigarette smoking and lung cancer. For obvious ethical reasons, researchers have never conducted a longitudinal study in which people are randomly assigned to either an experimental group, where they are expected to smoke a prescribed number of cigarettes per day, or to a control group, where they are not allowed to smoke. But in the absence of more rigorous studies, there are many other, less rigorous studies that have consistently pointed to smoking cigarettes as the main cause of lung cancer. On the basis of this research, scientists have concluded that there is a strong cause-effect link between cigarette smoking and lung cancer.

Types of Research Hypotheses

If a researcher predicts that variables will be found to be related (association, correlation, or causation), it is possible to express that relationship in one of two ways within a research hypothesis: either a directional or a nondirectional hypothesis may be appropriate, depending on what was learned from the literature review.

In a directional (also called one-tailed) research hypothesis, the researcher not only asserts that the variables will be found to be related, but also predicts the direction of their relationship. In contrast, in a nondirectional (or two-tailed) research hypothesis, the researcher asserts that the variables will be found to be related, but does not wish to hazard a guess as to the direction in which they will be found to be related (Weinbach & Grinnell, 2007). An example of a directional hypothesis is as follows: "Among adolescent psychiatric patients, those who received group treatment will reflect a higher rate of rehospitalization than those who received individual treatment." An example of a nondirectional hypothesis using the same two variables is as follows: "Among adolescent psychiatric patients, there will be a difference in rehospitalization rate between those who received group counseling and those who received individual counseling."

Sometimes, variables are commonly believed to be related, but the researcher, on the basis of the literature review and practice experience, is convinced that they really are unrelated. In this case, a research hypothesis would be stated in such a way that it reflects the prediction that the variables will be found to be unrelated. An example of a hypothesis that predicts no relationship between

Box 5.3 Three Types of Research Hypotheses

1. Directional — "Males learn computer skills faster than females" *or* "Females learn computer skills faster than males."

2. Nondirectional — "Males and females learn computer skills at different speeds."

3. No relationship — "There is no difference in the speed at which males and females learn computer skills."

variables is as follows: among adolescent psychiatric patients, those who received group treatment will have the same rate of rehospitalization as those who received individual treatment. In this example, the two variables were described as having no association. If they are not even believed to be associated, they could not be correlated, or a relationship of causation could not exist. Box 5.3 provides another example of the differences among these forms of research hypotheses.

Notice that the third type of research hypothesis is really just the opposite of the other two types. It states that two variables are unrelated. If they somehow appear to be related, it is because of one or more other explanations, for example, the influence of some confounding variable or some other flaw in the design of the research. The appearance of a relationship might exist because we deliberately or unintentionally drew an atypical sample of cases to study (see Chapter 9) or simply because we just drew an unusual sample—samples rarely look exactly like they would if all possible cases were to be studied. This latter phenomenon is why the third type of research hypothesis is sometimes (mistakenly) referred to as the null hypothesis. The null hypothesis (discussed in more detail in Chapter 13) is not a research hypothesis per se. It is more hypothetical than real. It relates only to the tendency of samples to naturally differ from each other and from the population from which they are selected and the degree to which that may have produced an apparent relationship between variables. It says nothing about all of the other reasons (including those just mentioned) why variables may appear to be related when they really are not.

Research-Based Practice

Using the two variables Gender and Marital Satisfaction, create a directional, nondirectional, and null hypothesis.

When Are Research Hypotheses Appropriate?

In some cases, there may not be enough known about an area to justify creating a hypothesis about how certain variables might be related or even which variables are relevant to the research problem, as in the case of many qualitative studies. Or, if there is enough information on which to base a hypothesis, the literature, research ethics, and/or researchers' knowledge of social work practice may reveal that it would be impossible to test the hypothesis. If either of these is the case, a testable hypothesis might not be appropriate.

However, if previous efforts have been made to study the research question, if at least a tentative statement about the relationship between variables seems justified, if finding or not finding support for such a relationship would be a valuable contribution to knowledge, and if it appears that a method can be devised to test that relationship, one or more hypotheses may be in order. Whether a research hypothesis should suggest a belief in causation, correlation, association, or no relationship between or among variables is a bit of a judgment call based on the researcher's assessment of just how much is already known about the answer to the research question, and what type of measurement of variables, control of potentially confounding variables, and data analysis is believed to be possible. Existing knowledge (and the researcher's belief in its credibility), as well as personal observations, would be used in deciding whether the research hypothesis should be stated in a directional or nondirectional form.

There is one additional guideline that should be used in formulating a research hypothesis. At this point, it should be obvious but probably bears mentioning anyway that when a hypothesis is tested, the results should produce a reasonable extension of existing knowledge as found in the literature. If it simply confirms what we already know, as in a replication study, it should be overtly recognized as a replication of a previous study. It is rare, however, that the knowledge generated by hypothesis testing represents a quantum leap from what we already know. The findings of most research make a relatively small contribution to filling a knowledge gap. Most good research hypotheses reflect this realistic expectation.

Although, as social work researchers, we might like to formulate and demonstrate support for research hypotheses, it is not essential to the goal of advancing our understanding of a research problem. One of the beauties of research is that, if it is conducted according to principles of scientific inquiry, which justifies our confidence in the research findings, we stand to advance knowledge by demonstrating either that the variables of interest probably are related or that they probably are not. For example, a researcher might hypothesize that one treatment intervention designed to reduce clinical depression is more effective than another. But if it is learned that both methods are really about equally effective (nonsupport for a directional research hypothesis), this knowledge can still inform practice decision making. An unsupported research hypothesis is just as valuable as one for which support has been demonstrated.

Wording of Research Hypotheses

It should be obvious by now that the way a research hypothesis is stated is important. Researchers should communicate exactly what they are predicting and nothing else. Goldstein (1969) offers some guidelines that continue to be used within the scientific community.

Consistency of Conceptualization

The variables within the hypothesis, the dependent (outcome) and independent (predictor) variables, should be stated at approximately the same level of abstraction or concreteness. For example, the research hypothesis, "People who hold college degrees have a high level of self-awareness, fails to meet this criterion of a good hypothesis." The first variable, education level, is easily measured and would fall on the concrete end of the continuum of conceptualization. The other variable, self-awareness, is far more abstract and difficult to measure with precision. A restatement of the research hypothesis that reflects greater consistency of conceptualization would be "People who hold college degrees will be more likely to receive a score of more than 80 on the Smith and Jones Scale of Self-Awareness than those who do not hold a college degree." Or, by moving education to a more abstract level, we could state "People with high achievement will have a higher level of self-awareness than those with low achievement."

Relevance to the Problem

Good hypotheses, when tested, will generate knowledge that has the potential to contribute to the alleviation of the research problem. This criterion seems obvious. Why would a researcher ever state and test a research hypothesis that is unrelated to the problem? It can happen, usually unintentionally. Sometimes, in the process of reviewing the literature, researchers can get sidetracked, losing sight of why they wanted to study the problem in the first place. They emerge with some very justifiable and logical research hypotheses that unfortunately have little or no relationship to the problem or its solution. This generally occurs because the broad research questions were not well formulated and did not provide enough focus. With good, broad questions, the problem is less likely to occur. This criterion should be thought of as a reminder, a check to make sure that the researcher did not forget about the problem while immersed in the literature.

Completeness

A research hypothesis should be stated as completely as possible. The person reading it should not wonder about the researcher's meaning or if it is missing key words. A sure indicator that a hypothesis is incomplete is the use of words that suggest comparison without the presence of a reference point. For example, the research hypothesis,"Women under age thirty are more assertive—lacks completeness. It leaves the reader in doubt about what exactly the researcher believes to be true about the assertiveness of women under thirty. Are they more assertive than women over thirty, than men under thirty, than all men, or than whom?" A research hypothesis that would be considered more complete is, "Women under age thirty are more assertive than women thirty and older. Phrases like "faster," "more frequently," and so on are useless in communicating the researcher's beliefs unless a reference point (for example, a comparison group) is included in the hypothesis."

Specificity

Specificity is closely related to completeness. Both criteria emphasize the importance of the researcher's saying exactly what is meant in a research hypothesis. Specificity requires that the words chosen to describe the variables in the research hypothesis and the relationship believed to exist between them should suggest only one meaning to the reader of the hypothesis. Many words and phrases in our language have more than one meaning; the researcher has the responsibility to ensure that a research hypothesis is stated so that no misunderstanding can possibly result. For example, the hypothesis, "Poorly timed marital counseling will reflect a low success rate—lacks specificity (in addition to having other problems)." The expression "poorly timed marital counseling" probably refers to other factors that may exist in a couple's life at the time that they seek counseling. But we cannot be sure. It may also refer to social workers' tendency to let their appointments run over the time scheduled for counseling sessions. Similarly, the word *reflect* in the hypothesis also contributes confusion regarding the researcher's meaning. It is sometimes used synonymously with *have*, and other times it is used to say that factors appear to be related when they really are not. Further confusing matters, it even has a special clinical meaning to social workers—an interviewing technique designed to help clients consider the meaning of what they have said. Given the context of the word in the research hypothesis, it is impossible to tell which meaning of the word is intended. The researcher's belief could be expressed with more

Specificity requires that the words chosen to describe the variables in the research hypothesis and the relationship believed to exist between them should suggest only one meaning to the reader of the hypothesis.

specificity if the hypothesis were restated. For example, it could have been worded: Couples undergoing bankruptcy proceedings are less likely to judge their marital counseling successful than those couples who have less severe financial problems.

Potential for Testing

In order to examine a possible relationship between or among variables, it is necessary to measure those variables with reasonable precision. Different cases must be able to be sorted into different groups (assigned value labels or values) in such a way that each case clearly falls into one and only one group. Some variables seem almost to defy objective measurement and therefore are inappropriate for inclusion within research hypotheses. For example, teachers and students continue to disagree on what constitutes effective teaching or on what the characteristics of good leadership are. A research hypothesis, "Good teachers will exhibit leadership within the classroom," would be a difficult one to test until we can achieve better agreement on how to measure both good teaching and leadership. Like beauty or a good personality, they remain a little too subjective to be able to measure objectively. However, another research hypothesis, "Teachers who post office hours are more likely to receive higher teaching evaluations than those who do not post office hours—is more testable." Here both variables are easily measurable.

Use of Subhypotheses

The use of subhypotheses can be used to make research hypotheses communicate more effectively what the researcher is saying. It is important not to try to say too much in a single hypothesis. If a relationship between variables is believed to exist, but is a difficult one to explain in a simple declarative sentence, several subhypotheses may be needed.

Subhypotheses often are helpful if there is an overall pattern of relationship between variables, but the pattern does not hold up for all case values or even reverses itself at some points. (Statisticians sometimes refer to this as a *nonlinear relationship* between variables.) For example, it may be hypothesized that social workers working in hospice settings exhibit certain patterns of degree of involvement with patients and their caregivers at various stages in the course of the patient's terminal illness. We might predict that they generally tend to be more involved when the patient first seeks hospice care and as the patient approaches death than during the time periods in between. The relationship between their degree of involvement and the stages of illness of their patients cannot be stated simply in one brief research hypothesis. An overall pattern believed to exist could be stated first as the central hypothesis, "Hospice social workers exhibit different degrees of professional involvement with their patients that are related to the stages of the patient's illness." Then, the different subhypotheses could be formulated to describe the specific trends within the central pattern. A series of simple statements expressing what the researcher believes to be the relationships between the variables is always preferable to a single research hypothesis that is so complex that few readers could understand it.

Research hypothesis construction, like problem identification (Chapter 3), is one of those steps in the research process that all too often is addressed hurriedly or taken lightly. A well-worded hypothesis can facilitate decision making at all subsequent stages of the research process. On the other hand, a research hypothesis that is vague or otherwise sloppy can cause difficulties later for the social work researcher. Time spent on hypothesis construction is rarely wasted; in the long run, it is a time saver. Overall, social work researchers should strive for simple, clear communication in stating research hypotheses. If they are successful in this effort, their hypotheses should be more than adequate to guide the subsequent stages of the research process.

SUMMARY

In this chapter, we examined two of the important products that may emerge from completing the literature search of existing knowledge: focused research questions and hypotheses. In both qualitative and quantitative studies, the researcher may use the knowledge gained from the literature review to state the research question or questions more precisely, reflecting a more specific focus of the research. In quantitative research (and much more rarely in qualitative studies), existing knowledge sometimes suggests a possible answer to one or more focused research questions. The researcher then goes even further and draws conclusions from the literature in the form of one or more research hypotheses that will be tested.

A well-worded hypothesis can facilitate decision making at all subsequent stages of the research process. On the other hand, a research hypothesis that is vague or otherwise sloppy can cause difficulties later for the social work researcher.

Researchers have developed their own language (and sometimes used existing language) to communicate certain key concepts. They use it both for clarity and efficiency of communication. We defined terms that are essential to the understanding of hypotheses: *variable, demographic variable, value label* or *value, frequency, dependent variable, independent variable,* outcome variable, and predictor variable. Terms used to describe the specific effects that other variables may have on the relationship between the principal variables of interest were also introduced. In future chapters, we will use the most generic of these terms, *confounding variable,* to describe any variable that might confuse researchers about the true relationship between the independent (or predictor) and dependent (or outcome) variables.

A research hypothesis was defined (among other things) as a prediction of a relationship between or among variables. It generally goes further, in predicting the way in which variables will be found to be related. Terms used to describe the nature of a relationship between variables (*association, correlation,* and *causation*) were differentiated, and the forms that a research hypothesis can take (*directional, nondirectional,* or *no relationship*) were explained. The importance of wording in hypothesis construction was emphasized throughout this chapter, and the appropriate use of subhypotheses was discussed.

Succeed with **PEARSON mysocialworklab**

Log onto **www.mysocialworklab.com** and answer the following questions. (If you did not receive an access code to **MySocialWorkLab** with this text and wish to purchase access online, please visit www. mysocialworklab.com.)

1. **Watch the Core Competencies Video: Diversity in Practice: Learning from the Client to Cocreate an**

Action Plan. Develop a focused research question and a research hypothesis with regard to the treatment of Alex.

2. **Read the Case Study: Foster Care: Dan.** After reading about Dan's history and problems, develop two focused research questions.

PRACTICE TEST

1. A variable that influences the dependent variable after the independent variable occurs is a(n)
   a. control variable.
   b. obscuring variable.
   c. antecedent variable.
   d. intervening variable.

2. A variable that interacts with the dependent and independent variables in such a way as to make them appear less closely related than they really are is a(n)
   a. control variable.
   b. obscuring variable.
   c. antecedent variable.
   d. intervening variable.

3. An example of a nondirectional research hypothesis is
   a. There is no relationship between grade in school and depression level.

   b. Freshmen college students experience more stress than sophomore students.
   c. 12-year-old girls and boys differ on their scores on the self-esteem scale.
   d. Women experience more depression during mid-life than men.

4. An example of a directional research hypothesis is
   a. Adolescents who participate in group therapy and those who participate in individual therapy will differ on their depression levels
   b. There is no relationship between type of therapy and success rate.
   c. Older people have a greater sense of life satisfaction than younger people.
   d. Men and women differ in their attitudes toward parenting.

5. Create a directional research hypothesis involving male and female children and prevalence of attention deficit hyperactivity disorder.

ASSESS YOUR COMPETENCE Use the scale below to rate your current level of achievement on the following concepts or skills associated with each competency presented in the chapter:

1	2	3
I can accurately describe the concept or skill.	I can consistently identify the concept or skill when observing and analyzing practice activities.	I can competently implement the concept or skill in my own practice.

_____ Understanding the process of creating focused research questions

_____ Understanding the different types of relationships between variables, including association, correlation, and causation

_____ Being able to distinguish between directional, non-directional, and null hypotheses

_____ Being able to create a clearly worded research hypothesis

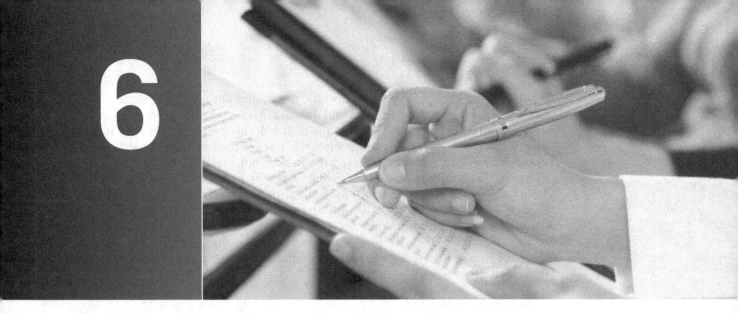

6

Group Research Designs

Core Competencies in this Chapter (Check marks indicate which competencies are demonstrated)

	Professional Identity		Ethical Practice	✔	Critical Thinking	✔	Diversity in Practice		Human Rights & Justice
✔	Research-Based Practice		Human Behavior		Policy Practice	✔	Practice Contexts		Engage, Assess, Intervene, Evaluate

In the previous chapter, we discussed how existing knowledge is used prior to data collection. In both qualitative and quantitative research, it is used to develop well-articulated, focused research questions. In quantitative studies, it often allows the researcher to develop research hypotheses as well. In all types of research, existing knowledge helps the researcher make decisions about how the research should be conducted, what is generally referred to as the *research design*. Chapters 6 through 8 will look at various research designs and methods. This chapter is devoted to research designs used in quantitative research studies. The next chapter will consider a specific form of quantitative research that looks at one case or individual at a time: single-system evaluation designs. Finally, Chapter 8 will turn to various methods that are used primarily to conduct qualitative research studies.

WHAT IS A RESEARCH DESIGN?

A literature review reveals what is already known about the research problem and the methods that have been used to study it. It thus suggests to the researcher what specific research methods and strategies are best suited to conduct further inquiry—a design for the current research study. A *research design* is a plan to attempt to find answers to the researcher's questions and/or to test any hypotheses that were formulated.

The design of a research study is a response to a series of questions:

- Where and when should the research be conducted?
- What data should be collected?
- From whom can the data best be obtained?
- What would be the best way to collect the data?
- How will research participants be located or selected?
- What information will be sought?
- What variables will need to be measured?
- How and when should they be measured?
- Are there other variables that will need to be controlled?
- If so, how should this be accomplished?
- What unavoidable methodological limitations will exist, and how can their effects be minimized?
- How should the data be organized and analyzed?
- How should research findings be disseminated?

The research design serves as a plan for the latter stages of the research. The answers to the preceding questions are not arrived at independently of each other. The decision-making process is made easier because these questions and their answers are interrelated. Having determined the answer to one or more of them, the answers to other questions often become quite obvious. For example, the selection of certain individuals to provide research data is likely to influence the general method of data collection used. Similarly, the way variables are measured and the way research participants are selected generally suggest the most appropriate type of statistical analysis to use. If one examines the ways that research has been conducted in the past, the interrelatedness of the preceding questions becomes readily apparent. Certain patterns emerge. Next, we will look at different ways research designs can be categorized and defined.

DIFFERENT CATEGORIZATIONS OF RESEARCH DESIGNS

The terminology used to describe the design of a research study can be confusing, because the design of a given research study can be (and often is) described in a number of ways and at several levels. We discussed two of the most general of these back in Chapter 1. Describing research as either *basic* or *applied* communicates how and when the knowledge derived from a study is intended to be used. The findings of a study are designed to either (1) contribute to our professional knowledge base (basic) or (2) be of immediate use for addressing a problem, answering a question, or making a pending decision (applied).

Another way to convey the general characteristics of a research design that was discussed in Chapter 1 is to describe it as either predominantly *quantitative* or predominantly *qualitative*. These terms suggest reliance on certain research methods, the nature of the data that are collected, and the method of analysis used, as well as other distinguishing characteristics (see Box 6.1).

We will examine several other terms throughout this chapter that offer additional understanding of how and why research is conducted, for example, how many times key variables are measured, what general methods for acquiring data are used, or what type of knowledge is sought. We will also look at specific research designs that have been developed and used effectively in past research. They have become *standards* or models for answering certain types of research questions. They can be displayed graphically to reflect certain key features of the design, such as the number of research samples that are used or the sequence in which certain events are supposed to take place. However, these research features do not provide a detailed description of how a given research study should be conducted. They merely describe a general framework on which to build the specifics needed to conduct the research. The researcher still needs to supply the specifics, and make sure they are properly executed.

It is often necessary to use several terms to completely and accurately describe the design of a research study. Some may be very general and some more specific, but each allows another researcher or the reader of a research report to get a clearer picture of exactly how the research was conducted.

Box 6.1 **Qualitative and Quantitative Research**	
Qualitative Research	**Quantitative Research**
▸ Is admittedly subjective	▸ Seeks to be objective
▸ Seeks to understand	▸ Seeks to explain, predict
▸ Uses inductive logic	▸ Uses deductive logic
▸ Produces hypotheses	▸ Tests hypotheses
▸ Data analyzed as received	▸ Data analyzed after it is collected
▸ Researcher is the instrument	▸ Reliance on standardized instruments for measurement

CROSS-SECTIONAL, PRETEST-POSTTEST, AND LONGITUDINAL DESIGNS

One way to describe a research design in general terms is to state the number of times observations or personal contacts will occur and/or key variables will be measured and, to a lesser degree, the length of time over which the research is conducted. Three terms are frequently used for this purpose: cross-sectional, pretest-posttest, and longitudinal research.

Designs that are described as cross-sectional make observations at one point in time, with all variables measured as simultaneously as possible. The researcher seeks to acquire *a snapshot in time*, and then to draw conclusions about what has been observed. Conclusions may include a description of the distribution of certain variables (e.g., how many people experience one problem as opposed to another one or how severe a problem is today). They may also answer questions or test hypotheses about the relationships between variables. For example, one group of social work researchers (Schwinn, Schinke, & Trent, 2010) analyzed cross-sectional data to explore gender and mental health influences on urban adolescents' use of alcohol, tobacco, and illicit drugs. While they found that substance use did not differ by gender, they found that it was associated with greater symptoms of depression, anxiety, and hostility.

In pretest-posttest designs (sometimes called *before* and *after* designs), the researcher conducts observations or interviews, or measures key variables, twice, generally before and after an event. In evaluation research, the event is likely to be a service or social program that is offered to clients or some other life experience to which people are exposed. A pretest measurement is used to determine just how much change occurred in the interim between the first and second measurements. That can be important information in helping to determine the effectiveness of a social work intervention. For example, social work researchers (Gonzales-Prendes & Jozefowicz-Simbeni, 2009) evaluated the effect of cognitive-behavioral treatment on anger and paranoid ideation for a group of men being treated for anger issues. By comparing pretest and posttest scores, they found that both anger and paranoid ideation were reduced after the treatment was completed.

If a research design is described as longitudinal, that means the researcher conducts observations or interviews, or measures key variables, more than twice, often many more times, and sometimes over a long period of time. All longitudinal research designs share a single characteristic—they entail the repeated study and/or measurement over time at predetermined intervals. Longitudinal studies are designed to study change, but they try to find out more than simply whether or how much change occurred. They seek to identify exactly when change occurred and what phenomena were associated with the change. Only longitudinal research can provide this type of useful knowledge. For example, in one longitudinal study, social workers McMillen and Raghaven (2009) interviewed foster care youth a total of nine times between their 17th and 19th birthdays to determine if their use of mental health services changed after they "aged out" of the foster care system. They found that all types of mental health service use dropped dramatically after these youth left foster care.

Three additional adjectives are often used in describing longitudinal research. They reflect differences in the way that a sample of research participants is selected. One variety, the *trend study*, entails drawing a sample of participants at different points in time from a group (pool) of potential participants. The pool tends to change over time. For example, a group of students may be selected at random from a social work program each year to participate in a study to assess changes in attitudes toward research. Although some students may be included in more than one stage of data collection (e.g., they may appear in the sample selected in two or more years), the sample of students will be different each year. An overall trend in changes in attitude within the program (but not within individual students) thus can be observed.

In a second variety of longitudinal research, the *cohort study*, the pool of potential research participants does not change, but the specific cases selected for study differ during the different stages of data collection. For example, a class of full-time students might be measured regarding their attitudes toward research over an academic year. Assuming that the class suffered no attrition or added no new members during the year, the class would be known as a cohort. Participants would be selected at random from the class at different points in time. No two groups selected for study would likely be identical in terms of which students would be included, but each group selected would represent the class at the various points of data collection.

In the third variation of longitudinal research, the *panel study*, the same group of research participants would be studied over time. In our example of a study to examine changes in student attitudes toward research, the same randomly selected students would be studied over their student careers to monitor any changes in their attitudes. Only attrition would result in any change in the composition of the group. The infamous Tuskegee studies, described in Chapter 2, provides an example of a longitudinal study that used the panel method.

Longitudinal studies can last for a few days or a few weeks, but more typically, they are conducted over a period of years. Some have gone on past the lifetime of the researchers who originally designed them and have been carried on by others, for example, studies on the status of women in the United States.

Most longitudinal studies are designed to document change. But they are also well suited to the needs of researchers who wish to document and learn more about the existence of a certain pattern of behavior and what is associated with it. Good examples of longitudinal research of this type are the studies of a large number of terminally ill patients that were conducted by Elisabeth Kübler-Ross (1989) and her associates over several decades. The researchers were able to identify five predictable stages in the dying process and describe them in detail. As a result, hospice social workers and others who work with people who have a terminal illness now possess greater insight into their patients' behaviors and are better able to help them come to successful resolutions relating to their impending death.

The findings of other longitudinal studies in the area of grief and loss (Benoliel, 1985) have similarly proven invaluable to the social work practitioner. For example, we now know that the time around the first anniversary of the death of a loved one often is accompanied by depression, and that anger at a deceased relative is a very predictable phenomenon at certain stages of the grieving process. Consequently, counseling now can focus on helping clients to anticipate and deal with anniversary depression, and to verbalize, better understand, accept, and work through their anger toward the deceased.

Longitudinal designs can yield knowledge not readily accessible using other designs. Slowly developing changes and up-and-down fluctuations in

Research-Based Practice

Using middle-school students as the sample, describe how a trend study, a cohort study, and a panel study would differ in how research participants are selected.

behaviors and phenomena, which can be identified and plotted by repeated measurements over long periods of time, might be missed using cross-sectional or pretest-posttest designs. Longitudinal designs alone tell us when changes occur and help us predict their occurrence with reasonable accuracy.

The major drawback to using longitudinal designs is cost. Researchers often are unwilling or unable to make the expensive, long-term commitment that is necessary to properly conduct them. Because they take so long to complete, researchers who hope to build an academic or scientific career around publication of numerous research papers tend to shy away from them. One can spend a decade on a longitudinal study that can result in a single published scientific paper. However, such studies may be more substantive and often produce more definitive answers to research questions than cross-sectional or pretest-posttest studies.

EXPLORATORY, DESCRIPTIVE, AND EXPLANATORY STUDIES

Still another way to characterize a research design in general terms is to describe them as exploratory, descriptive, or explanatory. They describe the primary type of knowledge that the study seeks to acquire and the primary methods used for acquiring the knowledge.

Knowledge building in a given problem area is a cumulative process. As we suggested in Chapter 1, uncovering and disseminating knowledge is a systematic process that occurs over time. It is rarely (if ever) the work of one individual. That's why social work researchers tie their research to existing knowledge, by reviewing the professional literature. They want to build on the work of others, and their findings will in turn help to facilitate the work of subsequent researchers.

Sometimes, the process of movement toward answers and at least partial solutions to problems occurs relatively rapidly, but more typically, progress in knowledge building is slow work. It entails the use of a variety of methods (designs) that occur most often in a certain logical sequence.

When very little is known about a problem and there are many more questions than answers, *exploratory* research designs are indicated. These designs are used when a researcher is exploring a subject area that is relatively new and unstudied. They can be either qualitative or quantitative, and are often a mixture of both. As knowledge in an area accumulates, *descriptive* designs are both possible and indicated. These studies attempt to describe situations and events. Once the general characteristics of a problem are understood, descriptive studies are in turn replaced by *explanatory* designs, which have the potential to provide more definitive answers to certain types of questions. Because there is a logical sequence in which different designs are employed in the study of a research problem, they can be placed on a continuum such as that shown in Box 6.2. Some writers (see Rubin & Babbie, 2007) add a fourth purpose to this continuum of knowledge or type of research, while others place evaluative studies in the category of explanatory research. *Evaluative* research seeks to evaluate social policies, programs, and interventions. Research designs attempting evaluation will often combine all three types of knowledge, exploratory, descriptive, and explanatory.

Orderly progress along the continuum is perhaps more of an ideal than a description of reality. There are numerous situations that suggest the need for exceptions. Sometimes, we mistakenly conclude that we have learned more about a problem than we really have. Explanatory research is conducted, and it presents us with surprises. It causes us to question the state of existing knowledge about a problem or question. Thus, we conclude that a return to descriptive or even exploratory research is indicated. Findings can then be used to fill in the gaps or attempt to explain some of the surprises that the explanatory studies produced.

An important task for the researcher reviewing existing knowledge is to locate just where on the continuum one's own research should fall. For example, if a review of professional literature reveals that virtually all of the past research on a problem has been of an exploratory nature, explanatory research may be premature. Research designed to expand the current description of the problem and the conditions that surround it would be more appropriate. Conversely, if the professional literature contains reports of explanatory research that have begun to isolate the cause of the problem, exploratory or descriptive research would not seem appropriate. The existing level of knowledge would suggest that such research would be unnecessary and redundant and that, perhaps, it is time to conduct evaluation research designed to test the effectiveness of interventions (prevention or treatment) in order to make a contribution to evidence-based practice.

Exploratory Research

Exploratory research is appropriate when problems have been identified but our understanding of them is quite limited. It is conducted to lay the groundwork for other knowledge building that will follow. Exploratory designs are predicated on the assumption that we need to know more about something before we can begin to understand it or attempt to confront it using intervention methods with high potential for success. In exploratory research, we often don't even know what it is we need to know!

In an exploratory study, the researcher begins his or her inquiry without much insight into the research problem, as is often the case in predominantly qualitative studies. Because the relevant variables have not been specified, there can be no hypotheses to test. However, a frequent goal of exploratory research is to derive hypotheses for future research endeavors.

Similarly, selection of research participants or cases for study is usually not a rigorous or exacting procedure when exploratory research designs are used. There may be few cases studied, or a large number may be selected to learn as much as possible about the problem. In either instance, because the population is often not clearly defined yet, there are usually no legitimate claims to the sample being representative of the overall population.

We do not wish to imply that persons who conduct exploratory research employ a more haphazard approach to knowledge building than those who use other designs. Good exploratory research is always carefully planned and conducted using specific methods and according to established guidelines. But researchers who conduct exploratory research must work with less "preknowledge" than those who use other research designs.

In exploratory research, we often don't even know what it is we need to know!

Thus, exploratory designs are employed to begin the process of knowledge building about a problem or focused question. For example, prior to the 1960s, exploratory research was used to study child abuse. In the early 1980s, it was used for studying spouse abuse and the problems of people with HIV infection. In the 1990s, it was used to study the phenomenon of bullying within school settings. Early in the twenty-first century, exploratory research was used to study cyber-bullying, as we were just beginning to recognize the existence of a problem that did not exist before the widespread availability of electronic communication. Exploratory studies try to conceptualize exactly what a problem is, the degree to which it is recognized as a problem, what forms it takes, and what variables might relate to it.

Descriptive Research

The accumulation of the findings derived from exploratory research makes it possible to design studies that allow us to gather *descriptive* knowledge. In predominantly qualitative descriptive studies, the researcher often seeks to describe the variety of ways that people experience or perceive something. In descriptive research that is predominantly quantitative, measurement and description of relevant variables (those identified using exploratory research designs) and the distribution of their values is usually the goal. For example, research on the problem of child abuse moved beyond exploration and into description by the late 1960s and early 1970s. Studies sought to measure its patterns of incidence and severity and chronicle its different forms. The major relevant variables had already been identified through exploratory research; it was now possible and desirable for researchers to measure how the variables were distributed and to see if there were any patterns of relationships between and among them.

Quantitative descriptive research seeks to better understand and measure how variables are naturally distributed. It does not entail introducing or manipulating variables to see how other variables are affected. Thus, support for a relationship of causation between variables would not be possible using descriptive methods. Although seeking support for relationships between variables is not a major objective of most descriptive research, we sometimes see hypotheses tested in quantitative descriptive research designs. When we do, they generally predict a relationship of association or correlation, rather than causation.

Even when hypotheses are not formulated prior to data collection, a relationship between and among variables sometimes appears to be obvious, especially in large-scale descriptive studies. For example, in one common type of descriptive study, the census, it is often possible to detect apparent associations or correlations that appear promising and worthy of additional study. Statistical analysis can be performed to determine the probability that the apparent relationship is the work of chance or sampling error (Chapter 13). It can be performed by the researchers who actually collected the data or by others who later have access to them.

In quantitative descriptive research, the researcher hopes to generalize from cases studied to those that are similar but were not part of the research study. Thus, it is critical that the researcher select and study cases that are typical of the entire group (see Chapter 9 for sampling techniques). Accuracy of measurement of variables also takes on great importance (see Chapter 10). Quantitative descriptive research is only as good or as bad as the representativeness of the sample of cases that are studied and the accuracy of the description that it produces. Just describing, if performed well, is an exact science that requires a great amount of knowledge and skill. There are rules and procedures that govern the conduct of good quantitative descriptive research, as in all other types of research.

In predominantly qualitative descriptive studies, acquiring a representative sample of research participants is less important than in predominantly quantitative studies. What is often sought instead is diversity, for example, the widest possible variety in the way participants experienced some event such as family violence, how they perceived it, the range of meanings they attributed to it, and so forth. We again want to emphasize that studies are often a combination of both qualitative and quantitative methods. Exploratory, descriptive, and explanatory research can all include both qualitative and quantitative components.

Explanatory Research

At some point, the knowledge about a problem may have advanced sufficiently to justify the use of explanatory designs. *Exploratory* and descriptive designs seek primarily to understand a problem and the factors that are associated with it. It is explanatory research that yields more definitive answers as to what might cause the problem and what intervention methods are effective in treating or even preventing it. Although some design variations of exploratory and descriptive studies may give hints as to which solutions might be effective, it is explanatory research that yields more definitive answers as to what might cause the problem and what intervention methods are effective in treating or even preventing it.

In explanatory research designs, the researcher uses hypothesis testing to try to verify possible relationships between variables. The dependent and independent variables have already been identified through exploratory research, and their distribution has been described through descriptive research. Cases are selected for study with the goal of making them as representative as possible of all cases, including those not studied. The researcher hopes to be able to verify the presence of important relationships between or among variables. Whenever possible, confounding variables, which might misrepresent the true relationship between dependent and independent variables, are controlled. This is accomplished through randomization, manipulation of variables, or through statistical methods. If they cannot be controlled, every effort is made to determine the degree to which they may have obfuscated the relationship between the independent and dependent variables.

Explanatory designs seek to uncover causal relationships between variables. As we indicated in the previous chapter, causality is a special kind of relationship. It goes beyond association and even simple correlation. In a causal relationship, exposure to an independent variable (and to its different quantities or qualities) actually brings about changes in the dependent variable. As noted previously, there are three conditions that must be present in relationships in order to conclude that one variable (x) causes the changes in the other (y). These conditions are that

Exploratory and descriptive designs seek primarily to understand a problem and the factors that are associated with it. It is explanatory research that yields more definitive answers as to what might cause the problem and what intervention methods are effective in treating or even preventing it.

1. x must actually precede y in time order.
2. x and y must consistently covary.
3. All other explanations for changes in y must be ruled out.

All three of these conditions must be present in order to conclude that x caused or produced the changes in the value categories or values of y.

PRE-EXPERIMENTAL, EXPERIMENTAL, AND QUASI-EXPERIMENTAL DESIGNS

Next, we will look at various research designs that have been widely used in social work research. These designs are generally labeled *pre-experimental*, *experimental*, or *quasi-experimental*, on the basis of the number of measurements taken and the type of comparison group, if any, that is used. Pre-experimental designs are those designs that do not attempt to control threats to the internal validity of the research study (see discussion of internal validity later in this chapter). These designs generally do not use a comparison group, and when they do, only one measure of the dependent variable is taken. Experimental designs are more rigorous designs and do attempt to control threats to the study's internal validity. Quasi-experimental designs attempt to control threats to internal validity but are different from true experiments in that they do not randomly assign participants in the study to either the experimental or comparison group.

We will use the following standard notations to describe these research designs:

> X = Exposure to the independent variable or treatment condition
> O = Measurement of the dependent variable
> O_n = nth measurement of the dependent variable in case of multiple measurements
> R = Random assignment of participants to a group

Pre-experimental Designs

1. Cross-sectional survey design. The cross-sectional survey design entails measurement of a characteristic in a defined sample or group at a given point in time. It is diagrammed rather simply as

$$O$$

where O represents one measurement of the dependent variable. For example, let's say the associate dean of a school of social work wishes to know what particular social work electives students might wish to take during the summer semester. A brief survey instrument describing proposed elective courses is developed and mailed to students to complete. A large percentage of these students complete the instrument and return it. The associate dean determines from their responses which courses should be offered during the summer semester.

The cross-sectional survey design, as used here, provides information about what individuals may want, feel, or believe at a given time. This is its primary usefulness. The alternative would be to guess what students might want for summer course work and run the risk of offering courses that no one is interested in taking or not offering courses that students may want or need.

2. One-shot case study or one-group, posttest-only design. The one-shot case study design, is schematically noted as

$$X\,O$$

where X represents exposure to a variable (such as a program or intervention) and O represents measurement of a dependent variable among participants.

Let's look at an example of how this design may be used in a social work research study.

Suppose a social worker in a neighborhood community center wishes to determine if eight weeks of English classes are helpful for teaching the English language to a group of Spanish-speaking residents who are seeking employment in an industry where a certain level of English fluency is required. The social worker identifies interested participants and arranges for them to receive the instruction. When the course is completed (eight weeks later), the group takes a brief paper-and-pencil test that measures knowledge of the English language. The social worker scores the tests and calculates the percentage of people who pass it. This process provides the measurement of the dependent variable.

The major advantage of this design is simplicity. However, it does not provide any comparisons between how much of the English language participants knew before exposure to the class and how much they knew following the eight-week course. Thus, one cannot conclude from this design that the program brought about any improvement in the participants' knowledge of English.

3. Longitudinal case study design. In the longitudinal case study design, research participants are exposed to an event or are introduced to the independent variable (e.g., they participate in a social program) followed by several repeated observations, interviews, or measurements. Thus, it is a form of longitudinal research. It may be diagrammed as follows:

$$X \; O_1 \; O_2 \; O_3$$

Using our previous example, suppose the social worker wanted to determine if the knowledge of the English language possessed by participants declines, is retained, or continues to grow over a six-month period. X represents participants' exposure to the eight-week language course. O_1 is the first measurement of their knowledge of English taken immediately following the course. O_2 is the second measurement of their knowledge of English, taken three months later, and O_3 the third measurement, at six months. From this design, the social worker is able to determine (1) the level of English knowledge after completion of the course and (2) the level of participants' knowledge of English over time. We still cannot determine if participants' English proficiency improved because of their completing the course. For that, we must turn to the next design.

4. One-group pretest-posttest design. The one-group pretest-posttest design represents an improvement over the preceding designs, as it adds an opportunity to compare pretest and posttest measures of the dependent variable. It is symbolized as follows:

$$O_1 \; X \; O_2$$

where O_1 represents the first measurement of the dependent variable, prior to exposure of participants to the independent variable (X). Afterward, the dependent variable is again measured O_2, and participants' pretest and posttest scores are compared. It is hoped that there will be a difference between measurements O_1 and O_2 and that this change may be attributed to the program or intervention (X). Let's look at our previous example and apply the one-group pretest-posttest design.

Using a paper-and-pencil test to measure the Spanish-speaking participants' knowledge of the English language, the social worker asks them to complete the test before the first session of the eight-week class (O_1). Following completion of this course (X), the participants complete the inventory again (O_2). Because of the pretest measurement (O_1), it is possible to know how much change in the dependent variable actually occurred over the course of the intervention. This is the major advantage of the one-group pretest-posttest design. We still cannot, however, make the dangerous leap to conclude that the intervention caused any improvements found. For this, an experimental design, discussed in the next section, would be required.

5. Static group comparison design or posttest-only design with nonequivalent groups. The static group comparison design allows the researcher to compare two groups on their measurements of a dependent variable, following exposure of one group to the independent variable. It is symbolized as follows:

$$X \; O \; O$$

where X is the independent variable and O is the only measurement, in this case, a posttest. A brief example illustrates the usefulness of this design. A social worker wishes to compare two groups on their levels of anxiety following a behavioral treatment program designed to reduce the anxiety symptoms in otherwise healthy adults. Group 1 consists of those people who are selected for inclusion in the treatment program, a cognitive-behavioral approach to treatment that lasts three months. Following completion of the program, the participants are measured on their level of anxiety using a standardized measuring instrument designed for this purpose. For comparison purposes, a group of similar adults who did not complete this program (perhaps they are on a wait list for receiving this service) is measured using the same instrument. Then a comparison is made between those who completed the treatment and those who did not. If the group receiving the treatment shows a lower level of anxiety than the comparison group, it is possible that the treatment had the desired effect. However, because there was no pretest for either group, we really do not know if the treatment group had a lower level of anxiety than the comparison group before treatment began. This is the major limitation of the static group comparison design.

Experimental Designs

Experimental designs seek to explain the variations (different values) of a dependent variable in relation to one or more independent variables. When reputable researchers use the word *experiment* to characterize their research, they are stating that their research design has specific features that justify their use of the word. An experimental research design is very rigorous. Its requirements make it the ideal design for generating cause-effect knowledge. In a true experiment, the following three requirements must be met:

▶ **The independent variable or variables are introduced or manipulated by the researcher.** This means, for example, that the researcher studying the relationship between enrollment in a specific job-training program and clients' success in finding employment must control who is enrolled in the program and who is not. Or another researcher studying the effect of hours of treatment time on recovery in an inpatient psychiatric facility should control the exact number of treatment hours given to patients participating in the study.

▶ **There are one or more control groups, which are not exposed to the independent variable.** In the first example described above, the researcher would select a group of individuals who would not enroll in the job-training program (a control group). They would be identified, but not given the training. Their success rate in finding employment (the dependent variable) would be compared to the success rate of those selected for the program and given training. In the second example, a control group would be selected, and their hours of treatment time might be set to the usual treatment time, while the treatment hours of the experimental group might be increased.

▶ **Research participants are randomly assigned to experimental and control groups.** *Random assignment* to groups, probably the key requirement of an experimental design that sets it apart from other designs, means that participants are assigned to the experimental and control groups in a completely random manner. In other words, each participant has an equal chance of being assigned to the control or experimental group. In the first example, nothing (other than random assignment to the groups) would influence whether potential trainees would be enrolled in the job-training program (experimental group) or selected for the control group. In the second example, assignment to either the experimental or the control group would have to be totally random.

Why is random assignment so important in an experiment? When experimental research designs are used, random assignment of research participants to experimental and control groups is the primary vehicle used for control of confounding variables. Random assignment relies on the laws of probability and what is likely to occur in the long run. It depends on the equalization effect that occurs naturally within groups (subsamples) randomly drawn from the same pool. As more cases are added to the two groups in a random manner, the groups become increasingly similar. In our first example, if the researcher assigned cases to the experimental and control groups randomly and if the two groups were sufficiently large (see Chapter 9 for further discussion of sample size), the groups should be similar in all respects. This means that characteristics that the researcher has reason to believe may affect participants' success in finding employment, such as motivation level, work experience, health, intelligence, physical appearance, or verbal skills, will tend to be similar in the two groups when they are viewed in as a whole.

But what if the literature review failed to reveal one or more other confounding variables that might affect participants' success in finding employment? They may be neither logical nor obvious, something that we might not have guessed to be potentially confounding variables (e.g., number of siblings or birth order). Can these variables also be controlled through random assignment of cases to relatively large experimental and control groups? Yes. A highly desirable effect of random assignment is that, if performed correctly (and a reasonably large sample size is used), it will control for the effects of all confounding variables, even those whose existence we have no reason to suspect! This is why random assignment is such an important feature of experimental designs.

The process of randomization is so useful a method for controlling for confounding variables that researchers frequently devise methods to use it in other ways within experimental designs. In our example of an experiment designed to measure the effectiveness of a job-training program, the researcher might randomly select trainers (from among those available) to facilitate the program. The researcher might also randomly select times of day to offer the training, rooms to be used, or any other potentially confounding variable that can be randomized without affecting the nature of the program being evaluated. This prevents the researcher from selecting trainers or times of day, for example, that could potentially bias the outcome of the research.

Experiments are the only research designs that possess the three characteristics listed above. True experimental designs help the researcher rule out the possible effects of any other factors (besides the independent variable) that may be affecting the dependent variable. Consequently, among the basic designs we have described, experimental designs do the most convincing job of providing evidence that a cause-effect relationship between variables exists. They can help the researcher conclude with reasonable certainty that the presence of a certain value of the independent variable caused a certain value of the dependent variable to occur.

Because all true experimental designs require rigorous control over certain conditions (assignment of people to groups, exposure to the independent variable, and so on), it sometimes can be difficult to implement them because of ethical concerns. In human services, social work researchers are committed to delivering the best possible services to each client, regardless of what a research design may indicate as desirable. Research must be of lower priority than service. However, with careful planning, experiments can be designed and implemented within human service organizations. We will describe three experimental designs that are used in social work research.

1. Classic experimental design or pretest-posttest control group design. The classic experimental design, also called the pretest-posttest control group design, does a good job of controlling for the possible effects of confounding variables. It is portrayed as follows:

$$R\ O_1\ X\ O_2$$
$$R\ O_1\ \ \ \ O_2$$

A highly desirable effect of random assignment is that, if performed correctly (and a reasonably large sample size is used), it will control for the effects of all confounding variables, even those whose existence we have no reason to suspect!

Practice Contexts

If you worked in a counseling center, what would be an ethical concern with regard to randomly assigning participants to either the control or the experimental group? Would the ethical concern change if you worked in a psychiatric hospital?

In this design, individuals are randomly assigned to one of two groups: an experimental group or a control group (the R denotes random assignment). The first line in the notation above denotes the experimental group and the second line denotes the control group. The dependent variable is measured for both groups (O_1). The experimental group is exposed to the independent variable (X), such as participation in a social program. Following completion of the program, the dependent variable is again measured for both groups (O_2). Then the following comparisons are made:

▶ **Comparison 1.** The researcher examines the O_1 scores for both groups, anticipating that these measures will be essentially equivalent. (They should be if research participants were randomly assigned to the two groups.) In addition, these measurements can be used to compute changes between O_1 and O_2 in each group.

▶ **Comparison 2.** The researcher examines the O_2 scores for both groups, anticipating that O_2 for the experimental group will have changed in a predicted direction, whereas O_2 for the control group will not, or will change much less, because this group was not exposed to the treatment program. Assuming the researcher finds the expected change in O_2 for the experimental group, with no or much less change in the control group, it can be concluded with some degree of certainty that the change is due to exposure to the independent variable rather than to some other factor.

The classic experimental design requires that the researcher has the authority to randomly assign research participants to one of two treatment conditions. It also requires that both groups are pretested and posttested. Finally, the design requires that individuals in the control group not receive the intervention being tested—a requirement that might be regarded as professionally unethical and therefore unacceptable. Given that the researcher may not know the effectiveness of the intervention being tested, however, it may not be regarded as unethical to either withhold treatment from the control group, wait list the control group or, in some cases, offer the control group "treatment as usual."

2. Posttest-only control group design. The posttest-only control group design uses random assignment of participants to either an experimental or a control group to equalize the groups. This design is used when the researcher believes taking the pretest may have an effect on the posttest measurement; therefore, neither group is pretested. For example, suppose the measurement involves timing how long it takes the participant to create a pattern using different colored blocks. Even if there are several weeks between the pretest and posttest, the participants might reduce the time it takes to complete the task the second time simply because they are familiar with the task. The researcher may, therefore, choose a posttest-only design symbolized as follows:

$$R \ X \ O$$
$$R \quad \ O$$

O is the only measurement of the dependent variable, which in this design is a posttest. The design allows the researcher to compare posttest measurements of the dependent variable by group. Specifically, the researcher is interested in discovering if the posttest measurement for the experimental group is either higher or lower than for the control group. It should be if the intervention had an effect. Even though there is no pretest to ensure equivalence of the groups prior to exposure to the independent variable, random assignment theoretically takes care of this. Pretests are required, however, when the measurement of the amount of change between pretest and posttest is important for the purpose of the study. In addition, pretesting is necessary if the groups are so small as to render random assignment ineffective in creating equivalent groups.

3. Solomon four-group design. The Solomon four-group design combines the classic experimental design and the posttest-only control group design. The two groups from the classic experimental design are used so changes between pretest and posttest can be examined. In addition, the two groups from the posttest-only control group design are used to determine if the use of a pretest may have contributed to changes in the dependent variable. The design is symbolized as follows:

$$R \ O_1 \ X \ O_2 \qquad \text{(Experimental group 1)}$$
$$R \ O_1 \quad \ O_2 \qquad \text{(Control group 1)}$$
$$R \quad \ X \ O_2 \qquad \text{(Experimental group 2)}$$
$$R \qquad \ O_2 \qquad \text{(Control group 2)}$$

Although the design may appear complicated, it is actually quite simple. Both of the experimental groups receive exposure to the intervention, while the two control groups do not. The experimental group 1 and control group 1 are pretested and posttested, while the experimental group 2 and control group 2 are posttested but are not pretested. At least four comparisons can be made using this design:

▶ **Comparison 1: O_1 and O_2 for both experimental groups.** What the researcher hopes to find is a change in both experimental groups, with no difference between scores of the two groups. If there is a difference, it might indicate the effect of the pretest measurement on the posttest measurement.

▶ **Comparison 2: O_2 for both control groups.** These measures ought to be similar, because neither group received the intervention. Differences here could also indicate that the pretest measurement has had an effect on the posttest measurement.

▶ **Comparison 3: O_1 for all groups.**
These measures ought to be similar, because random assignment has been used to assign participants to groups, and no one at this point had received the intervention, that is, the independent variable.

▶ **Comparison 4: O_2 for all four groups.** If the intervention was successful, posttest scores for experimental group 1 should be better than posttest scores for control group 1, and posttest scores for experimental group 2 should be better than posttest scores for control group 2.

Quasi-Experimental Designs

no random assign

Quasi-experimental research designs differ from true experiments primarily because they fail to randomly assign participants to either the experimental or control groups. Groups that are used for comparison purposes, but are not randomly assigned, are referred to as *nonequivalent control groups* or *comparison groups*. There are compelling ethical reasons for not creating true control groups, such as the need to assign clients to experimental or control groups on the basis of the judgment of professionals that they will likely benefit from (and not be harmed by) them. In other situations, true control groups may be logistically impossible because, for example, some interaction between members of control and experimental groups is inevitable or even desirable. Whole books have been written on various experimental and quasi-experimental research designs. The classic remains a 1963 work by Campbell and Stanley and its subsequent revisions. We will look at two quasi-experimental research designs.

1. Nonequivalent comparison groups design or pretest-posttest comparison group design. When random assignment is not possible for ethical or logistical reasons, the nonequivalent comparison groups design is an alternative. It is portrayed as follows:

$$O_1 \; X \; O_2$$
$$O_1 \quad O_2$$

In this design, individuals are assigned either to the experimental group or the comparison group. The dependent variable is measured for both groups (O_1). The experimental group is exposed to the independent variable, such as participation in a social program. Following completion of the program, the dependent variable is again measured for both groups (O_2). Then the following comparisons can be made:

 Comparison 1. The researcher examines the O_1 scores for both groups. The researcher hopes that these two measures will be equivalent. However, without use of random assignment, these measurements may be different. Any differences found between the pretests must be considered when evaluating the outcomes of the posttests. Pretest measurements will also be useful to compute changes in each group from O_1 to O_2.

 Comparison 2. The researcher examines the O_2 scores for both groups, anticipating that O_2 for the experimental group will have changed in a predicted direction, whereas O_2 for the comparison group will not, or will change much less, because this group was not exposed to the treatment program. Assuming the researcher finds the expected change in O_2 for the experimental group, with no or much less change in the comparison group, it can be tentatively concluded that the change is due to exposure to the independent variable. A further study using an experimental design could then be used to verify the outcome.

2. Time series design. In the time series design, several measurements are taken on a dependent variable over time, typically before and after exposure to the independent variable (another longitudinal approach). A typical time series design looks like this:

$$O_1 \; O_2 \; O_3 \; X \; O_4 \; O_5 \; O_6$$

These symbols indicate that three measurements of the dependent variable were taken prior to exposure of the group to the intervention. Following intervention, three more measures (over time) were taken of the dependent variable. An example will help illustrate the usefulness of this design in social work research.

A group of men meet weekly at a local mental health center to work on issues related to anger expression. During week 1, week 2, and week 3, the level of expressed anger is measured using a standardized measuring instrument designed for this purpose. The social worker introduces a new model of treatment at week 4. The model requires several weeks of group process. When enough time has lapsed for the new treatment to have taken effect, the men's expressed anger is again measured for three consecutive weeks.

Several comparisons are possible using a time series design. First of all, the three pretest measures allow the researcher to establish a baseline measurement of the dependent variable. Baseline measures taken in this way allow a researcher to measure a variable as precisely as possible before intervention. The baseline measurement would be the average expressed anger score of the group over the three-week period prior to the introduction of the intervention in week 4, which probably would be more accurate than a single score measured on one day because the variable is likely to fluctuate naturally over time.

In cases where a control group is not possible, a time series design can help evaluate the effectiveness of a program. By repeatedly measuring the outcome or dependent variable, trends in the data can be identified. If these trends change significantly when the intervention is introduced, support exists for the possibility that changes in the dependent variable were caused by the independent variable. We will look at this concept more in our discussion of single-system evaluation research in Chapter 7.

The time series research design allows the researcher to make at least two comparisons:

- **Comparison 1.** The average pretest measure can be compared to an average posttest measure to see if the intervention has possibly produced changes in expressed anger in the desired direction.
- **Comparison 2.** Changes between O_4 and O_5 and between O_5 and O_6 can be compared to see if any changes that occurred in the desired direction endured over time.

You have to remember that these are just example designs that have been used successfully in social work research. Many other designs can be found in the research literature. For example, a multiple time series design is created by adding a comparison group to the times series design. It would look like this:

$$O_1 \ O_2 \ O_3 \ X \ O_4 \ O_5 \ O_6$$
$$O_1 \ O_2 \ O_3 \ \ \ O_4 \ O_5 \ O_6$$

The time series design can be easily transformed into an experimental design by adding a randomly assigned control group rather than the comparison group in the multiple times series design. The control group would have the same pretest measurements and the same posttest measurements taken as the experimental group, but without the intervention. Another variation would be two experimental groups randomly assigned to compare two different interventions (X and Y). This design would look like this:

$$R \ O_1 \ O_2 \ O_3 \ X \ O_4 \ O_5 \ O_6$$
$$R \ O_1 \ O_2 \ O_3 \ Y \ O_4 \ O_5 \ O_6$$

Such a study, completed by Plow, Mathiowetz, and Lowe (2009), compared two interventions designed to promote health and physical activity among clients with multiple sclerosis. Research participants were randomly assigned to either individualized physical rehabilitation or group wellness intervention. Two pre-intervention measurements were taken and two post-intervention measurements were taken on all of the participants. They concluded that the clients benefited more physically from the individualized rehabilitation and more mentally from the group wellness intervention.

Y = is different intervention

The reader should not look at the designs described here as a definitive list of research designs. Designs are created to fit the needs of the researcher and the research study, not the other way around. These designs are just some of the more commonly used designs in the social work literature.

CHARACTERISTICS OF A GOOD RESEARCH DESIGN

The fact that experimental research is characterized by rigorous hypothesis testing and methods that attempt to control for the effects of confounding variables often has led to the erroneous conclusion that they are always appropriate or are a standard by which to judge other research. Historically, there has been a pronounced bias in this direction. High school science teachers still sometimes denigrate any student research proposals that lack a control group when they are entered in science fairs. The knowledge sought may suggest the need for an exploratory or descriptive study or for a more qualitative approach to knowledge building, but the student may pay the price for using a design that is still regarded by some as "unscientific" or otherwise inferior. Similarly, social workers seeking funding for their research from private foundations and government institutions have struggled to compete with others who submit research proposals describing experimental or quasi-experimental designs. Qualitative studies, even though they may be exactly what are needed to address a research problem, face especially difficult odds when grants are awarded. It is important to remember that designs should be selected based on the purpose and goals of each individual research study. It does a disservice to the field to conclude that one research design is always preferable over another rather than analyzing the needs of the study being proposed.

Although no design is ever perfect (compromises are inevitable), the researcher strives to come up with the best design, given unavoidable limitations. The advantages of different design features must be considered. For example, the popularity of many cross-sectional designs is based in part on their potential to control several of the threats to internal validity (described later in this chapter) that can be eliminated when a single measurement of all variables takes place at the same time.

Generally, the selection of an appropriate design should be guided by the following conditions:

▶ **It is based on a review of existing knowledge.** It should be obvious why the design was selected. The reader of the review of literature section of a report should not be surprised by any part of the research design. The design selected should suggest that the researcher has learned from the methodological successes and failures of others. A design may have come directly from a recommendation of the suggestions for future research section of another recent study, or it may represent a needed replication of research conducted years earlier.

▶ **It is appropriate for the level of knowledge that exists.** The design should promise to advance knowledge about a problem or question. As such, on the research continuum, it will generally fall at or slightly to the right of other recent scholarly research in the area. It should not threaten either to reinvent the wheel or represent a quantum leap by, for example, attempting experimental research on a problem that has barely been explored and adequately described. The design should suggest that the researcher has found the appropriate place on the design continuum.

▶ **It is internally consistent in each of its components.** As suggested earlier, certain design types can be recognized by groupings of characteristics. A design or design component should contain features that belong together, not a little bit of one and a little bit of another. For example, if a design claims to be both quantitative and descriptive and attempts to generalize from research participants to the larger population, it should reflect careful attention to selection of a research sample that will represent the group being studied. The use of a group of participants selected less rigorously (as they might be in more qualitative, exploratory research) would not be appropriate. An experimental or quasi-experimental design would be expected to test hypotheses and contain methods for control of confounding variables. One expects to find certain design features with certain designs or design components and not with others. When the researcher settles on a design type, the decision provides help in resolving such issues as the importance of obtaining a representative sample or the degree to which control of potentially confounding variables is critical in conducting the research.

▶ **It is feasible.** The ideal research design may be impossible to implement because of economic, political, ethical, or logistical obstacles. It may have to be compromised to deal with the realities that exist within the context of social work research. For example, descriptive research on gang members' initiation rites that is otherwise well designed probably will have to rely on sources of data other than firsthand observation. A feasible alternative might be to use interviews with community leaders or police officers who are closely affiliated with gang members. Such secondary sources, although probably not as good, would reflect a reasonable compromise. The research design would be *doable*.

Internal Validity

Internal validity refers to the amount of confidence the researcher has that only exposure to the independent variable produced changes in the dependent variable and that there are no other factors that accounted for these changes. Obviously then, internal validity is critical to any conclusions about causation drawn from experimental (or explanatory) research (but not for exploratory or descriptive studies). For example, suppose that a researcher asserts that, on the basis of research findings, "in counseling victims of rape, counseling method A produces a higher rate of success than counseling method B." Peers will agree with this conclusion only if they are convinced that, on the basis of the research design used, it seems to have internal validity; that is, if the differences in success rate that were observed appear to have been caused by the two counseling methods and nothing else. It was not client age, marital status, varying skill level of the social workers who counseled the clients, or any of the multitude of other potentially confounding variables that could affect the different rates of success. The research should have been designed so that they were all controlled in some way.

There are many factors that are generally acknowledged to threaten internal validity. Singleton and Straits (2005) offer a description of the most common ones.

Threats

- **Testing effects.** As we suggested in one of our earlier examples, the use of a pretest to measure the dependent variable may actually result in a change in measurements of the variable. Participants can learn from or be otherwise influenced by the process of completing a questionnaire or other measurement procedures. If feasible, the use of two or more experimental and control groups (as in the Solomon four-group design described earlier) can help the researcher assess the extent to which testing effects might represent a threat to internal validity.

- **Maturation or passage of time.** Some behaviors and problems seem to have a logical life cycle, or change naturally over time. For example, grief over the death of a loved one tends to subside over time with or without counseling. Any conclusion that the presence of long-term bereavement counseling may have resulted in improved survivor functioning would thus have to be tempered with an assessment of the degree to which time (the threat to internal validity) might have contributed to apparent treatment success.

- **History.** An event sometimes occurs during the course of a research study that might have a major effect on the dependent variable. It may have a much greater effect on the dependent variable than the intervention. Such a historical event may never make the newspapers. For example, it may be the firing of a popular coworker or the implementation of a new personnel policy that affects the job satisfaction of a group of clerical workers much more than the presence or absence of a new longer lunch break (the independent variable). Or the event may be truly historical in scope, such as a tsunami or a terrorist bombing. We could sympathize with researchers who, for example, might have been attempting to prove that "type of counseling affects anxiety level of clients" if one of these disasters occurred in the community during the course of treatment. The internal validity of their findings would almost certainly be questioned.

- **Statistical regression to the mean.** Sometimes, it is desirable to select research participants who exhibit only the most extreme measurements of some variable. Researchers might do this to be certain that their participants are those most in need of intervention and/or that they truly possess certain characteristics that researchers want to try to affect (e.g., low assertiveness or a high level of hostility). Participants will have exhibited the most dramatically high or low measurements of the dependent variable. Following completion of the intervention (the independent variable), the dependent variable generally would be measured again. The second measurement is likely to be less extreme than the first one. Would that mean that the intervention was successful? Maybe, but maybe not. Even if the intervention had no effect whatsoever, a less extreme measurement of the dependent variable might have occurred simply because participants were unlikely to repeat their extremely high or low measurement of the variable. There would be little room for the measurement of the variable to become more extreme, but plenty of room for it to moderate as part of its normal fluctuations.

The tendency of extreme measurements to regress or become more moderate over time can obscure and obfuscate the results of research that uses participants who were selected because of their extreme measurements of a variable. If feasible, a control group consisting of others possessing equally extreme measurements can be used to determine whether statistical regression threatened the internal validity of research findings. If changes in the control group are found to parallel those in the experimental group, it was probably statistical regression and not the independent variable that affected the dependent variable.

▶ **Instruments used.** If a pretest was completed using one version of an instrument and the posttest using another version, the researcher must be certain that any differences between the experimental and control groups did not result from differences in the instruments used. Were the pretest and posttest measurements equal in difficulty or otherwise comparable? Were the experimental and control groups given different versions, and were they comparable? Did they favor one group or the other? If not, any differences may have been caused by the different instruments used, not by the independent variable. Or if two observers were used to measure behaviors, the researcher must be sure that the measurement procedures were clearly operationalized so the same behaviors were consistently measured the same by the two observers.

▶ **Lack of sample comparability.** No comparison of an experimental group with a control group following the introduction or manipulation of an independent variable would be valid if the two groups were not comparable to begin with. As noted, researchers use random assignment in true experiments to improve comparability. But in quasi-experiments or other explanatory designs, they often must use experimental and comparison groups in which participants were not randomly assigned. The samples may deliberately or unintentionally have been constituted in such a way that one group might have a higher likelihood of success. For example, what if we compare clients who attend a substance abuse counseling program with those who do not choose to participate after being referred for counseling? The counseling offered (the independent variable) may not be the reason that the people in counseling had a lower rate of recidivism. Perhaps the participants who chose to participate were just more highly motivated to get better than those who chose not to participate. Their recidivism may have been lower even if they had not participated in the counseling. In cases where random assignment is not used to create true control groups, the researcher cannot be sure that the two groups are comparable on important variables.

▶ **Experimental mortality.** The fact that a researcher can lose research participants or objects over the course of research can offer a threat to internal validity. This is particularly true in longitudinal research (discussed earlier in this chapter), but it can occur in other types of research as well. If the reasons why cases are lost are related to the dependent variable, the results can be misinterpreted, and the findings may lack internal validity. For example, in a study of the effectiveness of a new method of addiction counseling, a control group may be used that receives the usual treatment. Clients could be randomly assigned to either the treatment as usual or the experimental intervention. At the time of the posttest interview, the experimental group (those who receive the new treatment) might reflect a much higher rate of success. But what if the experimental group lost 40 percent of its clients (those who are no longer available to be interviewed), whereas all clients in the control group agree to participate in the posttest interview. The lost 40 percent may reflect the same rate of treatment success as the remaining 60 percent in the experimental group that was interviewed. But, of course, they also may not. They may have dropped out of treatment because the treatment was so successful that it became unnecessary (although that would probably be an overly optimistic interpretation of their behavior). It is also possible that they left because they concluded that their treatment was doing them no good, and they decided to devote the time that they had been wasting to better pursuit of their addiction! If so, the conclusion that the experimental treatment was more successful than the usual treatment would be lacking in internal validity because of experimental mortality.

▶ **Ambiguity about direction of causation.** Sometimes in pre-experimental research designs, it could be argued that it was really the researcher's dependent variable that produced different values of the independent variable, rather than the other way around. For example, a researcher might observe that couples who completed a ten-week marital enrichment seminar have a higher level of marital satisfaction (the dependent variable) than those who dropped out before the seminar was completed. Does that mean that the seminar enhances marital satisfaction? Maybe. But perhaps satisfaction affected completion, rather than the other way around. Perhaps those who completed the seminar had fewer problems, making it easier for them to complete it, whereas those who had more problems had to drop out. (In this example, the threat to internal validity is closely related to the previous one.)

▶ **Diffusion or overlap of intervention methods.** If researchers hope to compare the effectiveness of two intervention methods, it is best if the methods are discrete and bear little or no similarity to each other. Unfortunately, this is not always the case. In the real world, blurring takes place over time, often because features of one intervention become imitated by practitioners of the other intervention method. Thus, any comparison is not a clean one.

For example, suppose a researcher wanted to find out whether support or confrontation is more effective in counseling spouse-abusing clients. Would the social workers assigned to use confrontation methods be able to stick to the method assigned to them? Would their treatment have elements of support? Would those assigned to be only supportive of clients occasionally lapse into a little confrontation? Perhaps both groups of social workers offering treatment will have learned over the years that certain elements of the opposite treatment method can be helpful on occasion and, consciously or unconsciously, they will inject them into their interventions. Then how will we be able to say that it was the treatment intervention (support or confrontation) that produced the different treatment success rates of the two groups of clients? Or if no difference in success rates were to be found, how do we know that the similarity between the two intervention methods used did not hide a real difference in the effectiveness of the methods?

These threats to internal validity should be regarded as the most common problems to be aware of, rather than a complete list. Experimental designs are more likely than other designs to produce findings with acceptable internal validity, because they use true control groups consisting of people or subjects that are randomly assigned to groups.

When findings in an experimental research study appear to have a high level of internal validity, it is possible to conclude that the values of the independent variable (and not something else) caused the values of the dependent variable among cases studied. But how far can the researcher generalize this relationship between variables? to all cases that were not selected for study? to all persons within the state who are similar in some way to those studied? to all persons everywhere who are similar? These are issues of external, rather than internal, validity.

External Validity

External validity refers to the extent to which findings are believed to apply beyond cases that were actually studied. Internal validity alone is not sufficient to guarantee the external validity of a study. External validity relates directly to the number and characteristics of the cases that were studied and to what degree they can be assumed to be representative of other cases in the population that were not studied. The keys to increasing external validity are *sample size* and *random sampling* (see Chapter 9). Using random sampling indicates that the researcher has randomly selected the research sample from the total population. For true random sampling to take place, every person in the population must have an equal chance of being selected as a participant in the research sample. In addition, having a large sample size increases the chance that the sample will be representative of the population. If the sample size is small, the chance of there being differences between the sample and the population increases. Therefore, randomly sampling a large sample from the population is the way to maximize a study's external validity.

Randomly sampling a large sample from the population is the way to maximize a study's external validity.

We want to emphasize here that external validity is not an either-or proposition. It is incorrect to say that a study either *has external validity* or *has no external validity*. The goal is to maximize the external validity by making sure the sample is as much like the population as possible. Suppose we want students at a university to complete a survey regarding their views on the economy. A method that would create very low external validity would be to interview the students in the Introduction to Social Work class. Obviously, this sample would be small and would not, in any way, represent the university student population. Students in this class, for example, might be older and more likely to be female, have children, and be employed than the average university student. Therefore, their views on the economy would not be representative of the larger population. If we randomly selected ten courses across the university and surveyed the students in those classes, the sample would be more representative, and the outcome would, therefore, have greater external validity. The sampling method that would maximize external validity would be to get a complete list of all students from the university (population) and randomly sample a large sample from the list. By using true random sampling and having a sufficiently large sample size (discussed in Chapter 9), we can be confident that the views held by the students in the sample are representative of the views held by the student population.

One mistake often made by researchers is to overstate conclusions made in a study. Consider a hypothetical study of the effect of the career goals of child protection workers (the independent variable) on the quality of services that they deliver (the dependent variable). Let us assume that a carefully designed and implemented explanatory study of a sample of workers within Erie County in western New York produces the finding that career goals of the workers in the study appear to directly affect the quality of child protection services within the county. On scrutiny of the researchers' methods, we conclude that the finding probably has internal validity; other variables and factors that might have caused the variations in the dependent variable were well controlled. To what degree does the finding have external validity? Is the relationship between the variables likely to be present among all child welfare workers (including those working in adoptions) within Erie County? among all public welfare social workers in Erie County? among all public welfare workers in all counties in New York? Would it hold up for any county organization with a heavy urban population, for both BSW and MSW social workers, for staff whose average age is fifty-two years or older, for those with no formal social work education, or for some other group of workers who may differ from those actually studied in some other way? Since the child welfare workers came from one county, the researcher cannot generalize the findings to other counties or states, or even to other departments in the same agency. If the workers were not randomly selected or if the sample size is small, the researcher cannot even generalize the findings to all of the child welfare workers in that county. These are all questions that relate to the external validity of the findings of the research.

Assessing the external validity of research findings and the design that produced them entails a judgment about the research sample that was studied. Specifically, it requires a conclusion about who (besides the participants in the research sample themselves) might also have the same characteristics of the participants in the sample. This is the issue of sample representativeness (discussed in detail in Chapter 9).

Obviously, good external validity (also referred to as broad generalizability) is important to the utility of explanatory research, which attempts to identify relationships between variables within research samples and provide evidence that the same relationships exist beyond those samples. If they are considered quite limited, research findings lose value. However, external validity is also often important to researchers conducting quantitative descriptive research studies, because they often study what they hope is a representative sample of people or objects to learn something about some larger group. In a descriptive study, a sample that is unique (biased) in some way can tell us little or nothing (or even mislead us) about the characteristics of participants not actually studied. But a descriptive study with good external validity can be useful to the social worker. It can provide tentative knowledge about clients or other people who may never themselves have been studied by researchers.

External validity is not nearly as important in exploratory studies as it is in explanatory or quantitative descriptive ones. In fact, many exploratory studies make no pretense of studying a representative sample of people or objects, often because one simply is not available. Internal validity, of course, is also a nonissue, because exploratory studies generally do not seek to find support for relationships between variables.

Critical Thinking

In obtaining a sample of high school teachers in Florida, describe one method of sampling that would have extremely poor external validity and another that would have very good external validity.

Research studies involving racial and ethnic groups raise some special concerns with regard to external validity. One issue is the use of generic labels when describing racial and ethnic groups in the United States. As the diversity of the American population continues to increase, the use of such labels in social work research is and will become increasingly problematic.

For example, the term *Hispanic* is essentially a linguistic designation that refers to people from countries where Spanish is the dominant language and where cultural aspects such as religion, music, art, dance, and food are influenced by traditions emanating from Spain. However, findings from studies on one Hispanic group may not be generalizable to other nationalities or ethnic groups that are included in this designation. There are distinct idiomatic differences, belief systems, and cultural patterns among and between groups, such as Cubans, Puerto Ricans, Dominicans, Mexican Americans, and Latin Americans, who make up the Hispanic mosaic in the United States. The failure to recognize these differences may lead to overgeneralizations from one group to another.

Within-group differences related to variables, such as nationality, social class, education, religion, language, immigration patterns, and degree of acculturation, influence responses in research and thereby determine the degree of external validity of a given research study. A similar issue must be addressed when using the term *black non-Hispanic*, which refers to people of African descent in the United States, South America, Africa, and the English-speaking Caribbean. The terms *American Indian* or *Native American* generally are used to describe 512 federally recognized tribes, who speak more than 200 dialects. *Asian, Pacific Islander* refers to more than 60 separate racial and ethnic groups. The desire of demographers and researchers to reduce this vast complexity into a few easily applicable labels can lead to a false sense of security in generalizing findings across and within racial and ethnic subgroups. Researchers are expected to help others assess the external validity of their research findings. In the research report, a detailed description should be provided of one's research participants and exactly how they were selected.

Any conclusions about the degree to which the findings of a research study possess both internal validity and external validity are always a bit subjective. Ultimately, they are based on one's individual judgment of the quality of the research design and the limitations that it contains. The responsibility of the researcher is to describe a research design honestly and completely, and let the readers of the research report draw their own conclusions.

Diversity in Practice

If you wanted to obtain a sample of Native Americans in the United States, what would be some of the challenges of trying to make your sample representative?

SUMMARY

A research design is a plan for conducting research. It is the way that a researcher responds to certain questions about how the research is to be conducted. The general characteristics of a research design can be conveyed in a number of ways. As noted earlier, research can be described as basic or applied, or as primarily qualitative or primarily quantitative. It can also be described as cross-sectional, pretest-posttest, or longitudinal, suggesting (among other things) how many times participants were observed or interviewed or certain key variables were measured, and what questions the researcher was attempting to answer. Research can be described as exploratory, descriptive, or explanatory, suggesting (among other things) the kind of knowledge that was sought and how the researcher went about seeking it. Box 6.3 summarizes some of what was discussed here and in Chapter 1.

Box 6.3 General Terms Used to Describe Research

Term	Major Differences	Decision Criteria
Basic/Applied	Purpose, application of findings	Knowledge requirements
Qualitative/Quantitative	Methods used; data and its analysis	Knowledge sought
Cross-sectional/Pretest-Posttest/ Longitudinal	Number and time of measurements	Knowledge sought
Exploratory/Descriptive/Explanatory	General nature of the research	Current knowledge level
Pre-Experimental/Experimental/ Quasi-Experimental	Use of control/comparison groups; number and time of measurements	Resources; feasibility of random assignment

Finally, specific research designs can be labeled as pre-experimental, experimental, *or* quasi-experimental. Sometimes, an existing design framework that has been used many times before will acquire a label that is widely understood. We examined a number of these designs in this chapter, including the best known one, the classic experimental design. Of course, even when using an existing design framework, it must still be "fleshed out" to meet the specific requirements of a given research study. Thus, every research design is different, tailored to answer the questions that are unique to the study.

Research designs are never perfect. They are limited by logistical, ethical, legal, monetary, political, time, and other factors. However, given these constraints, some designs are better than others. We examined the most common criteria used in evaluating the quality of research designs—the degree to which they produce findings that possess internal validity and external validity.

Succeed with **PEARSON** **mysocialworklab**

Log onto **www.mysocialworklab.com** and answer the following questions. (If you did not receive an access code to **MySocialWorkLab** with this text and wish to purchase access online, please visit <u>www.mysocialworklab.com</u>.)

1. **Watch the Core Competencies Video: Critical Thinking: Applying Critical Thinking.** If you were asked to evaluate this social worker's practice with this client and other clients like her, describe one possible group research study that you might design.

2. **Read the Case Study: Medical Social Work: Annie.** After reading about the homeless shelter and some of the issues facing the social workers, describe one possible group design research study that could help the social workers. Would your design be exploratory, descriptive, or explanatory?

PRACTICE TEST

1. In the standard notation for research designs, O stands for
   a. independent variable.
   b. measurement of the dependent variable.
   c. random assignment of participants to a group.
   d. nonrandom assignment of participants to a group.

2. In the standard notation for research designs, R stands for
   a. independent variable.
   b. dependent variable.
   c. random assignment of participants to a group.
   d. nonrandom assignment of participants to a group.

3. One of the following is not a requirement of an experimental design:
   a. Multiple measures must be taken before and after exposure to the independent variable.
   b. The independent variables are introduced or manipulated, one at a time, by the researcher.
   c. There are one or more control groups that are not exposed to the independent variable.
   d. Research participants are randomly assigned to experimental and control groups.

4. Quasi-experimental groups designs are distinguished from true experiments primarily because they
   a. always use only one measurement of the dependent variable.
   b. do not involve exposure to an independent variable.
   c. never use a comparison group.
   d. fail to randomly assign participants to either the experimental or the control groups.

5. Briefly describe the nine common threats to internal validity.

ASSESS YOUR COMPETENCE
Use the scale below to rate your current level of achievement on the following concepts or skills associated with each competency presented in the chapter:

1	2	3
I can accurately describe the concept or skill.	I can consistently identify the concept or skill when observing and analyzing practice activities.	I can competently implement the concept or skill in my own practice.

_____ Being able to distinguish between cross-sectional, pretest-posttest, and longitudinal research studies

_____ Understanding the different uses of exploratory, descriptive, and explanatory research

_____ Being able to use standard notation to describe group research designs

_____ Being familiar with the most common pre-experimental, experimental, and quasi-experimental research designs

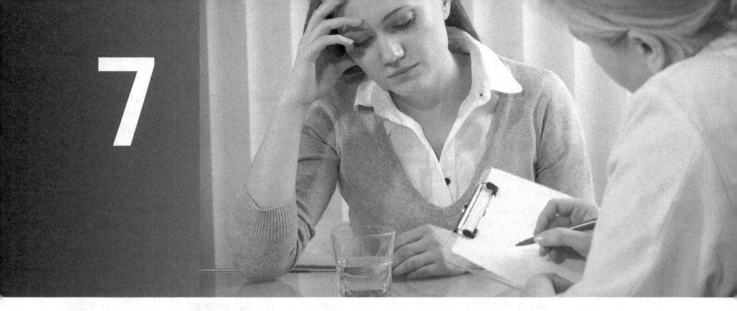

7

Single-System Evaluation Designs

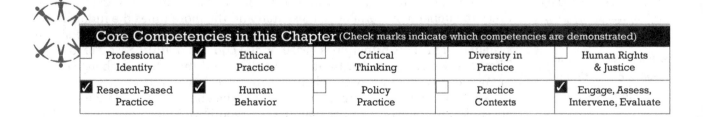

Core Competencies in this Chapter (Check marks indicate which competencies are demonstrated)				
☐ Professional Identity	☑ Ethical Practice	☐ Critical Thinking	☐ Diversity in Practice	☐ Human Rights & Justice
☑ Research-Based Practice	☑ Human Behavior	☐ Policy Practice	☐ Practice Contexts	☑ Engage, Assess, Intervene, Evaluate

In Chapter 6, we looked at group research designs that are used when groups of people or client systems (e.g., families, neighborhoods) participate in the research process. In the most rigorous designs (experimental), the participants are randomly assigned to either a control group or an experimental group, and data from both groups are compared. In less rigorous designs (pre-experimental and quasi-experimental), either no comparison group is available or the groups cannot be randomly assigned for ethical or logistical reasons. We looked at one group design, the time series design, which, in the absence of a control group, uses repeated measures before and after the intervention to allow for comparisons. By using repeated measures, we can look at the trend of the measurements before the intervention is introduced and compare it to the trend of the measurements after the intervention is completed. Although not as rigorous as using a control group, this design does allow the researcher to begin to evaluate the impact of the intervention on the participants of the study.

The use of repeated measures and the analysis of the trends of the data before and after the introduction of the intervention is the key concept in single-system evaluation research (also commonly referred to as single-subject designs, single-case designs, and n=1 research). Unlike the time series design, in which measurements are taken before the intervention is begun and after it is completed, single-system designs involve taking measurements before the intervention is introduced, throughout the time period while the intervention is being carried out, and sometimes after it is completed or withdrawn. Researchers look for significant changes in the outcome or dependent variable when the intervention is introduced or withdrawn. The more stable the trends of the data are, and the more pronounced the changes, the stronger the argument for inferring that the intervention may have produced the changes. Thus, single-system evaluation designs help researchers evaluate their practice effectiveness.

There are several differences between single-system designs and group research designs. The main difference, of course, is that group designs require that a group of research participants be involved in the study. Single-system designs use a single client or client system, whether that be an individual, family, school, community, or whatever system level is the focus of the practitioner/researcher's intervention. Another important difference is that while group design research is often conducted by research specialists who do little else but conduct research studies, single-system evaluations are often conducted by practitioners for their own use (feedback). It is important to remember that although single-system evaluations are generally conducted by social work practitioners and are integrated with their practice, in terms of priorities (and when ethical issues arise), a social worker conducting single-system evaluations is a practitioner first and a researcher second.

Single-system evaluation research is similar to group research in that, just as there are a variety of group research designs, there are different types of single-system designs, some more rigorous than others. Generally speaking, the more times the dependent variable is measured and the more times the independent variable is manipulated (introduced and withdrawn), the stronger the single-system design. This principle is based on the concept of unlikely coincidences. That is, if we can see clear trends in the data, and these trends change one or more times coinciding with when the intervention is introduced and withdrawn, it becomes increasingly unlikely that the changes are a coincidence (or are caused by something other than the intervention). Much of the terminology used in single-system evaluation research is common to all forms of research.

It is important to remember that although single-system evaluations are generally conducted by social work practitioners and are integrated with their practice, in terms of priorities (and when ethical issues arise), a social worker conducting single-system evaluations is a practitioner first and a researcher second.

Box 7.1 Research Terms and Their Equivalents in Single-System Evaluation

Baseline Phase (A phase) The measurements taken during the absence of the intervention. This can be before the intervention is introduced the first time (*true baseline*) or it can be during later phases when the intervention is withdrawn.

Treatment Phase (B phase, C phase, etc.) The time period(s) during which the intervention is being implemented and measurements are taken.

Design The number and sequence of alternating A (baseline) and B (treatment) phases.

Exploratory design A design with no A phase (baseline), e.g., BC or BCD.
Descriptive design A design with a true baseline and one or more interventions, e.g., AB or ABC.
Explanatory design A design that uses repetition or withdrawal of the intervention to observe whether a pattern among the measurements of the dependent variable occurs, e.g., BCBC, ABA.

Independent variable The intervention or its absence (or, less frequently, the magnitude of the intervention). It is almost always a nominal-level variable, a categorical variable with two or more distinct values (see Chapter 10 for a detailed discussion of the levels of measurement).

Dependent variable The severity of the target problem or its incidence as measured through all phases of the evaluation. It can be any level of measurement.

"Case" A single measurement of the dependent variable in either an A phase or a B phase.

"Sample" The total number of measurements of the dependent variable in a single A phase or B phase.

"Control group" The measurements of the dependent variable in an A phase.

"Experimental group" The measurements of dependent variable in the B phase that follows an A phase.

Sampling error The normal fluctuation of the dependent variable; a possible reason why measurements in an A phase may differ from those in a subsequent B phase.

Sampling bias The tendency of a sample of measurements of the dependent variable (especially in a true baseline) to be atypical for the client or client system.

However, in single-system designs, many terms have different, specific meanings. Still other research terms are not often used, but they are implicit in the designs of single-system studies. This can be confusing, so we have grouped some of the more important research terms in Box 7.1 along with how they are understood to exist in single-system evaluation research. The reader may wish to refer back to them in the discussion that follows.

WHEN ARE SINGLE-SYSTEM EVALUATIONS APPROPRIATE?

Single-system evaluations are best suited to those situations in which (1) a primary treatment goal is change in a client behavior, attitude, perception, or other characteristic; and (2) whatever the social worker is seeking to change (the target of the intervention) can be accurately measured. In order to conduct a single-system evaluation, the social worker must be able to specify exactly what change is sought and how it will be measured, as well as the intervention that will be used in an attempt to reach the goal. If progress toward attainment of a goal cannot be measured, or if the intervention method cannot be clearly specified, a single-system evaluation is not appropriate. See Box 7.2 for some of the practice situations in which single-system evaluation may not be appropriate.

In addition, the target for change should be something that the social worker can directly influence through work with the client or client system. The measure of the target for change must, as we stated earlier, be measured repeatedly. Research that entails only two measurements (e.g., a pretest-posttest design) is not a single-system evaluation.

Box 7.2 Some Situations Where Single-System Evaluation Is Not Appropriate

▶ When the target problem or problems cannot be easily and accurately measured

▶ When multiple measurements of target problems over time are not logistically possible, as is often the case with short-term or crisis interventions

▶ When the intervention is complex or otherwise cannot be clearly specified

▶ When the intervention is "one shot," as in making a referral or in conducting discharge planning

▶ When the intervention is "indirect," as in working with teachers around how to better manage classroom behaviors or in working with community members to help them to reduce gang violence

Single-system evaluation can be used by social work practitioners to evaluate their own practice, whether their practice involves individuals, couples, families, schools, hospitals, neighborhoods, or communities. This is why we have chosen to use the term *single-system* rather than one of the other terms, such as *single-subject*, as it emphasizes the fact that any level of system, micro (individual), mezzo (small group, including family, work group, social group, etc.), or macro (larger group, including communities, organizations, etc.), can be studied using this methodology. Single-system evaluations can also be used in situations where selecting a larger group of participants is either impossible or unethical. Mattaini (2010) argues that, in many cases, a single-system evaluation is the most appropriate form of research and evaluation for social workers:

> Single-system research is, in many ways, an ideal methodology for social work research. Social worker practitioners commonly work with one system at a time, under often unique contextual conditions, and single-system methods have the potential to make such work much more powerful. Every client's world and behavioral history are different, and . . . standardized treatments are unlikely to be widely applicable without individualization. (p. 268)

Over the past few decades, researchers and theoreticians have greatly expanded the number of practice situations where single-system evaluation can be used. Progress has come from at least three sources. First, social work researchers and practitioners have created and refined scales for the measurement of such hard-to-measure variables as marital adjustment and family relations. Corcoran and Fischer (2000a, 2000b) have compiled a two-volume book of hundreds of scales that can be used in single-system evaluation research. Many of these scales have been shown to possess both reliability (consistency in measurement) and validity (measurement of what is intended to be measured) when used repeatedly with the same clients or client systems. Second, scholars have designed highly sophisticated single-system evaluation designs. There is a design that is suitable for nearly every practice situation (Weinbach, 2005). Third, still other scholars have developed computer software to make the recording and analysis of data nearly effortless for the practitioner (Bloom, Fischer, & Orme, 1999).

ELEMENTS INVOLVED IN SINGLE-SYSTEM EVALUATION

There is a general sequence of steps that are followed in conducting a single-system evaluation. These steps are presented in Box 7.3. Notice that seven of the eleven steps are conducted before the data are collected. As we have emphasized

---

Box 7.3 The Usual Steps for Conducting Single-System Evaluations

1. Describe the client's problem (or at least its symptoms).

2. Specify the target problem—the behavior, attitude, and so on (the dependent variable) and how you propose to measure it.

3. Identify the pattern of the target problem believed to exist (stable, rising, falling, and so forth).

4. Identify professional literature that describes the problem or something similar and suggests the interventions that may be effective.

5. Briefly specify the precise treatment or intervention to be used and how it will relate to other, ongoing services to the client.

6. Select from among the various single-system designs the one that you will use. Justify why it is best, given such factors as time, ethical constraints, need to control for other variables, treatment goals, and so forth.

7. Determine which pattern of the target problem would indicate that your intervention may be related to a desired effect, that is, the treatment goal. Also determine which pattern(s) would suggest the possibility that your intervention may have promoted unhealthy dependency or some other unintended consequence.

8. Conduct the research, carefully graphing measurements of the target problem over time.

9. Analyze the results of the research relative to step 7.

10. If the intervention appears to have been associated with success, consider replicating the research with other similar clients or client groups who might also benefit from it.

11. Disseminate the results of the research to colleagues who might benefit from knowing them.

A slightly different version of this box appeared in Compton, B., Galaway, B., & Cournoyer, B. (2005) and Weinbach, R. (2005).

---

in earlier chapters, careful planning is critical to research success. With single-system evaluation, steps 2 and 4 take on special importance if researchers are to learn about their practice effectiveness. They need to know exactly what their intervention is (the independent variable) and what it is that they hope it is influencing (the dependent variable). Otherwise, findings would be of little practical value.

Before we look at the various single-system evaluation designs, let us examine the major elements of a single-system evaluation: (1) Defining the outcome or dependent variable; (2) Measuring the outcome or dependent variable; (3) Defining the independent variable or intervention; (4) Conducting the baseline phase(s); (5) Conducting the intervention phase(s); (6) Graphing and analyzing the outcome data.

Defining the Outcome or Dependent Variable

Defining the outcome or dependent variable as well as how it will be measured is key to single-system evaluation because it relates directly to the client's problem. The dependent variable is generally the main target (although it doesn't have to be) that the intervention is attempting to change. Whenever possible, it is preferable to define the goal of intervention (the dependent variable) in a positive way. This is consistent with practice values that stress building on client strengths (the *strengths perspective*). For example, it would be preferable to define a goal as "increasing the number of self-esteem–enhancing comments made by Ms. X to her son" rather than "decreasing the number of deprecating comments made by Ms. X to her son."

If the subject of the evaluation is an individual client, couple, or family, the dependent variable might be, for example, a score on a depression or anxiety inventory, the number or intensity of verbally abusive acts between a husband and wife, the number of times a child disrupts the classroom by yelling out

Engage, Assess, Intervene, Evaluate

How could you translate the goal "reduce the number of times the student with ADHD disrupts the class" to a more positive goal?

during class, the number of temper tantrums, or any of the myriad of possible targets of treatment. If the subject is a school, the dependent variable might be, for example, the number of students successfully passing an advancement test, the number of violent episodes in the school, or the number of students absent from school each day. If the subject of the evaluation is a community, the dependent variable might be, for example, the number of break-ins reported in the neighborhood or the number of children involved in a community center after-school program. There is no limit to the dependent variables that can be defined for single-system evaluations.

It should be noted that, in single-system evaluations, the dependent variable defined need not be the central problem or the major focus of the social worker's treatment plan. It can be just one symptom of the problem (it often is) or even something that may be only tangentially related to the central problem but is contributing to the client's or client system's problem in some way. For example, a social worker might use an intervention to attempt to decrease how frequently his client, a woman with a diagnosis of schizophrenia, talks to herself in public places.

Measuring the Outcome or Dependent Variable

Once the outcome or dependent variable has been identified and clearly defined, the practitioner must determine how the dependent variable is to be measured. When using single-system designs, regular measurements of the target problem are made over the entire course of the study. Ideally, this involves using more than one observer or method to ensure that the measurements have reliability and validity. Measurements are recorded as they are made, usually using standard graph paper or a computer software package designed to produce the line graphs that are characteristic of a single-system evaluation. A variety of types of measurements can be used in a single-system evaluation, including most commonly standardized questionnaires or instruments and behavioral observations.

There are many ways in which a target problem can be measured. Some common ways used in single-system evaluations are as follows:

1. **Frequency.** For example, we might measure the number of times that an inpatient psychiatric patient attends recreational therapy each week.

2. **Duration.** For example, we might measure the length of time that family members spend eating their evening meal together over a two-month period.

3. **Interval.** For example, we might measure the length of time between incidents of racial conflict within a community over a period of five years.

4. **Magnitude.** For example, we might measure the intensity of a client's depressive feelings each week as measured by a depression inventory.

5. **Presence or absence.** For example, we might record whether or not an adolescent attends school each weekday.

Which type of measurement of the target problem is most appropriate for a given evaluation? The answer to this question relates in part to research issues and in part to treatment issues. The availability of valid measurement instruments may be an important consideration, especially if the target problem is

Human Behavior

How could depression be measured using frequency, duration, interval, magnitude, and presence or absence?

one that is not easily measured. For example, we may find a standardized measurement instrument to measure the overall positive and/or negative intensity of a parent-child relationship, but it may be much more difficult to develop a log that will enable the parent and child to accurately (reliably and validly) document the number and duration of individual positive and negative interchanges throughout the day. In another example, the frequency of drug use may be difficult to measure with precision, but its presence or absence each day or the interval between occurrences may be easier to measure as well as more relevant to the intervention goals.

The goal of intervention is an especially important consideration in determining how the dependent variable will be measured. For example, suppose two parents have frequent, but superficial and brief, discussions with each other regarding their child-rearing practices. If the treatment goal is to increase the depth of their discussions, then measuring the duration of the discussions may be more consistent with the treatment goal than counting the number of times the parents discuss child-rearing practices. We operationally define our outcome variable on the basis of the desired target behavior, as well as on the best available measurement tool for measuring the target behavior.

A measurement issue that is unique to single-system designs (and time-series group designs) is that the measure will be used repeatedly throughout the study. This may eliminate measurement instruments or methods that would be too tedious or difficult to measure over and over (e.g., a questionnaire with 200 items). If repeating a measure over and over is likely to influence the measurement, this would constitute an internal validity threat to the study. In other words, something other than the intervention (the fact that we are repeating the measure over and over) is causing the change in the outcome measure. Measurement of a variable should be sensitive enough that it will record meaningful changes, yet not so sensitive that it will record changes that are meaningless in relationship to the goals of the intervention. It also should be as unobtrusive as possible, so that it does not interfere with the intervention itself.

Measurement also must be acceptable to the client or client system. This is in part an ethical issue. Because a power differential exists and because they may fear displeasing the social worker, clients might agree to provide data that they would prefer not to provide or to permit measurement in a way that they might otherwise resist. Thus, it is the social worker's responsibility to ensure that both the measurement itself and its method of collection are acceptable to the client or client system.

Issues of measurement will be looked at in much greater detail in Chapter 10. For now, it is sufficient to say that the outcome variable and the way it will be measured must be identified and operationally defined, that is, the variable and its method of measurement should be defined in such a way that it can be measured consistently (reliably) throughout the evaluation.

Defining the Independent Variable or Intervention

The next step is the selection of the independent variable or intervention to be introduced . This is consistent with social work practice. Once the target problem has been identified, the next step is to select the intervention. As in all quantitative research (and in evidence-based practice), this step should be undertaken after a review of the literature to determine the most effective treatment or intervention available for the target problem. Once the intervention has been identified, it should be operationally defined so it can be clearly described in the research report or case notes. This enables the practitioner or the reader of the report to replicate the study at a later time using the same intervention or a variation of the intervention.

The basic assumption underlying single-system designs is that, if an intervention makes a difference, a client or client system will show a response to it (change). With most designs, practitioners expect (hope?) that the target of the intervention will change when the intervention is introduced. The stronger the pattern of agreement between the presence or absence of intervention and corresponding changes in its target, the greater the evidence that the intervention makes a difference. For example, if one pattern is evident during the presence of the intervention and another pattern can be seen both before the intervention is introduced and after it is removed, the evidence that the intervention makes a difference is especially strong. Such consistent patterns would constitute an unlikely coincidence, and would suggest that the presence of the intervention and changes in the target problem are related. Of course, practitioners hope to demonstrate that the intervention is accompanied by a desirable change in the target, one that is consistent with intervention goals. But the observation that the presence of the intervention is accompanied by undesirable change or even that it makes no difference would still be valuable feedback to the practitioner. Either would suggest that the intervention was not successful, at least not with that particular client or client system.

Conducting the Baseline Phase

Baseline data are the measurements taken before the intervention is introduced. The time period during which the baseline data are collected is the baseline phase, referred to symbolically as the A phase. As you will see later in the chapter, not all single-system evaluations include a baseline phase, but most do. While the experimental intervention is withheld during the baseline or A phase, the client may receive no intervention or may receive other forms of assistance, such as the usual treatment.

If an A phase occurs before the intervention is first introduced, it is known as a true baseline or sometimes just a baseline. It is used to represent the usual pattern of the behavior or other target of the intervention, the starting point for the intervention. Depending on the design being used, there may be additional A phases later in the process. In these instances, the intervention is withdrawn to see how the dependent variable is affected. However, once the intervention has been introduced, any subsequent A phase is no longer indicative of the true baseline—the intervention may continue to influence it even after it is withdrawn. An A phase serves the same general function as a control group does in an experimental research design, providing a source of comparison by indicating what occurs with the target problem when the intervention either (1) has not yet been introduced or (2) is withdrawn. It has been suggested that in single-system evaluations, there is both the equivalent of an experimental group (measurements taken during the intervention phase) and a control group (measurements taken during the baseline phase).

There is no consensus as to what constitutes an adequate baseline. The rule of thumb is that at least three measurements should be collected during the baseline phase, although many researchers argue for at least 5 to 10 baseline data points. Ideally, the baseline should contain a large enough number of measurements so the practitioner can identify the normal fluctuations of the dependent variable in the absence of the intervention so it can later be determined if

An A phase serves the same general function as a control group does in an experimental research design, providing a source of comparison by indicating what occurs with the target problem when the intervention either (1) has not yet been introduced or (2) is withdrawn.

there was a change in the pattern after the intervention was introduced. However, because of time constraints and logistical problems, this is not always possible. So, can just five or ten measurements of the problem constitute a baseline? Or, are more needed? The answer is, it depends. Theoretically, a good baseline can be established using relatively few measurements if they accurately reflect the usual pattern of the target of the intervention. But more is generally better. Often, the decision on the adequacy of baseline data comes down to a social worker's subjective judgment, his or her answer to the question, Have I captured the usual pattern prior to offering my intervention?

Fortunately, a baseline containing a large number of measurements sometimes can be created retroactively. If good records have been kept and are available (e.g., school attendance records), baseline data that have already been gathered can be used to create the baseline phase. This entails secondary data analysis, which can have serious limitations (see Chapter 4). Among other things, it is dependent on the ways in which the problem was conceptualized and operationalized and how conscientiously it was measured. The researcher must determine if the retroactive data are reliable enough to be used or if additional baseline data must be gathered. Generally speaking, recorded data, such as grades, attendance records, doctors' records of appointments, diagnoses, and prescriptions, and other similar data are considered reliable data that can be used to create a retroactive baseline phase.

While the required number of baseline data points cannot be easily specified, the goal is to collect enough baseline data that the data trend becomes apparent. Once a clear trend has been established, it is more likely that any change in the trend that occurs after the intervention is started is due to the intervention itself. In other words, the internal validity of the design is improved if the researcher takes enough baseline measurements so that a clear trend is established. During the baseline phase, there are several possible trends that researchers might observe in the data: increasing, decreasing, stable or unchanging, cyclical, or unstable. *Increasing* is when the values of the outcome measure are steadily increasing, while *decreasing* is when the values are steadily decreasing. *Stable* is when the values are staying essentially the same, or changing very little. *Cyclical* is when there is an up-and-down pattern that is happening regularly over a certain time period. An *unstable* trend is when there is no clearly identified trend. If the data are unstable, it is preferable to keep collecting further baseline measurements until a trend is achieved. Otherwise, the baseline data offer practitioners little in the way of comparison once the intervention is introduced (See Figure 7.1 for diagrams of these trends).

Generally speaking, recorded data, such as grades, attendance records, doctors' records of appointments, diagnoses, and prescriptions, and other similar data are considered reliable data that can be used to create a retroactive baseline phase.

Conducting the Intervention Phase

In those designs where baseline data are gathered first (there is a true baseline), the intervention then follows The intervention phase is the time period during which the intervention is being applied and the dependent variable continues to be measured. The intervention phase is represented symbolically as the B phase. The behavior or other phenomenon that the social worker is seeking to influence is referred to generically as the *target problem* and is regarded as the dependent variable for research purposes. The presence (B phase) or absence (A phase) of the specific treatment or intervention that is used serves as the independent variable.

As we shall see later in the chapter, different single-system designs can also be used to compare the relative effectiveness of different interventions, attempt to learn which sequence of interventions worked best, and even to examine whether a given intervention seems to work more effectively with one

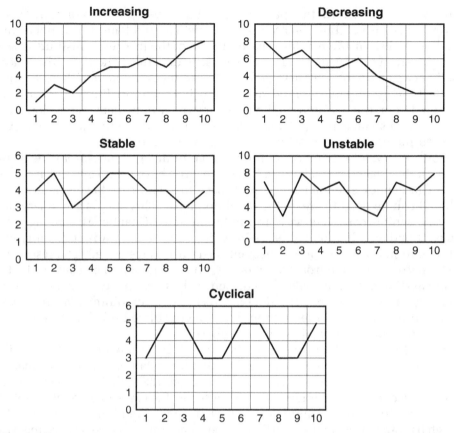

Figure 7.1
Possible Trends in Baseline Data

target problem than with another. In evaluations in which two or more inter-ventions are examined, subsequent intervention phases are referred to as the C phase, D phase, and so on.

Graphing and Analyzing the Data

As the measurements of the outcome variable are gathered during the baseline (A) and intervention (B) phases, they are graphed on a line graph. During the baseline phase, studying the graph enables the practitioner/researcher to deter-mine when a clear trend in the data has been established. During the interven-tion phase, the graph enables the practitioner to know whether desirable changes in the target problem are occurring and thus guides practice decisions.

In a line graph showing the data of a single-system evaluation, the appro-priate time periods are displayed along the *x* axis (horizontal axis) and the measures of the dependent variable are shown on the *y* axis (vertical axis). In this way, we can visually see if the trends of the dependent variable are chang-ing or remaining the same over time. The presence or absence of intervention at the time of each measurement is clearly indicated on the graph by labeling time intervals either as A (for a baseline phase) or B (for an intervention phase). If measurements of the target problem are numeric (e.g., score on a standard-ized instrument, number of times a child is disruptive in class, etc.), the pos-sible range of values of the dependent variable are displayed along the vertical axis and units of time along the horizontal axis. Thus, each dot on the graph reflects a measurement of the target problem and the point in time when the measurement took place. If the target problem is a dichotomous variable (e.g., attended/did not attend group treatment, complied/did not comply with medication, or completed/did not complete all homework), a horizontal line is placed on the graph with one value category above it (labeled, for example, "attended treatment") and one below it (labeled "did not attend treatment") on the vertical axis. Then an X or a dot is placed either above or below the line each time that the target problem is measured to reflect its measurement.

The most common form of data analysis used in single-system evaluation is visual analysis. In other words, the data are graphed on a line graph, and we look carefully for trends in the data and changes in these trends in relation to when interventions were introduced and withdrawn. Many social workers using single-system designs believe that only those effects that be easily seen on a line graph should be considered meaningful. If there is no improvement, or if there may be improvement but it is not obvious, the null hypothesis is deemed not rejected. In other words, the change in the outcome variable is so small that it appears the change could be due to chance rather than the intervention.

The data gathered during the intervention phase are interpreted on the basis of the trends in the data during the baseline phase. For example, consider a client whose score on a depression inventory is steadily increasing (indicating increased depressive symptoms). If the data even off after the intervention is introduced, the social worker could argue that the intervention may be helping in that the problem at least stopped getting worse. What if the target problem was getting slowly better during the baseline phase, and then continued to get slowly better after the intervention was introduced? On first glance, it might seem the intervention could be helping. However, since the client was already getting better before the intervention was introduced, the intervention may actually be having little or no effect on the dependent variable. We just want to emphasize the importance of the baseline data when analyzing the data collected during the intervention phase (see Figure 7.2 for examples of these and other data trends).

Figure 7.2
Interpreting Trends in B-Phase Data

In single-system evaluations where there is a baseline A phase followed by an intervention B phase, statistical analyses are sometimes used to determine the mathematical probability that differences in the dependent variable between the A and B phases represent nothing more than normal fluctuation. There are several easily computed tests that can tell us if the difference between the measurements in the A phase and the subsequent B phase is statistically significant, that is, it is large enough that the probability of its representing just normal fluctuation over time is quite small. While these methods are beyond the scope of this chapter, you can find a thorough discussion in Mattaini (2010). These methods are based on the following assumptions:

▸ The A (baseline) phase is an accurate representation of the dependent variable and its variability (it is a representative sample).
▸ The same pattern of variability of the dependent variable would continue following the A phase if the intervention were not introduced.
▸ Any difference between the pattern of the dependent variable in the A and subsequent B phases may be attributable to the presence of the intervention during the B phase.

SINGLE-SYSTEM DESIGNS

Just like the research designs that we discussed in the previous chapter, different single-system designs have been created to answer different questions. Some are exploratory. They lack an A phase and seek simply to answer the question, Do changes occur during the time an intervention is being applied? Other designs are descriptive. They contain a baseline (A) phase and are used to answer the question, How much change occurs when an intervention is introduced? Still others are described as explanatory. They contain a series of alternating A and B phases and attempt to answer the question, Did the intervention actually cause changes in the dependent variable? Explanatory designs tend to be the most complex because they must attempt to control for threats to internal validity. We will look at examples of all three types, paying special attention to their specialized uses.

B Design

The most basic single-system exploratory design is the B design. It consists of the introduction and continuation of the intervention while measurements of the target problem or dependent variable are carried out and recorded. It is exactly what most responsible practitioners already do to some degree. However, for the monitoring to be considered single-system evaluation, the practitioner would have to (1) operationally define the target problem and the intervention; (2) measure the target problem repeatedly throughout the intervention; and (3) graph and interpret the data.

Other exploratory single-system designs include the BC or BCD designs. In the BC design, the first intervention (B phase) is withdrawn and a second intervention is introduced during a C phase. The outcome or dependent variable continues to be measured throughout the completion of the second intervention to see if positive changes are being made. In a BCD design, a D phase is conducted during which the second intervention (C phase) is withdrawn and a third intervention is introduced. These designs allow the practitioner to explore the possible effects of a series of one or more interventions on a target problem.

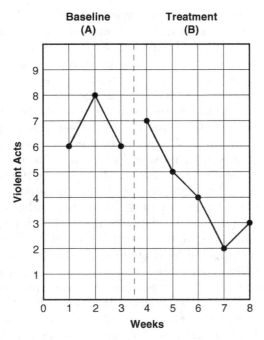

Figure 7.3
AB Design: Patient Violence toward Staff

AB Design

An AB design is slightly more complicated than B and is considered *descriptive*. It consists of two phases: (1) a baseline phase (A phase), during which the dependent variable is measured and graphed and the intervention being evaluated is not offered, and (2) an intervention phase (B phase), during which the intervention is carried out and the dependent variable continues to be measured (see Figure 7.3 for an example).

When using an AB design, the intervention being evaluated is not offered until a true baseline phase of measurement takes place or is constructed from available data. Thus, a social worker might have an ethical objection to using an AB design with a client or client system that is in imminent danger because the target problem is life threatening or otherwise destructive. For example, we would not use an AB design to see if a promising intervention is effective in reducing the number of times that a client at high risk for contracting an HIV infection engages in unsafe sexual practices. We could not ethically justify waiting to offer the intervention just because we preferred to use an AB design. However, if we already have or can acquire valid measurements of the client's usual sexual practices prior to seeking assistance, we might be able to use these measurements to create a retroactive baseline.

AB is often the design of choice when permanent learning or nonreversible behavior or attitudes are a likely consequence (and a goal) of the intervention. As we will discuss later, some single-system designs (withdrawal designs) withdraw the intervention and return to a second baseline phase. If the data reverts to the levels of the initial baseline, the practitioner can argue that the intervention is causing the data fluctuations. If, however, the behaviors, once learned, are not likely to spontaneously revert if the intervention is withdrawn, withdrawal designs are not appropriate. In these cases, an AB is more appropriate. For example, a social worker may select a specific intervention to

Ethical Practice

Give your own example of when taking the time to gather a baseline could be considered unethical.

increase the frequency of assertive behaviors in a client. The intervention may be accompanied by an increase in these behaviors, as reflected in the B phase of the design. The literature and experience tell the practitioner that the client is likely to continue assertive behaviors when appropriate, because they promote desired responses from others. If additional data are collected after the intervention is concluded, they would offer the practitioner follow-up data to see if the gains were maintained over time after treatment was ended.

In all single-system designs, the dependent variable (target problem) must be measured accurately. But it should not be measured so narrowly that another similar behavior can simply be substituted for it. In the example portrayed in Figure 7.3, an intervention was used to attempt to reduce or eliminate physical attacks by a client on nursing staff within an inpatient psychiatric setting. Suppose we define the dependent variable as the number of client attacks on nurses. A dramatic decline in the dependent variable during the intervention phase might have suggested a successful intervention. However, during the time that the patient stopped attacking nurses, increased attacks on social work staff or even other patients may have occurred. This phenomenon is referred to as *symptom substitution*. This undesirable behavior would not be measured in the social worker's evaluation because of the way the dependent variable or target problem was conceptualized and operationalized. It would have been better to define the target problem as "physical attacks on other people," thus including other staff, patients, and even visitors.

When using descriptive designs such as AB (or ABC or ABCD), a social worker does not control for other variables (besides the intervention) that might produce change in the target problem. In the evaluation portrayed in Figure 7.3, for example, the decrease in attacks on staff during the B phase may have been the effect of the intervention, but may also have been the result of changes in the patient's diet or medication, help offered by other staff, visits from the patient's relatives, pressure from other patients, the passage of time, and any of hundreds of other factors working alone or in concert.

Perhaps the A phase (baseline) was an atypical time for the patient and the B phase is simply more typical of the patient's behavior. Or perhaps the difference between the A and B phases just represents normal fluctuation for the client, and the B phase did not really reflect change at all. Descriptive single-system designs can only answer the question, How much change occurred? Answering this question is possible only if the practitioner has made good baseline measurements, which describe accurately the normal pattern of the target problem prior to the introduction of the intervention.

Successive Intervention Designs

Sometimes, as practitioners, we know of several interventions that may be effective, but none of them is clearly indicated to be the most effective. We seek some general guidance as to which may be best or, to be more precise, which intervention or series of interventions seems to work best with a given client or client system. Successive intervention single-system designs can examine several interventions, each introduced one at a time. These designs are used to examine the relationship between several interventions and a single dependent variable (a target problem).

Figure 7.4 illustrates the efforts of a public health social worker to evaluate the relative effectiveness of several interventions with a client in a smoking-cessation program.

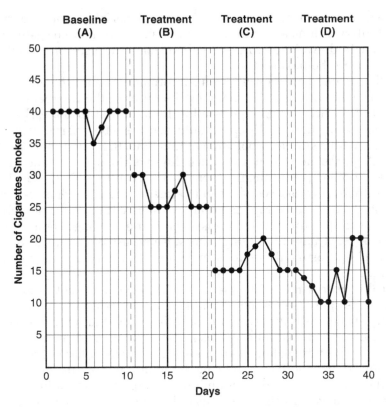

Figure 7.4
ABCD Design: Client Effort to Reduce Cigarette Smoking

This evaluation started with a baseline phase (A), during which the number of cigarettes smoked by the client was recorded and graphed for ten days. Next, three interventions were introduced consecutively (B, C, and D), during which time the dependent variable (cigarettes smoked) continued to be recorded. This constitutes an ABCD single-system design. If there had been four interventions used, the design would have been ABCDE, and so forth.

When using a successive intervention design, the potential for treatment carryover from one phase into subsequent ones can make it difficult to determine just which intervention produced the most change in the dependent variable (target problem). For example, the continuation of a desired behavior at approximately the same level following the shift from one intervention to another, as in the D phase in Figure 7.4, may mean that interventions C and D are equally effective. It may also mean that the effects of intervention C continued on through the D phase. If so, it may be this carryover effect and not intervention D that produced the level of the desired behavior in the D phase. Another interpretation may be that intervention D may simply be ineffective or may even promote smoking. If this is true, the social worker would have even further support for the effectiveness of intervention C. But how can we know this is what happened? The possibility of treatment carryover can severely limit any conclusions about the relative effectiveness of different interventions when successive designs are used. To avoid effects of treatment carryover, the social worker may want to add a baseline phase between each intervention to have a clearer idea of the effectiveness of each individual intervention. While the previous intervention may continue to affect the data during the baseline phase, there would possibly be some change once all interventions are withdrawn making it easier to analyze the affects of various interventions. When all interventions are withdrawn and data continue to be gathered, these are called withdrawal designs. We will discuss the uses and limitations of these designs in the next section.

Another method for gaining useful information about the effectiveness of individual interventions is by changing the order of the interventions in subsequent studies. If the smoking-cessation intervention in the earlier example was unsuccessful, the practitioner could use the same participant again (or another one with a similar problem), but this time, the practitioner could begin with an A phase and then introduce interventions C, B, and D, in that sequence. Another study might order the interventions D, C, and B, and so forth. Eventually, the best sequence of treatments might be identified, especially if the study were to be replicated many times with similar participants. In situations where problem recidivism is common (e.g., family violence, substance abuse, truancy, bullying), the repeated use of the ABCD design with the same client using different sequencing of interventions can be quite enlightening.

Ethical concerns related to use of ABCD designs are not as great as with some other designs. One issue sometimes voiced relates to withdrawing an apparently successful intervention to substitute one that may not be found to work as well. But this is not as problematic as it might seem at first, because most often the withdrawal of an apparently successful intervention is immediately followed by another promising intervention. A greater ethical issue occurs when the intervention is withdrawn completely and followed by a second baseline phase. Designs that use this method are called withdrawal designs.

Withdrawal Designs

Single-system withdrawal designs include any design that introduces an intervention (B phase) and then subsequently withdraws the intervention and returns to a baseline phase (A phase). In some cases, such as the ABA or ABAB designs, there is a true baseline phase at the beginning of the evaluation. In other designs, such as the BAB, there is no true baseline phase before the intervention is introduced.

ABA Design

An ABA design consists of an initial baseline phase (A), followed by the intervention phase (B), followed by a third phase in which the intervention is withdrawn to create a second baseline phase (A) of observation and measurement. This explanatory design attempts to address potential threats to internal validity. If the target problem shows improvement during the intervention phase and seems to get worse again during the second baseline phase, evidence exists that the intervention (and not something else) may have caused the problem to diminish. Of course, this type of design is useful only when the effects of the intervention are not expected to carry over once the intervention is withdrawn. For example, if cognitive-behavioral therapy is used to treat a client with depression, it would not make sense to use a withdrawal design, because, once the treatment is completed and withdrawn, it is hoped that the treatment effects will continue. In this case, subsequent measurements will offer follow-up measures to see if the treatment effects are long lasting.

Suppose, for example, children in a residential foster care facility are offered tokens for completing their chores each week. These tokens can be traded for television, computer, and video game time. If the token system is used for six weeks and seems to be working successfully, the social work researcher could withdraw the system for three weeks and return to baseline measurements to see how well the children complete their chores without the tokens. Because we would expect the effects of the intervention to significantly reduce after the intervention is withdrawn, the ABA design would be effective design (see Figure 7.5) in this scenario. If the second baseline data shows a reduction in chores done, the next step often would be to reintroduce the intervention and leave it in place indefinitely (making it an ABAB design).

Although an ABA design can tell the practitioner what happens to the target behavior after the intervention is withdrawn (which an AB design cannot do), there are possible ethical issues that must be considered. Many social workers question whether it is ethical to withdraw an intervention believed to be effective. But two things should be kept in mind. First, with only an AB design in place, the social worker cannot claim that the intervention has caused the improvement in the first place. Many other factors could be affecting the dependent variable. By withdrawing the design, the researcher can be more confident that the intervention really is helping. Second, researchers would not use a withdrawal design in situations in which discontinuing the treatment could be dangerous to the client. For example, in the situation above, the social work researcher was trying to encourage children in a group foster case home to complete their chores. By withdrawing the intervention, it became clearer that the tokens being offered were increasing the completion of the chores. Withdrawing the tokens for a period of weeks did not present any danger to the clients or to the social worker. It is up to the practitioner to decide when it is appropriate and ethical to use a withdrawal design. Because the issue for many social workers is ending the research in an A phase, the next design, the ABAB design, is is sometimes preferred by social work practitioners.

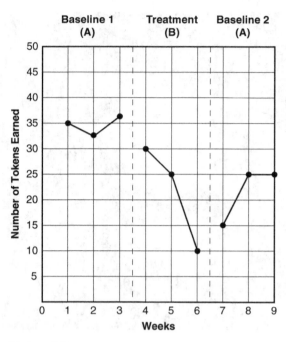

Figure 7.5
ABA Design: Token Economy

ABAB Design

The ABAB design is probably the most preferred withdrawal design because it ends with an intervention phase. The addition of one or more alternating A and B phases helps to provide additional evidence for a possible cause-effect relationship between the intervention and the target problem. When using an AB design, there is only one point in time that the intervention is introduced. Many other events could have taken place in the client's life to affect the dependent variable at that point in time. In the ABAB design, there are now three points in time the independent variable is manipulated: when the intervention is introduced, withdrawn, then introduced again. If the measures of the dependent variable change at each of these three points in time, one could argue that the intervention is indeed affecting the dependent variable. In other words, it becomes less and less likely that other factors could have coincidentally affected the dependent variable at all three of these points in time.

Let's continue our example of the token economy being used to encourage children to complete their chores. Figure 7.6 shows the graph of an ABAB design, in which the dependent variable (percent of chores completed by all children in home) is shown on the *y* axis and time is shown on the *x* axis. The baseline data are gathered for four weeks to see a relatively stable trend in the data. The intervention starts and data are gathered for the next four weeks. To justify the continuation of the program, suppose the social worker needs to present data to her supervisor in support of the program. To strengthen the data, she decides to use a withdrawal design. She stops offering tokens to the children, and continues to measure the dependent variable for four weeks. When it is clear that the there was a significant drop in the percent of chores being completed, she re-instituted the program, continuing data collection for four more weeks before showing the outcomes to her supervisor. Her

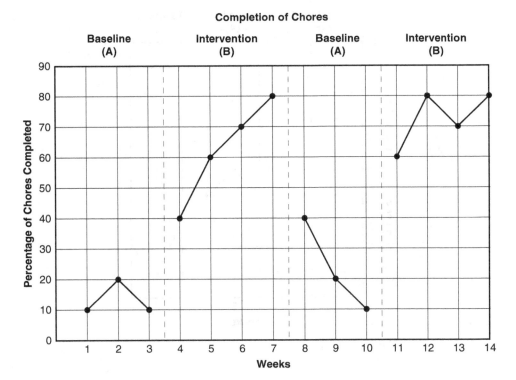

Figure 7.6
ABAB Design: Completion of Chores

supervisor agreed with her conclusion that the intervention was successful, and allowed the program to continue indefinitely.

BAB Design

The BAB design can be used in cases where a withdrawal design is desirable, but it is impractical to gather baseline measurements before the intervention is introduced. It is popular, because, like the ABAB design, it ends with an intervention (B) phase, a characteristic that appears to be consistent with social work practice values and ethics. This design is especially well suited to crisis situations where the social worker believes that conducting a baseline measurement prior to offering the intervention would be unethical, but where it is believed that the intervention can safely be withdrawn after a short period of time.

Figure 7.7 illustrates a BAB single-system evaluation design. Suppose a teacher asks the school social worker for help with a child who is hitting other children in the classroom. The teacher does not want to wait for the time required for baseline data collection. She is already convinced it is a serious problem, which is why she came to the social worker. The social worker helps the teacher implement an intervention that entails offering the child rewards contingent on the number of times each week he does not hit or physically hurt another child in the classroom. After three weeks, the data show a marked improvement of the boy's behavior. However, the social worker is aware that other factors in the boy's life may have caused the improvement (e.g., possible treatment outside of school; a new friend in the classroom; change in diet, sleep, or exercise). In addition, without baseline data before

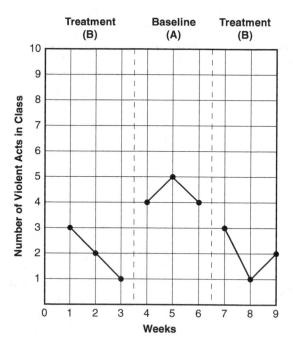

Figure 7.7
BAB Design: Client's Classroom Behavior

the intervention started, there is no way to know for sure (with only non-measureable reports from the teacher) how many incidents the boy was having before the intervention. To be more confident that the intervention is having a positive affect on the student's improved behavior, the reward program is withdrawn. Baseline data are gathered for two weeks. The number of incidents during the baseline phase increases significantly, giving the teacher more confidence that her intervention is having a positive affect on the boy's behavior. The reward system is then put back into place until the behavior improves, and the teacher decides whether it is appropriate to leave the intervention in place indefinitely or perhaps to slowly withdraw the intervention while monitoring the child's behavior.

In using a BAB design, ethical concerns center around the timing of the decision to withdraw intervention, that is, to move from the first B phase into the A phase. Without extensive foreknowledge of the client and the target problem pattern (unlike when a true baseline occurs first), it may be difficult to know when it should be considered safe to withdraw the intervention. What if the social worker's professional judgment suggests that ethically it would be detrimental to the client to withdraw the intervention at the time that the design calls for it to be withdrawn?

Because they begin without benefit of a true baseline, BAB designs are less likely to be completed than the other designs we have already discussed. A BAB design (as well as other designs, for that matter) sometimes has to be "scrapped" as contact with the client or client system reveals that the problem is either more or less of an emergency than it was believed to be, or that planned removal of the intervention would not be in the best interest of the client. Of course, the lack of a true baseline does not necessarily mean that the social worker has no knowledge of the client. There may be records or other sources of information that can be used to provide an accurate description of the severity of the problem. The client also may have been receiving services from the social worker for some period of time before the design was implemented. It is not at all unusual for social workers to decide to conduct single-system evaluations with clients or client systems who are already well known to them. Often, observation of a problem over time is the impetus for conducting a single-system evaluation.

Combined Successive Interventions/Withdrawal Designs

Look back at the example we used earlier (see Figure 7.4), in which the baseline phase was followed by three successive interventions (ABCD design). If the withdrawal method had been added to this study, we would have had another design (ABACAD). Such a design would give us a clearer indication of the relative effectiveness of the three treatments. But, its downside would be that the cumulative effect of treatments B, C, and D may have been more difficult to determine because of the presence of baseline phases between each treatment. Therefore, it would depend on the goal of the social worker in completing the study. If he prefers to keep the effects as separate as possible, the ABACAD design may be preferable. However, if he is more interested in looking at the cumulative effects of the interventions, the simpler ABCD design may be more beneficial. As we already pointed out, it is important to remember that the well-being of the client always remain our first concern even if it means using a weaker evaluation design.

Multiple-Baseline Design

In cases where it is not appropriate to withdraw the intervention, either because of possible detrimental effects on the client or because the intervention effects are likely to continue even after the intervention is withdrawn, the multiple-baseline design is a way to increase the evaluation's internal validity. In other words, this design offers another way to determine the likelihood that something other than the intervention has caused the observed effects on the dependent variable. This design can be used to observe the effects of an intervention on two or more clients, two or more (usually related) target problems, or two or more settings (e.g., school, home, church, child care setting).

When using a multiple-baseline design, an A phase precedes the introduction of the intervention for all of the clients, target problems, or settings. For the remainder of this discussion, we will use the term 'target' to refer to the clients, target problems, or settings being evaluated. During this phase, baseline measurements of the dependent variable or variables are taken. Then the intervention is introduced to attempt to influence one of the targets. Generally, it is applied first to the target that has reflected the clearest trend during the initial baseline (A) phase. As the intervention is offered to the first target, baseline measurements for the other targets continue, thus creating an extended A phase. After the intervention is used for some period of time with the first target, the intervention is introduced for the second client, target problem, or setting. During this time, the baseline measurements continue to be taken for the remaining targets. This continues until the intervention is introduced to all of the cases.

It should be noted that the intervention is the same across all of the targets, whether you are looking at multiple target problems, clients, or settings. If multiple target problems are being studied, then the client and settings also stay the

Research-Based Practice

Describe why the ABACAD can help the social worker see the individual effects of the interventions better than the ABCD design.

In cases where it is not appropriate to withdraw the intervention, either because of possible detrimental effects on the client or because the intervention effects are likely to continue even after the intervention is withdrawn, the multiple-baseline design is a way to increase the evaluation's internal validity.

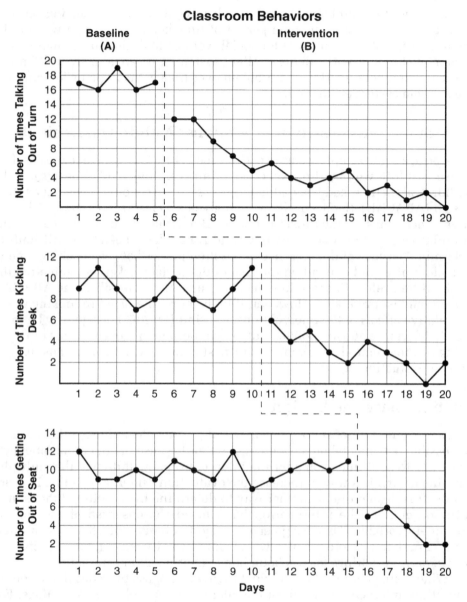

Figure 7.8
Multiple-Baseline Design across Problems

same across cases. Likewise, if multiple clients are used, the settings and target problems stay the same. Finally, if multiple settings are being examined, then the clients and target problems stay the same. In other words, in any one multiple-baseline evaluation, only one factor changes while the others remain constant.

Let's look at some examples of this design. Figure 7.8 illustrates an application of a multiple-baseline design that looked at one client across three target problems. In this study, a fourth grade boy with ADHD was having problems in his classroom, leaving his seat at inappropriate times, kicking the chair in front of him, and talking out of turn. Because these behaviors occurred very rapidly, the teacher decided to tackle them one at a time. The school social worker agreed to observe the boy for thirty minutes each day right after lunch, a time when the teacher said the boy's behaviors were particularly troublesome. After the social worker had observed and recorded the target behaviors for five days, the teacher started the intervention (stickers and rewards for not exhibiting the behavior) with the boy's habit of talking out of turn. This was chosen first because the baseline data was extremely stable after the first five days of recording. After five days, this behavior had subsided dramatically, so the teacher began the intervention with the boy's kicking the desk in front of him. Again, dramatic gains were observed, this time after ten days. Finally, the intervention was used to try to control the child's tendency to get out of his seat. Again, the intervention seemed successful, after one week. The teacher decided to continue the intervention indefinitely and asked the school social worker to come in periodically to measure the child's behaviors to make sure they did not reappear.

Figure 7.9 illustrates a multiple-baseline design across clients. In this example, a social worker conducted a crime reduction program in three high-crime neighborhoods in her city. Monthly crime statistics were gathered from city records for the six months preceding the start of the study, thus creating a retroactive baseline. The program was started in neighborhood A. Baseline data continued to be gathered for the other two neighborhoods. After three months, the program was started in neighborhood B, while baseline data continued to be gathered on the third neighborhood. Finally, three months later, the program was introduced to neighborhood C. As you can see from the data, the crime rates in each of the neighborhoods started to reduce soon after the intervention was started. This design offers a much stronger argument than a simple AB design would that the intervention actually caused the change. If, for example, the same program had been started in all three neighborhoods at the same time, the social worker would not have known whether something else had happened at the same time that caused the reduction in crime (e.g., new stiffer penalties, change in weather, road construction). It would be much less likely that something happened at all three times the program was initiated in the different neighborhoods to cause the reduction. This is the strength of the multiple-baseline design.

Figure 7.10 shows a single-system evaluation of an intervention across settings. The social worker is trying to help a young mother reduce the number of temper tantrums thrown by her 3-year-old son. Because the tantrums are occurring at home, in preschool, and at the grandparents' home where the child stays on weekends, the social worker decided to use a multiple-baseline design to evaluate the client's progress. The intervention was defined and clearly described to all of the authority figures in these three settings, the parents, the teachers, and the grandparents. After baseline data were gathered for three weeks, the intervention was started at the child's home. The temper tantrums reduced dramatically at home, but can be seen to actually increase slightly at the preschool and grandparents' home. After three weeks, the intervention was introduced into the preschool setting. The tantrums reduced, although not as dramatically as they had at home. Finally, the intervention was introduced at the grandparents' home, which also showed a reduction. Overall, the parents were satisfied with the intervention, and decided to continue using the parenting skills they had learned through the intervention.

Unlike the withdrawal designs, multiple-baseline designs do not present researchers with the ethical issue related to withdrawing a possibly effective intervention. Of course, when the intervention is used with one client across multiple problems or settings, there is the potential for treatment carryover. In

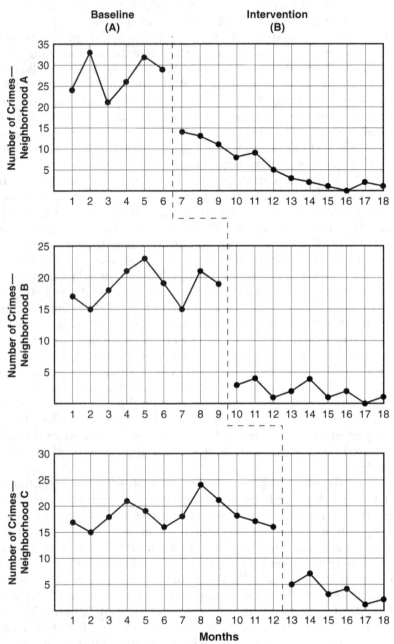

Figure 7.9
Multiple-Baseline Design across Clients

the previous example, the treatment applied in the child's home may affect his behavior at the preschool or grandparent's home before it is introduced in either of these settings. This is generally not considered a problem. If the behavior improves significantly in the other settings, the intervention may not need to be implemented there. If the behavior gets worse, the intervention is introduced at the other settings as planned and hopefully the behaviors will improve as in the example data shown in Figure 7.10.

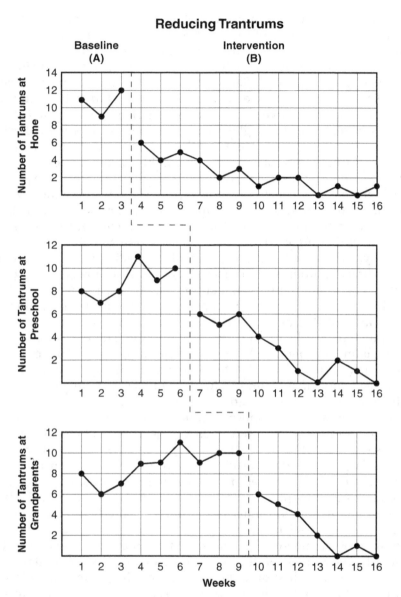

Figure 7.10
Multiple-Baseline Design across Settings

STRENGTHS AND WEAKNESSES OF SINGLE-SYSTEM EVALUATIONS

Single-system evaluations are not new. They have been discussed in the social work literature for more than thirty years. During the 1980s, single-system evaluation was rediscovered and touted as a logical bridge between research and practice.

An objective assessment of the place of single-system evaluation research in social work must recognize both its strengths and weaknesses. On the positive side of the ledger, single-system evaluations are inexpensive to implement. They cost little in time and other resources, something that generally cannot be said of many of the other forms of research we have described. Single-system evaluations are easily comprehended; a short workshop or staff development program is all that is needed to get staff started in using them to evaluate their practice. They offer almost instantaneous feedback regarding a social worker's practice effectiveness. There is no need to wait months or years to acquire and disseminate research findings—a phenomenon that is typical of other forms of research. In single-system evaluations, data are collected and interpreted on an ongoing basis while practice intervention continues. Application of findings is thus easily and quickly accomplished.

Findings from single-system evaluations are never obscure or esoteric; they are in a form that is amenable to utilization. They can provide useful early feedback about new or experimental intervention methods. The methods can be quickly evaluated and either discarded or, if they seem to be promising, evaluated more thoroughly using other types of research.

Single-system evaluations provide good feedback for evaluating the effectiveness of practice intervention methods, especially those that are primarily task centered or problem solving in nature. Sometimes, a series of studies using the same intervention, the same target problem, the same designs, and the same or similar participants can begin to suggest knowledge that transcends any one case. This method (replication) is the only way that single-system studies can make any claim to generalized knowledge building or to producing findings with external validity (being able to generalize findings to the larger population). However, any such claim is a tenuous one at best, given what we know about the uniqueness of people and their situations.

However, there are a number of inherent design weaknesses in single-system evaluation research. It often must depend on a client's own measurement and self-report of target problems or the reports of others such as friends or relatives (especially when used anywhere other than in institutional settings). The accuracy of this method of measurement can easily be questioned. Of course, this potential problem is no stranger to the social worker. Almost all intervention and evaluation must rely heavily on the belief that what others tell us is truthful and accurate.

Another problem related to single-system evaluation research is that it cannot be used productively unless work environments support its use. Even though this type of evaluation requires relatively little time and effort on the part of the practitioner, problems can occur unless administrators and supervisors are convinced of its value. A supervisor who fails to share a commitment to it and who does not understand it may view it with suspicion and even perceive a supervisee to be wasting time conducting it. No one will want to conduct single-system evaluations if a supervisor demands to know why the social worker is "fooling around with those graphs when you should be seeing clients or keeping your records up to date."

Single-system evaluations are vulnerable to misuse. A supervisor may attempt to use the evaluation findings (including graphs) as evidence of the supervisee's competence (or lack of it). They may be used for annual performance evaluations or to support personnel actions. This practice can be tempting for supervisors seeking "objective" criteria to justify their actions. But it is a gross misuse of single-system evaluation research. Evaluation data are not intended as a vehicle to assist the supervisor in evaluating the social work practitioner; it is intended as feedback for the researcher/practitioner. Use for any other purpose will quickly discourage a social worker from conducting it. However, on occasions when a supervisor has understood and appreciated the purpose of single-system evaluations, some supervisees have been able to discuss their findings safely and productively in case supervision conferences designed to help conference participants use their findings to become more effective practitioners.

Single-system evaluation research has proven vulnerable to misuse in another way also. Ironically, this misuse has occurred because of the increased popularity of and need for program evaluations. As evaluators and program managers have sought ways to demonstrate the effectiveness of services, they have sometimes turned to reports of single-system studies (conducted by social workers for their own use) as evidence of successful or unsuccessful programs. They have increasingly been used as indicators of outcome achievement. Like their use to evaluate individual professional competence, this trend could cause social workers to distort findings to look more favorable and thus to defeat the purpose of why they conducted single-system evaluations in the first place—to receive honest, objective feedback about their practice effectiveness.

ETHICAL ISSUES

We have alluded to a number of ethical concerns that have been voiced regarding the use of single-system evaluation research. Most of them, when examined carefully, are really nonissues. However, there are times when the practitioner must make decisions between what is best for the study and what is best for the client. Even the strongest advocates of single-system evaluation research would never suggest that the evaluation should take precedence over the welfare of those social worker practitioners are committed to help. Suppose that a single-system design requires a change, for example, the removal of an apparently successful intervention or the introduction of one that, on the basis of new knowledge of the client, may prove injurious. If so, the evaluation design must be altered, despite the fact that the decision may result in less valuable feedback to the social worker. Or, if the design calls for no change to occur and the current A or B phase appears to not be in the client's best interest, the design may have to be altered. Practice values should always take precedence over the researcher's need for knowledge. This same principle applies in all forms of research. Luckily, when single-system designs are used, the cost of ending the evaluation prematurely or changing the design for ethical reasons is rarely great. In contrast, in many other types of research, it can be expensive.

There are a few ethical issues that have yet to be resolved. They relate to what we discussed back in Chapter 2. Some claim that conducting evaluation research with one's clients comes dangerously close to a dual relationship and may therefore be unethical. Others suggest that the only way to avoid this conflict is to have clients sign consent forms, thus ensuring that the principle of voluntary informed consent has not been violated. Still others contend that single-system evaluation is just part of good practice; it is not research per se. Thus, a signed consent form is not necessary. They see nothing unethical about using a method to systematically monitor and evaluate one's practice to ensure that the best possible interventions are offered. In fact, they suggest, it would be irresponsible for a professional not to do so.

Different agencies have different rules and policies on the use of consent forms and the necessity of review of single-system proposals by institutional review boards (IRBs). Administrators in some settings (e.g., teaching hospitals) contend that a client receiving services has already agreed to participate in research and that no additional requirements must be met. Other settings may require consent forms and reviews by IRBs for their legal protection. Even universities have different policies on the issues. The university where one of the authors of this book once worked requires professors of students conducting single-system evaluations to submit a summary of all proposed studies to an IRB for approval and that all participants (clients) must sign an informed voluntary consent form. At the university where one of the authors now teaches, there are no such requirements, because single-system evaluation is seen more as a part of social work practice than as research.

Because there is a lack of consensus on a number of ethical issues related to single-system evaluation research, a social worker must be familiar with the rules and policies that are in force in the agency or other institution under whose auspices the research will be conducted. The rules or policies regarding single-system evaluation are generally not prohibitive and should not discourage social work professionals from using this method to evaluate their practice.

SUMMARY

In this chapter, we examined an evaluation method for practitioners who wish to receive feedback about their practice effectiveness. Single-system evaluation involves a careful monitoring of changes in certain behaviors, attitudes, perceptions, or other characteristics of clients or client systems. Design variations are employed to attempt to answer different questions, to attempt to control for the effect of other variables, and to be able to conduct evaluation in a way that is not in conflict with professional values and practice ethics. We discussed several of the designs that can be used, stressing their specialized usage and individual strengths and shortcomings. We demonstrated the importance (and the complexity) of interpreting the evaluation findings.

Log onto **www.mysocialworklab.com** and answer the following questions. (If you did not receive an access code to **MySocialWorkLab** with this text and wish to purchase access online, please visit www.mysocialworklab.com.)

1. **Watch the Core Competencies Video: Engagement, Assessment, Intervention, and Evaluation–**

Intervention. Describe a single-system design you might use to evaluate the progress of this client.

2. **Read the Case Study: Foster Care—Dan.** What are two problems you might work on with Dan in therapy? What is one way you might measure each of these problems if you were to conduct a single-system evaluation of this case?

PRACTICE TEST

1. Evidence-based practice dictates that the intervention be selected after
   a. statistical analyses are defined.
   b. a sample of participants is selected.
   c. a review of the available research literature is completed.
   d. measurement instruments are selected or created.

2. A research study that starts with a baseline phase and follows with an intervention phase is a(n)
   a. A design.
   b. B design.
   c. AB design.
   d. BA design.

3. A research study that has no baseline phase, introduces an intervention, withdraws the first intervention, and introduces a second intervention is a(n)
   a. ABC design.
   b. AB design.
   c. BA design.
   d. BC design.

4. A multiple-baseline design requires that
   a. the baselines are of differing length.
   b. all of the interventions start at the same time.
   c. more than one target problem must be measured.
   d. more than one measurement instrument must be used.

5. Describe an ABAB design that looks at a behavioral reward system used by a teacher to help reduce the number of outbursts by a student in class.

ASSESS YOUR COMPETENCE
Use the scale below to rate your current level of achievement on the following concepts or skills associated with each competency presented in the chapter:

1	2	3
I can accurately describe the concept or skil.	I can consistently identify the concept or skill when observing and analyzing practice activities.	I can competently implement the concept or skill in my own practice.

_____ Understanding how single-system research designs can be used to evaluate your practice

_____ Understanding the differences between the baseline and intervention phase

_____ Being able to draw a line graph using data gathered from a client

_____ Being familiar with the standard notation of single-system evaluations

8

Qualitative Research Methods

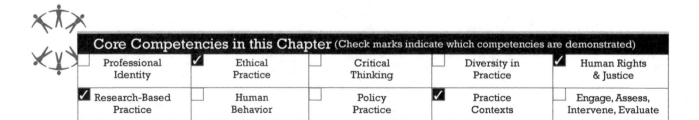

Core Competencies in this Chapter (Check marks indicate which competencies are demonstrated)									
☐	Professional Identity	✔	Ethical Practice	☐	Critical Thinking	☐	Diversity in Practice	✔	Human Rights & Justice
✔	Research-Based Practice	☐	Human Behavior	☐	Policy Practice	✔	Practice Contexts	☐	Engage, Assess, Intervene, Evaluate

We devote this chapter to an overview of qualitative research, describing specific qualitative research methods and offering criteria for evaluating qualitative research studies. Most qualitative researchers agree that there is no specific definition of *qualitative research*. It can be viewed more as a group of methods that follows certain key characteristics, such as studying the subjects in their natural settings, interpreting events through the meaning the subjects ascribe to them, and interpreting the data with an open-minded viewpoint. Anastas (2004) defines the key characteristics of qualitative research:

1. Flexibility of method and procedure during the conduct of the study, often in response to findings as they emerge;

2. The collection of relatively unstructured data to describe the phenomena of interest in the words or actions of those who live them;

3. A scope of study that includes the observational context of the study, usually the one in which the phenomena of interest naturally occur, as well as the decisions made during the conduct of the study;

4. A scope of study that includes the subjective experiences of the researcher and the research participant as data while also describing and analyzing them. (p. 58)

5. Many qualitative researchers advise locating a qualitative study within a specific epistemological tradition because there are significant differences among them. Five epistemological frameworks found in qualitative evaluation are postpositivism, pragmatism, phenomenology, interpretivism or constructivism, and critical, normative science. (p. 59)

As we discussed in earlier chapters, qualitative research studies generally do not include research hypotheses to be tested. Pure qualitative research is often interested in an ongoing process, event, or problem about which little is known; therefore, findings cannot be predicted. The researcher attempts to maintain a broad perspective in order to develop a comprehensive understanding of the phenomenon being studied, and the study is generally carried out in the setting where the phenomenon naturally exists. Holosko (2010) lists the following reasons why a researcher may select a qualitative approach to research: (1) one wishes to explore a topic or phenomenon of which little is actually known; (2) one wishes to study something that is sensitive and has emotional depth; (3) one may wish to capture an experience from the perspectives of those who live it and create meaning from it; (4) one may wish to delve inside a program and/or intervention; (5) one is a quantitative social work researcher who has reached an impasse in data collection, interpretation of data, and/or findings; and (6) one wishes to give voice to a group and merge social activism with research (pp. 345–346).

Qualitative data can consist of a variety of types, including words from an interview, field journals, minutes from meetings, television shows, newspaper or journal articles, and other historical documents. Some of the more commonly used techniques for gathering qualitative data follow:

▶ *In-person interviews.* Structured, semi-structured, or unstructured interviews are often used to collect qualitative data. Sometimes, data collection instruments are developed to assist in this process.

▶ *Focus groups and key informant interviews.* Discussion groups are often held in which a small group of people discuss the topic of interest. These can be structured or unstructured, and can allow the researcher to interview several people simultaneously.

The researcher attempts to maintain a broad perspective in order to develop a comprehensive understanding of the phenomenon being studied, and the study is generally carried out in the setting where the phenomenon naturally exists.

▶ *Systematic observations.* Observations are made and may be recorded on logs, in field journals, using audio/visual recordings, and so forth.

▶ *Secondary data.* Information that has already been gathered, including recordings or written materials, can be analyzed as qualitative data.

These data collection techniques are described in greater detail in Chapter 11. A variety of qualitative research methods have been developed to help the researcher accomplish the various goals of qualitative research. We will turn now to a discussion of some of the more frequently used methods.

THE CASE STUDY

The case study employs methods of data collection that rely heavily on the interviewing skills of researchers and their capacity to establish relationships of trust.

A case study is descriptive and generally more qualitative than quantitative. It combines observations of behavior with observations of attitudes and perceptions of research participants. The case study employs methods of data collection that rely heavily on the interviewing skills of researchers and their capacity to establish relationships of trust. As we shall see, there are some good reasons for the case study's continued popularity among social work researchers.

A case study is appropriate for situations where

▶ **little is known about the area being studied.** Topics for which there already exists a substantive body of relevant knowledge are better studied using other research designs;

▶ **it is impossible to draw a representative sample of participants.** Participants are selected on the basis of their availability and willingness to participate in the research. There is no way of knowing if they are typical of others who are involved in the same behavior.

Researchers conducting case studies collect their data from just one or a few cases. Usually the number does not exceed four or five. A case need not be an individual person; it can also be a family, a group, an organization, a community, or virtually any other system or entity that can be readily defined.

Case studies are a particularly good way to study areas that involve illegal behavior or some form of behavior that is not socially sanctioned, because the behavior is not available for study using more traditional research designs. Participants may be fearful about being found out and are usually very concerned about the confidentiality of what they reveal about themselves or their situation.

In a case study, interviewers must be receptive and nonjudgmental. They must be able to observe and interpret a wide variety of verbal and nonverbal communication, because data collected consist of both responses to preselected questions and the interviewer's observations of participants. Acquiring the trust of participants is absolutely essential. Relationships of trust are not easily developed and nurtured, because participants naturally tend to be guarded in what they say and to whom they say it. Participants may have learned how to give evasive answers to sensitive questions and may find it difficult to be candid. Social workers are ideally suited to conduct case studies. Their interviewing skills, nonjudgmental attitudes, and other professional values and ethics help to foster trust.

Case studies have often been misunderstood and sometimes maligned. Misunderstandings about case studies have sometimes led to a belief that they are less-than-scientific methods for knowledge building. Part of this misunderstanding may be attributable to misapplication of the label to research that is poorly designed and implemented. For example, sometimes, researchers have conducted some other type of research using a very small sample of research participants. In order to deflect criticism of their work and the credibility of their findings, they have erroneously applied the case study label to their research design.

Suitable Topics

There are many problem areas that are well suited to a case study design: different aspects of substance abuse, sexual deviance, white-collar crime, or any problem area about which little is known. It should be remembered that the list of problems suitable for a case study is ever changing. Once more is known about a problem, or once a problem is no longer considered socially unacceptable, researchers would be able to move to a different type of research to gather data from a larger sample. An example of this is a study by one of the authors (Weinbach, 1989), in which he conducted a case study on "secret survivors," people who had experienced the sudden death of a partner with whom they were involved in a long-term extramarital affair. At that time, the case study was appropriate for studying this problem, because extramarital affairs were not a topic that people freely discussed. A great deal of trust had to be developed between the researcher and participant before the participants would share feelings of grief over the death of their loved one. But less than a decade later, changing societal values and the accumulation of other exploratory studies of the problem had moved our understanding of the problem beyond the point where a case study would be appropriate. A more recent example is a study by Harding and Hamilton (2009), in which the researchers used the case study design to determine the extent that abuse and coercion influenced the decision of homeless women to engage in sex work. Another case study (Bergen & Ezzy, 2009) looked at the influence of mass media on the recent growth of interest in the Wiccan religion. Every year, problems emerge that are appropriate for research using a case study design, as others are deleted from the list.

Culturally sensitive social work practice is another area often studied using the case study approach. Research may look at interventions that have been studied with the dominant cultural groups, but have not specifically focused on certain minority groups. Other studies may look specifically at issues that are relevant to a particular ethnic or cultural group and analyze the effects of interventions taking these cultural phenomena into consideration. An example of this is a case study by Trinidad (2009) that studied the effects of colonization on Hawaiian youth, including persistent structural discrimination and loss of land and indigenous ways of knowing. This case study of a community-based youth program analyzed how these issues influence the risk, treatment and prevention of youth violence, suicide, substance abuse, and juvenile delinquency. Semi-structured interviews were conducted and then analyzed using content analysis (Chapter 4). The researchers used critical indigenous qualitative research to build a model for violence prevention that provides opportunities for active participation by the Native Hawaiian young adults.

Research-Based Practice

Once a substantial amount of research has been conducted on a subject area, why are case studies rendered less appropriate for further research?

Strengths and Limitations

Case studies enable researchers to achieve insights (such as how people feel about and experience certain phenomena) that cannot be obtained using more quantitative methods. They also are among the most interesting and gratifying types of research that can be conducted. A researcher conducting a case study can experience a feeling of being on the very cutting edge of knowledge building about a problem or question.

A major limitation of the case study is its inability to generate knowledge that could be described as definitive. Any conclusions should be carefully qualified. Because the number of participants is small and because they cannot be considered representative, few real conclusions emerge from case histories. Often, the most that can be said about data collected is something like "These are some of the problems that were found," "These are some of the ways that some people experience them," or "This is what some people think can be done about them." A case study does not allow the researcher to generalize beyond the research participants. Thus, the external validity of any findings is low or even nonexistent. Findings are often used as the starting point for other types of research.

GROUNDED THEORY

Grounded theory is one of the best known and one of the purest types of qualitative research. It falls in the exploratory-descriptive area. It is more likely to be cross-sectional than longitudinal in the purest sense; however, data collection can occur over an extended period of time and entail the use of multiple interviews with the same research participants. It relies heavily on skillful interviewing and a specialized form of data analysis. Grounded theory research seeks to learn what meanings people give to certain events in their lives. Like most qualitative research, it seeks to generate hypotheses, not test them, and attempts to build theory from data, in contrast to quantitative research, which often tests theories using data.

Researchers conducting grounded theory research constantly monitor and reshape their developing theories. The method involves a recurring process of proposing (on the basis of analysis of completed interview data) and checking and verifying what has been proposed (with subsequent interviews). In grounded theory research, sample selection, data collection, and data analysis occur simultaneously rather than in a preestablished sequence. Analysis of data gathered early in the study guides and shapes subsequent sample selection and the focus of future data collection. Researchers use emerging theoretical categories to influence both the ways in which subsequent data collection will be accomplished and from whom. For example, in early interviews, researchers may begin by asking general research questions on the basis of whatever clues the literature may provide as to what they might find. If some questions turn out to be irrelevant or nonproductive, they are dropped in subsequent interviews. Other, new questions, suggested by what they learned in earlier interviews, may be added. Similarly, if certain types of participants seem to be providing more enlightenment for the emerging theories than others, subsequent interviews may target only those people who show the greatest potential to verify (or refute) their theories.

Despite its somewhat unconventional approaches to data collection and case sampling, grounded theory is definitely not a haphazard or unscientific method of conducting research. It employs a systematic sequence of steps. For example, after one batch of data is collected (often using DVD recordings of interviews), the process of analyzing and conceptualizing it, referred to as coding, is begun. In the early stages of analysis, a process called open coding is used. It entails broadly conceptualizing what the data seem to mean and beginning to categorize them. It requires a careful dissection of interviews, sometimes word by word. Questions such as "What is this?" or "What does this seem to mean?" are common at this stage of the data analysis.

Later, two other types of coding, axial coding and selective coding, are used. Eventually, as proposed relationships between categories gain support as more data are collected, the researcher produces what is referred to as a story line, a brief narrative description of what was observed. This is analyzed and distilled further to form what is called a core category. Finally, a theory or hypothesis emerges as a product of the research. We looked at a study by Taylor (1998) in our earlier discussion of dual-role relationships in Chapter 2. In her research on parents who experienced the death of an adult child to AIDS, Taylor developed the theory statement, "Parents of persons with AIDS employ a combination of spiritual strengths and self-talk, along with a network of social supports and confidants, to arrive at a level of acceptance and confidence" (p. 237). Note that several terms in the statement (*spiritual strengths*, *self-talk*, *social supports*, *confidants*, *acceptance*, and *confidence*) were codes that the researcher developed through the process of analyzing the interviews and conceptualizing what was heard and observed.

Grounded theory is based on the premise that the meanings that people give to events in their lives are important in understanding their responses to the events and their resilience after. It is based primarily on theories of symbolic interaction, which hold that people construct their own meanings for events in part on the basis of their interactions with others. Grounded theory research thus seems especially well suited to acquiring the kinds of knowledge needed by social workers. Conducting it also requires many of the very attributes (interviewing skills, ability to form relationships, and so forth) that they possess.

Content analysis (see Chapter 4) is often used in conjunction with grounded theory as a way of analyzing all types of data, including interviews, journals, meeting minutes. One recent study (Takahashi et al., 2009) used the grounded theory approach along with content analysis to examine the effects of Internet-based social support groups on people with depression. Ayon (2009) used grounded theory methods to complete a content analysis of the paths to mandated child welfare services experienced by Mexican families who recently had immigrated to the United States.

ETHNOGRAPHIC RESEARCH

Ethnographic research is primarily descriptive research. It is most likely to be cross-sectional but is sometimes more longitudinal, that is, it is conducted over an extended period of time to record changes. Ethnographic research uses a combination of quantitative and qualitative research methods to answer research questions about individuals within their social context. It entails observations and measurement of behaviors (quantitative), but it also seeks to understand the beliefs, attitudes, values, social roles, social structures, and norms of behavior in social environments that are different from that of the researcher (qualitative). It often relies on various forms of systematic observation (see Chapter 11) to accomplish these goals.

Ethnographic methods were first developed in the field of anthropology to guide participant observation and qualitative field research of Western investigators studying behavior in primitive societies. However, ethnographic methods are now also used to understand subgroups within modern dominant cultures. Those subgroups may exist based on shared race, culture, class, religion, or some other characteristic that in some way differentiates the subgroup from the mainstream culture.

Two concepts embedded in ethnographic research methods are *emic* and *etic* perspectives. The emic perspective is that of the insider who is indigenous to the group being studied. This perspective is an experiential one based on an individual having been socialized to daily living in the culture and participating fully in all its psychosocial aspects. The etic perspective is that of the outsider—the stance traditionally assumed by researchers who study a culture that is not their own. An assumption of ethnographic research is that each perspective has advantages and disadvantages. For example, although the emic perspective permits an intricate understanding of even the most subtle cultural nuances, its requirement of familiarity with the cultural context may fail to raise critical questions about why things are the way they are or what maintains the status quo. On the other hand, although the etic perspective may miss important cultural nuances, it allows researchers to raise questions of context and purpose that would never occur to an insider. Ethnographic research attempts to blend these two perspectives by allowing the outside investigator to function as an insider, through participant observation and other methods that will enhance the understanding of the cultural context. As in other types of research that rely on participant observation, the extent to which the very presence of the outsider changes the natural order of the cultural dynamics of insiders (reactivity) is a potential source of distortion of data thus collected.

Goodson-Lawes (1994) describes a particularly useful application of ethnographic methods in social work research. The researcher used ethnographic research to study families of Mexican and Vietnamese immigrants. Researchers lived with the families to understand the consequences of immigration for family functioning and family structure. They learned their language and took part in the daily life of the families. They became a normal presence in their homes. Events, reactions, emotions, and interactions were carefully recorded in detailed journals.

Although participant observation is the data collection methodology most often associated with ethnographic research, there now are other methodological approaches that can help investigators understand different cultures. These include eco-mapping, geographic information system mapping, formal and informal interviews, life histories, kinship charts, and analysis of religious practices, myths, music, and other forms of folklore.

Because of negative historical and political encounters between ethnic communities and mainstream governmental or social welfare institutions, gaining access to study samples in ethnic communities may be problematic. Mistrust of motives for the research and fear of how the data may be used are frequently expressed concerns. Many ethnic communities have been used as study sites, with little or no feedback on study outcomes. Even when feedback has been given, it sometimes has not been in a form that is helpful in addressing community problems.

Many researchers conduct key informant surveys to assist them in conducting ethnographic research. They consist of completing unstructured interviews with or mailing open-ended questionnaires to knowledgeable individuals and community leaders. These data are used to gain the advice and support of people who can offer an insider's perspective on their research efforts. Such surveys or interviews may be especially useful when the researcher is undertaking an exploratory investigation that requires an understanding of an unfamiliar context or setting.

The emic perspective is that of the insider who is indigenous to the group being studied. The etic perspective is that of the outsider—the stance traditionally assumed by researchers who study a culture that is not their own.

Practice Contexts

In what ways would living with the research participants potentially change the data collected by the researcher?

Key informants can be helpful in several ways. They can provide guidance on where to find information and resources on topics of study interest, how to access and gain participation of study participants, and how to interpret study findings. Key informant surveys are also a way of forging alliances with community leaders and influential citizens who can endorse the research enterprise. Who is a potential key informant? The answer to this question sometimes is hard to determine in ethnic communities. Leaders designated by funding sources or university advisory boards may not be regarded as leaders by the members of their ethnic group. Butler (1992) notes, for example, that whereas funding sources may rely on academic credentials, work experience, or political connections to select leaders, members of some African-American communities are more likely to locate leadership in individuals who embody the community values of spirituality, wisdom, strength of character, and style. This suggests that key informants should be selected on the basis of a wide variety of criteria based on the values and ethics of the ethnic community involved in the research.

One example of recent ethnographic research is a study by Haight (2002), which focuses on the spiritual socialization of African-American children through the African-American Baptist church and Sunday school. Many researchers have discussed the sociocultural significance of the church in the history of the African-American community. Haight looked at adult-child interactions, storytelling, and elderly Sunday school teachers focusing on the role of religion in the development of resilience among African-American children and families.

Ethical Practice

What possible ethical issues might a researcher face in conducting an ethnographic study of a group of Mexican immigrants?

Smith (2009) completed an ethnographic study of Afghan refugees in California to illustrate effective ethnographic research methods. She demonstrates how to contact gatekeepers and other members within the community to help preserve autonomy, ensure confidentiality, build trust, and improve the accuracy of the results.

Some ethnic communities have set up stringent review and approval procedures before permission to conduct research is granted. Notable among these are some of the Native-American tribal groups. Any researcher wishing to conduct studies that are on tribal lands or involve people who are members of their tribal group must be prepared to comply with their particular approval process. Typically, researchers must present a proposal before a tribal, community, or village governing body that exercises some degree of control over the research process. Beauvais and Trimble (1992) found the following guidelines in place in one Native-American tribe: (1) assignment of a tribal or village member to monitor study implementation; (2) community's right to review and edit guidelines concerning respondent selection procedures; (3) community's right to review and edit questionnaires, interview schedules and field notes, and so on; (4) community's right to review and edit research reports and restrict or prevent the circulation and distribution of findings; and (5) ownership of the raw data and findings granted to the tribe or village. There are a few tribes that forbid any outside research within their boundaries; as sovereign states, they can legally do so.

It is to the researcher's advantage to understand the specific historical and cultural traits of the target community to (1) anticipate the degree and nature of resistance to participation and (2) seek advice from knowledgeable individuals on overcoming resistance to participation. For example, Kim, McLeod, and Shantzis (1992) looks specifically at factors that are necessary for the culturally competent evaluation of social service programs involving Asian-American and Pacific Island-American groups. They presented some practical

It is to the researcher's advantage to understand the specific historical and cultural traits of the target community to (1) anticipate the degree and nature of resistance to participation and (2) seek advice from knowledgeable individuals on overcoming resistance to participation.

issues that should be considered when developing and evaluating drug and alcohol abuse prevention programs within these communities, such as :

- Conduct data collection in private settings.
- Provide refreshments (because of the importance of food and communal meals in social gatherings).
- Use personal contacts, such as telephone calls or word-of-mouth invitations, to invite participation in the study, rather than sending formal letters for appointments.
- Compensate respondents for their time (because research and evaluation are less important to many Asian-Americans than work in exchange for compensation).
- Provide transportation and child care (because many Asian-American families are accustomed to having children present at semiformal gatherings).

Some recent research has looked at utilizing the Internet in gathering data for ethnographic research. Garcia, Standlee, Bechkoff, and Cui (2009) look at the strengths and weaknesses of technologically mediated communications. While such communications prevent the researcher from directly observing the participant, they enlarge the possible pool of participants and can allow the participant to remain anonymous. The authors offer suggestions on how to conduct participant observations and interviews, how to obtain access to settings and subjects, and how to deal with specific ethical issues related to Internet usage. For a more thorough discussion of the use of ethnographic research methods, see Lowery (2010).

CROSS-CULTURAL RESEARCH

Cross-cultural research is related to ethnographic research; it is primarily descriptive research, is it interested in looking at people within the context of their ethnic community, and it employs both quantitative and qualitative methods. However, it has its own unique focus—it seeks to describe cultural similarities (universalities that exist across cultures) and differences between and among cultures. It is being used more frequently than in past years because of a number of factors, including the opening of previously sealed international borders, large migration streams, globalization of the economic market, international tourism, increased cross-cultural communication, and technological innovations that make communication and scholarship in other countries possible (Van de Vijver & Leung, 1997). In cross-cultural research, investigators face some unique methodological challenges usually related to definitions of theoretical constructs and their valid measurement in different cultural contexts. Other problems relate to obtaining a representative sample and accuracy of translation of data collection instruments into foreign languages. Some of these issues will be addressed in more detail in later chapters in this text.

Social workers wishing to conduct research and/or practice across multiple countries will be especially interested in cross-cultural studies of human behavior, family systems, and other social organizations, as well as epidemiological studies of health and mental health disorders and their treatment in various cultural contexts. Some cross-cultural research may also apply to the study of ethnic and racial groups within the North American culture.

One recent cross-cultural study (Dwairy et al., 2010) analyzed the differences between adolescents in nine countries. The researchers specifically looked at psychological disorders and how they differ across cultures on the basis of the presence of different parenting factors, such as control, consistency, and rejection. Leenaars et al. (2010) conducted a thematic analysis of sixty suicide notes drawn from Turkey and the United States to identify common cultural themes as well as specific differences. They found more common factors than differences, although they did find that suicide notes written by Turkish subjects more often indicated that there were reasons for the suicide that were not included in the suicide note. The authors conclude that there is much to be learned through cross-cultural research in the field of suicidology.

Marin and Marin (1991) offer several suggestions for researchers who plan to undertake cross-cultural research. These suggestions are designed to reduce the risk of cultural encapsulation (i.e., depending entirely on one's own cultural frame of reference to formulate assumptions and define research constructs) and increase cultural relativity (i.e., the ability to understand behavior, attitudes, and values within the context of the culture in which it occurs). Suggested strategies include the following:

▶ Cultural immersion in the group to be studied.
▶ The obtaining of information directly from cultural minorities about values and normative behavior rooted in the culture (i.e., what is normal and what is pathological for that specific culture).
▶ Collaboration with key informants from the culture to be studied on all aspects of the study design prior to initiating the study.

FEMINIST RESEARCH

Feminist research is distinguished primarily by two things—its focus and its purpose. It is research that seeks to build knowledge about women, specifically, about their unique problems and the social institutions that affect them. When the label *feminist research* is used to describe a research study, it conveys little about what research methods were used. That is because feminist research employs all available methods, often in combination. Feminist research runs the gamut in relation to the broad descriptions described in earlier chapters. It can be predominantly quantitative or qualitative and exploratory, descriptive, or (less frequently) explanatory and employ cross-sectional, longitudinal, or pretest-posttest designs.

Goals and Assumptions

In her work on feminist research, Shulamit Reinharz (1992) points out that feminist research relates to "women's ways of knowing," a concept developed by others who have observed that women acquire knowledge differently than men. Feminist research is designed to hear the voices and other communications that more traditional, male-oriented approaches to knowledge building may miss. That would seem to suggest that (1) it is only qualitative research and (2) it can be conducted only by women. Both of these assumptions would be incorrect. However, it is conducted by people (men and women) who generally identify themselves as feminists or at least are concerned with the status and well-being of women.

Feminist research should be regarded as research both for and about women. It is often a form of action research: research designed to bring about change in women's lives by confronting sexism and attempting to alter those social institutions that may promote or perpetuate it. It results in consciousness raising and awareness of women's issues. The fact that feminist researchers study problems such as rape, sexual harassment, sexism, and salary inequity stimulates reflection and discussion about these issues by others.

Feminist research rests on the assumption that gender is critical to understanding women and culture. Thus, gender is a central focus. It has produced a wealth of data about women. For example, within the past two decades, knowledge about domestic violence, marital rape, women's health issues, and women's work at home and in the community has been developed. Knowledge derived from feminist research is used to validate women's lives and experiences and is useful for understanding women's issues, problems, and strengths. It also has been used to suggest additional needed research relevant to women and to influence the development of social policy that directly affects women.

A Response to Traditional Research Methods

Knowledge developed through feminist research is often contextual and relative. This is justified by feminist scholars on the basis of the assertion that traditional approaches to scientific research assume an objectivity about the world that is irrelevant to women's lives.

More traditional methods of inquiry are believed to ignore and distort women's realities. For example, many widely accepted measurement procedures were developed by and standardized using men, thus making their value in understanding women's experiences questionable. In addition, many life experiences that are important to the lives of women, such as sexual harassment in the workplace and post-partum depression, were historically neglected by researchers using traditional research methods.

Human Rights & Justice

Why do you think research has historically concentrated on men in our society?

Feminist researchers have described the more traditional methods of inquiry (especially experimental designs) as being antithetical to the purposes of feminist research. For example, experimental research generally is conducted "in the laboratory" under tightly controlled research conditions. Feminists have argued that these types of designs have a sexist bias in the ways that questions are asked and answered and the way that data are interpreted. They assert that the artificiality of the research laboratory is not conducive to a true understanding of people and their relationships. In addition, it is asserted that traditional research methods have tended to exploit and objectify women.

Feminist research, with its emphasis on more egalitarian approaches to interacting with research participants, is believed to be less exploitive than traditional methods in its approach to data collection. The relationship between the researcher and the person being studied is more one of equality. That is why research participants often are referred to as *research partners* rather than research participants.

Feminist research is conducted within the context of an understanding of feminist perspectives of culture; it uses these perspectives to select methods for study of a research problem and for interpreting data. Feminist researchers also argue that their methods of conducting research allow them to critique knowledge developed by others using more traditional models of inquiry and to attempt to reconcile their findings with those of others. Doing this can put a whole new meaning on what a researcher learns directly, how the researcher interprets the findings of others, and how the data collection experience mutually affects the research participants.

Design Characteristics

Methodologically, feminist research has been described using such terms as *open, contextual, relative, interpretive, experiential, empowering,* and *social change–oriented.* These descriptors suggest the wide range of research designs used by and for feminist scholarship. Feminist research relies heavily on a variety of qualitative (and, less frequently, quantitative) techniques. Feminist research designs are often hybrids, combining features of two or more approaches to knowledge building. For example, quantitative data may be collected and analyzed, but then participants may be asked if they would like to meet with a member of the research team to discuss their responses more fully to more clearly communicate the meaning of their answers to the researchers.

Like some of the other forms of research described in this chapter, feminist methods are characterized by relatively open relationships between researchers and research participants. Researchers may get involved with the lives of participants by establishing relationships with them that go beyond simple data collection. They often serve as resources to participants by providing information about community resources or may assist them in bringing about social change. The relationship between researchers and their participants is viewed as critical to the development of knowledge about women. Questions asked often emanate from researchers' own concerns and experiences, rather than out of some previously developed interview schedule or agenda. The knowledge acquired through this kind of interpersonal interaction leads to an interpretive approach to data analysis that makes no claims of total objectivity.

Feminist research usually does not emphasize the testing of prespecified hypotheses. It focuses instead on the development of a wide range of information and understanding. It has been described as emergent; it is not highly controlled. It often seeks to gather a wide array of descriptive, contextual information to provide data that are as complete as possible for analysis.

A predominantly qualitative approach to data collection and *analysis— naturalistic inquiry* (a form of unstructured systematic observation)—attempts to document and understand women's behavior as influenced by their social contexts. Observations may be made in a variety of field settings, such as women's health organizations, women's work and social groups, and other groups and communities to which women belong. The data in naturalistic inquiries, as in most qualitative research, are typically rich in detail. In naturalistic inquiry, the researcher allows the patterns and themes contained in the data observed to emerge naturally.

There are many excellent examples of naturalistic inquiries in the literature. Many of these studies have been conducted by feminist sociologists and anthropologists. One study (Gagne, 1992) sought to better understand wife abuse in a rural community. On the basis of the findings from her naturalistic inquiry of violence and social control, the researcher conceptualized three categories of control. She then used them to assert that domestic violence is dependent on cultural and social structures that condone men's domination of women and that, without them, violence would be less effective as a means of social control.

Examples

Virtually every research method described so far has been used in feminist research. On the basis of our description, it should come as no surprise to the reader that some of the qualitative methods described earlier in this chapter (e.g., grounded theory) are frequently used. Although feminist research has often used quantitative methods, since this chapter focuses on qualitative research methods, we will focus here on feminist research that has utilized mainly qualitative methods.

Semi-structured, open-ended questionnaires (administered by the researcher) are useful when the purpose of a study is to have participants respond to certain questions in their own words. Participants often become involved both in the interpretation of the meanings of their responses and in the refinement of data collection methods to be used in future research. Typically, this method of data collection entails the use of multiple sessions with participants. Because the researcher often cannot anticipate the type of information that will be shared, the interviews often are a process of discovery both for participants and the feminist researcher.

What are some examples of past descriptive feminist research? How was it conducted? Here, we will look at a few examples of the many areas that feminist research has explored: date rape, single mothers, and eating disorders.

Date Rape Research

Prior to the mid-1980s, there were few (if any) references to date rape in the social science literature. Studies looking at various forms of violence against women were developed partially as an outgrowth of earlier research and because of changing societal definitions of what connotes permissible levels of violence. One qualitative study (Lipman, 2002) used semi-structured clinical interviews to explore women's relational and sexual functioning after experiencing a date rape. Some of the major themes she found were distrust in men, feelings of powerlessness, and lack of desire and pleasure in the sex act. She also found the effects were more pronounced among women who were virgins at the time of the rape than among women who had previous sexual experiences.

Single Mothers

Other feminist research has focused on the challenges and needs of single mothers. Harmon (2010) completed interviews with thirty single white mothers who had children of mixed race and found that these mothers experienced significant levels of racism and prejudice aimed at their children as well as social disapproval themselves. Another qualitative study (Reid, 2009) explored the social support network of single African-American mothers living in a small town's public housing community. The researcher found that most of these single mothers identified family members as their primary source of support. In addition, while communication with neighbors in the public housing community was often limited, most of the mothers had exchanged vital resources, such as food or transportation, with at least one other single mother living in the same housing project.

Eating Disorders

Because eating disorders have historically affected more women than men, feminist research has focused some attention on this area. Malson and Burns (2009) have analyzed feminist approaches to eating disorders and the shifts in the way cultures define gender, body weight, body management, and food. The researchers contend that eating disorders should not be viewed as static individual mental illness. Instead, eating disorders are viewed as conditions that constantly change in response to cultural changes experienced by the individual.

Brown, Weber, and Ali (2008) use a feminist narrative approach to analyze cultural influences that not only shape the eating disorders but also can be used to guide the treatment of eating disorders. They argue that a combination of feminist and narrative treatment approaches can be more effective in working with women with eating disorders than more traditional approaches.

As we noted earlier, it is the specialized purpose and focus of feminist research that gives it its identity. Feminist research is designed specifically to develop needed knowledge about women and the social institutions that impact them.

PARTICIPATORY ACTION RESEARCH

Participatory action research offers research participants the chance to conduct research on their own behalf. The researcher serves as a resource to the participants in the study, while the participants not only define the problem(s) to be studied but also are responsible for the research design needed to study the problem. It is argued that research has too often been in the hands of the majority groups rather than in the hands of those in the groups who often benefit most from increasing knowledge in the problem area. By placing the information in the hands of those who most need it, research participants are empowered to find the answers and help themselves and others.

The focus of participatory action research is on some action or change based on the outcome or information generated by the research. It is used primarily to give a voice to marginalized groups of people. A recent study using participatory action research methods (Happell et al., 2009) explored and evaluated the mental health practices in the pediatric unit of a rural general hospital. Nursing staff were given the opportunity to actively participate in the design, direction, and outcomes of the research study. Focus groups with the nurses revealed that the nurses felt they were inadequately trained to provide mental health services to children. The participants (nurses) then requested further training by mental health specialists as well as the development of new policies and clinical guidelines to facilitate their care of mental health patients.

In another participatory action research study (Van der Velde, Williamson, & Ogilvie, 2009), focus groups with immigrants and refugees were conducted to identify practical strategies to encourage engagement and participation in immigrant and refugee communities. As in most of the methods described in this chapter, it is generally categorized as a qualitative research method, but the design of a participatory action research study can be predominantly qualitative, predominantly quantitative, or a mixture of both types of methods. For further information on completing participatory action research, see Blum, Heinonen, and White (2010).

EVALUATION CRITERIA FOR QUALITATIVE RESEARCH

It is clear that the research methods and epistemological frameworks used in qualitative research are diverse. Because of this diversity, it has been challenging to create a set of evaluation criteria for qualitative research. A group of social workers (Shek, Tang, & Han, 2005) evaluated research studies using qualitative methods that were published in the social work literature between 1990 and 2003. On the basis of their results, which showed the quality of many qualitative research studies to be not high, they concluded that social workers need additional training in qualitative evaluation and that social workers conducting qualitative research should be sensitive to issues of quality. Another outcome of this study was a set of criteria for evaluating qualitative research studies. Shek et al. combined a number of criteria that have commonly been adopted in the field of qualitative research to create a comprehensive list of criteria that covers the broad and diverse types of methods used in qualitative research. These criteria include the following:

1. Explicit statement of the philosophical base of the study (this includes a clear statement as to why specific approaches are chosen, such as grounded theory, ethnography)
2. Justifications for the number and nature of the participants of the study
3. Detailed description of the data collection procedures
4. Discussion of the biases and preoccupations of the researchers (this is particularly important since it is especially difficult to eliminate biases in qualitative research)
5. Description of the steps taken to guard against biases or arguments that should or could not be eliminated
6. Inclusion of measures of reliability, such as interrater reliability (the stability of interpretations across different researchers) and intrarater reliability (the stability of interpretations of the same researcher at different times)
7. Inclusion of measures of triangulation in terms of researchers and data types
8. Inclusion of peer-checking and member-checking procedures
9. Consciousness of the importance and development of audit trails
10. Consideration of alternative explanations for the observed findings
11. Inclusion of explanations for negative evidence
12. Clear statement of the limitations of the study (p. 184)

Since there is such a wide range of goals and procedures involved with the various qualitative methods, one should not expect every qualitative research study to meet all of these criteria. Criteria may have to be selected on the basis of the theory base of the researchers. However, all researchers using qualitative methods should keep these criteria in mind to ensure the highest possible quality of their study. Shek et al. (2005) also suggested four possible reasons why the quality of the qualitative research may have been lower than expected: (1) Some methods, such as peer checking and member checks, that could enhance the quality of a qualitative study can be extremely costly in terms of time and money; (2) Journals rarely provide guidelines or standards to report qualitative research findings; (3) Space constraints in academic journals may force qualitative researchers to report their findings in a truncated and inadequate manner; and (4) Inadequate training in qualitative research methods among social workers may lower the quality of subsequent qualitative research (p. 191).

SUMMARY

We focused on six types of research that rely most often on qualitative approaches to knowledge building: case studies, grounded theory, ethnographic research, cross-cultural research, feminist research, and participatory action research. Each is characterized by (1) a general purpose; (2) the data sources they rely on most frequently; and (3) the primary research activity that is employed. Box 8.1 summarizes the major characteristics of each of the methods that were discussed in the chapter. We also discuss evaluation criteria that can be used by researchers and the readers of research reports to evaluate the quality of qualitative research studies.

Box 8.1 Qualitative Research Methlods

Label	Purpose	Major Data Source(s)	Major Activities
Case study	Gain beginning insights	In-person interviews	Speaking, listening
Grounded theory	Develop theories, hypotheses	In-person interviews	Conceptualizing, verifying
Ethnographic	Understanding of a culture	Interviews, observation	Field research methods
Cross-cultural	Identify cultural differences	Interviews, observation	Field research methods
Feminist	Empowerment/advocacy	Widely varying	Widely varying
Participatory action	Social action/change	Interviews, focus groups	Suggesting new policies and guidelines

Succeed with **mysocialworklab**

Log onto **www.mysocialworklab.com** and answer the following questions. (If you did not receive an access code to **MySocialWorkLab** with this text and wish to purchase access online, please visit www.mysocialworklab.com.)

1. **Watch the Core Competencies Video: Diversity in Practice: Building Self-awareness.** If the social worker in this video had been Caucasian instead of one of African descent, how might have the early part of the interview process been handled differently?

2. **Read the Case Study: Community Practice: Golem, Albania.** What are two issues you may want to look at in an ethnographic research study on this community?

PRACTICE TEST

1. Case study would generally not be appropriate when
   a. the subject area involves some form of behavior that is not socially sanctioned.
   b. it is impossible to draw a representative sample of participants.
   c. there is a great deal known about the subject area.
   d. the subject of the study is a family or organization rather than an individual.

2. Which of the following statements does not apply to grounded theory?
   a. The design entails a recurring process of proposing and then checking and verifying what has been proposed.
   b. Sample selection, data collection, and data analysis all occur in a very definite sequence.
   c. Emerging theoretical categories influence the way subsequent data collection is carried out.
   d. The design seeks to learn what meanings people give to certain events in their lives.

3. All of the following are strategies for cross-cultural research except
   a. cultural encapsulation.
   b. cultural relativity.
   c. cultural immersion.
   d. obtaining information directly from cultural minorities.

4. The etic and emic perspectives in ethnographic research refer to
   a. who the participants in a research study are.
   b. whether the study is conducted in the clinic or in the natural setting.
   c. whether the researcher is an insider or outsider to the culture being studied.
   d. what data is collected in the study.

5. What are four commonly used data collection techniques used in qualitative research?

ASSESS YOUR COMPETENCE Use the scale below to rate your current level of achievement on the following concepts or skills associated with each competency presented in the chapter:

1	2	3
I can accurately describe the concept or skill.	I can consistently identify the concept or skill when observing and analyzing practice activities.	I can competently implement the concept or skill in my own practice.

_____ Being able to identify commonly used qualitative data collection techniques

_____ Being familiar with the qualitative research methods: case study, grounded theory, ethnograhic research, cross-cultural research, feminist research, and participatory action research

_____ Understanding the strengths and weaknesses of each of these methods

_____ Understanding the criteria for evaluating a qualitative research study

9

Sampling Issues and Options

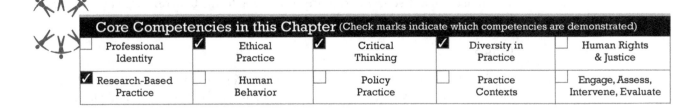

Core Competencies in this Chapter (Check marks indicate which competencies are demonstrated)				
☐ Professional Identity	☑ Ethical Practice	☑ Critical Thinking	☑ Diversity in Practice	☐ Human Rights & Justice
☑ Research-Based Practice	☐ Human Behavior	☐ Policy Practice	☐ Practice Contexts	☐ Engage, Assess, Intervene, Evaluate

In the previous chapters, there were numerous references to two important components of research design: sampling (sometimes referred to as *case sampling*) and measurement. Because of their importance (especially in quantitative research), we will examine them in greater detail in this chapter and the three that follow.

In social work research, a sample is often a group of people chosen to represent a larger group of people. For example, it might be a group of active clients with some problem who are chosen to represent all clients with that problem. Or it might be a group of staff members who are chosen to participate in a focus group. Samples can also be inanimate, for example, a group of

- case records selected to estimate the extent of some problem, such as the error rate in service eligibility determination;
- social agencies selected from among all agencies that serve a certain client population;
- research reports that meet certain criteria and are evaluations of a particular method of intervention in a meta-analysis (see Chapter 4);
- records of human communication, such as the minutes of business meetings, recordings of oral histories, television programs, or Internet Web sites, that are used for content analysis (see Chapter 4).

In exploratory studies in which the researcher hopes only to acquire a better understanding of a problem or the other phenomenon, samples are often chosen more for their availability than anything else. There can be little pretense that what is learned from them can be generalized to cases not studied. This is also the case in many studies that are primarily qualitative that, for example, seek to learn about the different ways that people perceive or experience a problem or an event and the meanings they attribute to it. In many descriptive studies and in explanatory ones that attempt to test hypotheses about relationships between variables (studies that tend to rely more on quantitative research methods), sampling methods are used that increase the likelihood that findings from the sample can be generalized beyond the sample, to the larger population. In short, every effort is made to produce findings that possess good external validity.

The reason for sampling is efficiency: by using one or more research samples, researchers hope to learn something at less cost using less time than would be involved if they had to study all of the people or objects in the population. Whether the research is designed to determine if there is support for hypotheses, describe a problem more accurately, or achieve any other purpose for which research is conducted, the composition of the research sample is important. Not just any sample will do. Researchers seek the sample or samples that will best accomplish their purpose, that is, samples that ensure to the extent possible the external validity of findings.

TERMINOLOGY

When used in a discussion of sampling, some terms take on very specific meanings. Let us look at some of the most important ones.

Case

A case (sometimes called an *element* if it refers to an inanimate object) is the basic unit of analysis in a given research study. If the unit of analysis is a person (as is often the situation in social work research), the term is used to denote each actual person who is selected for study. Collectively, those people selected as research participants for the study constitute the sample. The term *case* may also refer to many different units of analysis, for example, a family, a group, an organization, a community, or even a nation.

Universe, Theoretical Population, and Accessible Population

The word *universe* is sometimes used in discussions of sampling to refer to the entire collection of people (or elements) that share some defined characteristics. The universe is sometimes referred to as the theoretical population. Depending on the theoretical population being defined, the universe for a research study may never really be known. For example, suppose we try to define the universe of all incidents of child abuse in North America. We can never fully define this population, because (1) some incidents of child abuse are never reported; (2) there are always going to be cases that are currently being investigated; and (3) there are continually new cases being reported and others being closed. If we defined our population as all incidents of child abuse reported in the United States during a specific time period, we would come closer to being able to compile an accurate list. However, it would still be extremely difficult, because we would have to rely on records from hundreds of agencies across the country. The chance of our list of cases being completely accurate would be extremely low.

Another term, *accessible population* (we will use simply *population* after this initial discussion), has a somewhat narrower connotation. It refers to only those cases that theoretically might be selected as research participants, those that are potentially accessible to the researcher because of geography, time, methods of data collection, and budget limitations or other constraints. In the preceding example, we may be interested in the theoretical population of all incidents of child abuse in the country. However, it is obvious that we will never have access to those incidents that are not reported. Therefore, our accessible population will include only reported child abuse incidents.

Sampling Frame

When defining certain populations, we could create a perfect listing of all cases in our population. For example, if we wanted to survey all presidents of state universities in the country or all high school principals in our state, we could probably create a completely accurate listing as of some point in time. When defining other populations, such as all reported child abuse incidents, we would most likely never be able to compile a completely accurate listing. The actual listing of potential cases from which our sample is drawn is called the *sampling frame*. We hope that the sampling frame will be at least a reasonable approximation of the population. But we all know that lists, no matter how meticulously they have been compiled, often are incomplete or contain some people or objects that should not be included. For example, if we are interested in studying some characteristic of social work students, the population may be defined as all current BSW and MSW students at XYZ University, and the sampling frame may be an actual list of social work students supplied by the dean's office. It would not include all students who registered after the day the list was compiled, and it may contain the names of some students who recently have withdrawn from social work courses but have not completed the necessary paperwork or notified the dean.

A population is what we would like to use for selecting cases, whereas a sampling frame is an available list that is the next best thing to a population. Frequently, a sampling frame is all that is available. Then one has no choice but to use a sampling frame, knowing full well that it is not a 100 percent accurate representation of the population. When researchers study a problem that carries a social stigma or is illegal, use of a sampling frame is usually inevitable. In some cases, the sampling frame may not even be a close approximation of the population. For example, suppose that a researcher in Mississippi wishes to interview victims of date rape during the past six months to determine what percentage of victims seem to be suffering from post-traumatic stress disorder. No list of date rape victims in Mississippi for the time period may be available. But a sampling frame containing the names of at least some victims could be compiled with the help of local law enforcement officials within the state if they could be convinced that the researcher would protect participants' confidentiality and conduct the research ethically. The researcher might use this sampling frame, although it probably differs in some important ways from the population. For example, it would not contain the names of date rape victims who did not go to the police or refused to press charges against their attacker.

Sample

We have used the term *sample* many times in this book. What exactly does it mean? A sample is a subset of cases selected for study from among people or objects within a defined population. It is chosen to represent the population. If there are two or more groupings of cases within a sample, they are referred to as *subsamples*.

Generally, researchers conclude that it is unfeasible or unnecessary to study the entire population or all potential cases. The population may be too large and/or too costly to study. Or researchers may conclude that it is possible to learn almost as much (and at far less cost) by studying only a portion of the population (or sampling frame). So they select a sample of cases.

Representativeness

In Chapter 6, we mentioned the importance of using a representative sample in quantitative research. The representativeness of a sample impacts both the internal and external validity of research findings. Although it is desirable in all research, representativeness is less critical in most qualitative studies, which often do not seek support for hypotheses (so internal validity is not an issue) or to generalize their research findings from the sample to its population (so external validity is less of an issue).

Representativeness is one of two criteria generally applied in evaluating the quality of a research sample. It refers to the degree to which a research sample is similar to the population from which it was drawn. Thus, representativeness should be regarded as a relative term. Ideally, researchers would like to study cases that are identical in all respects to the members of the population from which they were selected. Of course, the only way that this can happen is if they do not sample at all, but study the entire population instead. But if they did, the major benefit of sampling (conservation of research resources) would be lost. Fortunately, perfect representativeness in every respect within a sample is not really necessary—a sample can be sufficiently representative of a population if it resembles the population as a whole with respect to a limited number of relevant variables, most often, the dependent, independent, and any potentially confounding variables.

In Chapter 6, we mentioned three sampling methods that are used in longitudinal studies: trend study, cohort study, and panel study. Generally, sample representativeness is important in this type of research. Longitudinal studies entail costly and time-consuming study of participants who, it is hoped, will provide an accurate picture of changes that occur within the population. A special problem in panel studies (which study the same group of participants over time) is the likelihood that participants may drop out or otherwise become unavailable as the study progresses. Because of death, participant mobility, or other forms of attrition, referred to as *experimental mortality*, the number of participants who are available over the entire course of the study often is much reduced from the number of participants who initially agreed to participate. If the causes for dropout are not related to central research questions, the problem can be handled by anticipating sizable participant loss and beginning with enough extra participants to absorb it. However, some participants may well drop out because of factors relevant to the central focus of the research. If this occurs, their presence can be missed and can affect the credibility of any research findings.

Size

The second criterion that is considered in assessing the quality of a research sample is the sample size. *Sample size* refers simply to the number of cases the sample contains, not to the percentage of the population or sampling frame that it contains. This is an important distinction and one often misunderstood. Although it seems logical that a sample that includes only a small percentage of the population could not possibly be a good sample, this is not necessarily true. Political pollsters using large samples (1,800 to 2,200) have been remarkably successful in recent years in predicting the results of most close national elections. Yet their samples consistently have included far less than 1 percent of registered voters. Why have they been so successful? A sample of 1,800 to 2,200 is large in the absolute sense. In addition, the cases within their samples were carefully selected using methods designed to increase the likelihood of the sample's representativeness.

In sampling, size and representativeness are interrelated. A sample's size affects its potential to be representative. For example, if we draw two samples, one larger than the other, and use the same method for drawing them, the larger sample is more likely to be representative of the population than the smaller one. However, the relationship between sample size and representativeness is not usually that simple and is not as direct as we might logically assume.

When is a sample considered to be large? When is it so small that it is almost surely not representative? Although these would seem like easy questions to answer, they are not. There is no general rule, no absolute definition of what is a large sample or a small one. To use one would be to rely on tradition, and as we discussed back in Chapter 1, that would be dangerous. A small sample is not one, for example, that is always less than 30, less than 100, and so forth; the same applies to what is a large sample. In short—it depends. However, there are several principles that address the issue of sample size and its relationship to representativeness. These principles assume that a sample is a random one (discussed later in this chapter) and relate to (1) the size of the population from which the sample is drawn and (2) the amount of variability within the population. For example:

1. If the number of people or elements in the population is small (e.g., less than 100), even a relatively small increase in sample size is likely to make the sample more representative. Conversely, if the number is large, adding a few more cases to the sample will most likely have little effect on its representativeness. A point of "diminishing returns" will have been reached.

2. If the number of people or elements in the population is small, the sample may have to include a fairly large percentage of the population (referred to as *sampling ratio* or *sample to population ratio*), perhaps 25 or 30 percent, to be sufficiently representative. If the population is very large (in the hundreds of thousands or even millions, as in the example of political polls mentioned earlier), a very small sampling ratio, 1 percent or even less, should provide a sufficiently representative sample.

3. If the population varies widely (heterogeneous) in relation to the variables being examined, a larger sample may be required to achieve sample representativeness than if the population is more similar in relation to the variables being examined (homogeneous).

These principles can be helpful in deciding what sample size is most likely to produce the degree of representativeness required. However, they still do not produce a formula for determining the correct sample size. Another factor to be considered in evaluating whether a sample size is appropriate for a given research study is the statistical analysis used. A sample can be considered too small if the sample or one or more of its subsamples is smaller than the size for which a statistical test was designed. Conversely, it is too large if it is larger than the size recommended for a given statistical test. If it is concluded that a sample is of an appropriate size for the statistical analysis being used and has been selected in such a way that it produces a high likelihood of representativeness, it is likely to be considered a good one, especially if the researcher hopes to produce findings that possess a high degree of external validity.

Sampling Error

There are two reasons why a sample may differ from its population: sampling error and sampling bias (see Box 9.1). The difference that occurs naturally when a sample is drawn from a population or sampling frame is referred to as *sampling error*. All samples, and especially smaller ones, are likely to differ from the population from which they are drawn. Even two or more identically sized samples drawn from the same population (e.g., two samples of twenty drawn independently from a class of social work students) are likely to differ regarding any variables that we may wish to study. The concept of sampling error is critical to an understanding of how certain types of statistical tests work (see Chapter 13). Sampling error can make variables appear to be related when they really are not, or it can hide true relationships between or among variables.

The relationship between sample size and the amount of sampling error present in a sample can be easily demonstrated by thinking of a class of fifty social work graduate students. Suppose the average age (referred to as the

Critical Thinking

Why would a population that varies widely in relation to the variables being examined require a larger sample size than a population that is more similar in relation to the variables of interest?

Box 9.1 Two Reasons Samples May Differ from the Population from Which They Were Drawn

1. **Sampling bias** The intentional or unintentional systematic distortion of a sample.

2. **Sampling error** The normal tendency of a sample to differ from its population.

mean in statistical analysis) of the class is 30, with most students being between 27 and 33. The oldest is 39, and the youngest is 21. The ages of the students might form a bell shape, or normal distribution, if we were to create a frequency polygon of everyone's ages.

If we were to draw a sample of five students from the class, we would not expect the average age of the sample of five to be exactly 30. It might be 28 or 32 or even 25 or 35. The difference between the mean of the sample and the mean of the class (population) would be the amount of sampling error in the sample. If we drew many repeated samples of five students from the class, most of the samples would not have a mean age of exactly 30. The average ages of the respective samples of five students would differ from the class mean (30) and from each other. Thus, most of the time, the mean age of any sample would be a poor estimate of the age of the class—the sample would not be very representative of the class for the variable "age."

Now suppose that we had drawn samples of fifteen students from the same population (class) of fifty. We would still expect the mean ages of most of the samples to not be exactly 30. However, we would expect that more of them to be closer to 30 than when we drew samples of only five. Why? Because with samples of fifteen, there is likely to be less sampling error than with samples of only five. A sample of five might contain, for example, five of the oldest students in the class. Then the sampling error might be large. In sampling fifteen students from the class, our first five selections might be the same five older students. But as we select more cases for the sample, the likelihood of drawing younger-than-average students (to balance off the first five) would now be increased, because the average age of the remaining pool of students would now be less than 30. As samples get larger, they begin to look more and more like their population. So, if we had drawn samples of forty-nine students each, we could expect that the average age of the students in the samples would be very close to the class average of 30. If we selected the entire population of all fifty students, there would be no sampling error. But this would defeat the purpose of sampling, which is to build knowledge in the most efficient way.

Since samples are likely to vary from their populations, we cannot assume that measurements of a sample's characteristics are the same as those of its population. But how much do they differ? An estimate of the similarity of a sample to its population can help us gauge to what degree a drawn sample is sufficiently representative of the population in relation to one or more variables. But how similar can we expect a given sample to be to its population?

There are methods and formulas to help us determine the minimum sample size that will produce an acceptably low sampling error (for more detailed discussions of these methods, see Cohen, 1988; Rosenthal, 2001; Weinbach & Grinnell, 2010). It is important to remember that it is the number of cases in a sample and the amount of variability within its population (and not simply the percentage of the population that a sample represents) that are important in estimating the amount of sampling error within a sample.

Research-Based Practice

Why are larger samples more likely to be representative of the population than smaller samples?

It is important to remember that it is the number of cases in a sample and the amount of variability within its population (and not simply the percentage of the population that a sample represents) that are important in estimating the amount of sampling error within a sample.

Sampling Bias

Even if a sample is relatively large and tables and/or statistical analysis seem to suggest that the amount of sampling error is estimated to be quite small, the sample still may not be adequately representative. It may contain too much *sampling bias*. Sampling bias refers to the systematic distortion of a sample. It can occur either intentionally or unintentionally. It is caused by such factors as the methods used to select a sample or when and where a sample was selected. A biased sample contains overrepresentation of some types of cases and underrepresentation of others (relative to the population from which it was drawn).

A biased sample can seriously limit the usefulness of the data collected by the researcher, especially in predominantly quantitative studies. If a sample does not adequately represent its population, nearly anything we find out about cases in the sample will be of limited value. We may know a great deal about a particular (biased) group of cases, but we will be unable to generalize this knowledge to the population from which the sample was drawn. Thus, the external validity of findings generated by a study of a badly biased sample (or of one containing too much sampling error, for that matter) would be low.

Some samples almost invariably contain sampling bias. For example, client satisfaction surveys tend to contain a disproportionately high number of responses from clients who are most satisfied with services. However, there are ways to decrease the likelihood that sampling bias will occur. By controlling the conditions under which a sample is selected using strategies discussed later in this chapter, we can increase the representativeness of research samples.

Statistic and Parameter

The terms *statistic* and *parameter* are closely related. Statistics describe the distribution of variables within samples. Parameters describe the distribution of variables within populations. In predominantly quantitative research studies, we often secure statistics from our sample data that we hope will tell us something about the parameters of the same variables within the population that the sample is supposed to represent. For example, we may calculate the mean (average) age of people within the sample (a statistic) and hope to be able to use that statistic as an estimate of the mean age of the population (a parameter). In those less common situations in which we attempt to study the entire population, we would summarize the findings of the research study as parameters. For example, if we conducted a thorough analysis of all active case records in a human service organization and then summarized the demographic characteristics of those clients currently being served, we would refer to our summaries as parameters.

Random Selection

Random selection entails drawing the cases for a sample or subsample so that all cases have an equal probability of being selected. It is designed to preclude sampling bias and produce a more representative sample. By enhancing sample representativeness, random selection can increase the external validity of research findings.

Random selection should not be confused with random assignment of cases to two or more subsamples, such as an experimental group and a control group. Random assignment relates more to design issues (Chapters 6–8) than to our discussion of sampling here. Random selection is used to increase the internal validity of research findings by controlling the most common threats to internal validity. In a research study, it is possible to have random selection without random assignment and vice versa. In experimental designs (Chapter 6), both are present.

Random Sample

A random sample is a sample or subsample that is drawn using random selection. There are distinct advantages to random samples. They control for sampling bias, by making it impossible for the researcher to inadvertently distort the sample in some systematic way. Random samples cannot eliminate sampling error. However, when random sampling has been done, researchers, using probability theory, can estimate the amount of sampling error within the sample and statistically determine the probability that certain relationships between variables within the sample were the work of sampling error (Weinbach & Grinnell, 2010).

Random samples are used in social work research when a representative sample is important. However, several factors explain why they are not used more frequently. To draw a random sample, we must have access to a list of all cases in a population or a sampling frame that is a good approximation of the population. Often such a sampling frame is not available, and even if it is available, the cost of acquiring a random sample from the sampling frame may be prohibitive. Many organizations that maintain such lists charge researchers who wish to use the list to draw random samples. Or it may simply be too expensive to collect data from cases in a random sample when cases are geographically scattered (e.g., when in-person interviews are the data collection method of choice).

There may also be ethical reasons why random samples are not used. For example, we could draw a random sample of current clients to receive an experimental treatment, but our knowledge of certain clients in the sample might suggest that they would more likely benefit from some other treatment or that they might likely be harmed by the experimental treatment. Ethically, such clients could not be included, and thus our sample would no longer be considered random.

Summary of Terms

We can now summarize how the preceding terms relate to each other in the context of research sampling:

- *Universe* or *theoretical population* refers to the entire collection of people (or elements) that share some defined characteristic(s) that a researcher wishes to study.
- A *population* is that portion of the theoretical population that is realistically accessible to the researcher.
- A *sampling frame* is an available list that approximates a population but is likely to differ from it in some ways.
- A *sample* is a group of *cases* drawn from a sampling frame that is actually studied. The purpose of selecting a sample is to efficiently study a group of cases that (to a greater or lesser degree) represents a larger number of cases within the population.

- Two criteria used to evaluate the quality of a sample are its *representativeness* (the degree to which it resembles the population) and its *size* (the number of cases it contains).
- Samples may not to be representative of the population because of (1) *sampling error*, which is the natural tendency of a sample to differ from its population and/or (2) *sampling bias*, which is the systematic distortion of a sample because of a variety of factors.
- In analyzing data collected from a *sample*, the researcher may calculate sample *statistics* and conduct statistical analysis as a way of estimating population *parameters* or, in explanatory studies, to determine the likelihood that sampling error might have produced a relationship between variables within the sample.
- *Random selection* entails selecting cases for a sample to ensure that all cases have an equal probability of being selected. Samples that are randomly selected are called *random samples.*

PROBABILITY SAMPLING

There are two general categories of sampling methods available to researchers: probability sampling and nonprobability sampling. Probability sampling uses random selection, and nonprobability sampling does not use random selection. With probability sampling, it is possible to calculate the statistical probability that any case within a sampling frame or population will be selected as part of the research sample. There are several methods that can be used to randomly select a sample using probability sampling techniques.

Simple Random Sampling

Simple random sampling is the most well known type of probability sampling. It entails randomly selecting a predetermined number of cases from the sampling frame or population. A researcher wanting to select 25 people from a sampling frame of 100 would write each person's name on an individual 3 by 5 file card and then randomly select 25 cards from a container. If the cards were identical except for the names on them and were mixed in the container in a way that each had an equal probability of being selected, a simple random sample would result.

For drawing larger samples, the researcher could consult a table of mathematically generated random numbers to assist in the selection of cases. Tables of random numbers are available in many research textbooks (see, for example, Rubin & Babbie, 2007). To use a table of random numbers, the researcher first assigns consecutive numbers to all cases in the sampling frame. Then the researcher enters the random number table at some random point (selecting any number off the table arbitrarily) and moves through the table in some systematic way until the required number of random numbers has been selected. The cases that correspond to the random numbers selected from the table would then be selected to be included in the sample.

Another common method for selecting a simple random sample is to use computer software designed to generate numbers at random. Many statistical software packages now offer a random number function. All cases in the sampling frame or population are assigned consecutive numbers. Then the researcher enters the size of the sampling frame and the number of cases that

Ethical Practice

Under what circumstances might simple random sampling be considered unethical?

will constitute the sample. The software produces a list of random numbers. The researcher then selects the cases assigned those numbers.

Systematic Random Sampling

Systematic random sampling is popular because of its simplicity. No table of random numbers is needed, and no computer programs are required. It uses a three-step process. An example will help to explain how it works.

Suppose that a researcher wishes to conduct a client satisfaction survey using a 25 percent sample of all 100 active clients in a human service organization. This would mean 25 cases. The case records for the active clients (the sampling frame) are stored in a locked file drawer or as a computer-generated file. The first 25 case records in the file could be selected, but they would not constitute a probability sample. Such a sample might be biased. For example, because files are stored alphabetically, the first 25 cases would include only those cases whose last names start with a letter early in the alphabet—that might produce a bias in terms of ethnicity. So, a systematic random sample would be preferable.

How would a systematic sample be drawn in this case? First, the necessary sampling interval (k) would have to be computed. The sampling interval is found by dividing the number of cases in the sampling frame by the number of cases needed for the sample. To select a sample of 25 cases from a sampling frame of 100, we would calculate our sampling interval as follows:

$$k = \frac{\text{number of cases in sampling frame}}{\text{number of cases desired for sample}}$$
$$k = 100/25$$
$$k = 4$$

Therefore, the sampling interval (k) would be 4. Next, we would randomly select a number from 1 to k (4 in this case). Let us say that it is 3. This number would be the starting point—the third case in the file would be the first case selected. Then, we would select every fourth case after that; that is, the seventh case, the eleventh, the fifteenth, the nineteenth, and so forth.

The initial, random selection of a starting point is an important step, and it cannot be ignored. It is necessary so that every case in the file has an equal chance of being selected for the sample.

Stratified Sampling

Stratified sampling is another probability sampling method, and can be used (1) to reduce the amount of sampling error when using a simple or systematic random sample or (2) simply to ensure that there are enough cases within different value or value label categories of a variable for comparison purposes. For either purpose, a two-stage sampling method is used.

The first stage of stratified sampling requires the researcher to divide the population into homogeneous categories, or strata. That is, people or objects are separated into two or more strata (subgroups of the population or sampling frame) on the basis of the variables of interest. Thus, within strata, members are homogeneous with regard to this variable (e.g., all social workers in one stratum and all physicians in another stratum for the variable "profession" or all women in one stratum and all men in the other stratum for the variable "gender"). In the second stage, the desired number of cases is selected from each stratum by simple random sampling or systematic random sampling.

Stratified sampling is a probability sampling method and can be used (1) to reduce the amount of sampling error when using a simple or systematic random sample or (2) simply to ensure that there are enough cases within different value or value label categories of a variable for comparison purposes.

There are two types of stratified random sampling: proportionate stratified random sampling and disproportionate stratified random sampling. They reflect (respectively) the two uses of stratified sampling that we mentioned previously. In *proportionate stratified random sampling*, the researcher stratifies cases on the basis of a variable that could distort the research findings if not proportionately represented in the research sample (i.e., one that is a potentially confounding variable). For example, a researcher wishing to study the effectiveness of treatment intervention on a group of clients who have been diagnosed as clinically depressed might have good reason to stratify the sample by gender. There might be concern that client gender may be a confounding variable that relates to treatment success. Thus, a method is needed to ensure that the sample does not consist of a disproportionate (relative to the sampling frame) number of either men or women.

Let us assume that the sampling frame from which the sample is drawn consists of 1,000 cases, of which 900 are women and 100 are men. A 5 percent sample (consisting of 50 cases) is to be drawn. To draw a proportionate stratified random sample, the cases would first be sorted into two strata consisting of (1) the 900 women and (2) the 100 men. Then 5 percent of the women (45 cases) would be selected from the group of women at random and 5 percent of the men (5 cases) from the group of men at random. The sample, like the sampling frame, would thus be 90 percent women—perfectly representative of the population with regard to gender. The sample thus produced might be biased in some other respects, but it is definitely not biased regarding gender. And every case in the sampling frame had an equal likelihood of being selected (0.05, or 5 percent), so the sample is considered to be a random one.

But what if the researcher wished to determine if the treatment intervention is more effective with men or with women? If a proportionate stratified random sample were used, it would require comparing the clinical depression level of one subsample of 45 women (probably an acceptable size) with the other subsample consisting of only 5 men. The researcher might be uncomfortable with allowing only 5 men to represent all male clients. Could only 5 cases be representative of all male clients? Five is a very small sample size; the likelihood of sampling error might be high, and certain potentially useful forms of statistical analysis that require larger samples would have to be eliminated.

Diversity in Practice

How would you use proportionate stratified random sampling to make sure your sample is representative of the population with regard to race?

An alternative method of sampling that also relies on the use of strata (homogeneous subgroups) is *disproportionate stratified sampling*. It can be used to produce subsamples of comparable size for comparison purposes by over-sampling from one group and under-sampling from another. For example, the researcher in the previous example might randomly select a subsample of 25 women and another of 25 men from their respective strata. In the total sample (men and women), there would be a disproportionate number of men relative to the sampling frame. In the sample, 50 percent of the cases would be men, although in the sampling frame the percentage of men is only 10 percent. Male and female clients clearly would have a different probability of being selected for the research sample. But it is still possible to calculate the likelihood of their being selected for the research sample—thus, the sample would still be a probability sample (but not a random one). Any male client would have a high chance of being selected for the sample (25 out of 100, or 25 percent); for any female client, the chance of selection would be less than 3 percent (only 25 out of 900).

Cluster Sampling

Cluster sampling involves a multistage process: a listing of cases followed by random sampling of groups of cases rather than individual cases. It is more likely to be used in large-scale surveys or studies that involve cases that are geographically distant from each other than in small, organization-based studies. There are some research situations where it is extremely useful for putting together a sample that is both representative and sufficiently large, while conserving the resources of the researcher.

In cluster sampling, researchers identify clusters of cases. Next, they randomly select a predetermined number of clusters. Then all cases (or sometimes a random sample of all cases) within each of the selected clusters is selected to constitute the research sample.

The following example should help clarify how cluster sampling is accomplished. Suppose a researcher wishes to collect data to describe the characteristics of a random sample of battered women in residence at domestic violence shelters within a state. For various reasons (e.g., the women's safety), there is unlikely to exist a master list of these women. Thus, a simple random sampling method cannot be used. However, a list of all shelters within a particular state may exist. Each shelter can be thought of as a cluster of cases. First, a random sample of these shelters (clusters) is selected. Then the administrators of the shelters selected could be asked to provide a list of all persons currently in the shelter (using numbers instead of names to preserve the clients' confidentiality). The lists from the shelters could comprise the research sample, or if the number of cases thus obtained is still too large, the desired number of cases could be selected from the lists using either simple or systematic random sampling.

Sometimes, even if a master list of potential research participants can be compiled, cluster sampling may still be the sampling method of choice. A major advantage of cluster sampling is that it allows the researcher to collect data in a timely and cost-efficient way, while not greatly increasing the likelihood of sampling bias. It allows a researcher to collect data on a large number of cases quickly and at relatively little cost. In our example, the researcher would be able to collect data about a large number of people in just a few locations (those shelters that were selected) using cluster sampling. Yet even if a simple random sample of all cases currently active in the shelters could have been drawn, a considerable amount of time and money would have been spent requesting assistance in acquiring data or even traveling around the state to collect data on just one or two cases in each of many shelters.

NONPROBABILITY SAMPLING

In a nonprobability sample, it is not possible to calculate the likelihood that a given person or element will be selected. It does not involve random selection, so some cases will have a greater likelihood of being selected than others. However, we cannot know how much greater. We also cannot estimate how much sampling error a sample contains using what statisticians call *confidence intervals*.

In many research studies, a method that produces a probability sample (random selection) cannot be used. This happens most frequently when no population list or even sampling frame is available from which to draw the sample. In such situations, it would be impossible to calculate the likelihood of a given case being selected. This was the situation when one of the authors was involved in an exploratory study of women who delayed childbearing until after age 30. No sample drawn could possibly be a probability sample, because the population could not be identified or specified and no acceptable sampling frame was available.

Even when it is possible to draw a probability sample, it might not be the best sample to use to study a given problem or research question. A nonprobability sample may be preferable. In some of the types of research described in Chapter 8, sample representativeness is not as important as other sample characteristics. For example, in research studies where the emphasis is on exploring the nature and impact of a problem, it may make sense to study only individuals who are likely to have the best in-depth understanding of the problem, whether or not they represent a cross-section of the population experiencing it. In this type of study, the researcher might deliberately exclude from the study those who might otherwise have been randomly selected as participants but who may contribute little or nothing new to an understanding of the problem.

There are four commonly used nonprobability sampling methods. All of these methods are suited to situations in which the researcher either (1) would prefer a representative sample but is unable to compile a population or sampling frame from which to draw one using probability sampling methods or (2) has decided that representativeness is less important to sample composition than one or more other characteristics.

Convenience Sampling

One type of nonprobability sampling method involves a very unscientific approach to sampling. Convenience sampling (sometimes called *accidental sampling*) entails selecting cases for study primarily because they happen to be readily accessible to the researcher. It is this type of sampling that is most likely to have been used when we hear on the evening news that a "random sample" of residents of our community was interviewed about their opinions regarding a news event. In fact, the sample was not at all random! Generally, the people interviewed were all in the same shopping mall or were sitting in the park near the television studio. They were selected mainly because of convenience. Clearly, some potential participants (those most readily available) had a greater likelihood of selection than others.

Like all sampling methods, convenience sampling may produce an acceptable level of representativeness but it is the method that is probably least likely to do so. The usefulness of convenience samples in social work research is limited. If the researcher is beginning to explore a new area of inquiry and it is hard to locate people with certain characteristics or obtain their permission to be research participants, it may be the only feasible alternative. But convenience samples present a major difficulty for researchers. How can they interpret the findings of their research? To whom do they apply? Under what conditions? Research designs that rely on convenience sampling have little or no claim to external validity. Findings generally are believed to be applicable only to those people or objects that were studied.

Purposive Sampling

Sometimes, cases are selected because researchers believe that the cases can provide them with access to a unique approach to a problem or situation or a special perspective, insight, expertise, experience, characteristic, or condition

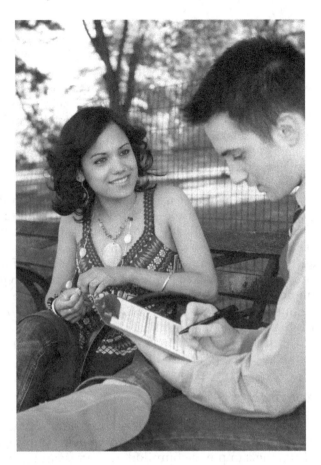

that they wish to understand. For example, suppose we wish to know more about the variations in coping strategies used by people diagnosed with early-stage Alzheimer's disease. Although we might be able to produce a sampling frame of people who have recently been diagnosed with the disease and draw a random sample from it, the sample thus selected might not be what is needed for our research. For our research objective, a purposive sample actually might be preferable to a more representative one. It would be more likely to help us describe the wide variety of coping methods used.

How would we acquire a purposive sample of people recently diagnosed with Alzheimer's disease? From informal conversations with medical staff, we might learn of a number of people being treated at clinics and hospitals who employ what staff members perceive as unique coping strategies. We might then select those twenty people with what seem like the most unique ways of coping and ask them to voluntarily take part in in-depth research interviews. Our sample would not be representative of the population or even of the available sampling frame. It would not contain the same distribution of coping strategies (percentage-wise) that exists within the population of people with Alzheimer's. For example, we might estimate that 40 percent of the people might all use the same coping strategy, but we might select only one person for our sample of twenty (5 percent) who uses that strategy. Because we would be seeking to learn about the diversity of coping strategies used by people (heterogeneity), there might be little value in interviewing more than one person who uses any one coping strategy. That would be redundant.

There are other variations of purposive sampling that are used less frequently in social work research. One, *expert sampling*, selects cases on the basis of the criterion that they have a certain desired expertise. Thus, we might select and bring together a panel of researchers, all of whom have studied, for example, the problem of weight-based discrimination or a group of primary care physicians who have set up their practices using a fee-based system (a system in which patients pay a fixed amount per year and are promised certain services at no additional charge). These "panels of experts" can then be surveyed, brought together in a focus group, and so forth in an attempt to tap their experience and expertise.

Sometimes, we might prefer a group of people who are "typical" in some way. We would use a type of purposive sampling known as *mode instance sampling*. For example, in conducting a needs assessment to determine the level of perceived need for a proposed social program, a researcher may want to assemble a sample of typical clients who might use the proposed program's services to collect their opinions or assess their needs.

Still another form of purposive sampling is the opposite of mode instance sampling. It is deviant case sampling, and it seeks the most atypical cases for study. For example, in an exploratory qualitative study, a researcher might wish to use a sample of investors who profited the most and/or who lost the most money by lying on home loan applications to acquire real estate that they planned to resell ("flip"). They might then be interviewed in order to learn how they were ethically able to justify their illegal behavior.

Snowball Sampling

Snowball sampling does not select a sample at one point in time. It bears some resemblance to both convenience sampling and expert sampling. When using snowball sampling, the sample is compiled as the research progresses. First, one or just a few people are identified as potential research participants. Then they are asked to provide the names of people they know or know about who, like themselves, have experienced a problem or who in other ways meet the necessary criteria for inclusion in the research study. The next potential participants are contacted by the researcher to determine whether they are indeed eligible for inclusion in the sample and if so whether they are willing to participate in the study. They may, in turn, be asked to provide the names of other potential participants. The process is repeated until enough participants are eligible and agree to take part in the study.

Snowball sampling is often used in the case studies such as those described in Chapter 8 and in the previously mentioned research study in which a sample of women who had given birth to their first child after age 30 were interviewed. In the latter example, an initial sample of women was identified by placing an ad in the paper (hardly a random selection procedure). Women who responded to the ad were interviewed by a member of the research team to ensure that they met the necessary criteria to be part of the research study and an early draft of a research data collection instrument was completed. At the conclusion of the interview, they were asked if they knew of other women who, like themselves, had borne their first child after age 30. These prospects were then followed up by the research team. The use of snowball sampling was appropriate because (1) the purpose of the study was to develop a research instrument for a subsequent study of delayed childbearing and (2) the researchers were not attempting to describe accurately the population of women who delay childbearing.

In exploratory studies designed to learn more about either a new problem or one that has only recently been identified, snowball samples are often used. The problem or behavior need not be illegal or carry some social stigma. For example, a sample of adolescents who are recent victims of *cyber-bullying* (harassment by peers using e-mail or other electronic communication) could be compiled by first identifying one victim and then asking him or her to provide the names of others who they know that have had similar experiences. Of course, as this problem grows and more and more victims are identified, a sampling frame of victims will be able to be compiled. Other, perhaps better, methods of acquiring research samples then will be used.

Quota Sampling

Another type of nonprobability sampling method, *quota sampling,* is used to obtain a sample that is (1) as representative as possible in relation to potentially confounding variables and (2) of a specified size (quota). The most common type of quota sampling, *proportional quota sampling*, begins with estimating the characteristics of the research population regarding selected variables. This description is built into a matrix, that is, a table displaying the percentage of people in the population believed to share each combination of characteristics. Then people are selected for study who have all of the characteristics described within each specific cell of the matrix. Sampling continues until there is a final sample of people selected that represents each of the cells. Then the people in each cell are assigned a "weight," a number based upon what is believed to be the portion of the total population that they represent. Quota sampling is generally used by political pollsters conducting exit polls. It has produced some accurate predictions but also some embarrassing, wrong ones. However, when the latter has occurred, it has usually been attributed to other factors, not a flaw in the sampling method used.

Sometimes, it is logistically impossible (cost, time, geography) to use a large research sample. However, the researcher still wants to be sure that certain variables are adequately represented in the sample. If proportional quota sampling were to be used, characteristics of cases that occur relatively infrequently might not be adequately represented. For example, a sample might contain only one person who is a Pacific Islander and has a disability. This one individual clearly cannot represent all people who have this combination of demographic characteristics—it would be better to have at least two or three cases. In such a situation, *nonproportional quota sampling*, a less common sampling method, might be preferred. It is considered the nonprobability equivalent of disproportionate stratified sampling. It entails determining the minimum number of cases required for each category or combination of characteristics (cell) and then sampling until that minimum is attained.

The use of nonproportional quota sampling, like many choices we make in research, is a trade-off. It is based on the assumption that sacrificing representativeness a little in the sample as a whole is preferable to the risk of having a category or combination of characteristics with a small number of cases and, thus, a high probability of sampling error within it.

There is one major problem that frequently precludes the more frequent use of quota sampling of either type. It is the absence of accurate estimates of the characteristics of the population of interest needed to develop a quota matrix. If some data are missing or are not believed to be accurate, a sufficiently representative sample cannot be obtained. Quota sampling should be used only when

(1) the researcher has confidence that the data needed to establish a quota matrix represent reasonably accurate estimates of the characteristics of the population and (2) an unbiased (ideally, random) method of selecting participants within each cell can be implemented after a matrix has been constructed.

SELECTING A GOOD SAMPLE

The sampling methods that we have just described might be regarded as options, or a menu of sampling alternatives. Sometimes, we simply select the one best suited to our needs and use it to draw a sample. Often, sampling is a little more complicated. We employ a *sampling plan*, a sequence of steps or stages that makes use of two or more of these methods. For example, in a study of the job satisfaction of social workers' in large outpatient mental health clinics, we might first (using systematic random sampling) select the names of twenty clinics from a statewide directory. The social workers in these clinics would then serve as a cluster sample. However, rather than selecting all of the social workers employed there to participate in our research study, we might draw a 20 percent simple random sample of them. After interviewing them, we might select ten social workers who are the most dissatisfied with their jobs (mode instance sampling) to participate in a focus group to discuss the reasons for their dissatisfaction. This multistage sampling plan would be designed to take advantage of the features of all of the different sampling methods used.

When selecting the sampling method or methods to be used and determining the appropriate sample size, a number of important, interrelated issues must be addressed. Some of them relate to practical matters that are easily understood; others are a little more technical. The major issues that the researcher needs to consider are (1) available resources for securing the sample, (2) the overall design and purpose of the study, (3) the type of statistical analysis that will be used, and (4) the relative importance of sample representativeness.

Available Resources

If the study is being funded by a human service organization or some other organization that has been contracted to have it designed and implemented, the size of the sample to be used may already have been specified. If this is not the case, the researcher is free to use judgment in selecting an appropriate research sample.

In general, larger samples are likely to be more representative of the population than are smaller ones. As previously illustrated, when larger samples are chosen, sampling error is reduced. But even in quantitative studies, where sample representativeness usually is critical to the credibility of the research, there is a point of diminishing returns. A researcher gets to the point where an increase in sample size does not appreciably reduce the amount of sampling error that may be present.

Using large samples can be costly. As stated previously, the processes of compromise and trade-off are ongoing activities in conducting social work research. Resources spent collecting data from a large number of research participants leaves less time and resources for performing other essential tasks in the research process. But if a smaller sample is used, some of that time and those resources can be used to perform those other tasks. The overall quality of the research study might actually be better.

A researcher gets to the point where an increase in sample size does not appreciably reduce the amount of sampling error that may be present.

Overall Design and Purpose of the Study

Generally, we expect to see different size samples (and different sampling methods) with certain types of research. For example, qualitative research studies often use nonprobability sampling methods with smaller sample sizes than predominantly quantitative designs. Often, a representative sample is impossible to obtain because of the absence of an adequate sampling frame. And it may not be considered important anyway if the research is primarily exploratory. In contrast, large-scale descriptive studies that are primarily quantitative often use large samples (to reduce sampling error) and strive for representativeness by using random sampling methods, because the external validity of findings is considered important. If, for example, the purpose of a study is to describe accurately the characteristics of a client population, such as older people who have admitted to having been victims of financial abuse, and a good sampling frame is available, a randomly selected sample consisting of several hundred cases may be used to ensure the likelihood of a sufficiently representative sample.

Other types of research use samples of various sizes, usually depending on financial resources available to support the research and the number of cases available for study. Research whose objective is primarily to develop measurement instruments to be used in subsequent research studies may use relatively small samples but may use many different samples representing different subpopulations and/or different times and settings for measurement. If a researcher wishes merely to pilot-test a research instrument that will be revised, a small nonprobability sample is likely to be used.

It is sometimes helpful to consult reports of other similar research and note how many cases were used. This kind of information can be used as a general guide, but it should be remembered that errors in sample size selection are quite common. We would not want to repeat another researcher's mistakes. For more in-depth discussion of sampling methods and issues, a text that is devoted solely to the topic of research sampling should be consulted (Levy & Lemeshow, 1999; Thompson, 2002).

Statistical Analyses to Be Used

In qualitative studies, statistical analysis usually is not an important consideration in designing a sampling plan. There currently are methods of analyzing qualitative data (primarily content analysis) that convert words to numbers that can then be analyzed statistically. However, since the sampling methods most frequently used (purposive, snowball, or even convenience) rarely produce samples that can be considered representative, there is usually little value in conducting statistical analysis. Any conclusions regarding, for example, relationships between or among variables would be highly suspect.

In primarily quantitative studies, the size of a research sample and the type of sampling method used are important factors in the selection of the form of statistical analysis to be used. But sometimes it works the other way around. In some instances, the researcher knows in advance what analysis will have to be used, for example, when conducting grant-sponsored research that specifies which statistical tests are acceptable or when replicating the research of others who used a specific form of statistical analysis. Then the size of the sample as well as the sampling method used (e.g., probability or nonprobability) is tailored to the requirements of the statistical analysis that must be used.

The relationship between types of statistical analysis and the most appropriate sample size is beyond the scope of this text. However, we should remember that sample size guidelines for various statistical analyses exist for a purpose. If a specific statistical test has been designed for a certain sample size, the sample size selected should be within the specified range, neither smaller nor larger. Samples that are either smaller or larger than recommended for a given statistical test can result in misleading conclusions regarding relationships between variables.

The Importance of Sample Representativeness

As noted earlier, quantitative studies place great importance on representative samples. There is a concentrated effort to avoid sampling bias and determine (statistically) the probability that sampling error may have produced a relationship between variables or obscured a real one. Thus, whenever possible, quantitative studies rely on probability samples and random sampling methods to increase the likelihood of representativeness within research samples.

Thus, whenever possible, quantitative studies rely on probability samples and random sampling methods to increase the likelihood of representativeness within research samples.

In predominantly qualitative studies, where representativeness is often impossible anyway, nonprobability sampling methods generally provide an adequate sample of cases. Both representativeness and size are less important than criteria such as the richness of data that a sample provides or the diversity (of perceptions, meanings, experiences, and so forth) contained within it.

SUMMARY

In this chapter, we focused on sample selection and its relationship to good research. Key terms relating to sampling were defined. Representativeness and size were identified as the two criteria most frequently used in evaluating the quality of a sample, at least in predominantly quantitative studies.

Sampling methods are characterized as either probability or nonprobability, depending on whether it is possible to calculate the probability that an individual person or object will be selected to be a case within the research sample. Random samples are often regarded as superior to nonrandom ones because they are more likely to be representative of the population from which they are selected and allow for the use of certain types of statistical analyses. Four types were described in this chapter: simple random sampling, systematic random sampling, cluster sampling, and proportionate and disproportionate stratified random sampling.

For some research studies, probability samples may be neither feasible nor desirable. In some qualitative studies, for example, nonprobability sampling methods may yield samples that are exactly what is needed. Four common nonprobability sampling methods were described: convenience sampling, purposive sampling, snowball sampling, and quota sampling.

Finally, we discussed four major issues that the researcher needs to consider when deciding which sampling method to use and how large a sample is needed. They are (1) available resources for securing the sample, (2) the overall design and purpose of the study, (3) the type of statistical analysis (if any) that will be used, and (4) the importance of sample representativeness to the research.

Succeed with PEARSON **mysocialworklab**

Log onto **www.mysocialworklab.com** and answer the following questions. (If you did not receive an access code to **MySocialWorkLab** with this text and wish to purchase access online, please visit www.mysocialworklab.com.)

1. **Watch the Core Competencies Video: Ethical Practice: Recognizing Personal Values.** If a school counselor wanted to conduct a qualitative study on the needs of pregnant high school students in her county, how would she go about gathering a sample? What sampling method would she probably use?

2. **Read the Case Study: Medical Social Work: Stephanie and Rose Doer.** If you wanted to conduct exploratory research on teenage girls who give birth to severely disabled infants, what are a couple of resources you might use to help you gather a sample? What sampling method or methods might you use?

PRACTICE TEST

1. What are the two criteria used to evaluate the quality of a research sample?
   a. Internal and external validity
   b. Sampling frame and universe
   c. Representativeness and size
   d. Statistic and parameter

2. A method for selecting a sample that ensures that all cases have an equal probability of being selected is
   a. random assignment.
   b. sampling bias.
   c. sampling error.
   d. random selection.

3. When just a few cases are initially identified, and these people are asked to provide the names of others who meet the criteria, the sampling method used is

   a. convenience sampling.
   b. snowball sampling.
   c. quota sampling.
   d. cluster sampling.

4. What is the major difference between stratified sampling and quota sampling?
   a. Stratified sampling uses random selection and quota sampling does not.
   b. Stratified sampling always uses a proportionate number of subjects from each group.
   c. Quota sampling uses random selection and stratified sampling does not.
   d. They are simply two different names for the same sampling method.

5. Describe the use of the cluster sampling method for selecting a sample of BSW graduates in the United States.

ASSESS YOUR COMPETENCE Use the scale below to rate your current level of achievement on
the following concepts or skills associated with each competency presented in the chapter:

1	2	3
I can accurately describe the concept or skill.	I can consistently identify the concept or skill when observing and analyzing practice activities.	I can competently implement the concept or skill in my own practice.

_____ Understanding how sample size, sampling error, and population representativeness are related

_____ Being familiar with the four types of probability sampling: simple random sampling, systematic random sampling, stratified sampling, and cluster sampling

_____ Being familiar with the four types of nonprobability sampling: convenience sampling, purposive sampling, snowball sampling, and quota sampling

_____ Understanding how available resources, the design and purpose of the study, the statistical analyses to be used, and the importance of sample representativeness all affect the selection of one or more sampling methods

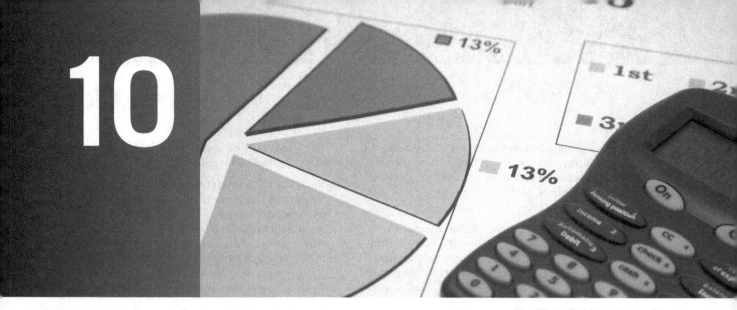

10

Measurement Concepts and Issues

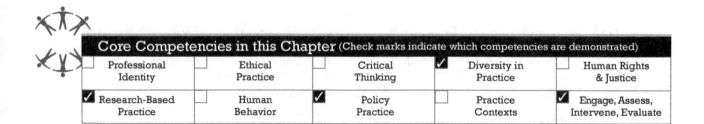

Core Competencies in this Chapter (Check marks indicate which competencies are demonstrated)				
☐ Professional Identity	☐ Ethical Practice	☐ Critical Thinking	✔ Diversity in Practice	☐ Human Rights & Justice
✔ Research-Based Practice	☐ Human Behavior	✔ Policy Practice	☐ Practice Contexts	✔ Engage, Assess, Intervene, Evaluate

Once researchers have determined how the sample research participants will be selected, they generally focus on measurement issues. Specifically, they decide (1) what data will need to be collected and (2) what instruments or methods will be used to collect it.

In quantitative research, accurate measurement is of paramount importance. Whether the goal is to describe a problem or phenomenon (as in descriptive designs) or test to see if two or more variables are likely to be related in the population from which a research sample was drawn, research findings will be misleading if key variables are not measured accurately. For example, how could we know if a report of the incidence and severity of family violence in a community is accurate if it is unclear what exactly was meant by the term *family violence* or if the methods for measuring its severity appear to be highly subjective? Or, how can we trust a researcher's conclusion that clients' motivation and degree of success in counseling are positively correlated if motivation was determined solely on clients' own assessments or success in counseling was measured solely on the basis of the subjective impressions of their social workers?

Measurement is also important in qualitative studies. Researchers conducting qualitative studies acknowledge, however, that their measurements may be biased by their own presence or other factors and will necessarily have a certain degree of subjectivity; they expect that. But that does not absolve them of the responsibility (1) to measure even highly subjective variables, such as impressions, perceptions, or the meaning of certain events to participants, as accurately as possible and (2) to measure more easily measured variables, such as their participants' demographic characteristics or behaviors, accurately. Thus, while Chapters 10 to 12 may seem to relate mostly to quantitative research, much of their content is equally applicable to predominantly qualitative research designs.

It is sometimes suggested that measurement issues should be resolved and decisions about how to measure certain variables should be made before sampling occurs or data sources are selected. Although there are compelling arguments for this sequence of events, we believe that it makes more sense to make measurement decisions after sampling issues have been resolved and the sources for data have been selected. Until it has been decided who or what cases will provide data and how they will be providing it (e.g., using written questionnaires, in-person interviews, direct observation), it is difficult to know what types of measurements are possible and the best ways to obtain them.

WHAT IS MEASUREMENT IN RESEARCH?

Most of us think we understand what measurement is all about and how it works. After all, we have used it almost all of our lives. But just to be sure we all agree on what it means, let's review it. In research, *measurement* is the process of sorting and, when possible, quantifying information in a systematic fashion. It entails collecting data in relation to certain variables and assigning the appropriate value categories or values to individual cases. In the social work literature, there is disagreement as to how precisely one can measure certain variables. Some writers have taken the position that, with enough effort, virtually all variables can be accurately measured (Rubin & Babbie, 2011). They believe that most variables can be *quantified*, that is, a number can be assigned to describe accurately the exact amount of the variable present within a case. Other writers, especially those who espouse qualitative research methods, point out that because of the nature of many of the variables that are of interest to social workers, they cannot be quantified using standardized measurement techniques. Our position is that for most (if not all) variables, a measurement strategy can be developed that will yield useful data for researchers. However, we also acknowledge that many variables of interest to social workers do not readily lend themselves to quantification.

PREPARATION FOR MEASUREMENT

Before any measurement can take place, two interrelated activities must take place. They are referred to as *conceptualization* and *operationalization*.

Our position is that for most (if not all) variables, a measurement strategy can be developed that will yield useful data for researchers.

Conceptualization

Conceptualization entails (1) selecting and specifying what a researcher believes to be the most important or relevant variables to measure and (2) stating the value labels or values that each variable can assume. It also involves (3) specifying as precisely as possible exactly what the researcher means by using those variables. In performing these tasks, researchers rely on both available knowledge (the literature) and their practice knowledge and experience. For example, the literature may have suggested that abuse (or nonabuse) of medication by terminally ill patients may be related to whether or not hospice care is given. It may have suggested the hypothesis that terminally ill patients who receive hospice care will be less likely to abuse medication than terminally ill patients who do not receive hospice care. Two variables that clearly would need to be measured are (1) involvement (or noninvolvement) with hospice care and (2) the presence or absence of medication abuse. Specification of the predictor variable (hospice involvement/noninvolvement) would be no problem. But the researcher would need to specify exactly what he or she means by *medication abuse* (the outcome variable). Would it be any use of medication—accidental or intentional—other than exactly as prescribed? Should it include taking less of a medicine than prescribed? What about the use of additional nonprescription medication? All of the preceding questions (and more) would need to be addressed before data collection begins, so that cases could be correctly and consistently assigned to value categories for both variables. There are no right or wrong answers to these questions. A researcher can answer them any way that seems logical.

Sometimes, the answers are summarized at this point in what is referred to as an *operational definition*. An operational definition tells the reader of a research report exactly what criteria were used to measure a variable in the current study. Another researcher might apply a different operational definition to the same variable in his or her research. An operational definition says, in effect, "When I use a term in this research, this is what I mean by it." For example, a researcher might construct the following operational definition:

> *Medication abuse is the intentional misuse of a prescribed, controlled narcotic substance on at least three occasions by a person who is terminally ill.*

Generally, several operational definitions must be constructed. Operational definitions of variables are presented (along with definitions of other terms that may need to be defined) at the end of a literature review or near the beginning of the methodology section of a research report. In our example, it would also be necessary to define operationally such terms as *terminally ill* and *hospice care.*

Operationalization

Operationalization is closely related to conceptualization and is the last step in preparation for measurement. It refers to specifying the actual measuring devices or methods that will be used to measure key variables. Thus, it further clarifies their meaning.

Generally, there are many ways that a variable can be measured. For example, measurement of the variable "medication abuse" might entail actual observations by nurses, social workers, caregivers, or aides. It might also include social workers' impressions based on mental alertness or other symptoms of medication abuse, self-reports of patients, or something as specific as a measurement of a certain chemical in the patient's bloodstream at regular intervals.

We noted that operational definitions of a term may vary from study to study. Similarly, different researchers may actually measure the same variable in different ways. Unless the researcher is replicating the research of others (in which case the same method of measuring the variable should be used), that is fine. The only requirements for operationalization of a given variable are that it should be logical and justified (usually through the literature). Sometimes, researchers choose to include the method of measurement (operationalization) of a variable in their operational definition of the variable (Neuman, 1997). An example follows:

> *Medication abuse is the intentional misuse of a prescribed, controlled narcotic substance on at least three occasions by a person who is terminally ill as reported by the patient's primary caregiver counting the number of pills missing from the medication dispenser.*

Cultural Sensitivity in Operationalization

Certain theoretical concepts may have different meanings for research participants, depending on their ethnic and cultural backgrounds. When this is the case, every effort should be made to operationalize a variable in a way that is consistent with the culture of those individuals who are providing research data. For example, what if a researcher needs to measure the educational attainment of a group of research participants? Traditionally, "years of formal schooling completed as reported by the research participant" is the operational definition of educational attainment. This definition, however, may underestimate the actual educational experiences and degree of knowledge attainment in certain groups of people. For example, for some African Americans, especially those from rural backgrounds, formal systems of education have not always been accessible. However, many (especially older) African Americans achieved both enhanced knowledge and skills through a combination of mentoring, apprenticeship, craftsmanship, and entrepreneurship. An accurate assessment of their educational attainment should include a measurement of these less formal venues for education.

Diversity in Practice

Identify another variable (similar to educational attainment) that might require the researcher be sensitive to cultural issues and/or definitions before creating the variable's operational definition.

LEVELS OF MEASUREMENT

Levels (sometimes called *scales*) of measurement refer to the degree of precision with which a variable is to be measured. Researchers must decide at what level each variable is to be measured, sometimes on the basis of the nature of the variable itself and more frequently on the method of measurement used. Determining the level of measurement is essential in deciding the most appropriate methods for statistical analyses of data (see Chapter 13). Researchers determine which of four forms of measurement is appropriate to apply to their measurement of a given variable. They represent a hierarchy of measurement precision.

Nominal Level

The nominal level represents the most basic form of measurement. It involves the use of a measurement scheme that simply sorts cases into exhaustive and mutually exclusive value categories of a variable. In a nominal-level measurement, a case must fall into one (exhaustive) and only one (mutually exclusive) category of a variable. The different value categories of a variable reflect only a difference in kind, not a difference in the amount of the variable present within a given case. Even if a number is used as a label for a value category to make data entry into a computer database easier, the number has no quantitative significance. For example, in measuring the variable "gender," the researcher may assign the number 1 for males and the number 2 for females, or the other way around. In either case, the numbers do not reflect a quantitative difference—just a qualitative one. They are merely labels, substitutes for words.

In measuring many variables, nominal measurement is all that appears possible. Variables such as gender, whether one voted in the last election, whether one owns a car or is an undergraduate social work major, or one's religious affiliation are nominal by their very nature. A researcher might be interested in measuring the number of cars owned or degree of religiosity, but those are different variables, ones that have the potential for more precise levels of measurement.

Ordinal Level

Ordinal measurement meets all the criteria for nominal measurement. In addition, the value categories possess a logical rank-ordering. The term *ordinal level* is assigned to variables that have been measured using a range of categories, such as "always," "sometimes," "rarely," and "never" or "not improved," "slightly improved," "somewhat improved," and "greatly improved." Note that these categories can be rank ordered—we would all arrange them in the same sequence to reflect the different quantities of some variable that each represents. But the value labels are not precise. For example, although we would all agree that "somewhat improved" reflects more improvement than "slightly improved," we cannot say exactly how much.

Ordinal measurement is used quite frequently in social work practice and research. For example, social workers may be interested in measuring the degree of cooperation displayed by families that have been court ordered to receive treatment. They might categorize degree of cooperation as (1) highly cooperative, (2) cooperative, or (3) uncooperative. Of course, it would be necessary to specify the criteria by which a rating (1, 2, or 3) would be assigned to a particular case. Note that the difference between successive points of measurement on the scale is not fixed. In other words, the difference between ratings of 2 and 3 on the scale is not assumed to be equal to the difference between ratings of 1 and 2. The numbers simply represent ranks.

Ordinal level variables in social work research include the many sociode-mographic variables such as age (when measured using the value categories "elderly," "middle-aged," "young adult," "adolescent," "preadolescent," and "child"); social class standing ("upper," "middle," "lower," and so on) and degree of educational attainment (when measured by the highest degree completed). Some measurement instruments that measure psychosocial variables, such as coping capacity or level of social functioning, may generate only ordinal-level scores. For example, an instrument measuring level of social functioning may produce numeric scores. They can be placed in the value categories of "poor," "fair," "good," and "excellent," once the appropriate range of scores for each category has been determined. The numbers also can be analyzed "as is," but any statistical analyses should be those designed for use with ordinal-level variables.

Interval Level

Interval-level measurements meet all of the criteria for ordinal-level measurement and additionally require that the exact differences between categories (values) of the variable are known and are equal to each other. Many standardized tests, especially those that have been refined over many years, are believed to produce interval-level measurements. For example, IQ tests, Scholastic Assessment Tests (SATs), or Graduate Record Exams (GREs) are believed to contain equal intervals. In theory at least, the difference between two equal intervals on an IQ test (say, between scores of 115 and 110 and between scores of 87 and 82) reflect equal quantities of the construct (intelligence) that the test is used to measure.

Interval-level measurement may use a zero as one of its values, but the zero represents a point on a range of measurement, not the total absence of the construct. For example, a scale measuring self-esteem may, for convenience, be scored on a range from 0 to 100. A person who scores a zero on this scale is not considered to be without any self-esteem. It would simply mean that the person answered every question on the scale in such a way as to suggest lower rather than higher self-esteem. Scores on an interval-level measurement may even be negative. A simple example is temperature. A temperature of 0 degrees Fahrenheit does not mean there is no heat. It is only one point on a range of equidistant measurements that can be higher (e.g., 85 degrees) or lower (e.g., −20 degrees).

Ratio Level

Ratio-level measurement meets all of the criteria for interval measurement—values can be rank ordered with fixed, equal differences between them. However, a ratio-level measurement also meets another requirement—the presence of an *absolute zero*. The value zero is assigned to the point where there is no measurable quantity of the variable. Thus, no value can be less than zero (negative). For example, if the variable "income" were to be operationalized as "the actual gross earned annual income of clients as reported on their previous year's income tax return," the variable could be regarded as ratio level. A value of zero would mean no earned income. In addition, a person with an income of $60,000 could be said to have an income three times that of one with an income of $20,000. We could not make such statements about nominal-, ordinal-, or interval-level measurements.

In social work research, we might be interested in measuring how many children a client has, how many times a social worker has met with the client, or how many other organizations have offered services to the client. Each of these measurements could be regarded as ratio level since a value of zero would be a "true" or absolute zero, that is, it would reflect the total absence of the construct.

More on Levels of Measurement

Research-Based Practice

List two examples (not listed in the chapter) of variables that could be measured at each of the four levels: nominal, ordinal, interval, and ratio.

The level of measurement of variables is often not a given in social work research. With many variables, the level of measurement is often dependent on how we ask a question or solicit data. For example, if we wanted to learn about research participants' life experiences with marriage using a self-administered questionnaire, we could ask, "Have you ever been married?" (yes or no). That would produce nominal-level measurement. If we ask married people the question, "How likely would you be to marry again?" (very likely, somewhat likely, not likely, very unlikely), answers would produce ordinal-level data. A standardized data collection instrument that measures marital satisfaction (with scores ranging from 25 to 100) included as part of the data collection instrument might produce interval-level data. Finally, the question "How many times have you been married?" would produce ratio-level data.

In general, we as researchers seek to measure a variable as precisely as possible so that we can use the more powerful statistical analyses (Chapter 13) that require higher levels of measurement. However, there are times when we might sacrifice precision for other priorities. Why would we ever do this? Sometimes, an estimate of a measurement is all that we require or can hope to receive, perhaps, because participants might not remember the exact, correct answer. It might be better to obtain an accurate estimate than an incorrect precise answer. Or, we might need to measure variables that are considered quite "personal," for example, "income," "number of marriages," or "number of illegal substances that have been used." They probably could be measured with reasonable accuracy, and responses to questions would yield interval- or even ratio-level data. However, to ask about them very directly and require specific numbers might cause some potential research participants to refuse to provide any data. Thus, it might be preferable to provide ranges of values for responses (which would result in only ordinal-level data) instead. The ranges would provide for a little more confidentiality for participants and thus might increase the percent of participants who would provide needed data. So, we might choose to trade off measurement precision for a higher response rate—often a good trade-off.

Some variables that would seem to be inherently nominal level (gender, religious affiliation, and so forth) do not have to remain so. For example, the variable "gender" can be converted into a new variable that we might call "femaleness." Then, a female research participant would be assigned the value 1, and a male would be assigned the value 0. If we chose to make the new variable "maleness," a male would be assigned the value 1, and a female would be assigned the value 0. Any new variables thus created (called *dummy variables*) are really measurements of the same variable or construct, but they are now considered ratio level for purposes of statistical analysis. Researchers sometimes do this to include the original variable in certain statistical analyses that require the more precise level of measurement.

The level of measurement of a variable is sometimes little more than a judgment call. Nominal-level variables usually can be easily distinguished from ordinal-level variables by our inability to rank order their value categories. However, distinguishing between ordinal- and interval-level measurements is especially difficult. Not surprisingly, even researchers sometimes disagree as to whether an item on a data collection instrument or a certain type of scale (see Chapter 12) yields interval- or ordinal-level data. It often comes down to a judgment of whether or not the intervals reflected in the measurement are really equal in size. For example, does the difference between one client's score of 75 and another's score of 70 on an assertiveness scale (5 points) reflect the same difference in assertiveness as that between the second client's score of 70 and a score of 65 of a third client (also 5 points)? If the scale has undergone many years of rigorous development and refinement, we might argue that it now yields interval-level data. However, it also could be argued that assertiveness cannot be measured with that much precision or that the construct is dynamic within a changing culture and thus the measurements produced by the scale are just not that precise. If that is the case, only ordinal-level measurement should be claimed.

While deciding whether a measurement is at the ordinal level or interval level is an important decision, the distinction between interval- and ratio-level measurement is relatively unimportant, at least for purposes of statistical analysis. In fact, in books on statistics, in describing the level of measurement requirements for using certain statistical tests, the terms *nominal, ordinal, and interval/ratio* (or *scale*) are frequently used.

CRITERIA FOR GOOD MEASUREMENT

In Chapter 6, we discussed two criteria used in evaluating many research designs, especially quantitative ones (external validity and internal validity). In Chapter 9, we presented two criteria for assessing the quality of a research sample (representativeness and sample size). There are also two criteria that are used to assess measurement quality (see Box 10.1). They are reliability and validity.

Reliability

Reliability is closely related to the concept of consistency. It asks the question, Does a measurement produce the same results under various conditions? If the object or person being measured has not changed, a good measurement procedure or instrument should not produce different results under different conditions. For example, one indicator of reliability (test-retest reliability, discussed

---

Box 10.1 Indications That the Measurement Procedure Is Good

1. **It is reliable**   We can demonstrate that it produces consistent results (e.g., 96, 96, 96, …) in a variety of situations and under different conditions.

2. **It is valid**   We can demonstrate that it actually measures what we claim that it measures (e.g., 96 = high level of aggression, not of assertiveness, anger, or some other construct).

Note: A measurement that is valid is both reliable and unbiased. Thus, a measurement that is valid is always reliable, but one that is reliable may not be valid.

in the next section) is related to the extent to which a measurement produces the same results when it is conducted at one time as opposed to some other time. If there is no reason why a research participant's measurement score on a variable (such as attitude toward capital punishment or sexist beliefs) should have changed, measuring the participant a second time using the same method as the first time should yield the same or nearly identical results. If not, the method of measurement is not considered reliable.

The degree to which a measurement is reliable is usually expressed in a *correlation coefficient,* a mathematical indicator of how much a measurement of a variable agrees (correlates) with a second measurement of the variable. A correlation coefficient reflects both the strength and the direction of the correlation between the two measurements. It consists of a number and a sign (– or +). Correlation coefficients range from –1.00 to +1.00. In using correlation coefficients as evidence of reliability, the researcher hopes to be able to produce correlation coefficients that are very high and positive (e.g., .85, .92).

High, positive correlation coefficients would result if, upon measuring people or objects twice (on two different days, by two different researchers, using two different versions of the test, and so forth) using the same method of measuring the variable, the measurements for all or at least most people or objects are the same or nearly the same on both occasions. For example, if we claimed to be measuring assertiveness, a high, positive correlation coefficient would result if people tended to receive the same or nearly the same assertiveness score when measured on Monday and again on Friday. That would demonstrate the reliability of our method of measuring assertiveness.

Probably no method for measuring variables that are human attributes is universally reliable. A method is generally limited to certain groups or segments of the population. For example, some methods for measuring characteristics such as assertiveness or hostility may be considered reliable when used with men, but not with women. Others may be reliable within one socioeconomic class, ethnic group, or culture, but not within another, or with people above a certain age, but not younger than that age. This is because the indicators of an attribute, what we use to measure a variable, tend to be more or less appropriate (they vary) on the basis of gender, socioeconomic class, ethnicity, culture, age, and so forth. For researchers, the message is this: Be sure that the methods of measurement that you choose have been found to be reliable with *your* research participants.

There are several types of reliability that a measurement can possess. The degree to which each is present is demonstrated using a different method. In any given research study, we are interested in the type of reliability that is best aligned with the purpose of the study and the appropriate use of the measurement instrument.

Fortunately, in recent years, a great amount of time and energy has been devoted to developing better ways to measure variables that are of interest to social work researchers (see, for example, Hudson, 1988). Part of this process has involved *reliability testing,* determining the various types of reliability that a method of measurement of a variable possesses and the degree to which it possesses them. There are entire books published on measurement instruments (e.g., Fischer & Corcoran, 2007) that include estimates of the amount of the different types of reliability that they possess (in the form of correlation coefficients) with regard to different subgroups of people and different settings. Often, it is possible to find exactly what we need—a measurement instrument that has been demonstrated to possess the type of reliability that we require.

If the object or person being measured has not changed, a good measurement system or instrument should not produce different results under different conditions.

For researchers, the message is this: Be sure that the methods of measurement that you choose have been found to be reliable with your research participants.

Even if none is quite appropriate, they can give us some beginning ideas for developing our own methods of measurement.

What are the different types of reliability that measurements of variables can contain? When is each of greatest interest? How do researchers and statisticians estimate the degree to which they are present? Next, we will examine each of the five types of reliability individually.

Test-Retest Reliability

An estimate of test-retest reliability requires testing the same participants twice, using the same measuring instrument to measure a variable both times, and then comparing the pair of measurements for each case. A correlation coefficient suggests the amount of agreement between the two sets of scores. The higher the positive correlation derived, the higher the test-retest reliability of the measurement instrument.

Test-retest reliability tells the researcher how consistently an instrument performs at different times. A time delay may occur between the first and second measurements of the variable, or they may be scheduled immediately after each other. If a delay between measurements is to be used, it can be as great as a week or even several months. Longer delays are most often used if (1) there is reason to believe that participants' measurements of the variable do not change naturally over time and (2) the researcher is concerned with a *testing effect*. A testing effect is the extent to which a participant's second measurement of the variable might be influenced by the experience of the first measurement if the two measurements occur too closely in time.

The degree to which this type of reliability can be demonstrated is often an important criterion in assessing the quality of measurement in social work research and, ultimately, the quality of the research itself. For example, suppose the research entails the measurement of personality traits or certain behavior patterns, variables that should not change over a reasonably short period of time. Unless the method or instrument used to measure them can be demonstrated to possess test-retest reliability, any findings about the relationship between them, or between them and other variables such as success in treatment, length of treatment, and so forth, will have little credibility.

Parallel Forms Reliability

Sometimes, for various reasons, it is necessary to have two or more forms of a data collection instrument or test. While individual items on them will differ, the different forms should be comparable so that regardless of which form an individual completes, the results will be the same, that is, there should be a high degree of parallel forms reliability. An estimate of the parallel forms reliability (also called *alternate forms reliability* or *equivalent forms reliability*) of a measurement instrument is calculated by administering two or more forms of the same instrument to the same participants, with or without a delay between administrations. If the scores on the different forms of the same instrument are identical or nearly identical, parallel forms reliability has been demonstrated.

Parallel forms of a test have been developed for many standardized achievement and knowledge measures (e.g., SATs or GREs), as well as for tests designed to measure many attitudes or perceptions. If the tests possess a high degree of parallel forms reliability, no matter which form (variation) of the test a person completes, his or her score would be about the same. A person also can take one form of a test, and the persons sitting to their right and left could complete different forms of the same test. None of the three would have an advantage over the others since the different forms would all measure the same variable and would contain the same amount of difficulty.

When parallel forms of a measurement instrument are used, demonstration of parallel forms reliability is generally expected. For example, the researcher might report that the different forms all produce distributions of scores that have the same or very similar means (averages) and a similar amount of variability.

While a demonstration of parallel forms reliability is important to people who develop and market standardized tests that require different forms of the same test, it is usually of less concern to social work researchers. However, it can be important in certain situations. Suppose a social worker is conducting longitudinal research to learn when and under what conditions changes occur in clients in an intensive anger management treatment program. He or she might need to measure anger management skills of clients on a weekly basis. To use the same instrument for measuring the variable each week might be problematic. Clients would eventually learn the "best" or socially desirable answers from being asked the same questions every week and possibly discussing them with other clients or family members. However, if different forms of the instrument (perhaps containing different but similar scenarios) could be found or developed and it could be demonstrated that they are comparable (parallel forms reliability can be demonstrated), potential problems might be avoided. For example, apparent improvement in clients' anger management skills could not be explained by either the fact that they took the same test repeatedly and learned how to respond to it or that they took different forms of the test that produced different results.

Split Half Reliability

An estimate of split half reliability entails dividing a single measurement instrument into two equal parts and correlating the score on one half with the

Engage, Assess, Intervene, Evaluate

Can you think of a way to measure anger that would be more accurate than using a client self-report instrument?

score on the other half. The two halves may be derived by, for example, placing the even-numbered items in one group and the odd-numbered items in a second group. The reliability estimate derived from using the split half method is really an estimate of the internal consistency of the measure, that is, the degree to which half of the measurements within an instrument are correlated with the other half. Split half reliability estimates have been popular in the past, primarily because of the simplicity of their calculation. They are quickly and easily calculated by hand.

Professors who develop short answer tests designed to measure knowledge of a subject are often interested in an estimate of split half reliability. It can suggest the degree to which the test is consistent in its level of difficulty. If individual students' scores on one half of the test are about the same as their scores on the other half, split half reliability is high; if they vary considerably, it is low.

In social work research, this indicator of reliability is most likely to be a concern if a variable being measured is the research participants' level of knowledge and the researcher wants the various items in the instrument to reflect equal difficulty. We might, for example, wish to measure social workers' knowledge of child abuse reporting laws by developing and administering a test to our research participants. It might consist of a series of forty true/false statements about current laws. The number of correct answers (out of forty) would be the participant's score. After administering the test, we could then determine its split half reliability by comparing the number of correct responses for even numbered statements for each social worker with his or her number of correct answers for odd numbered statements. If the estimate of split half reliability is high and positive, it suggests that the level of difficulty of the test items was consistent throughout the test. If it is not, the level of difficulty of items may vary too much to use them as intended.

An even more accurate estimate of this indicator of reliability could be achieved using the related method that we will describe next, coefficient alpha. It is mathematically more complicated than the split half method, but this is no longer a major concern now that computers are so readily available to do the work for us.

Coefficient Alpha

If a measurement instrument can be split in half, it also can be further subdivided into as many parts as there are items contained within it. Coefficient alpha, a better estimate of the overall reliability of the instrument than split half reliability, may be obtained by securing the correlation between every pair of its items (the answers to questions about child abuse reporting laws in the previous example). Coefficient alpha is a statistic that summarizes the results of this kind of analysis. It provides an estimate of the reliability of a measurement instrument by generating the average correlation among all pairs of items. If a coefficient alpha analysis produces a high, positive correlation coefficient, it can be inferred that responses to individual items or questions are highly correlated. Most personal computers have a statistical software package that can perform this operation.

Some measurement instruments are designed to be multidimensional in nature—for example, occupational inventories or tests that measure different aspects or dimensions of personality, each with its own subscale. For these instruments, it would not be appropriate to estimate reliability by using a measure of internal consistency such as coefficient alpha or split half reliability. One would expect to get a low correlation coefficient if they were used. Some other method of reliability estimation (such as the test-retest method) might be more appropriate, or each subscale could be treated as a separate variable using coefficient alpha or split half reliability to measure the consistency of the items within each individual subscale.

Interobserver Agreement

When more than one person makes observations or reviews data such as DVD recordings, interobserver agreement can be used to estimate the reliability of the measurement process. Interobserver agreement is an estimate of the degree to which two or more researchers agree in their measurements of a variable. As is true with other types of reliability, the higher the positive correlation between the measurements of two observers or interviewers, the greater the indication of consistency in measurement.

When is interobserver agreement considered to be important to the quality measurement in a research study? Traditionally, it has been more important in quantitative research. That makes sense because findings about the relationship between variables (more common in quantitative studies) are worthless unless the variables were measured in a way that provides consistent measurements. But reliability is important for qualitative measurement as well. For example, a study using grounded theory (Chapter 8) may entail video recording in-depth interviews with research participants who recently experienced an event. Then two or more judges can review the recordings and log how they think each participant experienced the event or whether he or she expressed some emotion. An estimate of the reliability of their measurements can be calculated (a correlation coefficient) using methods to estimate interobserver agreement.

Which Type of Reliability Is Most Important?

The importance of any one type of reliability depends primarily on what variable is being measured, how it is measured, and how the measurement is to be used. The test-retest reliability of a data collection instrument or scale might be desirable in many studies (especially quantitative ones), but in some cases, it may be too costly or too big an imposition on research participants to ask them to measure the same variable twice using the same method of measurement. Demonstration of parallel forms reliability would be important and relevant (and possible) only in research that uses equivalent forms of the same measurement instrument. Split half reliability and coefficient alpha would be important for measurement of knowledge or attitudes where internal consistency of measurement is desirable. We might expect some demonstration of either or both if a new test or measurement instrument was being used. It would be important to demonstrate interobserver agreement if more than one interviewer or observer is used to collect or analyze data. Inter-observer agreement would indicate that all of the interviewers or observers had been trained to observe and record the data in the same way.

Researchers can improve the overall reliability of measurement instruments by attending to a variety of factors. They include the following:

▶ **Standardizing environmental factors during measurement.** Many factors besides the measurement instrument used can negatively affect consistency of measurement of variables. When conducting cross-sectional research, data should be collected in similar settings, at similar times, and in similar ways from all participants. In longitudinal studies, all measurements of the same variable should be conducted in similar settings.

▶ **Conducting a pilot study of the instrument.** In addition to its other uses (discussed in Chapter 12), the process of pilot-testing a measurement instrument with a few individuals who are similar to the research participants can help to make measurement more reliable. For example, if a previously developed measurement instrument is to be used, pilot-testing it can either confirm or refute the researcher's belief that the instrument is reliable when used with different research participants than those on whom it was developed. If indicated, another measurement instrument can be substituted or revisions can be made in areas that appear to be unreliable. However, when using a standardized instrument with published validity and reliability statistics, if researchers add, delete, or change any items, they should reevaluate the validity and reliability of the new instrument.

▶ **Increasing the number of items on a test or measurement instrument.** In general, for unidimensional measures (those measuring just one variable), adding items will improve the reliability estimate. This occurs because coefficient alpha is a function of both the average correlation among items and the number of items on a test or other instrument. Even for instruments that are not unidimensional, adding additional, clear items can sometimes help to improve the reliability of measurement of the subscales that they contain.

Validity

When evaluating measurement, validity refers to the degree of fit between the construct we are trying to measure and the instrument or method we are using to measure it. Just to ensure we are on the same page, a definition of a construct might be useful here. A construct is something that is not tangible; it cannot be observed directly. It develops through a cognitive process, exists within human brains, and is defined by established theories. A construct might be an ability, a skill, an attribute, or (frequently in social work research) a problem or deficiency in one of these areas.

The presence of reliability is required for a measurement to be valid. But, as emphasized in Box 10.1, reliability is not in itself sufficient to guarantee that a measurement is valid. For example, a measurement instrument may claim to measure assertiveness among people, and it may produce consistent results (reliability). But it may, in fact, be measuring aggressiveness or anger, not assertiveness. A valid measurement is both reliable and it also measures what it claims to measure.

For example, suppose a researcher creates an instrument to measure the eating disorder, bulimia nervosa. The instrument contains items that measure binging behaviors only. While the instrument may consistently measure binging behaviors (good reliability), it would not be a valid measure of bulimia nervosa because it does not include other necessary symptoms of bulimia, such as purging behaviors and self-evaluation based on body shape and weight. It would also fail to distinguish between clients with bulimia nervosa, binge-eating disorder, and binge-eating/purging type of anorexia nervosa, all of which contain binging behaviors. Validity, like reliability, is not

The presence of reliability is required for a measurement to be valid. But reliability is not in itself sufficient to guarantee that a measurement is valid.

an all-or-nothing proposition. Validity is often a matter of degree. The researcher must be convinced (and be able to convince others) that a measurement possesses enough validity of the type most important to his or her research to produce an acceptable measurement of key variables within a given study.

Sometimes, it takes a long time before it is concluded that an instrument measures what it claims to measure. For example, the SAT examination was long held to provide a valid measurement of scholastic aptitude. Critics asserted that although it provided a reliable assessment of "something" (some said scholastic achievement), it was not a scholastic aptitude measure. The original name, Scholastic Aptitude Test, was changed to Scholastic Assessment Test in 1990, and finally to SAT Reasoning Test (to distinguish it from the SAT subject tests) in 1993, to reflect this position.

An instrument is said to be valid for a given use when data have been compiled and presented that provide evidence for the instrument's validity in that research situation. Thus, the burden of proof is on the researcher to show that an instrument may be appropriately used in the researcher's study to measure the desired construct with the research sample being used. It is important to remember that an instrument may be valid with one sample, but may not be valid or appropriate for use with another sample. For example, a hopelessness scale shown to be valid when used with teenagers may not be valid or appropriate for use with elderly people living in a hospice care center. Questions that suggest hopelessness for a teenager may simply suggest acceptance among residents in a hospice care center.

Evidence of the validity of a measuring instrument is developed in relation to its purpose. Instruments can be categorized as serving one or more of three purposes:

1. **To measure achievement in a content area.** Tests of knowledge (examinations) have this purpose.

2. **To predict performance in regard to some criterion.** Examples would be aptitude tests or tests used to screen for admission into an educational program.

3. **To provide a measure of a construct to learn if it relates to some other construct.** Attitude scales or diagnostic instruments would be examples of instruments used for this purpose.

As with reliability, there are certain criteria that are commonly employed to provide an estimate of validity. They are content validity, criterion validity, and construct validity. They correspond roughly to the three purposes of measurement instruments listed.

Content Validity

Demonstrating content validity involves an assessment of whether a measurement adequately covers all aspects or components of a particular body of content. It also involves a determination as to whether irrelevant or inappropriate content is present in the measurement. Content validity is the indicator of validity that is of special concern to the researcher when the purpose of a measuring instrument is to measure participants' learning or achievement in a content area. For example, to measure what participants learned in a workshop, seminar, or training session, tests need to be content validated.

Tests of knowledge that are believed to possess content validity pose questions that measure what was actually covered in a course, training session, or other curriculum package. They do not ask questions that do not relate to the curriculum's content. For example, an item on a test on this chapter that tested the reader's understanding of reliability in the context of measurement could be assumed to possess content validity; one that asked the names of the authors of this text (an old favorite among some professors) or one that required knowledge about content in Chapter 11 or about world history would not.

Tests are generally judged to possess content validity on the basis of how they were developed. Content validity is achieved by defining a hypothetical domain (or universe) of test items that fully cover the construct being measured. Items then are randomly selected so that they are believed to be representative of the domain. Researchers may not actually develop a hypothetical domain of test items (sometimes called a *test bank*). They simply define each content area, identify its major categories, and write items that correspond to the various categories or facets of the content area. This process is known as constructing a *blueprint* of the measure. When this is done well, it improves the likelihood that the measure will be content valid. Researchers reporting on the content validity of a measure are expected to describe the procedures used in instrument development that support their claim of content validity.

The use of content experts is also extremely helpful in providing evidence of the content validity of an instrument. They may be used to help define the content area so that a useful blueprint will emerge. In addition, content experts might be asked to evaluate a draft of the instrument to assess the usefulness of specific test items. Or they may be used to examine the completed instrument to state how content valid the test appears to be.

In truth, this assessment really does not provide hard evidence of the content validity of the test. What it provides is information about the *face validity* of the measure, that is, that the test looks valid on the face (or surface). Face validity is measured on the basis of how valid the measure appears to be to content experts and/or the people (or the type of people) who will be asked to complete the instrument. Some authors do not include face validity in their discussions of validity, because having face validity does not mean that a measure *actually* measures what it is supposed to measure, but only that it *appears* to measure what it is supposed to measure.

Criterion Validity

Evidence of criterion validity is important when the purpose of an instrument is to predict behavior or measure a characteristic of research participants. Evidence of criterion validity is achieved by demonstrating that scores on the measuring instrument are consistent with some other accepted indicator of the same variable. The second indicator (which may or may not be a standardized measurement instrument per se) is known as the criterion. As with reliability, evidence of criterion validity usually is presented statistically as a correlation coefficient.

There are two subcategories of criterion validity: concurrent validity and predictive validity. *Concurrent validity* is demonstrated by producing a high, positive correlation between two measures—measurements using the measurement instrument and the criterion—both of which are made at approximately the same time. For example, one might correlate scores on a newly developed measurement of student test anxiety with scores on some other well-accepted measure of anxiety. If the new measure has concurrent validity, statistical correlation with the older measurement instrument should be high and positive. Or, a researcher who has developed an instrument presumed to measure charisma might demonstrate its concurrent validity by pilot-testing it with two groups: people generally acknowledged to possess charisma and those who are believed to lack it. If the instrument has concurrent validity, the first group should achieve high scores, whereas the latter group should achieve low measurements of the variable.

Predictive validity provides evidence of the correlation between a measure and some future performance or behavior (the criterion). To develop evidence of predictive validity, follow-up data are gathered. For example, newly developed screening inventories to predict abusive behaviors might be correlated with the results of follow-up studies of research participants who completed the inventories to determine just how well the instruments were able to predict abusive behaviors.

One example of the concept of predictive validity that is well known to students is the use of standardized tests such as SATs or GREs to predict how students will perform in college or graduate school. The measure of how students actually perform in school is the criterion. Educational researchers interested in providing evidence of criterion validity for standardized tests would attempt to demonstrate a high correlation between scores attained by students on these tests and their later performance in school (usually as measured by grade point average or a similar indicator of academic success).

Construct Validity

As noted earlier, validity in measurement refers to the degree of fit between a construct and indicators of the construct. Then, isn't construct validity what validity is all about? Yes, in fact, it is. In some ways, it might be accurate to describe the other indicators of validity (content, criterion, and even face validity) as just different facets or subelements of construct validity.

A narrower definition of construct validity is the degree to which the measure of the construct of interest is related to other variables or constructs that are hypothesized to be either related or not related to our construct. It can be measured using *convergent validity*, *discriminant validity,* or both. Convergent validity is the degree to which the measure correlates highly to measures of other constructs or variables that researchers believe are related to the construct of interest. Discriminant validity is the degree to which the measure does not correlate to measures of other constructs or variables that are believed to be unrelated to the construct of interest. For example, the diagnosis of anorexia nervosa includes both disordered eating behaviors and unrealistic attitudes toward body and shape. Therefore, if we were testing the construct validity of a new scale believed to measure attitudes toward body and shape, we would look for a correlation between our scale and an established scale that measures disordered eating behaviors (evidence of convergent validity). Conversely, if there is no theoretical connection between disordered eating behaviors and, for example, conduct disorder, we would not expect to see a strong correlation between a scale measuring disordered eating behaviors and a scale that measures conduct disorder (evidence of discriminant validity).

Many of the variables that researchers seek to measure in social work research are really constructs. Psychiatric diagnostic categories, such as anorexia nervosa, bipolar disorder, attention deficit hyperactivity disorder, and schizophrenia, are constructs. Their presence is inferred when certain conditions exist. For example, schizophrenia is said to exist only when a certain group of symptoms or behaviors is identified as present (certain thought disorders, inappropriate affect, and so forth). Many other problems that social workers seek to address, such as unemployment, codependency, substance abuse, family violence, and homelessness, are also constructs. In many social work research studies, especially in single-system evaluation research (Chapter 7), these problems or constructs are usually defined as the dependent variable, the condition that researchers seek to alleviate or otherwise positively influence through their interventions. Some type of intervention (i.e., an individual service or social program) is what they hope will alleviate or positively influence the dependent variable. Thus, the presence or absence of the intervention is often the independent variable. These interventions might be, for example, community empowerment programs, behavior modification therapy, feminist therapy, supportive treatment, confrontation treatment, and reality therapy.

It is important to note that each of these interventions (the independent variable) is also a construct. Construct validity requires that all variables are measured accurately. Thus, in many social work research studies, the construct that is the independent variable (the intervention or its absence) must also be understood and explained and appropriate indicators used to determine the degree to which it exists or does not exist. Why is this important for producing accurate and useful research findings? Suppose that a research study attempts to learn whether a new recreational program whose outcome objective was to reduce youth gang activity in a community was successful. Obviously, we would have to find a way to accurately operationalize and measure the variable "level of youth gang activity" (the dependent variable) in the community, perhaps before and after implementation of the program. However, before we could conclude whether the proposed program was effective in achieving its objective, we would also have to use appropriate indicators to learn if the program that was implemented was really the program that was supposed to be implemented, that is, it remained true to its original design. Our measurement will lack construct validity unless we do this, and any conclusions drawn from the research will be unlikely to be valid. Suppose we did not do this (provide a valid measurement of the independent variable) and the program that was actually implemented drifted considerably from its original model (a fairly common occurrence). If youth gang activity declined following the onset of the program, we might erroneously conclude that the program (as originally conceptualized) was successful in reducing gang activity (a cause-effect relationship) and should thus be implemented in other communities. This conclusion would not be a valid one, since really a different program or other unknown factors may have produced changes in the dependent variable. What's more, our research would also lack *conclusion validity*; that is, the conclusion that the program that was designed and the level of gang activity are even related at all would be erroneous, because one of them wasn't even present.

If an instrument is to provide a valid measurement of a construct, it must measure the essential components of the construct. Thus, if a researcher designed a data collection instrument to classify participants as homeless or not homeless, the instrument should include all items that cover all indicators of the construct "homelessness." If the instrument, for example, provides no indication of whether the participant has a permanent address accessible through the U.S. Postal Service, that would suggest that the instrument is probably lacking in construct validity. Similarly, if the independent variable is the use or nonuse of a specific intervention, such as a new program designed to reduce homelessness, construct validity would require that the researcher ensure that the program that was implemented is really the one described in its design.

There is no simple, direct way to assess the degree of construct validity that is present. It is assessed by accumulating a variety of evidence, usually in the form of the other indicators of validity. This involves the use of several related types of information. Construct validity demonstrates that the construct being measured exists within a theoretical framework, thereby explaining the construct itself and how it relates to other variables. In a sense, a test of construct validity becomes both a measure of the construct and a test of its underlying theory.

Concurrent validity data can help to provide evidence of the construct validity of an instrument. For example, the researcher in the previous example could determine if people who have been classified as homeless by The Salvation Army are also classified as homeless using the current measurement instrument. If the instrument shows a pattern of relationships with criterion measures (classifications that agree with the Salvation Army classification), then there is some evidence of construct validity. Face validity—for example, the fact that it is just logical to conclude that a person living in his or her car is probably homeless—could also help to support claims of construct validity.

What about the measurement of the independent variable? How would we demonstrate the construct validity of its measurement? Suppose the logic model or other description of the program to address the problem of homelessness contains services such as job training or substance abuse counseling. Concurrent validity data could be used to see if the method of classifying these services by the researcher are the same as or similar to those offered in other programs that claimed to offer job training or substance abuse counseling. Face validity might be implied in the fact that a measurement instrument was used to determine if participants in the program were given instruction in how to prepare a job application form or how to dress for a job interview.

Some familiar words (e.g., *value, reliability, validity, normal*) have specific meanings in research and statistics, different from what they have in common speech or in social work practice. Sometimes, the same word even has different meanings within different research contexts. This can be especially confusing. In this chapter, we used one word, *validity*, which we used in Chapter 6 to discuss the internal and external validity of research studies. Box 10.2 should be helpful in clearing up any confusion that this may have caused.

SOURCES OF MEASUREMENT ERROR

The validity of measurement in a research study can be negatively affected in many ways. When it is affected, this is described as measurement error. In discussing reliability earlier in this chapter, we noted that virtually all methods of measurement and measurement instruments have their limits. For example, as mentioned before, a measurement instrument may be considered reliable for measuring a variable with males, but not with females. That may be because the data used to construct it was collected from only males and it is believed that females differ in some ways that relate to the variable. Caution should always be exercised when instruments are to be used with research participants who are different in important ways from groups with whom the existing instruments were developed and "normed." Before using an existing measurement instrument, social work researchers need to be familiar with how and on which population group(s) the measurement was constructed. It should never be assumed that established norms and benchmarks on which scoring is based

Box 10.2	**Different Types of Validity in Research**	
Type of Validity	**Research Activity**	**Question(s) Addressed**
Internal validity	Research design	If a relationship between variables was found, is it a causal one? Can I be certain that something else did not produce the measurements of the dependent variable?
External validity	Sampling	To what extent can I generalize the research findings beyond the research sample(s) in the current study?
Content validity	Measurement	Does the measurement instrument adequately cover all of the components of the construct being measured?
Face validity	Measurement	Does the measurement instrument appear to measure what it is supposed to measure?
Criterion validity	Measurement	Is the measure of the construct consistent with another accepted indicator of the same construct?
Concurrent validity	Measurement	Is the measure correlated with another indicator of the construct measured at approximately the same time?
Predictive validity	Measurement	Is the measure correlated with a future performance or behavior as measured by a second indicator or criterion of the construct?
Construct validity	Measurement	How well did I measure the variables/constructs that I claim to have measured? In particular, how does the measure of the variable correlate with other constructs that are theoretically related or unrelated to it?
Convergent validity	Measurement	Does the measure correlate highly with other variables theoretically related to it?
Discriminant validity	Measurement	Does the measure *not* correlate with other variables hypothesized to be unrelated to it?
Conclusion validity	Data analysis	Were the research conclusions correct? If hypotheses were tested, was an error made in determining whether or not there was found to be support for them?

apply uniformly to all participants across all settings and cultural contexts. When conducting cross-cultural research (Chapter 8), efforts should be made to find instruments normed on a variety of cultural groups or nationalities, or to look for instruments developed in a variety of cultural contexts that attempt to measure the same underlying construct. Such instruments are difficult to find. A few examples of instruments designed for and/or normed on specific ethnic and racial groups follow:

- The Acculturation Rating Scale for Mexican Americans (ARSMA-II) (Cuellar, Arnold, & Maldonado, 1995), which measures degree of acculturation for normal and clinical populations of Mexican Americans
- The Hispanic Stress Inventory (HIS) (Cervantes, Padilla, & Salgado de Snyder, 1991), which measures psychological stress in immigrants from Latin America and in Mexican Americans
- TEMAS (Tell-Me-a-Story) (Constantino, Malgady, & Rogler, 1988), which is a thematic apperception test developed for African-American and Hispanic children

♦ The Multigroup Ethnic Identity Measure (Phinney, 1992), which measures ethnic identity on elements that are common across groups

♦ The Cultural Congruity Scale (CCS) (Gloria & Robinson-Kurpius, 1996), which measures the cultural congruity of Chicano/a students in higher education in the United States

Special concerns about reliability and validity arise when instruments are translated from one language to another for use with linguistically diverse study populations. The nonequivalence of research instruments can limit the usefulness of data obtained in cross-cultural research. There are many ways to increase the likelihood that both the reliability and validity of a measurement instrument will be maintained throughout the translation process. Five suggestions follow:

1. Attempt to understand one's own values and cultural perspectives and how they might influence one's definitions of key constructs that the instrument is designed to measure.

2. Consult with members of the group of interest to determine the cultural relevance of constructs of interest within the target population and assess the face validity of the instrument items for measuring constructs of interest in that culture.

3. Translate the instrument from the first language to the second language, using skilled, bilingually fluent translators working individually, sequentially, or as a team. (The translators should be aware of idiomatic subtleties related to geography or social class.)

4. Translate the instrument from the second language back into the first language, using skilled translators. The back-translation should then be compared to the original version to determine the accuracy of the original translation.

5. Field-test the translated instrument using bilingual participants, to establish equivalence through parallel forms reliability coefficients (compare scores on the translated version versus scores on the original version).

Policy Practice

How could a politician purposefully word a question about abortion in order to attempt to sway the participants to be reflect a position in opposition to abortion?

What we have just described is a way to avoid something called cultural bias, a form of *systematic measurement error* often seen in cross-cultural research. However, systematic measurement error can easily occur within research in one's own culture as well. When measurement lacks construct validity, systematic measurement error will almost certainly occur. We might, for example, believe that we are measuring a construct such as clinical depression, but if the only questions we ask relate to physical symptoms, we may really be measuring our research participants' health status instead. Or, if we asked participants how they would respond in a crisis situation such as a hurricane or flood, they might respond very differently than if we actually observed how they reacted in such a situation. If we used their responses as indicators of how they would act, we would commit measurement error. Similarly, if we asked a group of social workers how they plan to vote in an upcoming election, they might be likely to say they would vote for candidates who are endorsed by NASW, yet many might do just the opposite when they got to the polls. Their responses would reflect what they think they should say (known as *social desirability bias*)—if we used them as an indicator of what they will do, we would again have systematic measurement error. Even the wording of questions can result in systematic measurement error if, for example, we word a question in such a way that virtually everyone feels they have to answer in a certain way.

Not all measurement errors are systematic and relatively easy to detect. There is also something called *random measurement error*, error that does not occur in any identifiable pattern or direction. If data are collected in a group setting, distractions such as cell phones ringing or the fact that the session is videotaped may affect some peoples' responses to questions, but not others. The problem is we have no way of knowing who was affected and who wasn't. Or, in a mailed survey, some people may just be tired and quit reading the items after a while. They complete the survey, just putting anything down to get finished. However, we will not know when this happened or with whom.

We have mentioned just a few ways that measurement error can occur—there are many more. As the reader has probably concluded, totally reliable and valid measurement may be unattainable. However, that does not relieve us of the responsibility to do the best we can to achieve it.

SUMMARY

Chapter 10 presented the concepts basic to measurement of variables. Two early tasks of the measurement process were identified: conceptualization and operationalization. Other measurement tasks of the researcher involve deciding just how precisely a variable can or should be measured and determining the level of measurement. The four levels of measurement (nominal, ordinal, interval, and ratio) were differentiated.

The criteria used to evaluate the quality of measurement were discussed. Reliability relates to the degree to which a measurement produces consistent results. Validity refers to the degree to which a measurement is successful in actually measuring what it has claimed to measure, that is, the construct that underlies a variable. A measurement that is reliable is not necessarily valid. However, a measurement that is valid will be both reliable and unbiased. We described the methods that researchers use to estimate the amount of various types of reliability and validity that a measurement instrument possesses. Their relative importance for different types of measurement and for different research objectives were identified and discussed. We emphasized the point that, if research findings are to be accurate, the measurement of all variables (the independent as well as the dependent ones) must reflect construct validity. Finally, we examined a few ways in which reliability and validity of measurement may be influenced by cultural differences and other sources of measurement error.

Succeed with PEARSON **mysocialworklab**

Log onto **www.mysocialworklab.com** and answer the following questions. (If you did not receive an access code to **MySocialWorkLab** with this text and wish to purchase access online, please visit www. mysocialworklab.com.)

1. **Watch the Core Competencies Video: Policy Practice: Building Alliances.** If you wanted to gather data on this prisoner, how could you operationalize his behavior into a variable? At what level of measurement will you measure the variable as you have defined it?

2. **Read the Case Study: Domestic Violence: Mikki's Story.** If you were to conduct a single-system evaluation with Mikki, what are three variables you might use to measure her progress? At what level of measurement would you probably define each of these variables?

PRACTICE TEST

1. This requires testing the same participant twice, using the same measuring instrument to measure a variable both times, and then comparing the pair of measurements for each case:
   a. Parallel forms reliability
   b. Split half reliability
   c. Test-retest reliability
   d. Criterion validity

2. This is calculated by administering two or more different versions of the same instrument to the same participants:
   a. Parallel forms reliability
   b. Split half reliability
   c. Test-retest reliability
   d. Criterion validity

3. This involves an assessment of whether a measurement adequately covers all aspects or components of a particular concept:
   a. Face validity
   b. Construct validity
   c. Content validity
   d. Criterion validity

4. This is determined by demonstrating that scores on the measuring instrument are consistent with some other accepted indicator of the same variable:
   a. Face validity
   b. Construct validity
   c. Content validity
   d. Criterion validity

5. Describe the difference between convergent and discriminant validity.

ASSESS YOUR COMPETENCE
Use the scale below to rate your current level of achievement on the following concepts or skills associated with each competency presented in the chapter:

1	2	3
I can accurately describe the concept or skill.	I can consistently identify the concept or skill when observing and analyzing practice activities.	I can competently implement the concept or skill in my own practice.

_____ Understanding how to conceptualize and operationalize a variable

_____ Being able to identify a variable's level of measurement

_____ Understanding the concepts of reliability and validity

_____ Being familiar with the major forms of reliability and validity

11

Methods for Acquiring Research Data

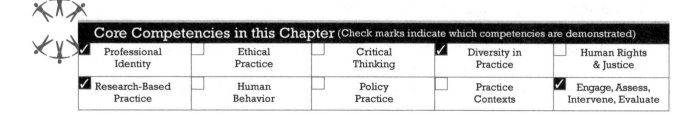

Core Competencies in this Chapter (Check marks indicate which competencies are demonstrated)				
✓ Professional Identity	☐ Ethical Practice	☐ Critical Thinking	✓ Diversity in Practice	☐ Human Rights & Justice
✓ Research-Based Practice	☐ Human Behavior	☐ Policy Practice	☐ Practice Contexts	✓ Engage, Assess, Intervene, Evaluate

One of the common characteristics of all types of research is that it seeks to increase our knowledge through the analysis of data. Data can come in many forms and have many origins. Some research designs (such as those used for evaluating social programs) require access to many data sources. Others rely on just a few or only a single source.

There is no one best data source. Each has advantages and limitations that are considered in answering the important research design question—what data source or sources would be most appropriate for my research study? In this chapter, we will examine the methods most frequently used in social work research (see Box 11.1 for overview of these methods).

SECONDARY DATA ANALYSIS

Sometimes, the time-consuming and expensive task of collecting original data for research studies proves unnecessary. Many research questions can be examined using data that already exist, often without leaving our place of employment. The reanalysis of selected data that were collected and stored for some other purpose is known as *secondary data analysis*. For reasons that will be evident, it is much more likely to be a viable option as a data source in quantitative studies than in qualitative ones.

Sources

There are many sources of research data within the public domain that can be useful to social workers for conducting research.

Human service organizations store great amounts of information about their clients and programs, which can sometimes be used to examine research questions and test hypotheses using quantitative methods. Extensive data banks exist within public social agencies, both to meet government requirements and to facilitate service delivery to clients. Smaller private and sectarian organizations also store a substantial amount of information about clients and client functioning. Increasingly, information is stored and retrieved via computerized data bases and information systems. However, in some smaller organizations, it still is maintained in the form of written files and records.

There are also many sources of research data within the public domain that can be useful to social workers for conducting research. For example, census

---

Box 11.1 Common Methods for Acquiring Research Data

Method	Definitions/Description
Secondary data analysis	Uses data collected for some other purpose
Oral histories	Recorded, firsthand descriptions of people who "were there" (Can be a source of secondary data or can be considered "original data")
Systematic observation	Watching, observing, recording (may include participation)
Mailed surveys	Data collected via postal service
In-person interviews	One-on-one conversations; structure varies
Group interviews	Several individuals provide data simultaneously; structure varies
Telephone	Data collected via telephone or fax
Electronic communication	Data collected via computer through e-mail, instant messaging, instant chats, etc.

data are a rich source of research-worthy information, collected at great expense to the taxpayer. However, they generally tend to be underused by researchers. The public documents section of libraries stores a wide variety of statistical data, such as labor and public health statistics. Federal grant reports and reports of demonstration projects also are available and frequently contain useful data.

More and more data, collected for a variety of purposes, are appearing on the Internet each year. These data are often the product of well-funded research studies by governmental agencies and relate to human conditions and problems that are often the focus of social work research. Organizations such as the National Science Foundation, the National Institute on Alcohol and Alcoholism, the National Institute on Child Health and Human Development, and the National Institutes of Health now place their research data in the public domain and encourage others to use it for their own research. It has been suggested that this has occurred, in part, because of the recognition that the high cost of federal research studies can be better justified if the data they produce can be made available for "mining" to answer other research questions besides those originally addressed (Sales, Lichtenwalter, & Fevola, 2006). Trustworthy research data on the Internet presents some excellent opportunities for social work researchers. Data that are within the public domain may be used with appropriate citation from their sources. Researchers do not need permission to analyze census data or data published by the National Center for Health Statistics and other federal agencies. They can be used, for example, to chronicle social changes, such as the rise and decline of various occupations and urban migration or the increased presence of women in the workplace over the past century. However, as we noted in Chapter 4, it is worth remembering that not all data that appear on the Internet can be trusted. Thus, it is always wise to *consider the source*.

NASW, CSWE, and other professional organizations also annually collect data about their members. Social workers interested in conducting research using selected characteristics of professional social workers, as well as social work educators, schools, and students can obtain permission to reanalyze these data.

Different Uses

Secondary analysis is used in descriptive and some explanatory quantitative studies. It is not used in experiments because, by definition, they require that the independent variable is either introduced or manipulated by the researcher. In secondary analysis, this would be impossible because data used typically are those collected by someone else for some other purpose. Some examples of use of social agency data may help to demonstrate the wide variety of ways that secondary analysis can be used in research if ethical and legal requirements can be met:

▸ In a private psychiatric in-patient facility, a researcher may wish to describe the participation of institutionalized clients in making discharge plans. A secondary analysis of data drawn from available case records might be used.

▸ In a child protection agency, case record data could be used to compile a picture of the disposition of cases that are referred for investigation of possible child abuse. They could be used to create a composite picture of patterns of service delivery.

    ◆ As part of a program evaluation of a battered women's shelter, agency record data could be used to learn if clients served by the organization are representative of the community in age, income level, ethnicity, and so forth. Data could be compared statistically to county- or community-maintained data on the same social indicators.

    ◆ In an alcohol rehabilitation facility, secondary data analysis could be used to seek support for the hypothesis that there is a positive correlation between the level of clients' participation in a given program and changes in some aspect of their functioning.

When large databases can be accessed by computer, there may be a temptation to select most or even all variables and to simply see if there are relationships between or among any of them. We recommend caution in using this approach as a method of secondary analysis. For both ethical and statistical reasons (beyond our discussion here), relationships between or among variables should be analyzed only after the researcher has justified hypotheses about their relationships (on the basis of the literature review). Computers should be used to statistically analyze relationships believed to exist, not to engage in a fishing expedition.

Tasks Required

There are many tasks that require special attention in research that employ secondary analysis of data. They include the following:

    ◆ **Operationalizing the variables.**   Methods used to measure variables in the original data collection should be identified, and if at all possible, the same operational definitions should be applied in the current study. Also, an estimate of the degree of reliability and validity (Chapter 10) of the original measurement should be made.

    ◆ **Specifying the sampling plan used.**   The source of data (case record, personnel file, monthly statistical report, and so on) and the strategy for selecting a sample of cases should be specified and justified.

    ◆ **Developing a data collection instrument and coding scheme for data collection.**   Typically, this is accomplished by using a data collection instrument that has been developed specifically for the research. Data are drawn from the original documents and recorded on the instrument. The researcher may decide to have more than one person read and record the same data from the original source. If this is done, an estimate of the interobserver reliability of the data gathering method can be made (Chapter 10).

    ◆ **Analyzing the data.**   The appropriate level of measurement for each variable must be determined (on the basis of information about how it was originally collected) before statistical analysis (Chapter 13) can be conducted.

    ◆ **Identifying the limitations of the study.**   Although most research reports typically include a section describing limitations of the study, the inclusion of a limitations section is particularly important in secondary analysis. Due to the nature of the data being analyzed (they were measured and recorded for some purpose other than the current study and usually by people other than the researcher), there is a greater-than-usual likelihood that they will have limitations regarding their application to the current study.

Advantages

Secondary data analysis is appealing to researchers for a number of reasons. First, the financial costs associated with it are often minimal compared with other data collection methods. Second, it generally requires less time than other forms of data collection and analysis. The data are already collected and recorded; the researcher needs only to develop a sampling method and an instrument for coding and recording them. If the data are already available in a form that is compatible with statistical analysis software, analysis can begin almost immediately following the literature review and the development of focused questions and/or hypotheses.

When ethically and legally feasible (under HIPAA, medical records now are generally inaccessible), secondary analyses are less intrusive than other methods that collect original data from participants. Permissions may not need to be secured, as people are not interviewed or observed in person by the researcher. However, when agency record data are used, clients' permission may be required because data were provided for use in receiving assistance, not for research. Problems related to anonymity may not be an issue if data are stored by case number or some other method that ensures that the researcher cannot possibly know who provided which data when it was originally collected. As a rule, one is less likely to encounter bureaucratic obstacles to conducting secondary analysis than when conducting other types of research that entail the collection of original data from clients or staff.

Limitations

Given the many advantages of conducting secondary analysis, why is it not used more frequently? For one thing, even when data are available for secondary data analysis, they are often quite limited. When planning to collect original data, researchers generally learn from the literature review what variables need to be studied (Chapter 4). Then they collect whatever data are needed. In secondary analysis, the existing data may fall short of providing all that is required to answer a research question or provide support or nonsupport for a hypothesis. If measurements of a variable are not in the record or document, the variable generally cannot be examined (unless it is possible for the researcher to go back personally and measure it). The researcher's plans for studying a question or testing a hypothesis may need to be modified to fit available data.

Another potential problem with the use of secondary analysis relates to the quality of measurement that was conducted. If the data are lacking in credibility, no amount of secondary analysis will improve their quality. A thorough examination of the context in which data were originally collected can help the researcher determine whether they can be trusted. An assessment of their quality should be made. Questions might include, for example, Who gathered them, using what kind of recording method? Was there possibly a hidden agenda that may have influenced what was recorded and what was not? What assurances of confidentiality or anonymity were given? If the people who originally recorded the information are available to the researcher, they should be consulted on these and other issues.

Most secondary data that are in the public domain or otherwise available for research tend to be relatively sterile. Thus, they cannot provide answers to the questions that are the focus of many social work research studies that seek an in-depth understanding of such phenomena as human emotions, perceptions, or behaviors. A notable exception is oral histories.

ORAL HISTORIES

One way to learn what it was like to experience some event or phenomenon is to ask people to describe it in their own words (and to preserve what was said). Oral histories are written, audio, or video recordings of people discussing an experience or life event from their own perspectives. These recordings are analyzed using a variety of research methods (e.g., content analysis as described in Chapter 4) to attempt to answer a variety of research questions.

Oral histories are firsthand accounts, what would seem to be, on the surface, a trustworthy data source. Who better to describe something than someone who "lived it"? However, when using oral histories as a data source, it should be remembered that what an oral history describes most accurately is how someone perceived or experienced something, not necessarily how it actually occurred. Even descriptions of perceptions and experiences may not be totally accurate if much time has lapsed. Pre-research meetings with participants (sometimes called *narrators*) are often used to develop comfortable relationships and determine which questions might be most productive to ask when oral histories are compiled. Then, the interviews are conducted and recorded, often over many sessions. Consequently, the person compiling an oral history can easily influence what the participant says. For these reasons, oral histories are generally regarded as qualitative data.

Oral histories preserve history. Thus, they enable us to learn from people who may no longer be with us or who are here now but will not always be around to tell their stories. For example, oral histories exist in which veterans of World Wars I and II, survivors of Nazi concentration camps, participants in the American civil rights movement, early labor union organizers, and people who worked in President Franklin Roosevelt's New Deal programs describe what these events were like from their perspective. The Columbia University Oral History Research Office is currently compiling oral histories of people who lived through the events of September 11, 2001, in New York and Washington, D.C. (Clark & Bearman, n.d.).

There are many examples of oral histories within the literature. Oral histories sometimes are used in ethnographic studies (described in Chapter 8). For example, the oral history data collection method was used in a study that examined life themes of native Hawaiian female elders (Mokuau & Browne, 1994). The elders, known as *kupunas* to native Hawaiians, play important roles in native Hawaiian culture. Three themes selected for emphasis in the study were relationships among people, peoples' relationships with nature, and their spiritual and religious beliefs. The data developed in interviews were transcribed and analyzed according to the themes and prepared in draft form for review by participants to aid in correcting any misinformation. Following the reviews, they were preserved by University of Hawaii's Center for Oral History.

In another study, Martin (1995) conducted in-depth interviews of elderly African Americans living in a community in the southeastern part of the United States. She gathered and recorded oral histories from members of fifteen families. The study evolved from Martin's concern with how the relative strengths of African-American families are portrayed. It documented African-American family adaptation systems.

Martin's interviewing schedule was an adaptation of Hartman's eco-map. A copy of the map was provided to all participants as a stimulus for discussion. The map was later used to help organize the oral history data that Martin had gathered.

Oral histories preserve history. Thus, they enable us to learn from people who may no longer be with us or who are here now but will not always be around to tell their stories.

Martin made extensive use of individual narratives to preserve the stories of her participants. All interviews were audiotaped and later transcribed. Themes related to adaptation, survival, and growth were identified in analyses of the transcriptions. The data were presented both in tabular form and thematically. Whenever possible, the respondents' own words were used to highlight important findings.

In the first phase of a more extensive project, Logan (2007) interviewed and recorded the experiences of ten African-American women who were involved in the civil rights movement, in South Carolina. Each participant's life narrative was captured in both booklet form and DVD.

In these oral histories and in many others, participants were encouraged to *tell their story*, interpret what it meant to them, and even describe their emotions and feelings surrounding it. Oral histories can be used to create a historical record of almost any event where participants were present. For example, members of the original board of directors of a social agency can be asked to describe their recollections of their early meetings and discussions. Their oral histories can be used at a later time to provide insight into why the organization began, what it hoped to accomplish, and how its mission evolved.

The examples that we have cited help to illustrate the many uses of oral histories. They also suggest why it is difficult to say exactly what an oral history is. Is it a product of some activity, an original data source, or a secondary data source? The answer to this question is that it can be all three!

For people who compile and preserve them, oral histories are often the end product of their work, a recorded description of how people experienced a life event, preserved for posterity. When this is the case, compiling and preserving them is an activity, but it is really more the work of a historian than a researcher. It is a valuable contribution to society, but it does not require most of the knowledge and skills that researchers use.

If the person compiling oral histories is more interested in answering research questions of immediate interest or, less frequently, determining if there is support for the research hypotheses (i.e., he or she is functioning more as a researcher), the compilation can be regarded as an original or primary data source. For example, a researcher could compile oral histories in such a way as to seek answers to a question such as "How do people from the Middle East perceive that they have been treated differently in North America following the terrorist acts of the early twenty-first century?" The histories that are compiled can be analyzed in search of an answer, using the skills of the researcher.

No matter why or by whom (historians or researchers) oral histories are created, once they are complied, they become a potential secondary data source for researchers who come along later. They can be used to seek answers to research questions that those who compiled them may have had little interest in or may never even have contemplated.

It is probably most accurate to simply state that oral histories are a good data resource for researchers. They may be either a source of secondary data *or* an original data source.

SYSTEMATIC OBSERVATION

When conducting either one-on-one interviews or group interviews such as focus groups, researchers have the opportunity to observe research participants. These observations often yield additional, unanticipated data for their research.

Sometimes, researchers observe a behavior or phenomenon in a more planned way. When a researcher makes a plan to observe a behavior or phenomenon, then follows the plan by observing and recording the data in a systematic way, it is called *systematic observation.* It is used in both qualitative and quantitative studies, but it tends to be less structured in qualitative research than in predominantly quantitative studies.

Observation is sometimes made in a created or contrived situation. The Zimbardo studies (Stanford prison experiment) of college students assuming the role of prisoner or prison guard (Chapter 1) are an example of this type of research. The created situation may also involve deception, as in the ethically questionable Milgram electroshock studies discussed in Chapter 2. However, most observation is conducted in a natural setting, one that is not created for purposes of the research.

Unstructured Observation

There are many instances in social work research where we may use observation as a data source. For example, we may wish to know more about parent-child interaction, group process, or task completion. Or, as part of a program evaluation, we may wish to learn what it is like to be a client in the program. If so, systematic observation can constitute a valuable source of data.

Unstructured observation is characterized by a lack of formal data gathering instruments. Typically, in unstructured observation, the researcher is either a passive observer (observes but does not participate in the activity) or a participant observer (observes and takes part in the activity). These methods are appropriate when the phenomenon being studied cannot be clearly specified in advance and when it is important to observe participants in their own environments rather than in a laboratory setting. For example, researchers who are interested in studying the behavior of a group such as Weight-Watchers or Alcoholics Anonymous might choose to join the group and make observations over a period of time. Of course, in such situations, the researcher would have to address certain ethical obligations, since deception may be involved. He or she should also adhere to the rules of the group. For example, the identities of members of the groups should not be revealed to others, or social interaction with members outside the group setting may be prohibited. Researchers in anthropology and social psychology have used unstructured observational methods in their studies of street gangs, homeless people, and various non-Western cultures.

In areas of inquiry where knowledge is limited, it is often best to observe behavior in an unstructured manner. In so doing, the researcher is not constrained by categories or checklists and is open to viewing all behaviors (or components of behaviors) that are displayed. Unstructured observation really falls somewhere between exploratory and descriptive research. It is often used to learn more about a behavior, culture, or environment of interest, often to lay the groundwork for subsequent studies that are more structured.

Unstructured observation requires researchers to maintain field notes. Usually, they either make mental notes for later recording or maintain a recorded running account or description of behaviors during the observation period. Developing and maintaining a note-taking procedure is crucial; otherwise, at the end of the observation, researchers would have to depend on their memory to recall what they observed.

Because unstructured observation tends to yield data that are primarily qualitative in nature, information collected often is presented in narrative

Professional Identity

What are some ethical considerations to be addressed when the researcher becomes a member of a group in order to make observations of the group's other members?

rather than statistical form. Running accounts, case vignettes, and anecdotes are often used. Direct quotations from participants are frequently included.

We will use an example to demonstrate how unstructured observation might be used in social work research. Suppose that a researcher is interested in developing an understanding of the psychosocial needs of family caregivers of older people. Unstructured observation might be used to study caregivers and the older people to whom they offer care in their homes. The researcher could observe the needs and demands of older people, as well as the responses of their caregivers. The interactions between the two would be observed and characterized. Particularly, the activities and emotional responses of the care-givers would be noted. The application of an unstructured observational method would allow certain kinds of questions to be addressed:

- Do caregivers seem able to perform the tasks required to provide needed care? If not, what are their emotional responses to not being able to meet the older peoples' needs?
- Do caregivers have opportunities to meet their own needs? What sacrifices do they appear to be making to care for the older person? How able are they to verbalize anger or frustration because of the demands of caregiving?
- What assistance is available to caregivers? Are there other people who are part of the caregiving network? If so, which ones appear to be most helpful to caregivers, and why?

Advantages

Unstructured observation is characterized by flexibility. During the observation period, researchers take note of behaviors, reactions, or environmental features that relate to the phenomenon being studied. Trained, sensitive observers are able to record data about many variables that may be impacting the phenomenon. During the course of an unstructured observation, researchers may become aware of the influence of other phenomena that were not originally identified or conceptualized. They may include observations of such phenomena in their study or make them the focus of a subsequent research study.

Findings from studies using systematic observation can often be generalized beyond those research participants who were studied. Especially in naturalistic observation—that is, in studies where data are gathered by observing large numbers of participants over an extended period of time in their own environments—the external validity of the research findings can be quite good. The researcher can be relatively confident that the behavior observed is characteristic of what people (at least in that setting) actually say and do. Of course, as in any method of data collection, the external validity of the findings can also be quite limited if the sample of individuals studied lacks representativeness.

Limitations

In systematic observation, the validity of research findings may be affected by participants' reactivity, that is, the degree to which they modify their behavior in response to the presence of the observer. When possible, the researcher should select an observer role that will at least minimize the impact of reactivity while still providing the needed access to data. For example, an observer watching a child's behavior in the classroom may choose to watch from behind a one-way mirror rather than from the back of the classroom to minimize reactivity.

Other disadvantages inherent in the use of unstructured observation (besides reactivity) relate to the consistency and objectivity of measurement procedures. Both can seriously damage the credibility of research findings. Consistency of data collection is a primary concern because, in unstructured observation, data collection is not standardized. When more than one observer collects data, variation in data collection procedures may be especially great. This is the issue of interobserver agreement (Chapter 10). The reliability of data can be enhanced by employing two or more observers to conduct the same measurement. Interobserver agreement can be assessed by using a form of statistical analysis that estimates the percentage of agreement between two observers.

Fatigue or boredom can also negatively affect the quality of the observations made, because observation generally occurs over an extended period of time. The potential for this problem can be reduced by using several observers, with each responsible for relatively short time segments of observation.

Because observers must be sensitized to a behavior before it is described and recorded, the likelihood exists that selective perception by observers will play a part in which behavior gets noted or the interpretation of what a behavior means. Training observers to increase sensitivity to the nature of the behavior of interest, use appropriate observational techniques, and use appropriate methods of recording data will minimize the major sources of measurement bias inherent in observation studies. However, subjectivity must be assumed to exist in all data collected using unstructured observation. That is why it is generally more suitable for use in qualitative research than in quantitative studies.

Structured Observation

If our goal is to accurately describe a behavior or phenomenon in a quantitative research study, structured observation is often used. Structured observation requires identifying a specific behavior or set of behaviors and systematically observing them over a given time period. A data collection instrument is used. Because of the structure imposed by this method, data are collected in the same format and therefore more easily sorted and analyzed than those collected using less structured observation methods.

In designing any form of observation, researchers must decide on the nature and degree of the researcher's involvement with the research participants. The most appropriate role for a given study depends on the purpose of the study, the researcher's assessment of how the most accurate data can be obtained, and legal and ethical issues. Observer roles may be understood as being located on a continuum from complete observer to participant observer. Possible observer roles follow:

- Concealed, nonparticipating (complete observer)
- Concealed, participating
- Not concealed, nonparticipating
- Not concealed, minimally participating
- Not concealed, participating (participant observer)

The two variables, concealment of the observer and degree of participation, can affect the quality of the data collected. When the presence of an observer is not concealed, participants may consciously or unconsciously alter their behavior (reactivity). However, when the presence of an observer is concealed, they are more likely to behave in their usual manner. Thus, if researchers wish to gather data without their presence affecting the participants, the observer should be concealed and nonparticipating. If the data are unlikely to be adversely affected by the observer's presence, the observer need not be concealed.

Concealing the observer from the participants does *not* mean the participants are not told they will be observed. As was noted in our discussion of research ethics in Chapter 2, not allowing participants to know that they are being observed may be considered unwarranted intrusion on their privacy. It might not be permitted by an IRB on ethical grounds because participants had not voluntarily agreed to be part of the research. Even if participants had agreed to participate in research but had not been told that they would be observed without their knowledge, that could be unethical. But if they voluntarily agreed to participate and were told that they would be observed but would not know exactly *when* they were being observed, this would not constitute deception and would probably be considered ethical.

How would the various roles be operationalized in social work research? Suppose a team of researchers is interested in studying the quality of interviewing skills of beginning social workers in a human service organization. If the researchers observe the interview sessions of new workers from behind a one-way mirror, they would be considered to be "concealed, nonparticipating." If the researchers observe from behind the mirror while using equipment that would enable them to prompt the interviewers, the observers would be "concealed, participating." They could also choose to observe a sample of client interviews conducted by beginning-level workers by actually sitting in on the interviews. If the researchers only record behaviors and do not influence the direction of the interview in any way, they are "not concealed, nonparticipating." But if the researchers provide occasional suggestions to the workers, communicate approval or disapproval of the workers' interviewing methods through nonverbal communication, or otherwise subtly influence them to conduct the interview differently, the researchers are "not concealed, minimally participating." However, if the interviews are conducted jointly by researchers and workers, and the workers' skills are later evaluated, the researchers would be "not concealed, participating."

Following are seven steps that are generally used to implement a structured observational design:

Engage, Assess, Intervene, Evaluate

What steps would you need to take before you observed a child's behavior in his classroom from behind a one-way mirror?

1. Define the behavior or list of behaviors to be studied. In structured observation, the researcher decides what behaviors to study on the basis of the literature review. They are those behaviors considered critical to an understanding of the research problem and answering research questions and/or testing hypotheses. Operational definitions of the behaviors are developed, and these definitions provide the basis for observation. Characteristics of the behaviors to be measured are also specified, for example, their frequency, duration, intensity, and so forth.

2. Identify a time frame during which the behaviors will be observed. The researcher has to know when specific behaviors are most likely to occur. This knowledge comes from a thorough understanding of the behavior under investigation derived from the review of literature, personal or professional experience, or an earlier research study. For example, if we are interested in studying verbal abuse by caregivers of older people, the researcher should have learned which times of day are most stressful for caregivers. This knowledge may have come from an earlier qualitative study that used unstructured observations to attempt to understand the caregivers' needs and problems.

In addition to identifying a specific time during the day to observe (or week or month), the literature review might also suggest a time interval during which the observation should occur. Will the observer observe for one hour at a time, for three hours, or for five minutes each hour? A time sample should be selected on the basis of the nature of the behavior under study (when and how frequently it is likely to occur) and the physical and emotional capacities of observers to gather accurate data. If observers are required to gather data for long periods of time, the quality of the data may suffer (referred to as *measurement decay*). Observers may get tired or bored and may require breaks and relief from their work.

3. Develop a data collection instrument. In structured observation, instruments typically take the form of behavioral checklists or category schemes. They are designed so that, when a behavior is displayed, its characteristics can easily be recorded. The instrument may also include demographic data on participants being observed, such as name, age, gender, or other identifying characteristics. As is true for new data collection instruments (Chapter 12), the instrument should be pilot-tested before use. This is done to see how effective and accurate the instrument is in describing the behavior.

4. Select an observer role. The observer role most appropriate to the behavior being studied is selected. Logistical and ethical issues (as previously mentioned) are addressed.

5. Train observers. Structured observation requires the use of trained research personnel. Unless the researcher is conducting all observations personally (a potential source of bias), observers usually are recruited or hired to observe. They need to be trained by the researcher in the method of observation to be used, and they need to gain experience with the use of the data collection instrument. Observers need to know what to look for, when to observe it, how to know if the behavior of interest is occurring, and how to record it using the instrument.

6. Conduct the observations. Observers observe participants' behavior, recording the data as they are obtained.

7. Verify the data. Data are checked for accuracy. One way to verify the data is to use two observers to observe and record the participants' behaviors. If the two observers generally agree on the behaviors observed, the researcher can be reasonably confident that the data are accurate.

Another way this is done is through the use of video recordings (with participant permission) to record behaviors. When recordings are made, an observer may or may not be present at the time the recordings are made. If an observer is present, then a second observer can watch the recordings later, and their findings can be compared to the original observer. In situations where it is more appropriate to not have an observer present during the recording, a team of trained reviewers can view the recordings later and arrive at a consensus as to what occurred. If such a consensus is not reached, a second review team may be used. If there is a serious discrepancy between the reviews of the two teams, the disputed data generally are discarded.

Advantages

A major advantage of structured observation is that the data acquired tend to be measured in a consistent manner and may be more accurate. They also tend to be better organized and in a more standardized format. It is easier to code them for computer analysis. Thus, quantitative analysis is possible, including statistical testing of research hypotheses.

Limitations

The downside is that, of necessity, they tend to be more sterile than data collected in less structured ways. Observations tend to be more limited in scope. Potentially valuable observations may not become part of the data if they were not planned for and included on the data collection instrument. Thus, structured observation is a more appropriate data source for quantitative studies, where the goal is to accurately measure a limited number of variables and examine possible relationships between and among them, rather than in qualitative studies, where the researcher is more open to receiving and processing the unexpected.

SURVEYS

Surveys have always been an important part of social work research. In program evaluations, a client satisfaction survey is almost always a requirement (even though, it should be remembered, client satisfaction is not always synonymous with program success). Most surveys are (1) cross-sectional, (2) used to collect quantitative data, and (3) descriptive. They are important tools in both basic and applied research, which are used to measure, for example, the demographic characteristics of people along with their opinions, preferences, and beliefs.

A good survey can answer many research questions. However, a poor one can lead to erroneous conclusions and actually be counterproductive toward attaining the goal of evidence-based social work practice. Planning to conduct a survey can be a painstaking process. It involves making many important decisions about, for example, sampling (see Chapter 9) and how data will be analyzed (see Chapter 13). It also requires an exacting process of word selection. Unless a previously developed, proven data collection instrument can be found that will generate the data required and offer valid measurements of key variables, a new instrument has to be developed and pilot-tested. Developing the instrument is not simply a matter of deciding what answers are sought and quickly writing a group of questions to elicit answers to them. The planning process entails considerable work and thought.

Even the best-planned surveys that rely on well-constructed data collection instruments can produce misleading findings. Because of their high potential for response bias (discussed later in this chapter), surveys that collect data by telephone or electronic data collection methods or rely heavily on mailed questionnaires are especially prone to producing misleading findings. This problem can also occur when acquiring data through in-person interviews, where reactivity can affect the validity of data. Next, we'll look at some of the challenges when conducting survey research.

Potential for Distortion

Distortion is likely to occur when any self-administered data collection instrument is used, but especially when data are collected by mail. When instruments are mailed to research participants, researchers do not know whether or not participants understood what was asked or if they responded honestly. A participant who does not need to face the researcher may be more likely to either inadvertently or deliberately misrepresent reality than one who participates in in-person interviews. That is why it is so important to word questions and statements well. For more information on constructing surveys, see Hutson and Kolbe (2010) or Rubin and Babbie (2011). Box 11.2 lists some of the common mistakes made when constructing surveys, along with examples of "how not to do it."

If inaccurate data are obtained because of poorly worded questions or statements, researchers may not be able to detect it. In the case of mailed surveys, researchers would not know if a participant took an hour to complete it or two minutes. They also have no way of knowing the state of mind of participants when the instruments were completed. They may well have been conscientious in completing them. However, they may also have "just put down anything," or even deliberately provided false information. Returned data collection instruments that contain clearly facetious or impossible responses can simply be discarded. But it is more difficult to determine what to do with a completed instrument that contains responses that are just a little unusual—it may contain valid data, or it may not.

Identity of the Participant

When using a mailed instrument, it may be impossible to know if the person to whom it was sent completed it. Did it fall into the hands of a mischievous

---

Box 11.2 What to Avoid When Constructing Survey Questions

Avoid

Leading questions – a question that suggests an answer through the use of certain "loaded" words, or includes the information for the answer the researcher wants.

Prestige bias – a question that could embarrass the respondent or encourage the respondent to give a false answer in order to look good.

Vagueness – the inclusion of phrases that may mean different things to different people or the use of answer choices that are unclear or difficult to understand.

Double-barreled questions – a question that has two questions joined into one question making it hard for the respondent to answer accurately.

Questions that are impossible to answer – questions that are impossible for the respondent to answer accurately.

Jargon, acronyms – the use of slang or abbreviations that may not have the same meaning to everyone.

Emotional language – the use of an emotional word or phrase that would bias the respondent toward one answer.

False beliefs – when a question assumes certain knowledge or belief held by the respondent.

"Loaded" responses – when the responses are loaded toward either a positive or negative response.

Examples of Poorly Worded Items*

Should innocent children have to do without needed medical care?

Do you regularly engage in unsafe sexual practices?

How often do you do things that risk your health?

Do you favor national health care supported through tax increases and a cut in social security benefits?

If you had not become ill, would you have finished college?

Do you think the NASA has finally jumped the shark?

Have abuses by welfare cheats and deadbeat fathers contributed to outrageous Medicaid costs?

When did you first learn that HIV is not a terminal illness?

Would you rate your current health care provider as OK, inferior, or very inadequate?

*Some of the poorly worded items may contain one or more additional problems.

child? Or was it deliberately delegated to another for completion? The identity of the respondent is almost certain to be a problem with some groups of people. For example, if a mailed questionnaire is sent to physicians, research respondents are likely to be staff members who work for the doctors and complete all of their paperwork.

Return Rate

A common problem with data collection by mail is a low rate of return of completed instruments. It is just too easy for potential research participants to discard a request for data or, with all good intentions, to set it aside and forget about it. The researcher who uses mailed data collection asks much and offers little. There is no potential for a pleasant interpersonal exchange with the researcher, only a letter from a person who is most likely a stranger and whose motives for seeking participation in the research are likely to be viewed with suspicion.

Although some research naturally draws a higher rate of return (e.g., research on emotionally charged topics or requests for data sent to college alumni or people who are fellow members of religious or civic organizations), the typical return rate for data collection instruments mailed to strangers is quite low. Hager, Wilson, Pollak, and Rooney (2003) looked at seventeen studies using mailed surveys and found a median return rate of 52 percent, with a range from 10 to 100 percent. Paxson, Dillmon, and Tarnai (1995) summarized the return rates for 26 studies using mailed surveys, and found an average return rate of 51 percent, ranging from 26 to 95 percent. A response rate that is much higher than an average response rate should be viewed with suspicion. For example, the researcher may have requested "interested volunteers" to complete a questionnaire. The implausibly high response rate reported may be misleading to the reader if this is not clearly stated in a research article or report. In fact, the researcher's findings may be more biased than another survey with a more typical return rate.

One obvious implication is that if a sample of responses of a given size is needed, the researcher should either (1) send out at least three times that many instruments to ensure having enough completed ones for data analysis or (2) go to extraordinary lengths to attempt to increase the usual, expected rate of return. The latter method is the preferred one. Here are some ideas that seem to work:

- ▶ **Keep it short.** The potential value of a well-designed study can be quickly negated if the researcher cannot generate a sufficiently high response rate. Excessive length probably results in more discarded instruments than any other feature of the instrument. Few potential participants will complete a ten-page instrument, no matter what the topic or their interest in it. Again, ten pages worth of questions jammed onto both sides of four or five pages, or use of a small font, will not fool anyone or fare any better. Such attempts at deception just make potential participants angry. Generally, if an instrument is longer than a few double spaced, easily read pages, it probably is trying to collect too much data at a single time. The researcher also should use as many fixed-alternative items (see Chapter 12) as possible. People are more likely to make a check mark or an X than to write one or more words.
- ▶ **Avoid bad times.** Although there is no ideal time to ask research participants to complete an instrument, some times of the year have been found to be worse than others. The December holidays should be

avoided. Among student participants, midterm and final examination times (and spring break) are not likely to result in a high response rate.

▶ **Provide incentives.** A small cash payment or a small gift as payment for participation will almost always result in more instruments being completed and returned. However, a promise of a reward after a completed instrument is received will be less effective in improving the response rate than an incentive mailed out with the instrument and cover letter. Why, then, are incentives not used more frequently? The costs of providing them may be great, and the costs may be more than just monetary. They may influence the responses received. Are participants who are paid for their responses more likely to provide either consciously or unconsciously those responses that they think are being sought by the researcher? The answer to this question is almost impossible to determine. Another type of incentive that can increase the response rate is an offer to share an outline or summary of the major research findings. If it is used, any requests for the summary (there are usually relatively few) must be honored, despite the cost of the additional correspondence. Not to do so would be unethical.

▶ **Provide postage-paid, preaddressed return envelopes.** People are unlikely to return an instrument unless they can do it simply and with no cost to them. Given the usual rate of return for mailed instruments, it generally is more economical to use metered envelopes than to affix a stamp to the return envelope. The postage for each response will be a little higher than if a stamp were provided, but one is charged only for those that are mailed back. Postage also affects return rate in another way. Generally, more expensive mailing methods yield higher rates of response. First-class mail is more likely to result in completed instruments than third-class mail. High-priority methods, such as overnight delivery, yield relatively high rates of response, but their cost can be prohibitive.

▶ **Use a carefully worded cover letter.** The cover letter should tell potential participants how they were selected to receive the instrument and that their response is important to the success of the research. Especially, if the research deals with sensitive matters (e.g., sexuality, religious or political beliefs, behaviors that are either illegal or not socially approved), potential respondents will need to know how the researcher got their names and how data will be used, and they will need to be assured that any confidentiality or anonymity promises will be kept.

The cover letter should reflect the researcher's genuine interest in the research problem and the assumption that potential participants may share that interest. Potential respondents will also need to be convinced that the instrument is not just being sent to millions of people and that their responses are important to the success of the research. If the researcher personally signs each cover letter, this impression will be likely reinforced.

Like the survey itself, careful wording of the cover letter is important. The wrong type of appeal for participation actually can reduce the rate of response. For example, a statement such as "I am a social work student who needs to collect data to meet my research course requirement" suggests that (1) the researcher probably is not really interested in the problem; (2) the researcher would not be conducting the research if it were not required; and (3) the findings are unlikely ever to be used for anything other than for helping a professor assign a course grade. Why would anyone want to take the time to respond favorably to such an appeal?

▶ **Use return addresses and letterheads.** The return address on an envelope used to mail out a data collection instrument and the inside address on the cover letter can affect the rate of return of mailed instruments. A home or business address can lend credibility to a research study; generally, a post office box number can harm it.

▶ **Use an agency address when it is likely to be beneficial.** The use of some agency addresses can help to increase the return rate; the use of others can decrease it. When an organizational affiliation is likely to increase the response rate, permission to use agency envelopes and stationery should be sought; they suggest written endorsement of and support for the research. However, some organizations, such as state departments of social services, mental health, or corrections, evoke certain emotional responses. Using their envelopes and stationery might negatively affect return rate and can even bias the data that are received.

Response Bias

It can easily be determined if a researcher has received a satisfactory return rate. A second and more difficult issue to be addressed is whether the data that are available for analysis were collected from a representative sample of participants. Although a high percentage of responses to a mailing of an instrument (e.g., 50 percent) is likely to produce a representative sample of those who were requested to participate, there is no guarantee that it does. The 50 percent who failed to respond may differ from the 50 percent who did respond in an important way that could have produced a biased sample. Conversely, although not likely, even a very low rate of return (e.g., 25 percent) theoretically could have produced a sample that is representative of the population being studied. The problem with using mailed instruments is that it is difficult to know whether those who did not return the instrument are similar to or different in an important way from those who did. Some follow-up calls to determine why the former group did not respond are sometimes informative. They can provide at least some insight into whether or not a response bias exists. However, they can also perceived as harassment by those people who already indicated their unwillingness to be research participants when they did not return their data collection instruments.

In some research situations, a response bias is quite predictable. For example, a follow-up survey to assess the vocational success of people denied admission to a job-training program would be expected to prompt a disproportionately high rate of return from three groups: (1) those who have been successful and wish to gloat about their success; (2) those who are still unemployed and wish to blame the denial of admission to them for their failures; and (3) those who receive the instrument, perceive that it means that they are still being considered for admission to the program, and therefore are careful to complete and return it. A lower rate of return might be expected from other people who are employed but have not been especially successful in their careers or otherwise have less emotional views regarding the program being evaluated.

A descriptive study (McQueen, 2000) of hazing rituals (emotional and physical abuse of students attempting to be admitted to membership in a

Research-Based Practice

If you wanted the parents of third grade elementary students to complete a survey and return it to their child's teacher, what are five things you would do to encourage the parents to respond?

group or an organization) among high school and college students provides a good example of how response bias can operate. In August 2000, many major newspapers reported that a large percentage of students had been victims of hazing. Although this conclusion was based on a study in which mailed questionnaires were completed and anonymously returned by a large number of students, the questionnaires had only a 12 percent return rate; that is, only 12 percent of the questionnaires mailed out were returned. The low return rate was reason enough for us to question the external validity of any findings drawn from returned questionnaires. However, we should also ask who was most likely to return the questionnaires and who was not. Wouldn't students who had experienced hazing be more likely to take the trouble to complete and return the questionnaires than students who had not experienced hazing and thus had no particular interest in it? It would probably be safe to assume that generalizations from this sample (at least any about incidence of hazing) are very suspect. In situations in which the use of the mail for data collection would likely result in response bias, other methods of data collection, such as in-person interviews, should be considered. A smaller (but more representative) sample of participants is almost always preferable to a larger, biased one.

While there are certainly weakness to acquiring data using mailed surveys, they are likely to remain popular for conducting certain types of research. What is a desirable stance to take in regard to them? We can recognize their limitations (primarily questions about the external validity of their findings), not assume that their findings are 100 percent accurate, and acknowledge their many contributions to our knowledge base.

Recently, there has been discussion of how traditional methods of conducting large-scale national surveys could be revised to yield high response rates and better data. One researcher (Trei, 2006) has proposed that a carefully selected, representative sample of 1,000 American households might be identified and provided with a laptop computer and high-speed Internet access to allow them to participate in a thirty-minute secure survey every month. The time blocks with these "professional research participants" could then be sold to researchers such as political pollsters or others who seek to measure American opinions and trends. Undoubtedly, the twenty-first century will see other innovative approaches to survey research, as the full capacity of the Internet is realized.

IN-PERSON INTERVIEWS

In-person interviews with research participants have always been an especially popular method of data collection among social work researchers. They are likely to remain so.

Differences between Quantitative and Qualitative Interviews

Interviews are essential to almost all qualitative research but often perform a valuable function in quantitative studies as well. However, quantitative and qualitative research interviews differ in several important ways. Box 11.3 summarizes some of the most important ones.

	Quantitative Studies	Qualitative Studies
Goal	Test hypotheses	Elicit perceptions, subjective meanings
Immediate objective	Accurate measurement	Insight, understanding
Reason for use	Verification, necessity	Method of choice
Relationship: participants	Detached, objective	Close, supportive, even therapeutic
Emotionality	Discouraged	Encouraged, supported
Structure	Highly structured	Unstructured, conversational, responsive
Discussion of sensitive issues	Avoided or delayed	Sought, encouraged early, supported

Box 11.3 In-Person Interviews in Quantitative and Qualitative Research

Goal and Objective

Of course, the primary purpose of all social work research interviewing is to collect data about a human phenomenon. In quantitative research, the researcher uses the interview most often to attempt to accurately describe a behavior, attitude, belief, or knowledge level by measuring one or more variables that are indicators of them. He or she wants to get accurate, factual information that will allow for the testing of research hypotheses.

In predominantly qualitative studies, the researcher is likely to be attempting to learn more about, for example, how research participants experienced an event, how they perceived it at the time, and what it currently means to them.

Reason for Use

In quantitative studies, interviews are often not the primary method of data collection. They are often used to verify the accuracy of data acquired in some other way, such as through a mailed questionnaire. The interview may just be a follow-up to verify or explain information provided by the primary data collection method. In quantitative research, interviews are also used to collect data that can only be obtained through oral communication or a combination of oral communication and first-person observation. Characteristics of research participants sometimes suggest that research interviews are the best way to obtain data. For example, very young children, some older people, people with learning disabilities, or people with minimal or no literacy skills all may require the use of an in-person interview.

Aspects of specific cultures may also favor the use of the in-person interview. Because cooperation in interpersonal interactions is important in cultures that are more collectivistic, research participants from such cultures, who adhere to these values, may respond more favorably to in-person data collection approaches than to less personal data collection approaches, such as questionnaires or Internet surveys. In many Hispanic cultures, *personalismo* is valued, that is, time is taken for people to get to know one another, and trust is established before information (especially that of a sensitive nature) is shared. The in-person interview is more conducive to this type of interaction and may increase rate of compliance with research protocols among people who hold this cultural perspective.

In qualitative research, interviewing is often the primary or even the only method of data collection. Through it (and the observations that accompany it), the researcher hopes to find out how people experienced a phenomenon or an event and learn its meaning or essence for them. The data that are provided are thus subjective. In addition, there is also a second layer of subjectivity present—the researcher's *interpretation* of its meaning. Consequently, since there is little pretense of objectivity, richness rather than factual information is sought, often through development of relationships of candor and trust with the participant. There is no pretense that the interviewer's presence did not influence the data; it is unavoidable.

Relationship with Research Participants

In a research interview in a predominantly quantitative study, the researcher does not seek to form a close or supportive relationship with research participants and may consciously try to avoid one. Thus, in a quantitative research interview, the researcher strives to not influence the responses of research participants by his or her choice of words, behaviors, facial expressions, and so forth. When a participant responds to questions, there is no indication provided in the form of either positive or negative reinforcement that would suggest that one response is preferable to another. Special attention is even paid to dress, mode of communication, manner of presentation, and overall demeanor. Researchers work to eliminate personal characteristics that may offend, intimidate, or otherwise influence the responses of participants. Of course, they cannot alter certain personal characteristics, such as age, gender, or ethnicity. However, they remain sensitive to them and attempt to determine how they may have influenced data collection.

In quantitative interviews, only necessary data are sought; any additional exchange of information is viewed as unnecessary and even undesirable. One common problem encountered is that requests for advice or other forms of assistance often occur, especially since the research participant generally knows that the researcher is a social worker. For example, it is difficult to collect factual data about participants' methods of child rearing without advice being sought at some point during the interview. To a quantitative researcher, promptly responding to such requests could compromise the role of "objective researcher"—it can affect the participant's subsequent responses. It can also disrupt the flow of data collection, making it difficult to get the interview back on track. The researcher may feel a professional obligation to provide assistance, if able, but probably would not do so during data collection. A reply that "I will be happy to talk about that with you after we complete our interview" is appropriate and usually is accepted by the participant. Naturally, such promises should be remembered and kept. Assistance may entail actually giving advice or, more commonly, making a referral to an appropriate organization or helping professional.

In contrast, in a qualitative research interview, the relationship with participants is likely to be close and even therapeutic, when needed. This represents no particular problem because, as previously noted, there are few pretenses to objectivity in data collection and therefore little concern that it might be compromised. Interpersonal exchanges, such as questions about the researcher's family or educational background or requests for assistance, are considered natural and expected. So the researcher responds to them when they occur. Providing requested help on the spot is viewed as both an ethical responsibility and desirable from a research perspective, since it will increase the likelihood that a participant will trust the researcher and thus be more open and candid in the conversation that follows.

Attitudes toward Emotionality

Emotionality in a predominantly quantitative interview represents a problem for the researcher. Even when measurements of attitudes and feelings are sought, emotional responses are assumed to provide unreliable indicators of them. Besides, emotionality in a quantitative research interview can seriously interfere with the collection of other needed data.

In qualitative research, displays of emotion by participants are not uncommon. In fact, sometimes, the researcher encourages emotionality to help better understand how the participant is experiencing or has experienced an event. They may be helpful in achieving the researcher's objectives.

Structure

In predominantly quantitative research interviews, major digressions by the participant are generally viewed as undesirable. The researcher exerts fairly tight control over the flow of the interview. Too long or too frequent digressions can interfere with the completion of data collection. Research interviews that run overtime can result in fatigue for participants or the researcher and may threaten the quality of the data acquired. Unnecessarily long interviews can also cause other appointments to be missed or delayed and thus jeopardize interviews with other potential research participants.

Usually, qualitative research interviews tend to involve relatively little structure and control by the researcher. Digressions by participants are expected and generally regarded as useful because they lead into topics that may prove to be more productive than those that the researcher might have introduced. Getting participants back on track is required only if it becomes apparent that the participants are avoiding topics that need to be discussed and seem to be within their emotional tolerance for discussion.

Discussion of Sensitive Issues

Both quantitative and qualitative interviews are likely to include discussion of behaviors or feelings of a personal or sensitive nature. Because this can provoke discomfort for participants, judicious placement of such content within the interview is important. In predominantly quantitative research, discussion of sensitive matters occurs only if necessary; that is, only if it relates to the research question and/or hypothesis. In such instances, it usually is planned near the end of the interview. Placed too early, there is a risk of losing potential participants who may decide that they have had enough, terminating the interview before much data have been collected. But if placed near the end of the interview, there is sufficient time for debriefing and the interview to end on a less emotionally charged note.

In a qualitative research interview, sensitive content is often addressed early in the interview, when there will be plenty of time to explore it and to provide support. The researcher does not like to see discussions about sensitive issues begin as the interview is about to draw to a close.

Advantages

Besides the fact that they allow the researcher to collect data from participants who might be unable to complete written data collection instruments, there are a number of other important advantages to collecting data using in-person interviews. As should be obvious from our previous discussion, they are generally more relevant to qualitative studies than to predominantly quantitative ones.

▶ **Opportunity to probe.** While talking with research participants, the researcher is able to initiate clarification about their responses by making such comments as "I wonder if you could tell me more about that" or "What led you to that conclusion?" These comments provide participants with the opportunity to expand on responses more fully, thereby allowing the researcher to acquire more in-depth, accurate data. It may thus be possible to understand and measure an individual's attitude about an issue and perhaps even determine the origins of that attitude. This type of insight is less likely to occur if a mailed instrument or other method that does not allow for interaction between the researcher and the participant is used for data collection.

▶ **High completion rate.** In-person interviews usually permit researchers to secure a completed return. If participants agree to be interviewed, they will usually complete the interview.

▶ **Access to supplementary data.** Interviewers are able to observe participants while they are responding to questions. Nonverbal communications may provide important data. They can indicate the participant's ease in responding, evasiveness in answering questions, or how seriously the participant seems to be taking the interview. They can be carefully observed, recorded, and used as part of later data analysis.

▶ **Opportunity to individualize data collection.** Interviews can be individualized as needed to facilitate data collection or aid in obtaining complete data from participants. Of course, the more interviews differ, the more difficult it becomes to compare responses of participants.

▶ **Use of interviewing skills.** Interviewing is natural for social work researchers whose professional education prepares them to conduct interviews about a wide range of topics. Thus, interviewing takes advantage of their strengths.

Disadvantages

If in-person interviews were the perfect data source, no other methods would be needed. But there are some major problems inherent in research interviews, especially in quantitative research. Although good preparation can minimize them, they cannot totally be eliminated.

▶ **Influence of the interviewer.** As we observed in discussion of other data collection methods, the fact that the researcher is present and posing questions directly to the participant may influence the responses of participants (reactivity). In some cases, participants may choose a response that they believe is sought by the interviewer. This type of distortion in responses is known as an *expectancy effect*. Participants also may choose a socially desirable response rather than provide their true response, leading to erroneous conclusions by the interviewer. Qualitative researchers regard such influence as inevitable, but quantitative researchers generally try to minimize this type of influence.

▶ **Potential for recording errors.** The accuracy of data collected in an interview also may be negatively affected by the manner in which responses are recorded by the interviewer. Participants may provide truthful and accurate data, but if they are forgotten, distorted, misinterpreted, or recorded in error by the interviewer, data quality will still be low. Careful preparation for data collection, which addresses how data are to be gathered and recorded, can reduce the potential for recording errors. If interviewers other than the researcher are to be used, they should be carefully trained to have a thorough understanding of the expected role and demeanor of the interviewer and the purpose of the study and its overall design. They should be given supervised practice in use of any interview schedule that is to be used and the correct manner of recording data.

Interviewer training can be expensive, but its cost is justified. If two or more interviewers are to be used, consistency in recording is enhanced if interviewers are trained together. They should be provided with the opportunity to ask any questions about the study that they may have. Interviewing simulations and role play can be part of the training package.

When research participants will agree to it, audio- or video-recording of interviews can greatly reduce recording errors and is a common practice in qualitative research studies. The recordings can be reviewed later, as many times as necessary, until the researcher is reasonably certain what was said or expressed. Others can also listen to or view the recordings (while respecting confidentiality) to verify or refute what was believed to have transpired. Recording of interviews is generally more feasible in qualitative studies than in quantitative ones, in which there may be more reluctance by research participants to allow it (less of a trust relationship), and researchers may have greater concern about how it might affect the truthfulness of responses.

▶ **Errors caused by demographic differences.** When interviewers and research participants are from different language, racial, cultural, or even socioeconomic groups, the possibility of flawed data due to either participants giving socially desirable responses or their unwillingness to provide or fear of providing frank answers may be increased. This is especially likely to occur when the research topic touches on areas related to the nature of differences between investigator and participant (e.g., racial prejudices and attitudes toward other groups). Under certain conditions, it may be preferable to match interviewers and participants by language, culture, and socioeconomic status. Use of same-ethnic data collectors can increase rapport and trust. Communication is also enhanced when bilingual interviewers are used for participants who are not native English speakers. Bilingual and bicultural interviewers are more likely to be aware of idiomatic variations among particular ethnic or nationality groups, as well as subtle differences in meaning for the same or similar words. They are also more likely to recognize and understand nonverbal forms of communication, which may be more critical than what participants actually say (Marin & Marin, 1991).

Butler (1992) cautions that simply matching interviewer and participant by race or ethnicity may be insufficient to guard against problems relating to demographics of the researcher and research participants. She notes, for example, that many African-American researchers are from the upper and middle classes and trained in mainstream educational settings, which may have removed them from the realities of African Americans from lower socioeconomic classes.

Interviewing Protocol

Whenever in-person interviews are to be used for data collection, researchers first contact potential participants and acquire their permission to be interviewed. Then the interview is conducted at a time and place mutually agreeable to both interviewer and participant.

Interviews can be conducted in a human service organization, a public place, or the participant's home. If participants are interviewed in their home, additional data can be collected and later analyzed. For example, observations can be made about the home environment and their interaction with significant others. These kinds of data can provide the researcher with additional (in some cases, serendipitous) information which may help to explain the participant's other responses more fully.

There are other practices that researchers try to follow to ensure that data received through interviewing are as complete and usable as possible. They include the following:

- ▶ **Provide complete identification.** Interviewers should appropriately identify themselves and remind the participant of the purpose of the study and their agreement to be interviewed. An appropriate introduction helps to confirm that the study is legitimate and thus helps to make the participant more willing to provide all requested data.

- ▶ **Promote pleasant interaction.** Respect and courtesy, of course, are appropriate in all research interviews. They are especially essential when interviews are conducted in the participant's home, where the researcher is a guest. Research participants often give much more than they hope to receive; an interviewer's demeanor should reflect an appreciation of this fact.

- ▶ **Use data collection instruments.** Because quantitative research interviewing tends to be more structured than interviewing used in qualitative research, data collection instruments (sometimes referred to as *interview schedules*) generally are used. In interviews in which a high percentage of items are designed to be read to participants, the specific wording of an item and the sequence in which items are covered take on great importance. Any deviation from the wording or sequencing of items could influence the responses received and invalidate any comparisons made between research participants. In less structured research, such as many qualitative studies, a schedule serves only as a general outline of topics to be introduced; wording and sequencing of items are less critical.

- ▶ **Record unobtrusively.** The method of recording research data and observations will vary from one study to another. The interviewer may be required to circle the appropriate responses on a data collection instrument or record verbatim what the participant says. If data are recorded, it should be done as unobtrusively as possible in order not to disrupt the flow of the interview.

- ▶ **Specify the progress of the interview.** As the interview progresses, the interviewer should periodically let the participant know about what percentage of the interview remains to be completed. This may help participants avoid becoming frustrated about the time required, help them remain focused, and give them a more positive feeling about the interview process. Interviewers might say something like "Now we have reached the halfway point," "We have just two more questions to go," or "We're nearly through now."

GROUP INTERVIEWS

Another useful method for acquiring research data is the *group interview*. It can occur in person, in a conference call or online, and can be an efficient and economical way of collecting research data.

Focus Groups

A common form of in-person group data collection in social work research (and one that is especially well suited to the skills of social workers) is the *focus group*. Focus groups are more likely to be used in qualitative studies than quantitative ones. They are used to gain insights from clients, staff, and others who have formed opinions about certain experiences, problems, or social programs.

How does a focus group work? People who share a similar problem or have experienced a similar life experience may be invited to participate in a group discussion led by the researcher. For example, a focus group of openly gay teenagers could be formed to discuss how they experienced the attitudes of teachers and other high school students, or a group of Native American students might meet with a researcher to describe their perceptions of how they have been treated in a predominantly White community.

Focus groups are sometimes intentionally formed of individuals who do not share the same experiences, beliefs, values, or demographic characteristics. For example, a researcher might lead a focus group of diverse people (ethnically, socioeconomically, educationally, and so forth) to assess the degree of support in a community for a proposed group home for people with developmental disabilities.

It is believed that a focus group has certain advantages over one-on-one interviews. Particularly, if the experience is one that is difficult to speak about, the group can be a source of emotional support. Members are especially likely to be candid among others who have had similar experiences or have similar values or opinions. The group also can be a stimulus for individual participants in another way. Members may think about and respond to issues brought up by other members that they might otherwise not have considered.

Focus groups are sometimes intentionally formed of individuals who do not share the same experiences, beliefs, values, or demographic characteristics.

Are there negatives associated with collecting data in a group of research participants? Yes. A major one is that the influence of the group can easily produce data of questionable validity. It is difficult to know when participants are speaking honestly about their own experiences and perceptions. In focus groups of members who are similar to each other, participants may be just joining in and revealing what they think the other group members expect them to offer. In diverse focus groups, they may just be so outraged by what others say that they may overreact and say things that may not be correct or reflective of their true opinions, or they may refuse to speak up at all. Because of the possibility of group influences on individuals, data collected in focus groups must be used cautiously.

The role of the leader (often called a facilitator) in a focus group is a little different from the role that the leader plays in other types of groups in which social workers participate (such as treatment groups). It is also different from the role researchers play in either qualitative or quantitative one-on-one in-person interviews. Leading a focus group to collect research data entails providing some degree of structure and direction to the discussion to acquire the data that are sought. At the same time, the researcher does not want to limit discussion excessively or lead it too much, thus missing out on unanticipated, valuable insights that participants might otherwise have provided. This requires a difficult balancing act.

Other Group Data Collection Methods

While focus groups are a common method of acquiring data in groups, they are not the only one. Other types of groups (e.g., social groups, committee meetings) are potential data sources as well, through interviewing, observation, or (most often) a combination of the two. Even treatment groups have this potential, but if they are to be used, additional ethical obstacles, such as the presence of dual relationships (Chapter 2), must be overcome.

Finally, not all group data collection involves interviewing at all. In studies that rely on standardized instruments or questionnaires (Chapter 12) for data collection, a researcher may use a group setting for their completion. When it is logistically feasible to gather a number of research participants in one place (e.g., in a social agency or at a college or university), group administration can be a cost-efficient way to collect data. In addition, there is the advantage of the researcher's presence—if any questions or items are unclear, participants can receive clarification, the same clarification that is provided to everyone else in the room.

TELEPHONE INTERVIEWS

The telephone and fax machine can sometimes be used for collecting data, even though this type of data collection has more limitations than advantages. If the amount of data required is small and not too personal and if the research participants have some connection or positive association with the researcher or a group that he or she represents, telephone calls and faxes can be an economical way (the primary advantage) to collect data from a large number of participants.

Two common examples of research that often use telephone interview surveys are client satisfaction surveys in human service organizations and alumni follow-up surveys in schools of social work. If an administrator is interested in determining to what degree a sample of clients is satisfied with services recently received, the phone can be used to contact former clients. Securing their responses to five or six questions can be performed quickly and inexpensively. Similarly, current students or faculty members can conduct a survey of a sample of a school's graduates to learn, for example, if they had difficulty in finding employment, what courses they found most useful in their practice, what curriculum changes they might recommend, and so forth. Notice that in both of these cases, the potential participants have an established relationship with the organization making the calls.

When should telephone interviews be conducted? Common sense and experience would suggest that it is a poor idea to call between 5:00 P.M. and, say, 7:00 P.M., when many people are returning from work or having dinner. Similarly, calling either late in the evening or very early in the morning is often resented by potential participants. Although these times are especially inconvenient for people to provide data over the phone, almost any time that the researcher calls he or she is likely to find potential participants doing something that they would prefer to do. Perhaps in earlier times, people enjoyed unanticipated phone calls, but few do today. Finding a time that is convenient is a difficult but important task in telephone interviewing. Therefore, it is prudent to schedule telephone interviews with participants in advance whenever possible.

Even if a phone call comes at an ideal time, any simple requests for information are now suspect. Telephone interviewers must overcome the annoyance and normal suspicions that people display when they receive a call from someone purporting to conduct legitimate research. The researcher can almost expect to hear "I don't have time for this!" or just a hang-up unless his or her credibility has been established in some way prior to the call.

Unfortunately, pseudoresearch has been used as a device to make a sale, to gain support of a position on some political issue or, even worse, to collect personal information to be used by the researcher for some self-serving (or even illicit) purpose. Telephone requests for information, even from a known reputable source such as a university or social agency, now often meet with suspicion. Although virtually anyone can memorize a few questions to collect telephone data, overcoming resistance to providing information over the phone is the hardest part of telephone interviewing.

Most of the same principles that apply to in-person interviews apply to the telephone interview as well. However, because participants may be naturally suspicious of why they have been called and of the true purpose of the caller, researchers conducting telephone surveys have an especially hard sell. It is necessary that interviewers identify themselves and tell what organization is supporting or endorsing their research. They should also ask permission to conduct the interview. If a participant indicates that the call has come at an inconvenient time, a request to reschedule the interview should be made.

Diversity in Practice

If we were to complete a survey using telephone interviews between 10 A.M. and 2 P.M. on Mondays and Wednesdays during the month of February, what are two populations that might be over-represented? Two populations that might be underrepresented?

Telephone requests for information, even from a known reputable source such as a university or social agency, now often meet with suspicion.

An important limitation of data gathered through telephone interviews and fax is the difficulty of obtaining a group of participants who are representative of the group being studied. Therefore, as we suggested earlier, the external validity of research that uses this type of data collection often is regarded as poor.

Any time of day when telephone interviews are conducted has the potential to interfere with sample representativeness. For example, people employed outside the home tend to be unavailable during daytime hours. The representativeness of the sample can be hindered in other ways, too. An organization administrator might have access to all case records (containing phone numbers) to conduct a follow-up client satisfaction survey. But some former clients may have moved or had their phones disconnected and would thus be unavailable to be contacted. These people may disproportionately be the very people who either are doing very well and have moved out of state or are having the most problems and are most dissatisfied with their services. Similarly, an alumni follow-up survey might get the participation of only those alumni who are most satisfied with their education (and want to express their appreciation) and those who are most dissatisfied (and want to take the opportunity to vent about it). The alumni who are more neutral may have little interest in providing data. They are more likely to refuse to provide it and therefore will be underrepresented in the data collected.

Often, the researcher who lacks access to current agency or university records is even less fortunate. If numbers are punched at random or selected randomly from a phone directory, a biased sample is almost certain to result. A telephone directory is not a good sampling frame from which to draw a research sample. It automatically excludes people who use only their cellular phones, do not have phones, or do not have listed numbers. In addition, the widespread use of voice mail and answering machines (often used to screen calls) has made it difficult to get through to many of those who have listed home phone numbers. All of these factors can severely bias a sample in relation to occupation, gender, ethnicity, socioeconomic class, and other related variables that may be important to the research. Of course, many of these same factors are related to access to fax machines.

Despite the likelihood of sampling bias, telephone interviews continue to be used for research data collection. "Unlimited minutes" for long-distance calls have made them a more economical alternative than most other methods. When they are used, certain rules can be applied (e.g., asking the person in a household who most recently celebrated a birthday to provide data) to at least minimize sampling bias and even to calculate the true response rate (Risley-Curtiss, Holley, & Wolf, 2006).

ELECTRONIC COMMUNICATION

The widespread use of electronic communication (e-mail, voice-over IP, instant chats, online groups, and instant messaging) has made it a tempting alternative as a method for data collection. There is software available, such as Survey Monkey, that makes it relatively easy to create online surveys (after the survey itself is developed). After the online survey is created, a link is sent to the intended participants through their email accounts. Data can be collected quickly and at minimal cost. Many people (especially younger ones) rely heavily on the use of electronic communication (try taking it away from them!) and would rather communicate by e-mail than by, for example, completing a written questionnaire on paper and mailing it back to the researcher.

Like the land telephone or fax, electronic communication has a major problem relating to sampling bias and the external validity of some findings. Some people still do not have regular access to a computer or cell phone, or if they do, they may not have e-mail or instant messaging. Others have them, but still lack necessary skills or are uncomfortable using them. Differences in relation to gender, ethnicity, and age are not as pronounced as they once were, but they still exist. Thus, the likelihood of acquiring a representative sample in relation to such variables is likely to be reduced when using electronic communication as opposed to some other methods. Of course, as suggested earlier, some people's preference for communicating electronically may leave them disinclined to participate in research that requests data in any other way.

Because of obvious limitations, electronic communication is used most effectively as a method for data collection only when certain conditions exist:

1. A reasonably complete list of potential research participants is available, along with their electronic addresses.

2. The majority of potential participants are likely to be people who regularly use electronic communication as their primary method of daily communication (such as social work students).

3. Variables that are believed to relate to differences in ownership and usage are unlikely to be relevant to the research questions that are being examined.

4. The data sought are such that they lend themselves to a questionnaire format and are not personal (do not arouse suspicions about viruses or spoof mail).

5. The research is primarily quantitative.

Of course, electronic communication (like the other methods for acquiring data that were discussed in this chapter) can also be used in conjunction with other methods, as preliminary to one or more of them, or as a follow-up to them. For example, an e-mail or text message survey can be used to identify potential participants who have certain characteristics and are willing to participate in an in-person interview or to seek bits of data that may have not been collected for some reason during a prior interview.

SUMMARY

This chapter presented some of the most common ways that social work researchers acquire the research data that they hope will provide answers to their research questions and/or allow them to test their hypotheses. It should be obvious by now that some of these methods are more suited to some types of research design (e.g., quantitative or qualitative; exploratory, descriptive, or explanatory; and so forth) than others. The primary advantages and disadvantages of each method that make them better suited for a particular type of research are summarized in Box 11.4.

Box 11.4 Common Methods for Acquiring Research Data: Primary Advantages and Disadvantages

Source	Primary Advantage	Primary Limitation
Secondary data analysis	Cost	Validity issues, sterility
Oral histories	Access to firsthand observations	Subjectivity, bias
Systematic observation	Less reliance on others	Distortion
Mailed surveys	Accessibility of participants	Low response rate, response bias
In-person interviews	High response rate, researcher presence	Cost, measurement bias
Group interviews	Efficiency, group support	Group pressure
Telephone interviews	Cost	Sampling bias, suspicion
Electronic communication	Cost	Sampling bias, suspicion

Each option presented in this chapter should be viewed as a data source to be considered. Together, they form a kind of menu from which to select one or more. Each method can be used alone to acquire data, or the methods can be used in combination.

Succeed with

Log onto **www.mysocialworklab.com** and answer the following questions. (If you did not receive an access code to **MySocialWorkLab** with this text and wish to purchase access online, please visit <u>www. mysocialworklab.com</u>.)

1. **Watch the Core Competencies Video: Engagement, Assessment, Intervention, and Evaluation: Assessment.**

After meeting with this client, identify two of the client's symptoms that we might be able to measure using Rapid Assessment Instruments?

2. **Read the Case Study: Mental Health: Dee.** If Dee were to complete self-report questionnaires, do you think the information would be completely truthful? Why or why not?

PRACTICE TEST

1. All of the following are advantages of secondary data analysis except one.
   a. Secondary data is usually cheaper to gather than other types of data.
   b. Gathering secondary data is less intrusive than other types of data.
   c. The researcher is able to define exactly what variables will be collected.
   d. Data are already gathered so secondary data takes less time to gather.

2. "Do you think the teacher and the school counselor do a good job with career counseling (yes or no)?" is an example of a
   a. double-barreled question.
   b. false belief.
   c. loaded response.
   d. leading question.

3. "Do you think the state should go after deadbeat fathers to collect child support?" is an example of a
   a. double-barreled question.
   b. false belief.
   c. leading question.
   d. prestige bias.

4. "Do you think your service was excellent, great, or okay?" is an example of
   a. an emotional language.
   b. a loaded response.
   c. a false belief.
   d. a double-barreled question.

5. Describe five roles the researcher (observer) can take in structured observation.

ASSESS YOUR COMPETENCE Use the scale below to rate your current level of achievement on the following concepts or skills associated with each competency presented in the chapter:

1	2	3
I can accurately describe the concept or skill.	I can consistently identify the concept or skill when observing and analyzing practice activities.	I can competently implement the concept or skill in my own practice.

_____ Understanding the advantages and disadvantages of using secondary data

_____ Being familiar with structured and unstructured systematic observation techniques

_____ Being able to create good survey questions, avoiding some of the common pitfalls

_____ Understanding the advantages and disadvantages of in-person, telephone, and electronic interviews

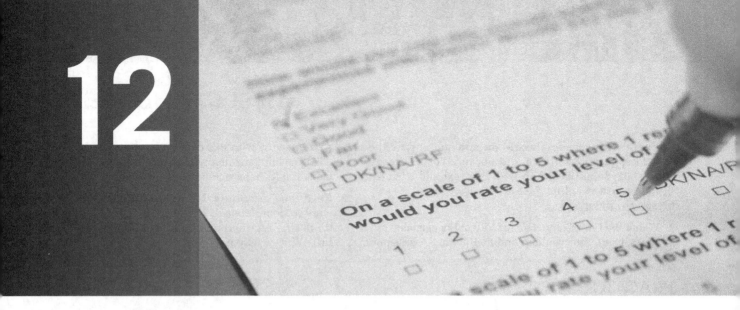

12

Data Collection Instruments

CHAPTER OUTLINE

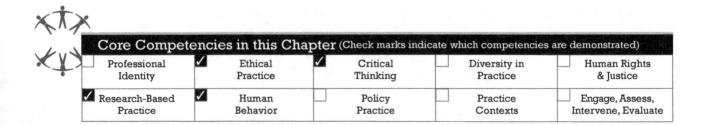

Core Competencies in this Chapter (Check marks indicate which competencies are demonstrated)				
Professional Identity	✔ Ethical Practice	✔ Critical Thinking	Diversity in Practice	Human Rights & Justice
✔ Research-Based Practice	✔ Human Behavior	Policy Practice	Practice Contexts	Engage, Assess, Intervene, Evaluate

---

Box 12.1 Components of Data Collection Instruments

1. One item; one variable
   A. Fixed-alternative items, simple indexes
   B. Open-ended items

2. Two or more items; one variable
   A. Composite indexes
   B. Scales,* for example, Likert, Thurstone, semantic differential

   ---
   *A scale may contain subscales, each of which contains two or more items. Each subscale may measure a different variable or construct.

In Chapter 11, we discussed data collection methods. Sometimes researchers rely on secondary analysis of sources, such as crime records, census data, or social agency records. Other times, they gather the data themselves, using in-person or group interviews or surveys completed through either the mail or via telephone or electronic communications. Systematic observation of people's behaviors is another unobtrusive way to conduct measurement. Other methods of measurement, called *indirect measurement*, require no direct contact between a researcher and research participants. For example, researchers might get permission to check public recycling bins to attempt to learn which electronic items are considered obsolete or not worth repairing, or count the number of people using seat belts by observing cars driving by a busy intersection.

Whether they make measurements directly or indirectly, researchers generally use some form of data collection instrument to record their measurements of variables and organize their data into a more or less standard format. As we shall see, data collection instruments vary widely in length, structure, and content. In this chapter, we will focus on the creation, selection, and use of data collection instruments.

As Box 12.1 suggests, data collection instruments usually consist of a combination of (1) individual items, each of which provides a measurement of a single variable, and/or (2) a group of items that together provide a measurement of a single variable. We will look at the less intricate of these—one item, one variable—first.

Whether they make measurements directly or indirectly, researchers generally use some form of data collection instrument to record their measurements of variables and organize their data into a more or less standard format.

FIXED-ALTERNATIVE AND OPEN-ENDED ITEMS

When variables or constructs can be measured using only a single item or question, the items may be classified as either fixed alternative (also called *closed-ended*) or open ended. An example of a fixed-alternative item follows:

Please indicate your current legal marital status by circling the letter of one response below:

a. Married
b. Single, never married
c. Separated
d. Divorced
e. Widowed

A slightly different form of fixed-alternative item, a *simple composite index*, is sometimes used for collecting data that are a little less factual, that is, more of a subjective judgment on the part of the person providing the data. An example of a simple composite index follows:

How would you rate your marriage overall? (Circle one number.)

Very Good	**Good**	**Fair**	**Poor**	**Very Poor**
1	2 3	4 5 6	7 8	9

Note that when using a fixed-alternative item, the respondent is given a limited number of choices from which to select a response. In contrast, an open-ended is a less structured item for which participants provide their own response in their own words. The following would be an open-ended item:

In your own words, please briefly describe your experience with marriage and your current attitudes toward it.

_____

_____

_____

Most frequently, fixed-alternative items are used in instruments when the range of responses to the item can be anticipated, that is, when the researcher is quite sure what the range of different responses will be. They are also sometimes used when the researcher wants the participant to consider certain responses that the participant might otherwise fail to consider.

In contrast, open-ended items are more likely to be used when the range of responses is likely to be great and/or the researcher cannot possibly anticipate all of them. A researcher may select an open-ended item format to avoid suggesting possible responses to research participants. Open-ended items also allow the researcher to collect data in the form of direct quotations. Sometimes, these can be meaningful in presenting participants' attitudes or opinions.

It is not unusual for a researcher to develop the first draft of a data collection instrument using an open-ended item. After pilot-testing the instrument (discussed later in this chapter), if it is observed that answers tend to fall within a small range of value categories, a fixed-alternative item is inserted instead in the final draft of the instrument. Conversely, a pilot-testing of a data collection instrument that uses a fixed-alternative item may produce a larger number and range of responses than anticipated. Many of them may be in the "other" value category that is frequently offered as an alternative response. Then the researcher may decide to revise the instrument to use an open-ended item instead.

Open-ended items provide a more in-depth understanding of a topic than do fixed-alternative items. They are especially useful when the purpose of an item is to secure qualitative data. However, this advantage may be offset by a number of potential disadvantages of open-ended items that should be considered:

- Participants are less likely to complete items that require them to develop and write their responses. Thus, the overall return rate may be low.
- The researcher cannot precode response categories for computer data entry as it is impossible to anticipate responses by participants.
- The researcher may experience difficulty in analyzing data that reflect wide variation and are not readily amenable to quantitative analysis. Although there are data analysis software programs for analyzing qualitative data, these programs are complex and require additional expertise on the part of the researcher.

Critical Thinking

Write a fixed-alternative item and an open-ended question regarding sexual orientation.

COMPOSITE INDEXES AND SCALES

Although it is often possible to measure a variable, such as age, gender, or marital status, by using a single fixed-alternative or open-ended item, there are many other variables that are not so easily measured. For example, many attitudes, beliefs, and behavioral patterns generally cannot be accurately measured by a response to a single fixed-alternative or open-ended item. They may be constructs that, by definition, possess multiple indicators, or they may be something else, for example, an attitude about people with a certain disability that individuals would not readily acknowledge through a response to a single direct item—more subtlety may be needed. In either case, to accurately measure the variable, multiple items may be required. The items frequently are organized in a format that is referred to as a *composite index* or a *scale.* In a composite index or scale, the response to each item contributes to the researcher's understanding of the participant in relation to the variable being measured. Ultimately, all the relevant responses viewed as a whole make it possible for the researcher to assign a value or value category representing his or her measurement of the variable.

Composite indexes and scales (especially the latter) tend to be highly structured and refined. They can be used as independent data collection instruments or as a component of a larger instrument. Although composite indexes and scales both perform measurements of more complex variables, they do so in different ways.

Composite Indexes

A composite index consists of a number of items that are believed to be important indicators of the construct being measured. In general terms, the more items that participants indicate as applying to them, the greater the quantity of the construct they are presumed to possess. An example of a composite index to measure "clinical depression" might be the following:

Place a check mark in front of each feeling that you have experienced during the past week:

_____ Sadness

_____ Hopelessness

_____ Powerlessness

_____ Just not caring

_____ Wanting to be alone

_____ Anxiety

A composite index requires a research participant to respond to each item in a dichotomous manner, often by simply checking or circling those items that apply (as in the preceding example) or by indicating "yes" or "no" for each. The number of check marks or "yes" answers then becomes his or her measurement of the variable. The measurement thus produced is, at best, ordinal level. Although measurement produced by composite indexes is sometimes adequate, often it is not. That is why researchers prefer to use scales.

Scales

A scale is constructed so that it addresses one or both of the following requirements of measurement:

> ▶ Not all indicators of a variable or construct are equal in importance. Thus, they may not carry the same weighting in the overall measurement of the variable. The degree or intensity of an indicator is an important factor. For example, the amount of agreement that a person feels with a statement or how frequently a behavior occurs should be a factor in the measurement of a variable or construct.

Linear or Summated Scales

A common form of scale, known as a linear or summated scale, is similar to a composite index in that it allows the researcher to derive a measurement of the variable for each participant by adding up the responses to individual scale items. An example of a linear scale to measure clinical depression follows:

> Indicate how often you experienced each of these symptoms by circling the appropriate number.

	Never				*Often*
1. Sad/down	0	1	2	3	4
2. Hopeless	0	1	2	3	4
3. Powerless	0	1	2	3	4
4. Apathetic	0	1	2	3	4
5. Withdrawn	0	1	2	3	4
6. Anxious	0	1	2	3	4

On the preceding scale, participants would be asked to circle a number for each item, and these numbers would then be totaled. Thus, the highest possible score would be 24, and the lowest possible score would be 0. On this type of scale, lower scores are operationalized to mean a lower level of the variable being measured (clinical depression); relatively higher scores indicate a higher level.

Linear or summated scaling is popular among social science researchers. Many variables (especially constructs) that social work researchers are interested in studying can be scaled using this model. It is appropriate whenever the researcher can construct multiple items that reflect various dimensions of the variable or construct.

The best known type of a summated scale is the *Likert scale.* In a Likert scale, a set of attitude items is supplied. Participants indicate their level of agreement with each item to indicate the intensity of their feelings. For example, a Likert scale might be used to measure client satisfaction with worker services.

> Indicate your level of agreement with each of the items listed below by circling the appropriate number: 1 = strongly disagree; 2 = somewhat disagree; 3 = undecided; 4 = somewhat agree; 5 = strongly agree

	Strongly Disagree				Strongly Agree
1. My worker seemed prepared for sessions.	1	2	3	4	5
2. My worker was considerate of my schedule.	1	2	3	4	5
3. My worker seemed preoccupied.	1	2	3	4	5
4. My worker acted professionally.	1	2	3	4	5
5. My worker did not care about me as a person.	1	2	3	4	5
6. My worker tried to understand me.	1	2	3	4	5
7. My worker really wanted to help me.	1	2	3	4	5

Likert scales generally contain a mixture of items, the so-called positive and reversal items. *Positive items* are those where a high level of agreement with the item would reflect a high quantity of the variable being measured and where a low level of agreement with the item would reflect a low quantity of the variable (such as items 1, 2, 4, 6, and 7 in the preceding example).

Reversal items (such as items 3 and 5) are worded in such a way that a high level of agreement with the item reflects a low quantity of the variable being measured, and vice versa. In scoring reversal items, scoring is reversed; that is, responses of "strongly agree" are given a 1; "strongly disagree," a 5; and so forth. In other words, if the participant responds with "strongly agree" to the item "My worker seemed preoccupied," less satisfaction is reflected rather than more. Therefore, the answer (5) is converted to a 1 to reflect the least amount of satisfaction.

Why do researchers include reversal items in a scale? They are included primarily to determine whether the participant has answered honestly. When reversal items are included, an individual completing the scale is less likely to determine what is being measured, gauge about where they fall in relation to the variable, and simply circle the same number for all items. To further ensure honesty, the researcher would not want simply to alternate positive and reversal items, a pattern that could soon be identified by the participant. A random mixture of positive and reversal items allows a researcher to determine whether participants really read and carefully considered each item before responding to it. If they did, a relatively consistent pattern of responses (reflecting a measurement of the variable) should be evident in both types of item.

In a Likert scale, all items contribute equally to the measurement of a variable. Although this characteristic makes scoring simple, it is also the scale's greatest weakness. Invariably, no matter how much time and effort has gone into the construction of a Likert scale, some items continue to reflect "more" of the variable than others or are a stronger indicator of it than other items. Yet this is not reflected in the scoring of the scale—the items are not weighted in any way. Thus, measurements are less precise than they might be. For this reason, Likert scales are generally considered to produce ordinal-level rather than interval-level data. Nevertheless, it is common in research reports and professional journal articles to see measurements produced by a Likert scale that were treated as if they were interval-level for purposes of statistical analysis. This is a practice that is questionable at best, and can hurt the credibility of a researcher's findings. What's more, it is unnecessary. There are plenty of good statistical tests available that can be used to examine the relationship between variables when the measurements of one or both are only ordinal level.

Thurstone Scales

Like linear or summated scales, Thurstone scales can be used to measure constructs such as attitudes or other personal attributes. In developing a Thurstone scale, a large number of potential items are constructed. Judges (often people knowledgeable about scale construction and/or the construct being measured) are then asked to indicate how strong an indicator each item is of the attitude or attribute. They can rate each item between 1 and 11, with 1 being "extremely strong" and 11 being "extremely weak." Some items will be eliminated because there is little consistency in their ratings between judges. On the basis of the median (middle) rating for each remaining item, the item is assigned a weighting, a number reflecting its relative importance to measurement of the construct. Responses of agreement with some items "count" more or less than others. For example, a Thurstone scale might be constructed to measure the severity of behavioral problems reflected by preadolescent children. It might ask parents if their child had engaged in any one of ten behaviors during the past month. On the basis of the opinions of experts and a long, time-consuming series of tasks leading to its development, the scale would contain different weightings for different behaviors reflecting their severity. For example, "fought with other children" or "refusing to obey parental requests" might get a low weighting, say, 3.7 or 2.1. In contrast, a behavior judged to be more symptomatic of serious difficulties, such as "torturing animals" or "starting fires," might have a weighting of, say, 9.9 or 10.2.

In a Thurstone scale, there are both positive and reversal items. The weightings are known to the researcher and are used in computing the measurement of the variable but are not included on the research instrument so that they are not available to the research participant. Items are placed randomly, not in the order of their weightings, to avoid revealing the rankings of the items to the respondent. If the scale measures an attitude (as is frequently the case), participants are asked to indicate their level of agreement with each item (e.g., strongly agree, agree, disagree, or strongly disagree). Less frequently, when the variable is a behavior, as in our hypothetical example, frequency of the behavior or some other words representing gradation is often added. A Thurstone scale for our example might look something like this:

> During the past week, did your child engage in any of the following behaviors? (Please circle "yes" or "no.")
>
> (Yes/No) 1. Fighting with other children.
>
> (Yes/No) 2. Intentionally destroying property.
>
> (Yes/No) 3. Showing kindness toward others.
>
> (Yes/No) 4. Refusing to obey your requests.

(Yes/No) 5. Starting fires.

(Yes/No) 6. Volunteering to help with chores.

(Yes/No) 7. Torturing animals.

(Yes/No) 8. Swearing or using vulgar words.

(Yes/No) 9. Throwing things at others.

(Yes/No) 10. Touching others inappropriately.

If this were a real Thurstone scale (which it is not!), scoring would consist of taking the concealed weighting for each item to which the respondent answered "yes" and adding them to produce a total score. A "yes" answer for items 3 or 6 would be "reverse scored," since they represent positive behaviors. Thus, if a parent circled a "yes" for either item, its weighting would be a negative number and would reduce the total score by the amount of its weighting.

Thurstone scales are time consuming to develop. Social work researchers rarely develop them, preferring instead to use the more easily constructed Likert-type scale. However, when existing ones can be located and used, Thurstone scales provide greater precision of measurement than do Likert scales. Although, as we noted earlier, Likert scales are generally believed to produce only ordinal-level measurement, Thurstone scales can approximate interval-level measurement (Miller, 1991). This increases the number of options for statistical analysis of data (Chapter 13).

Bogardus Social Distance Scales

A Bogardus Social Distance Scale (Bogardus, 1947) measures one specific attribute of people—the degree to which they would be willing to interact with people who are different from themselves, such as people of a different ethnic group or people with a different sexual orientation. Participants review a group of rank-ordered statements, each of which describes a closer interaction with the other group than the previous one. The participants then indicate if they would be willing to tolerate each level of interaction. The researcher would note at what point each participant "draws the line." The number of tolerable interactions as marked by participants would give a good indication of each participant's willingness to interact with people in the other group. It is important to note that while the researcher knows the rank-ordering of the statements in the instrument, the order of the statements are often changed in the actual instrument so that the progression is not obvious to the person completing the scale.

For example, if we were looking at people recovering from crack addiction, the items in their rank order might look like this:

It would be OK if a person recovering from a cocaine addiction:

1. _____ lived in my town.
2. _____ lived on my block.
3. _____ lived next door.
4. _____ became friends with one of my family members.
5. _____ became my son's or my daughter's best friend.
6. _____ dated my son or daughter.
7. _____ married my son or daughter.

The researcher would probably rearrange the statements in the final scale so the respondent would not immediately see the progression of the statements toward greater and greater interaction.

Semantic Differential Scales

Likert, Thurstone, and Bogardus Social Distance scales all measure a variable quite directly. That is fine, if the variable is not an especially personal or sensitive one. However, some variables of interest to social work researchers require a more indirect measurement. Simply to come out and ask straightforward questions (e.g., "How homophobic are you?" "Do you consider yourself racist?") might produce only politically correct or socially desirable responses, not a true measurement. In these cases, a semantic differential scale might be appropriate. A scale of this type is characterized by the following:

- It is used to measure variables when direct questions might not produce honest answers.
- It provides a subtle, indirect measurement of the variable.
- It is "projective" and often seeks unconscious feelings or attitudes.
- Respondents are instructed to respond quickly, not think too long or look for the "right" answer.

A semantic differential scale provides a list of word opposites (e.g., slow/fast, simple/complicated, old/new, and so forth). They may seem to have only a vague or indirect relevance to the construct being measured. The words may be placed on opposite ends of equal-length lines. The research participant is instructed to place an X on each line to indicate his or her response in relation to the construct being measured. Often, numbers (e.g., the numbers 1 through 9) may be placed between the two words at equal distances and the respondent is asked to circle one number per pair of words. Then the numbers are added up to determine the respondent's score, using reverse scoring where appropriate.

A semantic differential scale is a kind of word association game. The assumption underlying it is that, in completing it, the participant will somewhat unintentionally reveal something about himself or herself in the responses to the pairs of word opposites—often his or her true attitudes. For example, suppose that our research required us to measure two variables, attitudes toward corporal punishment and attitudes about old age among social work students. To be successful, we would have to avoid responses that reflect "attitudes that social workers *should* have." We might use two semantic differential scales that look something like these:

Attitudes about Corporal Punishment

Good	1 2 3 4 5 6 7 8 9	Evil
Pleasant	1 2 3 4 5 6 7 8 9	Unpleasant
Sour	1 2 3 4 5 6 7 8 9	Sweet
Happy	1 2 3 4 5 6 7 8 9	Sad
Healthy	1 2 3 4 5 6 7 8 9	Sick
Love	1 2 3 4 5 6 7 8 9	Hate
Fair	1 2 3 4 5 6 7 8 9	Unfair

Attitudes about Old Age

Pleasant	1 2 3 4 5 6 7 8 9	Unpleasant
Sour	1 2 3 4 5 6 7 8 9	Sweet
Happy	1 2 3 4 5 6 7 8 9	Sad
Healthy	1 2 3 4 5 6 7 8 9	Sick
Love	1 2 3 4 5 6 7 8 9	Hate
Fair	1 2 3 4 5 6 7 8 9	Unfair

Like composite indexes and Likert scales, semantic differential scales do not provide very precise measurements. Thus, they produce what is generally regarded as ordinal-level data. Not surprisingly, semantic differential scales are most often designed by psychologists. After all, they are just a variation of the projective testing methods clinical psychologists often use for diagnostic purposes.

Of course, psychologists are not the only professionals to use various forms of composite indexes and scales in their professional practice. While we have focused on their use for measurement of certain variables in research, they have utility in social work practice as well. Social workers are likely to encounter different forms of them, especially in clinical work with individuals, families, or groups.

Goal Attainment Scaling

Another type of scale that is sometimes used to evaluate the success of an individual social worker's intervention methods is goal attainment scaling (GAS). GAS has a relatively long history of use by social workers; it was first used back in the 1960s among therapists working with psychiatric patients. Since then, it has been used in a wide variety of settings where social workers are employed. When using it, a social worker identifies (along with the client or client system) a small number (usually, three to five) of specific behavioral problems. They should be problems of importance to the client and ones for which it is reasonable to expect that social work intervention might produce some positive changes. Although GAS is used most frequently to evaluate the success of interventions with individual clients, it is also applicable when working with problems within groups, families, institutions or communities, as long as the problem and its incidence can be easily quantified. For example, a social worker employed in a community agency might use it to assess her effectiveness in increasing the percentage of the local population who register to vote in an upcoming presidential election.

Once having identified and specified a small number of problems and the goals of intervention associated with them, a range of five levels of goal attainment are specified and listed in rank order. They are assigned a number between −2 and +2. Zero is assigned to what will be the expected outcome if intervention is successful. Plus scores are assigned to goal attainment that is greater than expected and minus scores to goal attainment levels that are less than expected. To return to our previous example, the social worker attempting to increase voter registration prior to a presidential election in a community where current registration is only 20 percent might use the following scale:

Most unfavorable outcome (−2)	20% or less
Less than expected outcome (−1)	21–25%
Expected outcome (0)	26–30%
More than expected outcome (+1)	31–35%
Most favorable outcome (+2)	over 35%

The decision as to which percentage of registration would represent expected outcome (0) and which percentage would be appropriate for the other four levels would be based on an assessment of what was realistic, given the time available for the intervention, and what past experience has taught the social worker about the likely impact of the intervention. Setting them at the appropriate levels requires a good understanding of both the client group and the likely impact of the intervention method being used.

Human Behavior

Suppose that you are treating a third grader with ADHD; construct a goal attainment scale to help you evaluate your client's progress.

The results of goal attainment in addressing different problems (perhaps, in our example, participation at community meetings or attendance at PTA meetings) can be combined mathematically to suggest, overall, how effective a social worker has been in working with a client or client system. The different problems can also be weighted to reflect their relative importance. Methods are even available to convert results to a scale with scores ranging between 1 and 100.

GAS is designed for use with well-motivated clients who will work to set realistic goals and honestly report their behaviors, as well as with larger client systems where valid measurement of behaviors is possible. It is also designed for social workers who want honest feedback about their effectiveness, not social workers who just want to appear successful. If, either unintentionally or deliberately, the different levels of success are scaled too high or too low, or if the measurement of success is inappropriate for some other reason, the results of GAS will be of little value as feedback to the social worker. For example, if both the social worker and an adolescent with a problem of severe shyness in social situations set an expected goal of two Internet chat-room conversations per week (+2 = 4; –2 equals none), a 0 level or even a +2 level might be accomplished. It would make the social worker appear successful, but would this really represent successful intervention for the client's shyness? Probably not, because the goal levels were set so low that they could easily be achieved. In addition, the goals may have been inappropriate, because there is little reason to believe that increased Internet conversations might help the problem of shyness in social situations.

USING EXISTING DATA COLLECTION INSTRUMENTS

GAS is designed for use with well-motivated clients who will work to set realistic goals and honestly report their behaviors, as well as with larger client systems where valid measurement of behaviors is possible.

The generic term *data collection instruments* is used to describe documents used to assist the researcher in acquiring necessary data and recording them. As we noted at the beginning of this chapter, data collection instruments vary widely in length, structure, and content. In many qualitative exploratory studies, instruments may consist of little more than a group of topics to be covered in interviews in no particular order, or just a list of questions to be addressed. At the other extreme, perhaps in a quantitative study designed to discover if there is support for several research hypotheses, a long, carefully worded data collection instrument or group of instruments may be used. They are likely to contain a mixture of fixed-alternative items, open-ended items, and/or indices and scales.

When we discussed data collection methods in the previous chapter, we suggested that secondary analysis of data collected for some other purpose can be a real time- and effort-saver in some situations. Similarly, if it is possible to use a data measurement instrument or even part of one that was developed by another researcher, a great deal of time and effort can be saved. The process of developing new instruments often represents a major research project in and of itself. Thus, where appropriate, researchers should consider using instruments or portions of instruments that have already been developed.

Another major advantage of using existing data collection instruments is that their validity and reliability may have been assessed and reported in previous research studies. In addition, *norms* (the distribution of scores that can be expected for members of specific populations) and *cutting scores* (the score that separates two levels of a condition, such as having or not having a certain condition) may have been identified for the instrument. When data collection instruments possess established validity and reliability (and frequently norms and cutting scores), they are called *standardized questionnaires*. Some standardized questionnaires are designed to be "self-reports"; others must be completed by the researcher.

In determining if an existing measurement instrument would be appropriate to use in a given research study, a number of issues need to be examined. First, the researcher needs to determine if the instrument can appropriately be used with the population of interest. Is it likely to provide reliable measurement with the researcher's participants? Measures are developed for specific uses with specific research populations. Are the proposed research participants similar enough to the participants for whom the instrument was developed and tested that the instrument will yield reliable data? Cultural differences, especially the meaning of words within subcultures or within different ethnic groups, should be given special attention.

> *A major advantage of using existing data collection instruments is that their validity and reliability may have been assessed and reported in previous research studies.*

The question of validity requires a comparison of conceptual definitions. Before using an instrument developed as part of another study, the researcher would want to be sure that what the instrument purports to measure is the variable that needs to be measured. To use an existing measure, a researcher has to (1) find one that was developed using the same (or similar) conceptual definition of the variable that needs to be measured or (2) adapt a current conceptual definition to that which was used in the development of the existing instrument. For example, a researcher interested in measuring parenting skills could try to find a measurement tool that was developed using a conceptual definition of parenting skills that is the same as the conceptual definition suggested by the researcher's review of the literature. If this proves to be impossible, it may still be possible to find a measurement tool that seems to measure most aspects of parenting skills of interest and then conceptually redefine the variable to be consistent with the conceptual definition of parenting skills used by the developer of the instrument. Fortunately, reference material regarding specific measures often includes the conceptual definition of the variable that was used by the author of the instrument. Information about the instrument may also include how to contact the author of the measure or how to obtain it. If the instrument is copyrighted (most composite indexes and scales are), it may have to be purchased from the publisher or directly from the author. If it is not copyrighted, it can usually be used with the author's written permission. Of course, if the instrument is in the public domain, it may be used without permission of the author.

There are many data collection instruments available for use by social work researchers. Box 12.2 lists some reference volumes that contain and/or describe scales and other data collection instruments that might be appropriate for use in social work research. A specific type of standardized instrument, called a *rapid assessment instrument* (*RAI*), is particularly useful for evaluation of social work practice. RAIs are instruments that can be completed and scored quickly and easily and are designed so that they can be completed multiple times, making them applicable for single-system research designs (Chapter 7).

Let's look at an example RAI (visit http://www.walmyr.com/CASSAMPL.pdf). Westhuis and Thyer's (1989) Clinical Anxiety Scale (CAS) measures dysfunctional anxiety associated with agoraphobia and panic disorder. The client is

CLINICAL ANXIETY SCALE (CAS)

Name: _____ Today's Date: _____

This questionnaire is designed to measure how much anxiety you are currently feeling. It is not a test, so there are no right or wrong answers. Answer each item as carefully and as accurately as you can by placing a number beside each one as follows.

1 Rarely or none of the time
2 A little of the time
3 Some of the time
4 A good part of the time
5 Most or all of the time

1. _____ I feel calm.
2. _____ I feel tense.
3. _____ I feel suddenly scared for no reason.
4. _____ I feel nervous.
5. _____ I use tranquilizers or antidepressants to cope with my anxiety.
6. _____ I feel confident about the future.
7. _____ I am free from senseless or unpleasant thoughts.
8. _____ I feel afraid to go out of my house alone.
9. _____ I feel relaxed and in control of myself.
10. _____ I have spells of terror or panic.
11. _____ I feel afraid in open spaces or in the streets.
12. _____ I feel afraid I will faint in public.
13. _____ I am comfortable traveling in buses, subways or trains.
14. _____ I feel nervousness or shakiness inside.
15. _____ I feel comfortable in crowds, such as shopping or at a movie.
16. _____ I feel comfortable when I am left alone.
17. _____ I feel afraid without good reason.
18. _____ Due to my fears, I unreasonably avoid certain animals, objects or situations.
19. _____ I get upset easily or feel panicky unexpectedly.
20. _____ My hands, arms or legs shake or tremble.
21. _____ Due to my fears, I avoid social situations, whenever possible.
22. _____ I experience sudden attacks of panic which catch me by surprise.
23. _____ I feel generally anxious.
24. _____ I am bothered by dizzy spells.
25. _____ Due to my fears, I avoid being alone, whenever possible.

Box 12.2 References for Scales, Tests, and Other Types of Measurement Instruments

Beere, C. A. (1990). *Gender roles: A handbook of tests and measures.* New York: Greenwood Press, Inc.

Beere, C. A. (1990). *Women and women's issues: A handbook of tests and measures.* San Francisco: Jossey-Bass.

Buros, O. (1978). *Eighth mental measurements yearbook.* Highland Park, NJ: The Gryphon Press. This is an annual publication by the Buros Institute. The *18th Mental Measurements Yearbook* is due out August 2010.

Corcoran, K., & Fischer, J. (1987). *Measures for clinical practice: A sourcebook.* New York: The Free Press.

Fischer, J., & Corcoran, K. (2007). *Measures for clinical practice: A sourcebook* (4th ed.; 2 vols.). New York: Oxford University Press.

Goldman, B. A. (1978–1995). *Directory of unpublished experimental mental measures* (vols. 1–6). New York: Human Sciences Press.

Goldman, B. A., Mitchell, D. F., & Egelson, P. E. (2002) *Directory of unpublished experimental mental measures* (vol. 7). Washington, DC: American Psychological Association.

Hammill, D. D., Brown, L., & Bryant, B. R. (1992). *A consumer's guide to tests in print.* Austin, TX: Pro-Ed.

Holman, A. M. (1983). *Family assessment: Tools for understanding and intervention.* Newbury Park, CA: Sage Publications.

Hudson, W. W. (1982). *The clinical measurement package.* Homewood, IL: The Dorsey Press.

Miller, D. C., & Salkind, N. J. (2002). *Handbook of research design and social measurement* (6th ed.). Newbury Park, CA: Sage Publications.

Rauch, J. B. (1994). *Assessment: A sourcebook for social work practice.* Milwaukee: Families International Incorporated.

Touliatos, J., Perlmutter, B. F., & Straus, M. A. (2001). *Handbook of family measurement techniques* (3 vols.). Newbury Park, CA: Sage Publications.

asked to complete the scale by placing a number (1–5) by each of the 25 statements. To score the instrument, the social worker must first *reverse score* the items that are listed at the bottom of the instrument (items 1, 6, 7, 9, 13, 15, 16). If you look at these items, you will notice that they are positively worded. For example, number 16 reads, "I feel comfortable when I am left alone." For the seven positively worded items, answering with a higher number actually indicates less anxiety. The eighteen remaining items are scored in such a way that higher numbers indicate more anxiety. Therefore, to add up the scores to represent the amount of anxiety being experienced by the client, these seven positively worded items must be reverse scored. To reverse score an item, 5 becomes 1, 4 becomes 2, 3 remains the same, 2 becomes 4, and 1 becomes 5. In this way, the answer that represents higher anxiety becomes a higher number. After reverse scoring these items, you can calculate the total score (S) by summing all 25 items and subtracting 25. This will produce a score of 0 to 100. If the client fails to answer all 25 items, the formula for calculating the score is a bit more complicated. You must add up all of the items that were completed, subtract the number of items completed, multiply by 100, and then divide by the number of items completed times 4. The advantage of this formula is that it will always produce a score between 0 and 100, regardless of how many items the client completes.

Reliability scores for the Clinical Anxiety Scale were 0.90 and higher, and validity scores were 0.60 and higher. A cutting score of 30 was established to help clinicians differentiate between anxious and non-anxious clients. In other words, clients who score above 30 on this scale are likely to have a problem with phobic anxiety, and clients scoring under 30 are not likely to suffer with this type of anxiety. This RAI is a self-report instrument and was designed specifically for repeated use for the purpose of evaluating change in the client's experience of anxiety over time, such as pre-treatment to post-treatment (for further information on this instrument, see Fischer & Corcoran, 2007).

REVISING EXISTING DATA COLLECTION INSTRUMENTS

Research-Based Practice

Complete and score the Clinical Anxiety Scale. Is your score above or below the cutting score?

If the researcher is unable to locate an existing measure that is appropriate for use without revision, he or she may still be able to find an existing instrument that could be modified and used. For example, an instrument may be available that measures client satisfaction with services received from an out-patient mental health clinic. If the researcher is interested in measuring client satisfaction with services received within an in-patient mental health setting, the existing instrument may possibly be modified for use. Several items may be borrowed from the instrument exactly as written and others reworded for use in the current study. The revised instrument should then be pilot-tested with a sample of participants, similar to the intended study group, to see if measurement problems have been introduced by the revision.

If the research study is exploratory or if the instrument is to be used as a guideline for the researcher (e.g., in a qualitative study in which data collection is conducted using unstructured interviews), modifications of existing instruments can be made with little concern about the effects of the changes. When these data collection methods are used, parts of different instruments may be freely borrowed and changed as deemed appropriate. There is little reason to be concerned about how a change in wording might affect the validity of measurement. Instead, an assessment of the quality of measurement is often based on the researcher's judgment of the degree of candor and truthfulness that participants seemed to display in response to its use.

In predominantly quantitative studies, which rely heavily on accurate measurement of variables to test hypotheses, rewording of existing instruments or changing them in any way should be undertaken with extreme caution. When using revised instruments, advice regarding the possible effects of the modifications in wording on quality of measurement may be obtained by contacting the author of the original instrument. If large sections of a data collection instrument are borrowed from an existing instrument (especially if it is copyrighted), the researcher must gain permission to use the instrument from the author or publisher. If only a few items are used, and if the original wording is substantially altered, permission is usually not necessary.

When borrowing items from an existing instrument, we should remember that assessments of its reliability and validity were based on the instrument as a whole. Thus, it would not be correct to alter items and assume that those assessments would be accurate for the revised instrument as well. Composite indexes and scales are especially sensitive to revision. If any items are changed, added, or deleted, assessments of reliability or validity for the original instrument should not be used.

CONSTRUCTING NEW DATA COLLECTION INSTRUMENTS

If it is not possible to use an existing data collection instrument, a new instrument will have to be developed. In those predominantly qualitative studies that rely on a data collection instrument to ensure that certain topics will be addressed but do not seek to standardize data collection methods, it is often simplest to create a new instrument from scratch, rather than to try to revise an existing one that is likely to have been developed to study some other question with some other group of research participants. The process of developing such an instrument may be relatively simple. It may consist primarily of thinking through and discussing with others what areas should be explored within the context of an in-person interview, focus group, and so forth, as well as, perhaps, the best sequence in which to explore them.

In predominantly quantitative studies, which rely more on careful, standardized measurement of variables, construction of a new data collection instrument is an exacting and demanding task (Nunnaly & Bernstein, 1994). Whichever formats and methods are selected, the task requires careful attention if one is to derive reliable and valid measurements.

Scales generally are developed by researchers following rigorous rules and procedures. Many scales have been developed, tested, and repeatedly revised and honed over decades. Up to this point, we have described only some of the general methods employed in constructing the various types of scales mentioned in this chapter. However, scale building is an exact science. It is the focus of graduate courses in statistics and measurement. Only rarely would a social worker attempt to construct a new scale as part of a research study. But to gain an appreciation of the effort that goes into their construction, we will mention briefly the usual sequence of events in constructing a scale.

1. **The variable to be measured is operationally defined.** The definition should refer to all relevant indicators of the variable. A clear definition enables the researcher to write an *item pool,* a preliminary set of items (ideally, 80–100) that may be included in the scale. The item pool should be as exhaustive as possible, so that less relevant items later can be eliminated while leaving enough items to constitute the scale. The items are then reviewed by judges. Their role is to evaluate the items for clarity, relevance, appropriateness, and ease in responding. Then items should be revised as needed. A draft instrument is produced, and a pilot test of the instrument is conducted. Pilot-test participants are asked to respond to the items and provide a critique of them. They are encouraged to make comments about the items themselves, for example, which items are not clear, which contain words they do not understand, and so on.

2. **Data from the pilot test are analyzed.** This is accomplished using statistical analyses known as *item analyses.* The process typically involves the calculation of two statistics by computer: item-to-total-scale correlations (for each item) and a reliability coefficient that provides a measure of the internal reliability of the scale (such as coefficient alpha). They are calculated to ensure that all of the items that are to comprise the scale are measuring the same construct and that the items, when taken together, represent the unidimensional measure that is sought.

The item-to-total-scale analysis determines how responses to each item correlate with how participants responded overall to the scale. (It is similar to the item analysis that professors sometimes use on multiple-choice or true/false tests to eliminate bad test items—those that were missed by students who did well on the test overall and/or were answered correctly by students who did poorly.) A researcher would want to retain only items with the highest positive item-total correlations. Items with low or negative item-total correlations are usually deleted. The analysis required for item-total correlations is conducted using statistical software packages specifically designed for social science data. When this is done, a reliability estimate of the scale describes the statistical effect of deletion of individual items. This assists the researcher in deciding which scale items to keep and which ones to delete.

Coefficient alpha, we will recall, reflects the degree to which individual items correlate with each other. Scales that are designed to measure a unidimensional construct should reflect a high degree of internal consistency. Scales that are multidimensional in nature (e.g., the MMPI [Minnesota Multiphasic Personality Inventory]) would not be expected to have a high degree of internal consistency overall, but their various subscales would.

3. **The scale is modified as needed.** Items are deleted or revised, often as a result of a statistical procedure known as factor analysis. If items are added at this stage, they should be subjected to pilot-testing and further statistical analysis. Once the scale is fully developed, data about the reliability and validity of the scale and of individual items are retained for reporting and for future analysis.

When a scale (or at least a portion of it) is published in a book of data collection instruments or a professional journal, the process of its development is described, along with a description of the people who contributed data for its development. Conclusions about the scale's reliability and validity (based on statistical analyses) as well as its limitations are noted. For example, we might read that "The scale was found to have a test-retest reliability of 0.89 among a sample of Latin Americans under age 65 who reside in the United States and Canada for whom Spanish is a first language. However, its reliability among other Spanish-speaking people was only 0.45."

Issues in Development

There are many issues that should be considered in developing a new data collection instrument. They relate to its intent, formatting, and sequencing of questions, as well as to its length, clarity, wording, and presentation.

There are many issues that should be considered in developing a new data collection instrument. They relate to its intent, formatting, and sequencing of questions, as well as to its length, clarity, wording, and presentation. Although these issues are most relevant to mailed or participant-completed instruments, most of them are equally relevant to data collection in which participant responses are recorded by the researcher.

Intent of Items

One issue relates to the nature of what is being measured: Is an item or series of items designed to measure (1) knowledge, (2) attitudes or beliefs, or (3) behaviors of participants? The intent of the measurement determines the way in which a question or series of items is worded. Often, when measuring complicated constructs, we require a composite index or a scale consisting of several items. However, sometimes, it is possible to measure knowledge, attitudes or beliefs, or behaviors using one question:

▶ Can a friend call the hospital to learn your room number so that he or she can visit you (knowledge)?

_____ Yes _____ No

▶ How helpful was your social worker during your hospitalization (attitude or belief)?

_____ *Very helpful*
_____ *Somewhat helpful*
_____ *Not helpful*

▶ During your hospitalization, how many times did you meet with your social worker (behavior)?

_____ Never _____ Once or twice _____ Three times or more

Of course, for reasons discussed earlier in this chapter, it is sometimes preferable to use an open-ended question to measure knowledge, attitudes or beliefs, or behaviors. Then the items might look more like this:

▶ Please describe your understanding of the HIPAA laws and how they affect visitors to the hospital (knowledge).
▶ Do you think that your social worker was helpful to you during your hospitalization? Why or why not (attitude or belief)?
▶ What were some of the questions that you asked your social worker (behavior)?

Clarity of Items

If items are not clearly understood by participants, their responses may not provide an accurate measurement of a variable. The best items generally are those that ask participants for a simple response, are unambiguous, and are phrased positively rather than negatively. People do not always notice a qualifying word in a question (e.g., words such as *hardly*, *never*, *not*, or *barely*); therefore, it is to avoid them.

Use of Contingency Instructions

When using self-administered data collection instruments, contingency instructions are sometimes appropriate. They are used to direct the participant through the instrument in an efficient manner (or, if it is administered by an interviewer, to assist him or her). They also provide a way to reduce the number of items that participants are asked to respond to and to avoid asking participants to answer items that are not applicable to them. They reflect consideration on the part of the researcher and help to organize the data that are collected. An example of a contingency instruction follows:

If you answered "yes" to question 2 above, please respond to questions 3 through 7; if you answered "no" to question 2, please skip down to question 8 on page 3.

Sequencing of Items

In developing new instruments, there are two perspectives on sequencing of items. Some researchers prefer general-to-specific sequencing—begin with the most general (and least controversial or personal) items and then move to the more specific ones. Placing demographic and/or less threatening items first may help to gain the trust and confidence of the participant. It also may be helpful to the researcher to have some understanding of the participants being studied prior to covering more specific items. The more personal or more threatening items can be placed near the end of the instrument.

If the researcher is not concerned that some items in the instrument might be offensive to or otherwise alienate participants, the specific-to-general sequence may be preferable. Then, the most important and the most specific (to the study) items are placed first. The more general data (often, demographic information) can be secured at the end. An advantage of this sequencing pattern is that if the instrument is not fully completed, some of the more important data will still be available to the researcher.

Instructions for Responding

In securing useful data, especially if the instrument is to be self-administered, the wording of instructions is equally as important as the wording of the items themselves. Participants must understand how they are expected to respond to items. This seems self-evident; however, researchers frequently assume that the correct method to respond to items is as obvious to the participant as it is to them. Consequently, they fail to provide complete instructions for responding. If there are two or more distinct sections and/or question types used, separate instructions should be included directly above each section or question type.

Length of the Instrument

Length is perhaps best addressed through use of common sense. As we suggested earlier, the longer the instrument, the less likely people are to complete it. The researcher needs to collect enough data to be able to answer his or her research questions and/or test hypotheses. Necessary items must be included, but unnecessary ones should be omitted. Frequently, the length of an instrument can be reduced through the elimination of demographic items that are not relevant to the focus of the research. As we indicated in Chapter 5, there is no such thing as a "usual" or standard group of demographic variables that must be included within every instrument.

Presentation

A self-administered data collection instrument should not appear crowded. Leaving adequate space for people to respond to items and not crowding questions helps participants to complete it. In addition, instruments should be error free. The goal is to make their completion a pleasant (or at least a nonstressful) experience, so that a high percentage of fully completed responses will be received.

Pilot-Testing

Even though the researcher may think that all of the preceding issues have been addressed, newly developed data collection instruments almost always produce some surprises. Even experienced researchers are not able to anticipate just how items on a data collection instrument will be perceived or interpreted by the participant or how a participant might respond overall to the instrument. A panel of experts consisting of people knowledgeable about instrument construction can provide good advice and suggestions. But what these individuals can contribute may be no substitute for the feedback provided by people similar to the research participants themselves. A pilot-testing of an instrument provides information on many factors that relate to the quality of a data collection instrument. Feedback is likely to provide insights about the following:

- Clarity/misinterpretation of wording of items
- Errors in grammar and spelling
- Juxtaposition of items that may bias measurement
- Potential offensiveness of items
- Redundancy that may annoy participants
- Indication that more structure is needed
- Indication that less structure is needed
- Time required to complete the instrument

Some of the preceding feedback areas can be gleaned from the way that the pilot-study participants complete the instrument. Some of it may require one or more additional broad questions that are not a part of the measurement instrument per se. For example, the researcher might add an extra question, such as "What parts of the instrument were difficult for you to complete and why?" Another good question would be, "Do you feel that the instrument gave you an opportunity to represent yourself accurately and, if not, why?" Such questions reflect an awareness of the possibility that the newly developed instrument may somehow lead participants to answer in certain unanticipated ways, or that questions or items that should have been included as part of the instrument may have been inadvertently omitted. A good pilot test and the thoughtful revisions that it generates can result in fewer problems and better measurement when data are subsequently collected from research participants.

There is an ethical issue that often comes up when using people as participants in the pilot-testing of a data collection instrument. If no additional questions are added to the proposed instrument (that is usually a "giveaway"), participants might not be aware that they are not "real participants" unless they are told so. Should they be told why they are being asked to complete the data collection instrument or be allowed to misunderstand their role? Not to tell them seems dishonest and deceptive, but to tell them may influence the seriousness with which they approach the task. In many instances, the pilot test includes giving participants the same introduction or cover letter that will be given to other participants, to see how effective it is. And that is almost certain to mislead them. If no changes are made to the data collection instrument on the basis of the pilot test, the data that pilot study participants provide can be aggregated along with that of other participants, thus avoiding the issue. But in other situations, the researcher must decide the most ethical way to approach the issue. It may entail telling participants in general terms what their role is, stressing the importance of their unique contribution to the research effort, and asking them if they still wish to participate.

USE OF SELF-ADMINISTERED DATA COLLECTION INSTRUMENTS

Ethical Practice

Do you think participants who are really just pilot-testing an instrument should be told that they are not actually participating in the research study? Why or why not?

Many of the issues we have discussed relate most directly to data collection instruments that are self-administered, that is, they are completed without the presence of the researcher. Self-administered data collection instruments are commonly associated with surveys (Chapter 11). In surveys, the researcher generally is interested in aggregating data about the characteristics, behaviors, feelings, attitudes, or opinions of a given population. The term *questionnaire* is widely applied to self-administered instruments when they are used in surveys.

Other types of knowledge building (besides surveys) also use self-administered instruments. They are used to collect data for all levels of research. Social work practitioners also use them to secure a measurement of an aspect of client functioning in their practice. For example, a clinician may wish to get an objective measure of the level of clinical depression that clients are experiencing and may either find or develop a data collection instrument that clients can complete without any in-person instructions or supervision.

Advantages

Because they are highly structured, self-administered instruments have several advantages:

- ▶ **Presence of the researcher is not required.** Once the instruments have been developed and distributed, the researcher is free to work on other research tasks while awaiting their return.
- ▶ **Responses and response categories can be precoded.** Analysis of the data is greatly facilitated when the researcher collects data that are presorted into computer-ready categories.
- ▶ **Data can be collected using fixed stimuli.** All participants are asked to respond to the same questions, worded in the same way. Thus, at least one aspect of data collection is standardized. This is especially important in quantitative studies.
- ▶ **There is the perception of anonymity.** Even though instruments may be precoded with identifying information, generally participants do not write their names anywhere on them. The appearance of anonymity (if not the reality of it) is thus maintained. This may increase participants' willingness to provide data. Most research that uses questionnaires for data collection reports data in aggregate form, enhancing confidentiality of responses. Participants can be reasonably confident that their individual responses cannot be attributed to them. This is an advantage to the researcher, both for securing truthful information and increasing the likelihood of a larger percentage of completed questionnaires.

Supervised Administration

A major reason for supervising data collection either individually or in a group situation is to secure a high rate of completion. If the researcher is present and distributes and collects the data collection instrument from participants, more fully completed instruments will be received than if the instruments were mailed out.

There are sometimes other reasons researchers wish to be present during data collection, for example, to clarify the intention of items, or to observe whether the instruments were completed conscientiously or in a haphazard way. This latter determination would be impossible if a mailed questionnaire were used.

Supervised individual completion of instruments (perhaps in the research participant's home, office, or a neutral site—whatever is most convenient) can produce a high completion rate. But if comparisons of participants and their responses or hypothesis testing is part of the research design (as in most

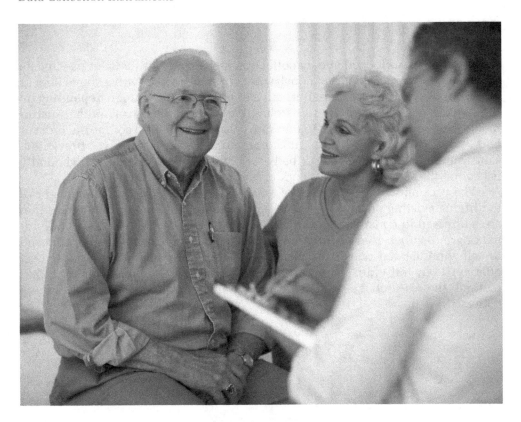

quantitative research), individualized data collection arrangements may not be desirable. In such cases, the same setting should be used for data collection with all research participants to ensure that the setting of data collection will not be a potentially confounding variable.

A useful alternative to the one-on-one, supervised method of data collection is instrument completion in a group setting. For example, the researcher might supervise the completion of an instrument by all members of a focus group or by all participants in a social program. Or a group meeting consisting of the sample participants might be constituted specifically for the purpose of data collection. When group supervision of data collection is used, instruments are distributed, participants complete them at their own pace or within a prescribed time limit, and they are collected. The researcher is available for clarification and to address questions related to the data collection instrument.

The major benefit of this kind of administration is efficiency—a large amount of data can be collected in a relatively short amount of time. Its relatively low cost and high rate of return are advantages that the researcher should consider when selecting a data-gathering method. However, like individually supervised completion of data collection instruments, the researcher's presence can have the potential to influence the data received. In addition, responses may be influenced by the reactions (e.g., anger, embarrassment, boredom) of others in the room.

SUMMARY

In this chapter, we looked at data collection instruments as tools for use in data collection. Some variables and constructs can be measured with a single item or question, using either a fixed-alternative or an open-ended item, depending on the specific data needs of the researcher. We discussed the use of other instruments that require many items to measure complex variables: composite indexes and scales. An overview of the most common types of scales was presented. Construction of scales was described as a highly complex process; it generally is beyond the scope of a social work research study.

The pros and cons of the use of existing data collection instruments or of modifying existing ones were discussed. We examined many of the issues that are addressed in constructing new instruments. Finally, the option of individual or group-supervised completion of data collection instruments (as opposed to self-administered ones) was discussed. Group administration is more cost efficient than individual supervised data collection, but when using either method, the researcher's presence can have the effect of biasing data that are collected.

Log onto **www.mysocialworklab.com** and answer the questions below. (If you did not receive an access code to **MySocialWorkLab** with this text and wish to purchase access online text and wish for you, please visit www.mysocialworklab.com.)

1. **Watch the Core Competencies Video: Professional Identity: Professional Roles and Boundaries.** What are two variables you might want to measure to evaluate the progress of this client?

2. **Read the Case Study: Mental Health: Alice and Eric.** Use goal attainment scaling to create scales to measure treatment progress for Alice and Eric.

PRACTICE TEST

1. The following is an advantage of using open-ended questions:
   a. Participants are more likely to complete open-ended questions.
   b. They are easy to analyze using quantitative data analysis.
   c. They allow the researcher to precode response categories for computer data entry.
   d. They allow the researcher to collect data in the form of direct quotations.

2. Items that are worded so that a high level of agreement with the item would reflect a high quantity of the variable being measured and a low level of agreement would reflect a low quantity of the variable are
   a. reversal items.
   b. positive items.
   c. linear scales.
   d. summated scales.

3. A Thurstone scale is characterized by all of the following except one.
   a. It is time consuming to develop.
   b. It can approximate interval-level measurement.
   c. It is easier to develop than a Likert scale.
   d. It can produce more precise measurements than a Likert scale.

4. Random assessment instruments are
   a. not particularly useful for evaluation of social work practice.
   b. completed and scored quickly and easily.
   c. designed so that they should be completed only one time.
   d. not applicable for single-system research designs.

5. Develop a simple Likert scale to measure student satisfaction with this textbook (construct at least three items).

ASSESS YOUR COMPETENCE
Use the scale below to rate your current level of achievement on the following concepts or skills associated with each competency presented in the chapter:

1	2	3
I can accurately describe the concept or skill.	I can consistently identify the concept or skill when observing and analyzing practice activities.	I can competently implement the concept or skill in my own practice.

_____ Understanding the difference between open-ended and fixed-alternative items

_____ Being familiar with composite indexes and the various types of scales used in social work research

_____ Understanding how to score a rapid assessment instrument (including reverse scoring)

_____ Understanding some of the issues involved in developing an original data collection instrument

Analyzing Data

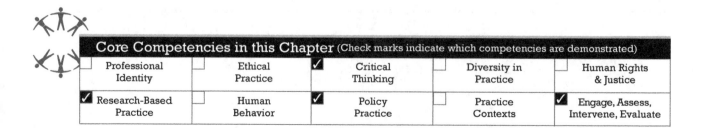
Core Competencies in this Chapter (Check marks indicate which competencies are demonstrated)				
☐ Professional Identity	☐ Ethical Practice	☑ Critical Thinking	☐ Diversity in Practice	☐ Human Rights & Justice
☑ Research-Based Practice	☐ Human Behavior	☑ Policy Practice	☐ Practice Contexts	☑ Engage, Assess, Intervene, Evaluate

Data can take many forms. In predominantly qualitative studies, they may take the form of audio or video recording of interviews, or field notes of interaction with participants. In secondary analysis, they may be completed data collection schedules compiled from case records or some other source. In meta-analysis, they may be the reports of many studies that examined a similar problem or question. Or, when a mailed survey method of data collection is used, they may consist of a stack of completed questionnaires.

No matter what form data assume, they must be organized, summarized, and analyzed, often with the help of computer-assisted statistical analysis. Generally, we associate statistical analysis of data with more quantitative research methods. However, methods for statistical analysis of qualitative findings have also been developed. A number of computer software packages are now available to assist researchers in the tasks of classifying, ordering, and analyzing both quantitative and qualitative data.

THE DATA IN PERSPECTIVE

In order to begin to make sense of the data collected, it helps to first understand their source by asking certain questions. The answers to these questions and other related ones help to put research findings in perspective. For example, if original data were collected from research participants,

- Who were they?
- Under what conditions did they provide data?
- What assurances about anonymity or confidentiality were given?
- What understanding did they have about how data would be used?
- What prior relationship, if any, did they have with the researcher?
- As a research sample, do they appear to be representative of the sampling frame or accessible population from which they were drawn?
- Was the sample biased in some way?
- How might any possible bias affect the quality of the data?
- Given the size of the sample, how much might sampling error have affected the quality of the data?

When appropriate, a good place to start is to calculate the percentage of completed responses, also called *response rate*. This is done by dividing the actual number of cases for which there are reasonably complete data by the potential number of cases (all cases that the researcher sought to include in the sample). A high percentage of completed responses are more likely to produce a representative sample than a low response rate, but a high percentage of usable responses does not guarantee representativeness. For example, a researcher could post a notice in shopping malls or run an advertisement in a newspaper asking for volunteers to complete a questionnaire about a personal problem they might have. Over time, he or she might acquire quite a few volunteers and would probably get an impressively high response rate (perhaps 90 percent or more) of complete, usable questionnaires from among those who volunteered. However, we could think of several reasons why the usable responses would not be representative of any group other than the volunteers in the study, and perhaps not even of them if the 10 percent who volunteered to complete the questionnaire but failed to complete all of it differed from those who completed it in some important way!

Generally, it is helpful to try to identify patterns of response that may suggest the presence of sampling bias. Certain questions can be helpful in this regard, for example,

- Among the potential cases within the sample, which ones contain complete data and which do not?
- Do they differ in any meaningful way?
- If so, should this be reported and discussed, or is the difference one that is probably unrelated to any research findings?

Most researchers summarize the most relevant characteristics of their data sources in a separate section of their reports. The summary helps both researchers and the readers of their reports to estimate whether their data sources were typical of the accessible population or sampling frame from which they were drawn. If research participants provided the data, a description of them often is presented in group form as a broad demographic profile. Sometimes, a brief description of a typical participant is provided.

A demographic profile of research participants can help the researcher put the findings of a research study into perspective. It can suggest the degree of the study's external validity. For readers of a research report to be able to assess the relevance of the research findings to their own specific practice situations, a clear picture of those who provided data is necessary. For example, a report of a study based on a sample of low-income mothers needing assistance in developing parenting skills might include a demographic summary of the research participants in relation to the variables age, income, presence of a father or father figure, number of children, and degree of support from extended family. Readers of such a report can assess how closely the participants resembled their own clients and thus can help them determine whether the findings and any recommendations might be useful for their own practice.

In more qualitative research, data are less likely to be aggregated. Instead, the demographic characteristics of each individual research participant may be included in a narrative description of the researcher's interaction with him or her. For example, we might see something like this:

> Lucretia W. is a 62-year-old Caucasian woman with three adult children, all of whom live out of state. Her husband (who was ten years older) passed away six months ago from advanced stage Alzheimer's disease. She has a high school education and worked as a cook in various restaurants until she decided to quit work about one year ago to care for her husband. She is an active church member and states that "my faith got me through it all." Her first explanation for her husband's illness was "it was God trying to make me stronger," but the longer that she and I talked over coffee in her kitchen, I began to detect that . . .

In both quantitative and qualitative studies, researchers generally describe the setting in which the research was conducted. It allows readers of their reports (1) to judge to what degree the setting in which data were collected might have influenced findings and (2) in the case of organization-based research, to assess whether the nature of the organization (and its services) in which the research took place is similar enough to their own that the findings of the research may be helpful in informing their own practice decision making. For example, readers of a report who work in an outpatient clinic, where federal reimbursement usually limits services to only four treatment sessions, may quickly conclude that a research finding that individual treatment is more effective than group treatment is of little relevance to them. They would base this conclusion on the researcher's description, which states that the research was conducted in a private, inpatient psychiatric setting that offers primarily long-term intensive psychotherapy.

PREPARING FOR DATA ANALYSIS

Prior to conducting data analysis and attempting to draw conclusions and findings from them, it is helpful to revisit the purpose of the study. It suggests the general type of analysis that would be appropriate. For example, was the research designed to assess the relative effectiveness of various treatment interventions for addressing a problem that clients were experiencing? Or was it designed merely to describe the effects that the problem has on specific client groups? In the first instance, the researcher would be expected to conduct and report on statistical analysis that would provide evidence of the relative effectiveness of the various intervention methods. In the second, only analysis that provides a clear description of the range of effects of the problems observed and some indication of their distribution within the research sample might be required.

The presence of other research purposes would suggest other approaches to analysis of the data. For example, if the purpose of a study was to describe group performance before and after exposure to an independent variable, or compare two or more groups in relation to a behavior or an attitude, the method of data analysis used would be different from that if the study's purpose was to determine to what degree several variables, viewed together, may explain or predict a problem or phenomenon. Or if the purpose was to assess how effective an individual's or a program's intervention was, another method of analysis might be used.

A review of how research questions and/or hypotheses were stated can help in selecting the most appropriate method of data analysis. For example, sometimes questions are posed in such a way that it is clear that differences between or among groups are being sought; other times, it is clear that the degree of association or correlation between or among variables is the primary focus of the research.

There are other interrelated issues associated with the choice of methods used to answer research questions and/or seek statistical support for hypotheses. They require the researcher to recall and review many aspects of the research design that produced the research data. Once again, certain questions can be helpful, for example,

Critical Thinking

How does the purpose of the research study affect the data analysis techniques selected?

> ⬦ Were the research methods used and the kind of data that they produced primarily quantitative or qualitative?
> ⬦ What general category of sampling was used (probability or nonprobability)?
> ⬦ How many samples or subsamples were used?
> ⬦ How large was each sample?
> ⬦ How (specifically) were participants selected?
> ⬦ Are the variables of interest believed to be normally distributed (they would approximate a "normal curve") within the population, or is their distribution badly skewed?
> ⬦ What levels of measurement were generated for each variable that will be used in statistical analysis?

DATA ANALYSIS: AN OVERVIEW

An in-depth discussion of methods of data analysis is beyond the scope of this book. However, we will examine the conceptual underpinnings that are critical to understanding how statistical analysis is conducted and how it assists the researcher in drawing conclusions on the basis of research data.

Qualitative Analysis

If the researcher employed primarily qualitative research methods, the data are also primarily qualitative in nature, perhaps in the form of summaries of indepth interviews, participant observations, video recording, or something similar. Data analysis then tends to be less standardized than that used in more quantitative designs. While it may rely on some widely practiced methods, it also may be highly creative and even unique to a given research study.

Qualitative data analysis seeks to make sense out of the data—to learn what actually occurred during the data collection process and what it might all mean. Even verbal qualitative data, such as recordings of in-person interviews, can have meaningful numbers (values) or labels (value categories) assigned to them. From the outset, the assignment process may be a little more subjective and a little less precise than when quantitative data are present, but once assignment is finished, the values and value categories can be manipulated and sometimes even analyzed using statistical analysis. However, the design of most qualitative studies (e.g., use of nonprobability samples, lack of control groups, reliance on interviewing or observation for data collection, lack of emphasis on measurement of variables) seriously limits the number and type of statistical tests that can be used for data analysis.

Assignment of values or value categories often entails a certain amount of counting (quantification) of behaviors, use of certain words, or emotional responses—content analysis (Chapter 4). Content analysis can be performed with the assistance of software packages that have recently been developed for this purpose. Or, it may entail more "human" methods, such as the use of two or more judges, all independently examining the same data and drawing their own conclusions as to what they saw in them. Afterward, the judges may meet to attempt to arrive at a consensus as to what they observed, or the researcher may attempt to reconcile any differences in the judges' observations. Sometimes, a majority rules method is used. For example, if two out of three judges perceived that in a videotape a person seemed anxious but a third judge did not, it would be concluded that the research participant was indeed anxious. Alternately, the decision may be made beforehand that an emotion or behavior will not be reported as a research finding unless all judges reported it—it must be a unanimous observation.

A wide variety of computer software packages, such as NVivo, XSight, EZ-Test, ATLAS.ti, and Ethnograph, are now available to help analyze qualitative data. Weitzman and Miles (1995) compiled a sourcebook for computer programs for qualitative research analysis. It is still useful, although it is somewhat outdated. Other books have also looked specifically at using computer software to aid in the analysis of qualitative data (e.g., Fielding & Lee, 1998; Gahan & Hannibal, 1998; Kuckartz, 2004). In addition, there are books that offer more general information on the analysis of qualitative data (e.g., Auerbach & Silverstein, 2003; Marshall & Rossman, 2011; Patton, 2001; Saldana, 2009; Warren & Karner, 2009).

Quantitative Analysis

In research studies that are more quantitative in nature, statistical analysis continues to play an important part in answering research questions and concluding whether there is adequate support for research hypotheses. It is often the final step in the process of elimination used to determine whether a relationship between or among variables within a research sample is likely to be a real one that exists beyond the sample.

If the amount of data being analyzed is small and the type of statistical analysis that is to be performed is relatively simple, researchers sometimes choose not to use a computer to assist in data analysis. However, because of the many user-friendly statistical software packages now available for use with personal computers and other handheld electronic devices, statistical analysis is now almost always conducted electronically.

Complex statistical computations are performed flawlessly when electronic methods are used for data analysis, assuming that the data have been entered accurately and the appropriate method of statistical analysis has been selected. Probably the most time-consuming step in statistical analysis has always been data entry. However, even this tedious operation may soon be eliminated as technology allows us merely to scan the data into a computer for analysis. Once data are entered into the computer, a wide variety of statistical analyses can be performed, each in just a matter of seconds. Some of the more widely used computer software packages for the analysis of quantitative data include Statistical Package for the Social Sciences (SPSS), Statistical Analysis System (SAS), Stata, Minitab, and Systat. There are also several books that offer help to researchers using these and other statistical software (e.g., Bryman & Cramer, 2005; Cramer, 2007; Greasley, 2008; Norusis, 2003).

The ease with which statistical analysis can be performed by a computer represents both a bonanza and a danger for the researcher. Statistical tests that would have been outside the mathematical competence of many researchers just a few years ago are now possible for anyone with even average data-processing skills. However, because hundreds of statistical analyses can be performed easily and quickly, there is a real danger that either (1) findings will not be interpreted correctly by researchers or (2) they will be misleading to readers of research reports. Unfortunately, computer programs cannot always determine if a given statistical test has been used appropriately. They also cannot know whether a researcher has even a beginning understanding of how the results of statistical analysis should be interpreted in light of a research question or hypothesis. They cannot know how the sample that provided the data was selected, and how it may have affected results. They also cannot alert the reader of the report that the researcher stumbled on a spurious (i.e., not real) relationship between variables simply by trying an almost infinite number of combinations—something that is now quite easy to do because of the ease with which computer analysis of data can be performed.

There are a few basic understandings that are central to the successful use of statistical analyses by the researcher. We will present an overview of them in this text and suggest that they be studied in greater depth elsewhere.

Uses of Statistical Analyses

Statistical analyses are versatile and can be used at several points in the research process to assist in decision making. In quantitative studies, they play an important role (1) in the design of research, (2) in summarizing the distribution of

Complex statistical computations are performed flawlessly when electronic methods are used for data analysis, assuming that the data have been entered accurately and the appropriate method of statistical analysis has been selected.

Policy Practice

Think of an instance when a politician used statistics to support his or her platform. Can you think of a way the statistics could have been "slanted" to serve the politician's needs?

variables within research data, (3) in estimating the characteristics of the population from which a sample was drawn, and (4) in drawing conclusions and interpretations about answers to research questions and the presence or absence of support for hypotheses. In this chapter, we will discuss only briefly the first and third of these uses, focusing most of our discussion on the second and fourth.

Designing Research

Some statistical methods are helpful to the researcher for making decisions related to the design of research. For example, statistical analyses can tell researchers when a simple random sample is sufficiently large that the impact of sampling error is acceptably low, or they can tell them the mathematical probability that a sample is sufficiently representative of a known population in relation to a variable (Sudham, 1976). As we noted in Chapter 11, statistical analyses also are used to help design and refine data collection instruments such as scales and indexes. They perform operations such as coefficient alpha to help assess the overall reliability of a data collection instrument. They also can be used to identify items in the instrument that appear to measure the same component of a variable, items that may be redundant or unnecessary, or that can be used to construct parallel forms of the instrument.

Summarizing the Distribution of Variables

Researchers use descriptive statistical analyses (sometimes referred to as data reduction) to reduce large amounts of data to a manageable size so that he or she (or the reader of a research report) will be able to visualize the major characteristics of the participants and the data that they provide.

Descriptive statistical analysis is used to provide a concise summary of data accumulated about and from those persons or cases that were studied. Researchers use descriptive statistical analyses (sometimes referred to as *data reduction*) to reduce large amounts of data to a manageable size so that he or she (or the reader of a research report) will be able to visualize the major characteristics of the participants and the data that they provide.

Descriptive statistical analyses may involve the construction of frequency distributions or graphs. A *frequency distribution* is a table displaying how many participants or cases fell in each value or value category (measurement) of a variable. The frequencies are displayed alongside the various values or value categories of the variable. Also, if the variable is at least ordinal level, frequency distributions may include additional columns for *cumulative frequencies* (how many cases had a measurement larger or smaller than a given value). Another column may reflect percentages of all cases represented by the cases in a given value category or what percentage of all cases had a measurement above or below a given value (*cumulative percentages*). Sometimes, values are grouped, that is, ranges of values are used instead of individual values, to make a frequency distribution table smaller. When this is done, the researcher seeks to make the table simpler to understand without giving up too much detail. See Figure 13.1 for an example of a frequency distribution table (including frequencies, percentages, and cumulative percentages) showing the results of a client satisfaction survey. The cumulative percentage allows us to easily see that 62 percent of the clients were either satisfied or extremely satisfied.

Graphs are also frequently used to describe the distribution of variables within a sample or population of cases studied. They can be simple or complex. The simplest forms portray the same data that are contained in frequency distributions, that is, the distribution of values of a variable. Some commonly used examples are bar charts, line diagrams, histograms, and pie charts. Bar charts and line diagrams use bars or lines of lengths that are proportional to the number of cases that possess a given measurement of a variable. Figure 13.2 provides an example of the data from Figure 13.1 displayed in a bar chart. For

Research-Based Practice

Create a frequency table to show the number and percentage of males and females in your research class.

	N	%	Cumulative %
Extremely satisfied	12	24%	24%
Satisfied	19	38%	62%
Neutral	7	14%	76%
Dissatisfied	8	16%	92%
Extremely dissatisfied	4	8%	100%
TOTAL	50	100%	

Figure 13.1

Example Client Satisfaction Frequency Distribution Table

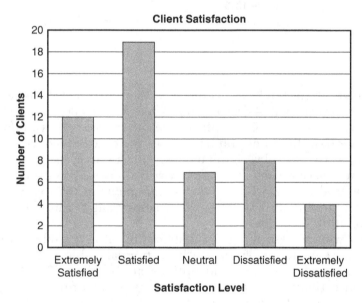

Figure 13.2

Example Client Satisfaction Bar Chart

the variable "client satisfaction," notice that twice as many clients were dissatisfied as were extremely dissatisfied; therefore, the bar is twice as tall for the value category "dissatisfied."

Histograms are graphs that portray the shape of the distribution of a variable. They can be created simply by connecting the tops of the lines or bars in a line diagram or bar chart to form a shape. Then the overall distribution can be described in summary form. For example, if the shape thus created is essentially bell shaped with most values clustering around the middle and then tailing off similarly to the right and left, the variable is regarded as normally distributed within the sample or population that provided the data.

Pie charts use areas of a circle to correspond to the percentage of all cases that were found to have a given measurement of a variable. Figure 13.3 shows a pie chart based on the data from Figure 13.1. In our example, 24 percent of participants in the study were extremely satisfied; therefore, the pie chart for the

Client Satisfaction

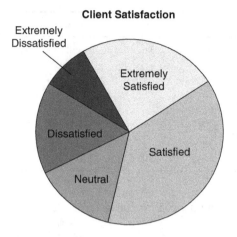

Figure 13.3
Example Client Satisfaction Pie Chart

variable "client satisfaction" is constructed with a slice labeled "extremely satisfied" that is 24 percent or 86.4 degrees (360 degrees × 0.24 = 86.4 degrees) of the pie.

Another commonly used graph is the scattergram that we referred to in Chapter 5. Unlike the other graphs that we have described, it portrays the distribution of two variables simultaneously. Each dot on the graph represents a case and its measurement for each of two variables. The overall pattern of dots can be used to suggest whether measurements of the two variables are positively or negatively correlated and, somewhat crudely, how strong a linear correlation they possess.

Another way of describing the distribution of a variable within a data set is to report what was found to be a typical value category or value among its measurements. Several options are available for this purpose. They are collectively referred to as *measures of central tendency.* One or more measures of central tendency for variables of interest may be computed and included in the research report. The most commonly used ones include the following:

- **Mode.** The value category or value that has the largest frequency (occurs most often) within the data.
- **Median.** The midpoint in a rank-ordered distribution of an ordinal-, interval-, or ratio-level variable.
- **Arithmetic mean.** The average of the values of all cases for an interval- or ratio-level variable (sum all values and divide by the number of cases).

In describing the distribution of a data set, it is also helpful to describe to what degree cases were *homogeneous* (similar) in relationship to a variable and to what degree their value categories or values reflected *heterogeneity* (difference). Descriptive statistics (referred to as parameters when describing populations) that do this are collectively referred to as *measures of dispersion* or *variability.* The larger a measure of dispersion is calculated to be, the more variation there is among values, and vice versa. When reported along with one or more measures of central tendency, measures of dispersion offer a fairly complete summary description of the distribution of a variable among cases in a research sample or population. Some of the more commonly used measures of dispersion follow:

- ▶ **Range.** The distance that encompasses both the highest and the lowest values. You can either simply state the *minimum* and *maximum* values or you can calculate the range by subtracting the minimum value from the maximum value and adding one.
- ▶ **Interquartile range.** The distance between the 75th percentile (where three quarters of values are smaller) and the 25th percentile (where one quarter of values are smaller) in a rank-ordering of values. In other words, how spread out is the middle 50 percent of the values?
- ▶ **Mean deviation.** The mean deviation is, simply speaking, the average distance from the mean of all the values in a distribution.
- ▶ **Variance.** Variance is obtained by subtracting the mean from each case value, squaring the difference, adding all the squared differences together to obtain the *sum of squares*, and then dividing it by the number of cases (for population data) or the number of cases minus one (for sample data).
- ▶ **Standard deviation.** The square root of the variance.

Statistics books provide more details on how to calculate measures of central tendency and dispersion, how they differ, and criteria for determining when each should be used (Weinbach & Grinnell, 2007).

Although descriptive statistics such as measures of central tendency and measures of dispersion can be ends in themselves (e.g., they are used to describe the number of times that research participants engage in a certain behavior or the variations in scores on a standardized scale), they are much more. They are important tools in each of the other three uses of statistical analyses. They provide the numbers that make it possible to do the mathematical calculations that each requires.

Estimating the Characteristics of a Population

In studies (primarily quantitative) in which random samples have been drawn, it can be useful to estimate (within a certain range) what the likely (true) measurement of a variable would have been if the researcher had studied the entire population. For example, if a random sample of clients of a given size were drawn, and their mean (average) level of satisfaction with services received were calculated with a standardized instrument, statistical analysis could tell us with different degrees of confidence a range in which the true mean satisfaction level of all clients would lie. This is known as constructing *confidence intervals.* Reporting a confidence interval in a research report can help the reader of the report to understand how much sampling error the measurement of a variable may contain.

Answering Questions and Testing Hypotheses

In research designs, such as descriptive research that seeks to learn if there is support for an association or correlation between variables, and, of course, in explanatory research, the researcher generally wishes to do more than simply describe the characteristics of the participants. For example, suppose that the existence of a relationship between variables has been predicted and stated as a hypothesis. A sample of research participants has been selected using methods designed to maximize the likelihood that they accurately represent members of the population, and they have been studied with the goal of determining if there is support for the hypothesized relationship.

Perhaps, on first blush, there is an apparent relationship between variables—it can be seen within the data collected from the research sample. Is that sufficient proof of the relationship? No. Before we can conclude that a relationship is a real one that probably exists within the population from which the sample was drawn, we must be reasonably certain that something else did not cause the apparent relationship.

Consider a rather typical scenario in which there appears to be support for a researcher's hypothesis that an experimental treatment is more effective than the treatment generally used. Within the data collected from a sample of clients, the experimental intervention method seems to have produced better results than the usual treatment. For example, researchers might have observed that one group of ten randomly selected clients with a diagnosis of alcoholism receiving an experimental counseling method reflected a 60 percent rate of treatment success (operationally defined as alcohol abstinence for one month) as compared with members of a control group who received the usual treatment and reflected only a 40 percent success rate.

Suppose that the research was well designed (using a classic experimental design) and implemented. The researchers are reasonably confident that their design has good internal validity, that is, they are reasonably certain that something else besides different treatments (the independent variable) did not cause the different results (measurements of the dependent variable). Another way of saying the same thing would be to say that "all threats to internal validity were adequately controlled." Does that mean that the relationship between the variables is a real one that exists beyond the sample? Not necessarily. What about sampling error? Wouldn't we expect to have some difference in success rates with any two relatively small groups of clients selected randomly, even if the two treatment methods were really equally effective? Yes. Remember, only sampling bias, not sampling error, was controlled by random selection and random assignment to the two treatments.

The question is, is the difference in the success rates of the two groups of research participants (the experimental and control groups) large enough that it can safely be assumed that it is not simply the work of sampling error? Statistical analysis can determine how safe it would be to make generalizations about the relative effectiveness of the two treatments that would go beyond the participants in the current research. This third use of statistical analysis employs methods that are broadly referred to as *inferential statistical analysis*.

Using a theoretical concept called a *sampling distribution*, inferential statistical tests can tell the researcher the mathematical probability that the apparent relationship between or among variables that can be seen in the research data is the work of sampling error. They are based on probability theory. They can tell us the mathematical probability that the difference between a 60 percent success rate and a 40 percent success rate using two groups of only ten participants each could exist because of sampling error. Thus, inferential statistical analysis can be used to help us draw conclusions about the relative effectiveness of the two treatment methods used in our hypothetical research example. Any one of several statistical tests (there is usually one that is most appropriate) could be used to determine the exact probability that a 20 percent difference in success rate would occur with two subsamples of ten cases drawn at random just because of sampling error. If that probability is very low and since the usual threats to internal validity are believed to have been controlled, we would be able to conclude that the relationship between the type of treatment received and success rate is probably a real one.

Before we can conclude that a relationship is a real one that probably exists within the population from which the sample was drawn, we must be reasonably certain that something else did not cause the apparent relationship.

Using a theoretical concept called a sampling distribution, inferential statistical tests can tell the researcher the mathematical probability that the apparent relationship between or among variables that can be seen in the research data is the work of sampling error.

Most of the time, being more than 95 percent certain that an apparent relationship within a research sample is not the work of sampling error is good enough for researchers to claim support for a relationship between variables. (As we noted in Chapter 1, all scientific knowledge is tentative anyway.) Of course, as in our example, researchers also must be reasonably certain that threats to internal validity have been adequately controlled by the research design.

When inferential statistical analysis demonstrates that the probability of sampling error having produced an apparent relationship between variables is less than 5 percent or one time in twenty (referred to as $p < 0.05$), researchers customarily describe the relationship between variables as *statistically significant* (see Box 13.1). Of course, the researcher may (with justification) set the level of statistical significance at some other level (referred to as a *rejection level* or *alpha level*), such as 0.025, 0.01, or even 0.001. If so, statistical significance would require demonstration that the likelihood of sampling error having produced the relationship between variables within the two samples is even smaller.

It is possible to imply that a statistically significant relationship was found to exist without actually using the words *statistically significant*. For example, in a report, a researcher might summarize the findings of a study simply by stating, "Among low-income women without extended family support, women who used casework services were more likely to possess a higher level of awareness of the medical needs of infants than those who did not use casework services. However, clients who used casework services were no more likely to use outpatient medical facilities for their babies' treatment than those participants who did not receive casework services."

It is important that we not make too much of a finding of statistical significance. First of all, as we have suggested, a finding of statistical significance, like all of the findings of scientific inquiry, is only a tentative conclusion based on reasonable certainty. It says only that sampling error is a very unlikely explanation of the apparent relationship between or among variables that occurred among cases that were studied. It never totally rules it out.

As we also suggested, even if there is a statistically significant relationship between variables, a true relationship between them or a strong or an important relationship still may not exist. A finding of statistical significance says nothing about the other possible causes of the relationship within the research sample (besides a true relationship) that might make the variables appear to be related. For example, some other variable or variables or a badly biased sample may have produced it.

Box 13.1 Statistical Significance: What It Is and What It Is Not

It is mathematical evidence, based on probability theory, that the relationship between or among variables within a sample is very unlikely to be the work of sampling error (chance).

It is not evidence that the strength of the relationship in the sample is the same as that within the population.

It is not 100 percent proof that the relationship within the sample was not the work of sampling error.

It is not 100 percent proof that the variables are related at all.

It is not proof that something else (a threat to internal validity) did not cause the relationship.

It is not proof that the relationship is necessarily a strong one.

It is not proof that the relationship is necessarily a meaningful one.

Engage, Assess, Intervene, Evaluate

How might the difference between statistical significance and the true importance of the relationship between variables affect your practice decision making?

Sometimes, statistically significant relationships between or among variables that are not the work of sampling bias or any of the threats to internal validity are real. But they still are not terribly valuable! They reflect real relationships, but they are relationships between or among variables that are virtually worthless because they are not very strong (Weinbach & Grinnell, 2007). This is especially likely to happen if the researcher is using relatively large research samples. Statistical significance is achieved quite frequently and easily if very large samples are used. But statistical significance thus achieved may be of limited or no practical value to the social work practitioner. For example, suppose several hundred students participated in an SAT preparation course and their average scores increased by 15 points, while the average scores of the students who did not participate in the course did not increase. This relatively small difference in scores may be statistically significant because of the large sample sizes. The social worker in charge of the program probably can safely conclude that there is a relationship between the scores on the SAT and participation in the class. However, he might also conclude that the difference, while statistically significant, is not large enough to warrant the time required to offer the class and its cost to students.

Researchers can minimize the likelihood of achieving statistical significance when the relationship between variables is so weak as to be meaningless if they use a sample that does not exceed the size recommended for the statistical test that they use. However, even if the appropriate sample size is used and statistical significance is achieved, interpretations of conclusions regarding the value of the results may still require a dose of common sense. A good question to ask prior to statistical analysis is, if a statistically significant relationship between variables is found, how strong would the relationship have to be in order to be considered meaningful? While a statistically significant relationship says that the variables probably are related beyond the sample, it says nothing about the strength of the relationship. Fortunately, there are types of statistical analyses that produce something called *measures of association* that are indicators of the strength of the relationship. They can be helpful in putting a finding of statistical significance in perspective.

There is still another reason why meaningless statistical significance is sometimes found even when the recommended sample size is used and the analysis is performed correctly. The problem is that the research finding is simply nothing new or unexpected! This occurs fairly frequently when statistical tests are used to determine if a correlation between two variables is probably a real one. Some correlations are valuable; but many others are not, even if they are real. For example, among a group of human service organization clients, we could almost certainly demonstrate a statistically significant positive correlation between income and the amount of money spent on groceries. But would such a finding be valuable? It is highly predictable, because one generally has to have money (or at least good credit) to spend it. Besides, would the finding help us to be more effective in our intervention with human service organization clients? Probably not. These types of findings are more common with the advent of computer statistical software. It is so fast and easy to run statistical tests that researchers are tempted to conduct analyses that may show statistical significance, but are unlikely to offer us any new or useful knowledge.

All statistical tests have assumptions (requirements) that underlie their use. However, there also are certain situations in which it is acceptable to ignore one or more of the usual assumptions for the use of a statistical test—the results will still be quite accurate. Even the selection of a frequency distribution, graph, or other descriptive statistic to report central tendency or dispersion is not always simple. Statistical analysis requires that the researcher be knowledgeable about rules and conditions that must be met. It also requires an ethical commitment to report the findings of research as accurately as possible. As we all know, it is easy to lie with statistics, by selecting a type of analysis that portrays the data the way we want them to look.

Fortunately, even the process of identifying the correct statistical analyses is becoming easier thanks to advances in computer technology. Software packages and Web sites are now available that use a series of questions to help the researcher narrow the list of analyses that might be appropriate. However, they still require a good basic understanding of research design. For example, to use them correctly, we have to understand factors specific to our research study, such as the sampling methods that were used, the level of measurement that was produced, and how certain variables tend to be distributed.

Finally, while it should be obvious, we would be remiss if we did not remind the reader that findings of statistically significant relationships between and among variables are not the only findings that are valuable. A lack of statistical significance (referred to as a *null finding*) may be just as valuable or even more valuable! For example, learning that the difference in success rate between group counseling and individual treatment for a particular client problem is not statistically significant could be helpful to a social work administrator in attempting to adjust to budget cuts without reducing the quality of services.

INTERPRETING AND REPORTING THE RESULTS

Once data have been analyzed and, where appropriate, statistical analyses have been performed, the results still must be interpreted. Any limitations of the methods of data analysis used should be identified and interpreted as to their possible effects.

The results are first examined in relation to the focus of the research. What do the results suggest about the answer to the research question or questions?

What do they indicate about any hypotheses? Were they supported? If so, what does that mean? If not, how could the researcher's prediction have been wrong? How can the results of data analyses be used to better understand the research problem or even to suggest effective prevention or intervention methods for alleviating it? What are the implications for the social practitioners who are seeking to provide better social work services? How will any findings make them better evidence-based practitioners?

Data analysis generates many findings. Often, they can be interpreted in a variety of ways. The specific meaning of each individual finding must be determined. Often, individual findings may need to be reinterpreted in light of other findings from the current research study or from the studies of others. This often requires researchers to make use of their practice experience. It also often requires them to look again at the relevant literature (or in predominantly qualitative studies, to immerse themselves in it more than they did initially) in an attempt to reconcile their findings with those of other researchers. Eventually, they must use their best judgment, knowing that they can always be wrong in their interpretations.

Especially in predominantly qualitative studies, it is often expected that there will be a strategy for early feedback of study results to participants and their communities. Researchers share major study findings with them (in non-technical language) and enlist their help in interpretation. This can be especially important since the researcher's own biases and life experiences can lead to some erroneous conclusions. This "checking and verifying" should occur before publication of the results in formal reports or scholarly journals. There are several advantages to doing this, especially in cross-cultural research (Chapter 8). First, people who know the community well offer a unique perspective on a study's findings. They often can suggest differences in interpretation that might never occur to the researcher. They can also help to determine how best to use the study findings to address community concerns and problems. Finally, sharing the data prior to dissemination reinforces the notion of partnership in the research enterprise and communicates respect for study participants and the communities they represent.

Interpreting research findings is not easy. For example, how do we interpret the descriptive finding that adolescents have such widely differing attitudes toward the use of contraception to prevent unwanted pregnancies? Or that the staff perceives a program to be highly successful while community leaders express resentment about it? Or that a software program that is used to perform content analysis of transcribed conversations with college students shows that anti-Semitic attitudes still persist among them? Or that a test of statistical significance fails to support a hypothesis that two groups of research participants respond differently to a type of intervention as is commonly assumed? Or that another statistical finding suggests that one variable really is associated with another in a consistent pattern? Does it suggest that one variable really is contributing to variations in the other variable? Or is it the other way around? Is the strength of the correlation really all that strong?

Because of the difficulty of drawing definitive conclusions from research data, researchers sometimes simply report findings, suggest several possible interpretations, and let the readers of their report draw their own conclusions. When inferential statistical analysis has been used, both findings of statistically significant relationships between variables and findings of nonsignificance are reported. All research findings from soundly designed and implemented research are potentially valuable to others. They can help them to make better decisions and become better evidence-based practitioners.

SUMMARY

This chapter described the general processes involved in analyzing research data so that they can be used to inform practice. Some of the more commonly used methods of data reduction (frequency distributions and graphs, measures of central tendency and dispersion) were described. It was emphasized that the researcher has an obligation to describe accurately the research sample or population from which data were collected. Results of descriptive statistical analysis usually are reported to portray participants' relevant demographic characteristics.

If hypothesis testing is undertaken (as is the case in most quantitative studies), inferential statistical analysis of data is performed to determine the likelihood that sampling error may have produced a relationship between or among variables within a research sample. An overview of both the theoretical underpinnings and the limitations of statistical testing were presented. The limited meaning of statistical significance was discussed. It was explained how, in some situations, a finding of a statistically significant relationship between variables may be of little practical value or a lack of statistical significance may be valuable.

All statistical tests of significance have assumptions—conditions relating to sampling methods, level of measurement, and so forth that are requirements for their use. They are described in books on statistics and are also addressed in the many Internet sites and "help" menus of statistical software packages that are now available to assist the researcher in selecting the appropriate test.

Log onto **www.mysocialworklab.com** and answer the following questions. *(If you did not receive an access code to **MySocialWorkLab** with this text and wish to purchase access online, please visit* www.mysocialworklab.com.*)*

1. **Watch the Core Competencies Video: Engagement, Assessment, Intervention, and Evaluation:**

Assessment. If we were to conduct a content analysis on Mrs. Davis' words, what do you think two of the themes might be?

2. **Read the Case Study: Community Practice: Organizing Social Work in the Republic of Armenia, Part I.** What are three statistics you would expect to see in the final report of this project?

PRACTICE TEST

1. One disadvantage of using computers to perform statistical analysis is
   a. computers make performing complex statistics much more difficult.
   b. complex statistical tests can be easily run on a computer but may be misinterpreted by the novice researcher.
   c. data entry is much more time consuming.
   d. computer analyses create more sampling bias.

2. The distance between the 75th percentile and the 25th percentile is the
   a. range.
   b. interquartile range.
   c. standard deviation.
   d. variance.

3. The probability that sampling error has produced an apparent relationship between variables is called all of the following except
   a. alpha level.
   b. rejection level.
   c. measure of association.
   d. level of statistical significance.

4. When a finding is statistically significant, it means
   a. there is no chance that the relationship between variables is caused by sampling error.
   b. the chance that the relationship between variables is caused by sampling error is small.
   c. the relationship between the variables is an important one with regard to your practice.
   d. there is no chance that sampling bias has created the relationship between variables.

5. Describe three measures of central tendency and four measures of dispersion.

ASSESS YOUR COMPETENCE
Use the scale below to rate your current level of achievement on the following concepts or skills associated with each competency presented in the chapter:

1	2	3
I can accurately describe the concept or skill.	I can consistently identify the concept or skill when observing and analyzing practice activities.	I can competently implement the concept or skill in my own practice.

_____ Understanding how the purpose of your research study affects the selection of data analysis techniques

_____ Being able to create and interpret a frequency table, including frequencies, percentages, cumulative frequencies, and cumulative percentages

_____ Being familiar with the three basic measures of central tendency and the four basic measures of dispersion

_____ Understanding the concept of statistical significance and how it is used to test research hypotheses

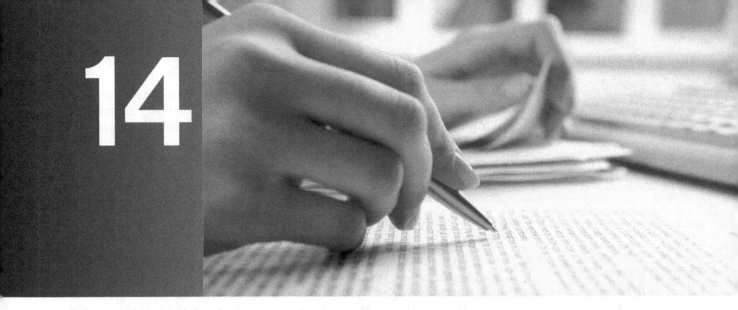

14

Disseminating Research Findings

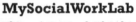
Core Competencies in this Chapter (Check marks indicate which competencies are demonstrated)				
✔ Professional Identity	✔ Ethical Practice	☐ Critical Thinking	☐ Diversity in Practice	☐ Human Rights & Justice
✔ Research-Based Practice	☐ Human Behavior	☐ Policy Practice	✔ Practice Contexts	☐ Engage, Assess, Intervene, Evaluate

A major reason for conducting research is to contribute to the social work knowledge base. For this to occur, research findings must be summarized and communicated to interested audiences in the research and practice communities.

There are many vehicles that can be used to share research findings. We will mention some of the more commonly used ones.

REPORTS AND MONOGRAPHS

Sufficient information is offered so that readers can replicate the research and/or evaluate whether the researcher's conclusions appear to be justified and the recommendations seem appropriate for implementation in their own practice.

If research is sponsored (funded) by an organization or designed to meet a graduate degree requirement, it is usually written (and often bound) using a standardized format developed by the organization or university involved. The report generally is quite lengthy. In the case of funded research, it may be distributed to interested parties as a research monograph (Chapter 4). If the research was a degree requirement, it may be called a thesis (master's degree) or a dissertation (doctorate). The report is placed in the library of the university where the student completed the degree. It is also made available to others through interlibrary loan systems in either hard copy or via electronic communication. A complete research report provides a detailed description of all aspects of the research study, including the participants, research design, outcome measures, results, and conclusions. Sufficient information is offered so that readers can replicate the research and/or evaluate whether the researcher's conclusions appear to be justified and the recommendations seem appropriate for implementation in their own practice.

Reports of Quantitative Studies

Most quantitative research reports, including journal articles (discussed later in this chapter), follow the same general format. The researcher is expected to address each of the following areas, although sometimes two or more can be combined under one heading.

1. **Title.** Developing a title for your study can be challenging. A good title reflects the main purpose of the study, often including information about the intervention and the population being studied. Titles often include a subtitle, which allows the researcher to share more information to interest potential readers. For example, Louden-Gerber's (2009) dissertation title, "A Group Forgiveness Intervention for Adult Male Homeless Individuals: Effects on Forgiveness, Rumination, and Social Connectedness," informs the reader of the study's intervention, population, and outcome variables. When looking through a long list of article titles to select articles of interest, titles like this can quickly draw the reader's attention.

2. **Abstract.** Most research reports, including journal articles and dissertations, include an abstract, which summarizes the research study. Thyer (2008) points out that the abstract will probably be read far more times than the complete article, and should include (a) the issue or problem under investigation; (b) information about the participants, listing age race, gender, and other pertinent features; (c) the research method, the intervention(s), and the outcome measures; (d) the results, including statistical significance and effect sizes; and (e) the

conclusions and any applications to practice (pp. 40–41). *The Publica-tion Manual of the American Psychological Association*, Sixth Edition, recommends that abstracts be 150 to 250 words long.

3. **Introduction.** The historical background of the study is described, and the origin of the researcher's interest in the topic noted. The research problem is specified and a description of its scope and signif-icance is stated and documented. The broad research question that was the focus of the study is stated.

4. **Review of the literature.** A summary and synthesis of literature rele-vant to the research question is presented (see Chapter 4 for a more thorough discussion of conducting a literature review). The literature assembled is used to summarize what is already known about the research question and to identify how the current research study promises to build on and extend knowledge previously available. It provides the rationale for research hypotheses and/or more specific research questions and for the design of the research.

5. **Statement of research questions and hypotheses.** Related to the pur-pose of the study and following logically from the review of the litera-ture, the specific set of research questions and/or hypotheses that were examined are stated. Operational definitions of key terms (also derived from the review of literature) may be included here, or may appear early in the methodology section.

6. **Methodology.** A detailed description of the research design is pre-sented. It generally includes subsections that describe the setting of the research, the research participants, the treatment or program being evaluated (if applicable), the outcome measures, and the statistical analyses that were used. The subsection on participants should include a description of the research sample or samples as well as the methods of their selection and the rationale for that method. The outcome measures subsection should include a description of the methods for conducting measurements of the key variables and a dis-cussion of the selection and/or development of any data collection instruments that were used. When describing previously published measurement instruments, there should be at least one reference in which the psychometric properties (reliability, validity, norms, cutting scores, etc.) are described. The methodology section reports in detail what was done, to whom or what, and by what method(s). The ration-ale for all major methodological decisions is presented (sampling, measurement, data collection methods, and choice of methods for sta-tistical analysis). The section enables the reader of the report both to assess the credibility of the researcher and the research findings and to replicate the research, if desired.

7. **Results.** The principal findings derived from the research are pre-sented. Outcomes of statistical analyses are summarized and inter-preted. The findings section generally contains tables, graphs, or other methods of summarizing the results of analyses to help the reader visualize what was found.

8. **Discussion.** The findings are discussed in relation to the research questions and/or hypotheses. Answers to questions are proposed, and, if applicable, evidence of support or nonsupport for hypotheses is presented. Findings are also discussed in relation to the findings of

others as reported in the literature. Findings that corroborate those of other researchers and theoreticians are identified, and findings that conflict with what has been reported elsewhere are discussed and, where appropriate, reconciled.

9. **Limitations.** The researcher lists and discusses the study's methodological shortcomings of which he or she is aware. No research is perfect—all research tends to be limited somewhat by one or more inherent design constraints or obstacles encountered in attempting to implement the design. For example, an explanatory design may contain inherent problems because of the ethical impossibility of using a true control group or because of the researcher's need to draw a sample from an available sampling frame rather than from the accessible population. Limitations also can result as a function of other methodological difficulties, such as the need to use a data collection instrument that had not yet been demonstrated to be reliable with the participants used in the research or because of constraints on the kinds of data that were allowed to be collected. There are many issues in research that prevent studies from being designed and/or executed flawlessly. The reader requires an honest description of these limitations to know how to interpret and evaluate findings. A useful format for the discussion of each major limitation consists of (a) a specific description of the nature and scope of the limitation; (b) an explanation of why the limitation was unavoidable; (c) the researcher's speculation on how the limitation may have negatively affected the research and its findings; (d) a description of what, if anything, was done to minimize the potential negative effects of the limitation on the research; and (e) an assessment of how successful the effort was.

10. **Conclusions and recommendations.** A description of how the study is believed to have advanced knowledge in the problem area is presented. The researcher also identifies needs for further research and suggests ways in which it might be designed and implemented both to build on the achievements of the current research and to avoid its shortcomings. The implications of the findings for social work practice are an especially important component of this section of the research report. Generally, the researcher makes specific suggestions as to how the findings might be implemented to improve the delivery of services to social work clients, that is, what changes in intervention methods appear to be indicated on the basis the findings of the study.

11. **References.** The reference list is placed immediately after the body of the manuscript in most research reports. The writer of the report should ensure that the references in the text of the report as well as the references in the reference list follow the appropriate formatting style. It is also important that every publication referenced in the body of the report is included in the reference list, and every publication in the reference list is referenced at least once in the text of the report.

12. **Appendices.** Appendices, which may be of interest to just a few readers, also may be included in the report. They may contain, for example, copies of data collection instruments that were used or materials developed by agency personnel to describe the program that was evaluated.

Reports of Qualitative Studies

If the research was primarily qualitative, the same general format may be used. However, there are likely to be several important differences in the report:

- The introduction section is likely to be briefer and contains fewer facts and numbers, since less is generally known about the problem than in predominantly quantitative studies.
- The review of literature section is shorter, because (a) there often is relatively little known about the problem and (b) the literature may have been reviewed less thoroughly prior to data collection to avoid biasing the collection and interpretation of the data.
- There are research questions but, very rarely, research hypotheses.
- The methodology section is likely to be shorter than in a report of a quantitative study. Since replication of a qualitative study is not likely to occur, there is generally less need to describe the research design in great detail. A notable exception might be if the design employed grounded theory (see Chapter 8), which prescribes certain tasks and a specific sequence of events. The reader may want to know whether they were adhered to in order to evaluate the credibility of the research findings.
- The results section may be quite long, often containing case vignettes or extended narrative descriptions with verbatim quotations from research participants. It may contain some descriptive statistics and rarely inferential statistics. In a qualitative study, the researchers are often looking for the deeper meaning of the phenomenon being studied, something that cannot be condensed into statistics, which are more characteristic of a report of a predominantly quantitative study.
- The discussion section may be quite long and contain numerous references to the literature as the researcher attempts to relate his or her observations and conclusions to what was previously known about the problem. It may contain one or more story lines, theories, or hypotheses that have evolved from the research and are now proposed for testing by other researchers.
- The limitations section may be shorter than in the report of a quantitative study, or even nonexistent. Since there are usually no claims to objectivity or, for example, sample representativeness or control of confounding variables in most qualitative studies, there is no need to speculate on their likely effects.
- While there are conclusions and recommendations, they may be more tentative and cautious than in reports of quantitative studies. They often contain ideas for future research, both qualitative and quantitative, and suggestions as to how the insights achieved might help to inform social work practice.
- In general, qualitative reports are likely to use more creative formats than quantitative reports. It is recommended that writers of qualitative reports look for outlets for their research that encourage submission of qualitative research.

The reader of a research report should receive a clear picture of what the research was designed to accomplish, how it was conducted, and what was learned from it. A research report reveals both the communication skills of its author and his or her knowledge of research methods.

The reader of a research report should receive a clear picture of what the research was designed to accomplish, how it was conducted, and what was learned from it.

The technical aspects of research report writing, such as footnoting and referencing style, use of certain terminology, whether or not to include data collection instruments in the appendices, and so forth, are beyond the scope of this book. However, there are entire books devoted to these topics (e.g., Pyrczak & Bruce, 2007; Thyer, 2008). The most common formatting style used in social work research reports is the American Psychological Association (APA) format. For a detailed description of this formatting style, one can turn to the manual of the American Psychological Association (2009). Several other books have been written in an effort to present the APA formatting style in an easier-to-use format (see, for example, Houghton & Houghton, 2009; Rossiter, 2009). One APA formatting book (Szuchman & Thomlison, 2010) was written specifically for social work researchers.

In addition, several Web sites are now available to answer your APA formatting questions, for example,

> ▶ http://owl.english.purdue.edu/owl
> ▶ http://www.apastyle.org
> ▶ http://www.writinghelp-central.com/apa.html

There are also computer software programs that assist the writer in creating documents following the APA formatting style. Some of these are Scholarword, PERRLA, Dr. Paper, StyleEase, FormatEase, and Reference Point Templates. Sometimes, these software packages lag one or even two editions behind the most current APA manual. Therefore, when using software to format a manuscript, it may be necessary to make additional changes to it in order to comply with the newest formatting rules.

INTERNAL CORRESPONDENCE
AND IN-SERVICE TRAINING

There are many reasons why researchers may choose to disseminate research findings through internal correspondence or in-service training sessions. Research studies with limited external validity, research on unique client populations, or unreplicated evaluation studies all may be appropriately disseminated through venues internal to the organization. Many organizations, have monthly or quarterly newsletters, (often available on-line) and their editors are looking for materials to publish. As vehicles to disseminate research findings, these outlets have several advantages. When researchers submit a summary of their research (emphasizing its findings) to the editor of such a publication, it is almost certain to be published, especially if an inquiry to see what form it should take has been made in advance. If published, the summary is likely to be read because staff members generally like to read about what is going on in their work setting. In addition, any recommendations will be put to use with only minimal time lag following completion of the research.

If the researcher's organization has a regular in-service training or staff development program, it can be used to disseminate research findings. Some organizations prefer to do this informally, for example, in a brown bag lunch program, where staff members take turns leading discussions about various work-related issues. This type of program attracts those who have a genuine interest in a researcher's findings and increases the likelihood that findings will be disseminated quickly and put to use.

Practice Contexts

Select a social service agency with which you are familiar. What are three topics that could probably be best addressed through an in-service training at the agency?

Research studies with limited external validity, research on unique client populations, or unreplicated evaluation studies all may be appropriately disseminated through venues internal to the organization.

MAJOR CONFERENCES

Research findings of a more general interest can be disseminated through presentations at professional conferences and symposia. Many national and international social work organizations—for example, NASW, SSWR, American Public Welfare Association, Child Welfare League of America, CSWE, the International Federation of Social Workers, and the Human Services Information Technology Applications—hold conferences at various locations throughout the United States and (in some instances) the world. However, some of them sponsor conferences that may be more geographically limited, such as state conferences, or that may be more narrowly focused on a topic or population, such as conferences relating to services to people with HIV, family support and preservation programs, long-term care, family violence, or homelessness. In addition, there are many other major conferences in fields related to social work, such as psychology, sociology, public health, public administration, or education, that often include presentations that are of multidisciplinary interest.

The largest and most prestigious conferences usually solicit proposals and abstracts for presentations about a wide range of topics that are loosely related to a theme. A "call for abstracts" or "call for proposals" and a deadline for their receipt is published in professional journals or newsletters, or mailed to the organization's members along with advertisements for the conference. Typically, a prospective presenter is asked to write an overview or abstract of what is to be presented and indicate the area of the program in which it would best fit. Many major conferences now have a separate grouping for proposals for presentations that are empirically based and another for those that are more conceptual or theoretical in nature. Proposals for presentations of research generally are expected to follow a specified outline—usually a miniversion of a traditional research report—plus descriptions of the methods for presentation. The author may be asked to indicate those individuals who would most likely benefit from and be interested in the presentation. The presentation overview or abstract itself generally does not include any identifying information, allowing it to be reviewed anonymously. A separate or detachable cover page includes the proposed presenter's name and affiliation, phone number, e-mail address, and other identifying information.

Generally, the major conference planning committees receive many more proposals for presentations than there are places for them on the program. It is not unusual for a major conference to accept only 10 or 20 percent of all proposals received. The review process takes time. Often, there is a lag time of several months between the proposal's receipt (acknowledged through e-mail or on a postage-paid card supplied by the proposer) and notification of a decision by the planning committee.

The major conferences tend to use a large number of volunteer reviewers who are generally accomplished professionals. A proposal may be read anonymously by two or three reviewers who provide a numerical rating on a scale devised by the conference planning committee. The system is likely to give points for such criteria as the proposal's relevance to the conference theme, the potential interest of conference participants in the topic, the quality of the research described, and how well the proposal is written and conforms to guidelines. The review criteria to be used usually are listed in the call for abstracts.

Professional Identity

Look up NASW and CSWE on the Internet. When will the next national conferences of these two organizations be held, and what are the themes of each of the conferences?

The system is likely to give points for such criteria as the proposal's relevance to the conference theme, the potential interest of conference participants in the topic, the quality of the research described, and how well the proposal is written and conforms to guidelines.

All people who submit proposals are notified at the same time of the decisions of the planning committee. Those who are invited to present are asked to respond in writing whether or not they can commit to attend. Audiovisual equipment can be requested, if needed, usually at some cost to the presenter, or the presenter can bring the needed equipment.

Presentations can take different forms. A researcher may be asked to write and present a formal paper, leaving time for discussion and questions from those in attendance. Although it is possible to simply read the paper, this is not very enjoyable for anyone involved and is now rarely done. The single-paper presentation is less popular today than it once was. Now it is more common to group two or three related papers in one session where each individual has an allotted period of time to present. A moderator introduces the presenters, monitors the time, and generally makes sure that all presenters are treated equitably. Presenters offer a brief overview of their work, usually in an informal manner. Especially in international conferences, presenters tend to use slides or, most frequently, PowerPoint. Handouts summarizing major findings are sometimes given to those in attendance.

Another format is the poster session. It is similar to how high school students showcase their research in science fairs (only without the seedlings, household products, or batteries!). The presenter is located in a large hall with many others who are also there to present and discuss their work. Typically, presenters are provided with a mobile display board to exhibit their research visually and a table and a few chairs to discuss informally their research methods and findings with interested conference attendees.

Presenters or their employers generally are expected to pay for travel expenses and accommodations. Only invited speakers and those who give keynote addresses usually are reimbursed for expenses by the conference sponsor. Some conferences provide a reduced registration fee for those who are presenting.

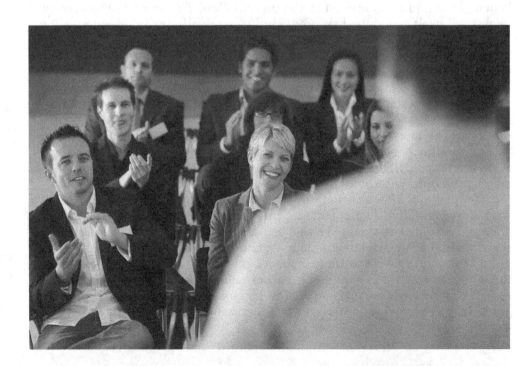

Even if presenting at a major conference costs the researcher some of his or her own money, the expenditure may be justified and productive. It can be intellectually stimulating to discuss your research with colleagues, some of whom invariably challenge some aspect of the research design and/or question your findings and recommendations. Those who choose to attend a researcher's presentation generally have shared interests and may even be doing research in the same problem area. Opportunities to share findings and to collaborate in a future research project can develop. In addition, a researcher learns a great deal about research from attending others' presentations.

The presentation of research at a prestigious conference can enhance a social work career. This is especially true for academicians or those who work for research-oriented organizations, such as teaching hospitals. In addition, continuing education units (CEUs) can be obtained to help meet state licensure requirements. Because major conferences also tend to be held in interesting places, there are also opportunities for sightseeing and recreation. Attending them can be just plain enjoyable.

Many larger conferences also help with the dissemination of research knowledge in another way. Presentations or a summary of them are often put together in electronic or monograph form and are sold (or sometimes distributed at no charge) to members who either attended the conference or were unable to attend. If the sponsoring organization has its own professional journal or journals, presenters may be asked to submit (for publication consideration) a paper based on their presentation.

OTHER PROFESSIONAL GATHERINGS

There are many other smaller conferences—for example, local and regional meetings—where researchers can disseminate their research findings. Getting on the program of, for example, a state NASW symposium or regional conference may be a less prestigious achievement than presenting at a major national or international conference. However, especially if the findings are primarily of local interest, a local or regional conference may be the best vehicle to share newly acquired knowledge.

Local and regional meetings have certain advantages. Costs associated with presentation (travel, registration fees, lodging, and so forth) tend to be lower at smaller conferences, which have fewer attendees and are held in less exotic locales. Opportunities to meet and network with fellow professionals may be better in some respects. At local and regional conferences, researchers can interact with those individuals whose help may be valuable for meeting daily job responsibilities or for acquiring needed support for future research projects.

PUBLICATION IN PROFESSIONAL JOURNALS

The most traditional and potentially the most effective way to disseminate research knowledge is through publication in a professional journal. Journals can be purchased by individual subscribers. Some journals are given as a benefit to the members of a social work organization, and thus tend to reach more potential readers.

Professional journals are also purchased by libraries, where they are increasingly available to students, scholars, and researchers to use in their research literature reviews and thus in their own research. Journal articles are also available on-line. They remain available for use indefinitely, long after a conference presentation has been forgotten.

When writing a manuscript for possible publication in a professional journal, researchers follow the general outline presented in the Reports and Monographs section discussed earlier. However, research reports in a professional journal are much shorter, usually between twelve and twenty printed pages. Thus, reports of many qualitative studies may not be suited to publication in professional journals, since they tend to exceed the maximum length of manuscripts accepted.

A potential journal article should be sent to only one journal at a time. Anything else is considered unethical. Most journals use volunteer, unpaid reviewers who give their time as a service to their profession. It would be a major imposition for an author to send a manuscript to several journals simultaneously, perhaps getting it accepted by two or more. Because only one ultimately can publish it, the reviewers from the other journals would have wasted their time reviewing and critiquing it. However, once one journal has rejected a manuscript, it is ethical to send it elsewhere. It is not unusual for a manuscript to be rejected by several journals until finally it is accepted by one.

Getting an article published in a professional journal can be a tedious, time-consuming, and sometimes frustrating experience. Among the most prestigious journals, many more manuscripts are submitted than are accepted for publication. Many people want to publish in them; academicians want and sometimes need to be published in them to maintain or advance their careers. While the best-known journals publish only a small percentage of manuscripts submitted for publication, in contrast, some of the more narrowly focused and less well-known ones may accept up to 50 percent of the manuscripts submitted, or even more.

There are reference books available to help prospective authors find the journals most likely to publish a report of their work (Beebe, 1993; NASW Press, 2009). Colleagues who have been published (especially academicians) often are another good resource. Most journals describe the procedure for submission of a manuscript in each issue of the journal and on their Web sites. The procedures are more alike than dissimilar.

Journals that use a *blind review procedure* use a group of consulting editors, usually relatively accomplished academicians and other professionals who serve limited terms. They have agreed to anonymously read and review manuscripts that have been submitted for publication. Two or three reviewers, selected by the editor on the basis of their expertise or interest in the topic, read and critique the manuscript and make an assessment of its publication potential. The final decision, however, generally remains with the editor, a small committee, or an editorial board.

What can happen when a manuscript is submitted to a professional journal? Usually, the author can expect one of three possible responses:

1. The manuscript is accepted for publication without revision. This happens rarely, especially among the best-known, most prestigious journals.

2. The manuscript is rejected by the journal. This can happen in one of three ways. Depending upon the journal, the length of time between submission and rejection may suggest which one occurred.

    i. The editor, in a cursory reading, may have concluded that the manuscript is either simply not publishable at all or not appropriate for

Ethical Practice

Why is it considered unethical to send a manuscript to more than one journal at a time?

Research-Based Practice

Why does the blind review process help ensure the quality and integrity of the articles published in professional journals?

the journal. Thus, the decision was made not to send it out to reviewers. If the author gets a rejection letter in a very short time, say, just a few weeks, this is most likely what happened.

   ii. If rejection takes longer, the editor may have decided that the manuscript might have publication potential and sent it out to reviewers, but a majority of them decided that the manuscript should not be published.

   iii. If an even longer period between submission and rejection occurs, it generally means that the initial reviewers may have read the manuscript but disagreed as to whether it should be published. It was then sent to another reviewer who cast the deciding vote not to publish it.

3. The manuscript is not accepted in its present form but the author is provided with suggestions for revisions. He or she is encouraged to make the requested revisions and then resubmit it. The author can then choose to (a) seek publication elsewhere or (b) inform the editor that he or she will make all or most of the required revisions. As a general rule, the latter alternative is the better choice. While not a guarantee of publication, if the author is conscientious in responding to suggestions by either making revisions as suggested or (occasionally) explaining why they should not be made, the manuscript usually will be accepted for publication. The research findings will be disseminated sooner than if the manuscript were to be submitted to another journal where the review process would begin anew. However, if the author believes that the suggestions for revision are incorrect or otherwise unacceptable, it makes more sense to seek publication elsewhere than to refuse to make many of the requested changes and resubmit the manuscript to the same journal. This stonewalling generally just results in rejection.

Even in instances in which a manuscript is rejected outright, it has become common practice to provide the author with limited feedback and, sometimes, suggestions for other methods for dissemination. This is both a professional courtesy and a useful service. It acknowledges that (1) a considerable amount of work went into preparing a manuscript for possible publication and (2) it may still be possible to find another venue (such as those we have discussed) where at least some of the author's efforts will be rewarded. For example, it may be tactfully suggested that, while the manuscript may not be publishable, the research findings might be better suited for a poster presentation at a conference.

Although the quality of the research methods employed, the importance of the findings, and the quality of writing displayed are major considerations in whether a manuscript is accepted for publication, luck and timing also play roles. For example, assuming that the manuscript meets all these criteria, its acceptance for publication may still depend in part on *when* it is submitted to a journal. Its chances are enhanced if it arrives when the journal needs another good article to complete an upcoming issue. The situation wherein the journal already has accepted but not published another manuscript on a similar topic or problem area could prove fortuitous, or it could work against the researcher. The journal may decide to accept the manuscript along with the previously accepted one, to complement it or make the topic the focus of a special issue including other articles related to the same problem area. But the other, already accepted manuscript on the topic may also work to the researcher's detriment. The editor may decide that the manuscript that the researcher submitted, although otherwise publishable, is simply not needed. The editor may reject the manuscript or possibly publish it in a later edition of the journal.

There are intangible rewards for having a published article in a professional journal. There is something gratifying about seeing the results of one's research in print and perhaps cited in someone else's work and hoping that it is being read, appreciated, and used by others. But journals do not pay authors for their articles when they publish them; in fact, publishing an article can be expensive in terms of the time and effort entailed. Unfortunately, publication in journals also does not result in rapid dissemination of research findings. Getting a manuscript accepted can take a year or more. Once accepted, it may not be published for another year or two. Despite these disadvantages, publication of one's research methods and findings in a professional journal probably remains the most generally accepted acknowledgment that a researcher has met an obligation to the scientific community.

SUMMARY

The sections of a typical research report were described along with the differences between qualitative and quantitative reports. The research report or monograph was proposed as just one vehicle that researchers use to communicate research findings to interested audiences. Other alternatives for research dissemination are internal correspondence and in-service training, major conference presentations, other professional gatherings, and publication in professional journals.

Succeed with **PEARSON mysocialworklab**

Log onto **www.mysocialworklab.com** and answer the following questions. *(If you did not receive an access code to* **MySocialWorkLab** *with this text and wish to purchase access online, please visit* www. mysocialworklab.com*.)*

1. **Watch the Core Competencies Video: Critical Thinking: Demonstrating Effective Oral and Written**

Communication. What are two topics that the social worker and client talked about that would make good topics for in-service training at the agency setting being portrayed?

2. **Read the Case Study: Mental Health: Carletta.** Compare and contrast the outline of this case study with the outline suggested for research reports.

PRACTICE TEST

1. Qualitative reports tend to differ from quantitative reports in that
   a. qualitative reports tend to be shorter overall.
   b. qualitative reports tend to have a longer review of the literature with more facts and numbers.
   c. qualitative reports usually include research hypotheses.
   d. the results section tends to be longer in qualitative reports.

2. The methodology section would include all of the following except description of the
   a. participants.
   b. research method.
   c. results.
   d. outcome measures.

3. Which of the following is not a possible response an author may get from a journal after submitting a manuscript for publication?
   a. The manuscript is accepted without revision.
   b. The manuscript is rejected.
   c. The manuscript is sent by the editor to another journal he or she feels is more appropriate.
   d. The reviewers make suggested revisions and the author is encouraged to make the changes and resubmit the manuscript.

4. When the editor makes suggestions for revisions and asks the author to resubmit the manuscript, the author should generally
   a. immediately seek publication elsewhere.
   b. make all or most of the revisions and resubmit the manuscript.
   c. resubmit it to the same journal without making the revisions.
   d. start over on another manuscript that seems to be more what the editor is looking for.

5. What five things should be included in the discussion of each major limitation of a research study?

ASSESS YOUR COMPETENCE   Use the scale below to rate your current level of achievement on the following concepts or skills associated with each competency presented in the chapter:

1	2	3
I can accurately describe the concept or skill.	I can consistently identify the concept or skill when observing and analyzing practice activities.	I can competently implement the concept or skill in my own practice.

_____ Being familiar with the general outline of a quantitative research study report

_____ Understanding the general differences between qualitative and quantitative reports

_____ Being familiar with the advantages and disadvantages of presenting research at national conferences, local and state conferences, and in-service training sessions

_____ Understanding the process of submitting a manuscript to a professional journal

References

Chapter 1

Anderson, R. C. (2000, November). We are all casualties of friendly fire in the war on drugs. *Utah State Bar Journal.* Retrieved from http://www.utahbar.org/barjournal2000/html/november_00_bar_journal_articl_15.html.

Begun, A. L., Berger, L. K., Otto-Salaj, L. L., & Rose, S.J. (2010). Developing effective social work university-community research collaborations. *Social Work, 55,* 54–62.

Briar, S. (1979). Incorporating research into education for clinical practice: Toward a clinical science in social work. In A. Rubin & A. Rosenblatt (Eds.), *Sourcebook on research utilization* (pp. 132–133). New York: Council on Social Work Education.

Bronson, D. E. (2009). Critically appraising studies for evidence-based practice. In A. R. Roberts (Ed.), *Social worker's desk reference* (2nd ed., pp. 1137–1141). New York: Oxford University Press.

Burkett, B. G., & Whitley, G. (1998). *Stolen valor: How the Vietnam generation was robbed of its heroes and its history.* Dallas, TX: Verity Press, Inc.

Corcoran, J., & Littell, J. H. (2009). Meta-analysis and evidence-based practice. In A. R. Roberts (Ed.), *Social worker's desk reference* (2nd ed., pp. 1149–1152). New York: Oxford University Press.

Council on Social Work Education. (2008). *Educational policy and accreditation standards.* Alexandria, VA: CSWE.

Day, N. L., & Richardson, G. A. (1993). Cocaine use and crack babies: Science, the media, and miscommunications. *Neurotoxicology and Teratology, 15,* 293–294.

Denzin, N. K., & Lincoln, Y. S. (Eds.). (1994). *Handbook of qualitative research.* Thousand Oaks, CA: Sage Publications, Inc.

Drug Policy Alliance. (2004). *Cocaine and pregnancy.* Retrieved from www.lindesmith.org/library/research/cocaine.cfm

Gambrill, E. (2009). Integrating information from diverse sources in evidence-based practice. In A. R. Roberts (Ed.), *Social worker's desk reference* (2nd ed., pp. 1120–1126). New York: Oxford University Press.

Gambrill, E., & Gibbs, L. (2009). Developing well-structured questions for evidence-informed practice. In A. R. Roberts (Ed.), *Social worker's desk reference* (2nd ed., pp. 1120–1126). New York: Oxford University Press.

Garvin, C. (1981). Research-related roles for social workers. In R. Grinnell, Jr. (Ed.), *Social work research and evaluation* (pp. 547–552). Itasca, IL: F. E. Peacock.

Gelso, C. J., & Lent, R. W. (2000). Scientific training and scholarly productivity: The person, the training environment, and their interaction. In S. D. Brown & R. W. Lent (Eds.), *Handbook of counselling psychology* (3rd ed., pp. 109–139). New York: Wiley.

Glasser, M., Kolvin, I., Campbell, D., Glasser, A., Leitch, I., & Farrelly, S. (2001). Cycle of child sexual abuse: Links between being a victim and becoming a perpetrator. *British Journal of Psychiatry, 79,* 482–494.

Grinnell, R., Jr., & Siegel, D. (1988). The place of research in social work. In R. Grinnell, Jr. (Ed.), *Social work research and evaluation.* Itasca, IL: F. E. Peacock.

Guyatt , G., & Rennie, D. (2002). *Users' guides to the medical literature: Essentials of evidence-based clinical practice.* Chicago: American Medical Association.

Hamilton, S., Nelson Goff, B. S., Crow, J. R., & Reisbig, A. M. J. (2009). Primary trauma of female partners in a military sample: Individual symptoms and relationship satisfaction. *American Journal of Family Therapy, 37,* 336–346.

Howard, M. O., Perron, B. E., & Vaughn, M. G. (2009). Practice-guidelines and evidence-based practice. In A. R. Roberts (Ed.), *Social worker's desk reference* (2nd ed., pp. 1157–1162). New York: Oxford University Press.

Israel, N., & Jozefowicz-Simbeni, D. M. H. (2009). Perceived strengths of urban girls and boys experiencing homelessness. *Journal of Community & Applied Social Psychology, 19,* 156–164.

Kirk, S. (1979). Understanding research utilization in social work. In A. Rubin & A. Rosenblatt (Eds.), *Sourcebook on research utilization* (pp. 1–15). New York: Council on Social Work Education.

Littell, J. H., & Corcoran, J. (2009). Systematic reviews and evidence-based practice. In A. R. Roberts (Ed.), *Social worker's desk reference* (2nd ed., pp. 1152–1156). New York: Oxford University Press.

Lynam, D.R., Milich, R., Zimmerman, R., Novak, S.P., Logan, T.K., Martin, C., Leukefeld, C., & Clayton, R. (1999). Project DARE: No effects at 10-year follow-up. *Journal of Consulting and Clinical Psychology, 67,* 590–593.

Mears, S. L., Yaffe, J., & Harris, N. J. (2009). Evaluation of wrap-around services for severely emotionally disturbed youths. *Research on Social Work Practice, 19,* 678–685.

Montgomery, P., & Mayo-Wilson, E. (2009). Randomized controlled trials and evidence-based practice. In A. R. Roberts (Ed.), *Social worker's desk reference* (2nd ed., pp. 1142–1148). New York: Oxford University Press.

National Association of Social Workers. (2010). http://www.socialworkers.org/research/naswresearch/0108evidencebased/default.asp

O'Neill, J. (2000). Practice-research sync "crucial for survival." *NASW News, 45,* 3.

Parish, S. L., Rose, R. A., & Andrews, M. E. (2010). TANF's impact on low-income mothers raising children with disabilities. *Exceptional Children, 76,* 234–253.

Petrosino, A., Turpin-Petrosino, C., & Buehler, J. (2005). Scared straight and other juvenile awareness program for preventing juvenile delinquency. *The Scientific Review of Mental Health Practice, 4*(1), 48–54.

Prentky, R. A., Nien-Chen, L., Righthand, S. Schuler, A., Cavanaugh, D., & Lee, A. F. (2010). Assessing risk of sexually abusive behavior among youth in a child welfare sample. *Behavioral Sciences & the Law, 28,* 24–45.

Proctor, E. (2003). Evidence for practice: Challenges, opportunities, and access. *Social Work Research, 27,* 195.

Rank, M.R. (1994). *Living on the edge: The realities of welfare in America.* New York: Columbia University Press.

Roberts, A. R. (2009). *Social worker's desk reference* (2nd ed.). New York: Oxford University Press.

Rosen, A. (2003). Evidence-based social work practice: Challenges and promise. *Social Work Research, 27,* 197–208.

Rotheram-Borus, M. J., Desmond, K., Comulada, W. S., Arnold, E. M., & Johnson, M. (2009). Reducing risky sexual behavior and substance use among currently and formerly homeless adults living with HIV. *American Journal of Public Health, 99,* 1100–1107.

Rubin, A., & Parrish, D. (2009). Locating credible studies for evidence-based practice. In A. R. Roberts (Ed.), *Social worker's desk reference* (2nd ed., pp. 1127–1136). New York: Oxford University Press.

Simpson, R. (1979). Understanding the utilization of research and other applied professions. In A. Rubin & A. Rosenblatt (Eds.), *Sourcebook on research utilization* (pp. 16–28). New York: Council on Social Work Education.

Strauss, S. E., Richardson, W. S., Glasziou, P., & Haynes, R. B. (2005). *Evidence-based medicine: How to practice and teach EBM* (3rd ed.). New York: Elsevier.

Thyer, B. A., & Myers, L. L. (2007). *A social worker's guide to evaluating practice outcomes.* Alexandria, VA: Council on Social Work Education.

Thyer, B. A., & Myers, L. L. (2009). N=1 experiments and their role in evidence-based practice. In A. R. Roberts (Ed.), *Social worker's desk reference* (2nd ed., pp. 1176–1182). New York: Oxford University Press.

Thyer, B. A., & Myers, L. L. (2010). Cultural diversity and social work practice: An evidenced based approach. In B. A. Thyer, J. S. Wodarski, L. L. Myers, & D. F. Harrison (Eds.), *Human diversity and social work practice: An evidenced-based approach* (3rd ed., pp. 3–28). Springfield, IL: Charles C. Thomas.

The United States Conference of Mayors. (2005). *A status report on hunger and homelessness in American cities.* Retrieved from www.rihomelessness.co.

Van Burgh, J., Redner, G., & Moon, C. (1995). *A report of project DARE with eighth grade students.* Retrieved from www.eduref.org/plweb-cgi/fastweb.

Wakefield, J., & Kirk, S. (1996). Unscientific thinking about scientific practice: Evaluating the scientist-practitioner model. *Social Work Research, 20,* 83–95.

Zimbardo, P. (2010) *Stanford prison experiment.* Retrieved from www.prisonexp.org.

Chapter 2

Anastas, J. W. (2010). Quality in qualitative evaluation: Issues and possible answers. *Research on Social Work Practice, 14,* 57–65.

Annas, G. (1992). *The Nazi doctors and the Nuremberg Code: Human rights in human experimentation.* New York: Oxford University Press.

Associated Press Report. (1997, September 18). Experts blast AIDS studies that endanger poor subjects. *The State,* A14.

Council on Social Work Education. (2007). *National statement on research integrity in social work.* Alexandria, VA: CSWE Publications.

Delva, J. (2007). The human subjects review process: A subjective view. *Social Work, 52, 2,* 101–102.

Eisner, R., Vasgird, D., & Hyman-Browne, E. (n.d.). *RCR responsible authorship and peer review.* Retrieved from http://ccnmtl.columbia.edu/projects/rcr/rcr_authorship/

Ellenberg, S. S. (2009). The use of placebo-control groups in clinical trials. In V. Ravitsky, A. Fiester, & A. L. Caplan (Eds.), *The Penn Center guide to bioethics* (pp. 259–270). New York: Springer Publishing Company.

Falit, B. P., & Gross, C. P. (2008). Access to experimental drugs for terminally ill patients. *Journal of the American Medical Association, 300,* 2793–2795.

Florida State University. (2010). *Human Subjects Committee.* Retrieved from http://www.research.fsu.edu/humansubjects/

Health and Medicine. (1994). UCLA didn't ask schizophrenic patients' consent for experiment. *New York Times,* pp. B9–B10.

Humphreys, L. (1970). *Tearoom trade: Impersonal sex in public places.* Chicago: Aldine Press.

Jones, J. H. (1982). *Bad blood: The Tuskegee syphilis experiment.* New York: Free Press.

Milgram, S. (1963). Behavioral study of obedience. *Journal of Abnormal and Social Psychology, 67,* 371–378.

National Association of Social Workers. (1999). *Code of Ethics.* Washington, DC: NASW Press.

National Commission for the Protection of Human Subjects of Biomedical and Behavioral Research. (1979). *The Belmont Report.* Retrieved from http://ohsr.od.nih.gov/guidelines/belmont.html.

Office of Research Integrity, Department of Health and Human Services. (2006). *Responsible conduct of research.* Retrieved from http://ori.dhhs.gov/education/

Pittenger, D. J. (2002). Deception in research: Distinctions and solutions from the perspective of utilitarianism. *Ethics and Behavior, 12*(2), 117–142.

Pryce, N. (1995). *A heuristic study using an evolutionary perspective of the experience of adolescents adapting to the head injury of a parent.* Unpublished dissertation, Columbia, SC: University of South Carolina.

Sieber, J. E. (1992). *Planning ethically responsible research.* Newbury Park, CA: Sage Publications.

Taylor, L. (1998). Parents who lost an adult child to AIDS. In A. Godenzi (Ed.), *Abenteuer forschung* (pp. 189–258). Freiburg, Switzerland: University of Freiburg.

Vasgird, D., & Hyman-Browne, E. (n.d.). *RCR mentoring.* Retrieved from http://ori.dhhs.gov/education/products/columbia_wbt/rcr_ mentoring/

Chapter 3

Agee, J. (2009). Developing qualitative research questions: A reflexive process. *International Journal of Qualitative Studies in Education, 22,* 431–447.

Anastas, J. W. (2010). Quality in qualitative evaluation: Issues and possible answers. *Research on Social Work Practice, 14,* 57–65.

Bellomy, P., Berstein, H., Bickley, S., et al. (1989). *Factors affecting child protection workers' decision-making in Sumter County.* Unpublished MSW research project. Columbia, SC: University of South Carolina, College of Social Work.

Creswell, J. W. (1998). *Qualitative inquiry and research design: Choosing from among five traditions.* Thousand Oaks, CA: Sage Publications, Inc.

Creswell, J. W. (2007). *Qualitative inquiry and research design* (2nd ed.). Thousand Oaks, CA: Sage Publications, Inc.

Denzin, N.K. (1989). *The research act: Theoretical introduction to sociological methods* (3rd ed.). Englewood Cliffs, NJ: Prentice Hall.

Fennig, S., & Hadas, A. (2010). Suicidal behavior and depression in adolescents with eating disorders. *Nordic Journal of Psychiatry, 64,* 32–39.

Frankfort-Nachmias, C., & Nachmias, D. (1992). *Research methods in the social sciences* (4th ed.). New York: St. Martin's Press.

Kartalova-O'Doherty, Y., & Doherty, D. T. (2008). Coping strategies and styles of family carers of persons with enduring mental illness: A mixed methods analysis. *Scandinavian Journal of Caring Services, 22,* 19–28.

Ramos-Lira, L, Gonzalez-Forteza, C., & Wagner, F. A. (2006). Violent victimization and drug involvement among Mexican middle school students. *Addiction, 101,* 850–856.

Rortveit, K., Astrom, S., & Severinsson, E. (2009). The feeling of being trapped in and ashamed of one's own body: A qualitative study of women who suffer from eating difficulties. *International Journal of Mental Health Nursing, 18*(2), 91–99.

Rothery, M. (1993). Problems, questions, and hypotheses. In R. M. Grinnell, Jr. (Ed.), *Social work research and evaluation* (4th ed., pp. 17–37). Itasca, IL: F. E. Peacock.

Rubin, A., & Babbie, E. (2008). *Research methods for social work* (6th ed.). Belmont, CA: Brooks Cole.

Shields, J. J., Broome, K. M., Delany, P. J., Fletcher, B. W., & Flynn, B. M. (2007). Religion and substance abuse treatment: Individual and program effects. *Journal for the Scientific Study of Religion, 46,* 355–371.

Shontz, F. (1986). *Fundamentals of research in the behavioral sciences.* Washington, DC: American Psychiatric Press.

Smith, C. (2007). Support services for students with Asperger's Syndrome in higher education. *College Student Journal, 41,* 515–531.

Vrabel, K. R., Ro, O., Martinsen, E. W., Hoffart, A. & Rosenvinge, J. H. (2010). Five-year prospective study of personality disorders in adults with longstanding eating disorders. *International Journal of Eating Disorders, 43,* 22–28.

Walsh, R. A, & Tzelepis, F. (2007). Adolescents and tobacco use: Systematic review of qualitative research methodologies and partial synthesis of findings. *Substance Use and Misuse, 42,* 1269–1321.

Chapter 4

Bem, D. J. (1991). Writing the research report. In C. M. Judd, E. R. Smith, & L. H. Kidder (Eds.), *Research methods in social relations* (6th ed.). Fort Worth, TX: Harcourt, Brace & Jovanovich.

Bengtsson-Tops, A., Saveman, B-L., Tops, D. (2009). Staff experience and understanding of working with abused women suffering from mental illness. *Health and Social Care in the Community, 17,* 459–465.

Corcoran, J., & Littell, J. H. (2010). Meta-analyses. In B. Thyer (Ed.), *The handbook of social work research methods* (2nd ed., pp. 299–312). Thousand Oaks, CA: Sage Publications, Inc.

Dauz Williams, P., Piamjariyakul, U., Graff, C. J., Stanton, A., Guthrie, A., Hafeman, C., & Williams, A. R. (2010). Developmental disabilities: Effects on well siblings. *Issues in Comprehensive Pediatric Nursing, 33,* 39–55.

Franklin, C., Kim, J. S., & Tripodi, S. J. (2009). A meta-analysis of published school social work practice studies. *Research on Social Work Practice, 19,* 667–677.

Galvin, J. (2006). *Writing literature reviews* (3rd ed.). Los Angeles: Pyrczak Publishing.

Hart, C. (1998). *Doing a literature review.* Thousand Oaks, CA: Sage Publications, Inc.

Krippendorf, K. (2004). *Content analysis: An introduction to its methodology.* Thousand Oaks, CA: Sage Publications, Inc.

LaGuardia, C. (Ed.). (2003). *Magazines for libraries* (12th ed.). New York: Bowker.

Littell, J. H., & Corcoran, J. (2010). *Systematic reviews.* In B. Thyer (Ed.), *The handbook of social work research methods* (2nd ed., pp. 313–337). Thousand Oaks, CA: Sage Publications, Inc.

Litschge, C. M., Vaughn, M. G., & McCrea, C. The empirical status of treatments for children and youth with conduct problems. *Research on Social Work Practice, 20,* 21–35.

Moncrieff, J., Cohen, D., & Mason, J. P. (2009). The subjective experience of taking antipsychotic medication: A content analysis of Internet data. *Acta Psychiatrica Scandinavica, 120,* 102–111.

National Association of Social Workers. (2008). *Encyclopedia of social work* (20th ed.). Silver Spring, MD: NASW Press.

National Association of Social Workers. (2009). *An author's guide to social work journals* (5th ed.). Silver Spring, MD: NASW Press.

Neuendorf, K. (2002). *The content analysis guidebook.* Thousand Oaks, CA: Sage Publications, Inc.

Pignotti, M., & Thyer, B. A. (2009). Why randomized clinical trials are important and necessary to social work practice. In H-W. Otto, A. Polutta, & H. Ziegler (Eds.), *Evidence-based practice: Modernizing the knowledge base of social work* (pp. 99–109). Farmington Hills, MI and Opladen, Germany: Barbara Burdich.

Pyrczak, F., & Bruce, R. (2005). *Writing empirical research reports* (5th ed.). Los Angeles: Pyrczak Publishing.

Rubin, A., & Babbie, E. (2007). *Essential research methods for social work.* Belmont, CA: Thomson Brooks/Cole.

Ryan, M., & Sheehan, R. (2009). Research articles in *Australian Social Work* from 1998–2007: A content analysis. *Australian Social Work, 62,* 525–542.

Scherrer, K. S. (2009). Images of sexuality and aging in gerontological literature. *Sexuality research and social policy: A journal of the NSRC, 6*(4), 5–12.

Sowers, K.M., Ellis, R., & Dessel, A. (2010). Literature reviews. In B. Thyer (Ed.), *The handbook of social work research methods* (2nd ed., pp. 504–516). Thousand Oaks, CA: Sage Publications, Inc.

Thyer, B. A. (1989). First principles of practice research. *British Journal of Social Work, 19, 309–323.*

Thyer, B. A. (1991). Guidelines for evaluating outcome studies on social work practice. *Research on Social Work Practice, 1,* 76–91.

Thyer, B. A., & Myers, L. L. (2010). Cultural diversity and social work practice: An evidenced based approach. In B. A. Thyer, J. S. Wodarski, L. L. Myers, & D. F. Harrison (Eds.), *Human diversity and social work practice: An evidenced-based approach.* (3rd ed., pp. 3–28) Springfield, IL: Charles C. Thomas.

Timmerman, G. M. (2006). Restaurant eating in non-purge binge-eating women. *Western Journal of Nursing Research, 28,* 811–824.

Chapter 5

Acker, G. M. (2010). The influence of managed care on job-related attitudes of social workers. *Social Work in Mental Health, 8,* 174–189.

Beck, A. T., Steer, R. A., Ball, R., & Ranier, W. (1996). Comparison of Beck Depression Inventories –IA and –II in psychiatric outpatients. *Journal of Personality Assessment, 67,* 588–597.

Bellomy, P., Berstein, H., Bickley, S., et al. (1989). *Factors affecting child protection workers' decision-making in Sumter County.* Unpublished MSW research project. Columbia, SC: University of South Carolina, College of Social Work.

Bonewell, K. J. (2009). Intrinsic and extrinsic religiosity and sexual compulsivity with Christian males: Understanding concepts and correlations based on race, age, socioeconomic status, and marital status. *Dissertation Abstracts International, 69,* 7802. Doctoral dissertation, Capella University, 2009.

Donate-Lopez, C., Espigares-Rodriguez, E., Jimenez-Moleon, J. J., Luna-del-Castillo, J. D., Bueno-Cavanillas, A., & Lardelli-Claret, P. (2010). The association of age, sex and helmet use with the risk of death for occupants of two-wheeled motor vehicles involved in traffic crashes in Spain. *Accident Analysis and Prevention, 42,* 297–306.

Fernandez-Aranda, F., Nunez, A., Martinez, C., Krug, I., Cappozzo, M., Carrard, I., Rouget, P., Jimenez-Murcia, S., Granero, R., Panelo, E., Santamaria, J., & Lam, T. (2009). Internet-based cognitive-behavioral therapy for bulimia nervosa: A controlled study. *CyberPsychology & Behavior, 12*(1), 37–41.

Goldstein, H. (1969). *Research standards and methods for social workers.* Northbrook, IL: Whitehall Company.

Hogan, T. P., Awad, A. G., & Eastwood, R. (1983). A self-report scale predictive of drug compliance in schizophrenics: Reliability and discriminative validity. *Psychological Medicine, 13,* 177–183.

Leung, A. W.-H. (2007). Shyness and social anxiety: Causal modeling of developmental antecedents. *Dissertation Abstracts International, 68,* 626. Doctoral dissertation, State University of New York at Albany, 2007.

Marmorstein, N. R. (2010). Longitudinal associations between depressive symptoms and alcohol problems: The influence of comorbid delinquent behavior. *Addictive Behaviors, 35,* 564–571.

Smith, B. C. S. (2009). Job burnout, spirituality and social support in women who are perinatal social workers: A quantitative and qualitative study. *Dissertation Abstracts International, 70,* 1035. Doctoral dissertation, Tulane University, 2009.

Townsend, L., Floersch, J., & Findling, R.L. (2009). Adolescent attitudes toward psychiatric medication: The utility of the Drug Attitude Inventory. *Journal of Child Psychiatry and Psychology, 50,* 1523–1531.

Weinbach, R. W., & Grinnell, R. M., Jr. (2007). *Statistics for social workers* (7th ed.). Boston: Allyn & Bacon.

Chapter 6

Benoliel, J. (1985). Loss and adaptation: Circumstances, contingencies, and consequences. *Death Studies, 9,* 217–233.

Campbell, D., & Stanley, J. (1963). *Experimental and quasi-experimental designs for research.* Chicago: Rand.

Gonzales-Prendes, A. A., & Jozefowicz-Simbeni, D. M. H. (2009). The effects of cognitive-behavioral treatment on trait anger and paranoid ideation. *Research on Social Work Practice, 19,* 686–693.

Kübler-Ross, E. (1989). *On death and dying.* New York: Macmillan.

McMillen, J. C., & Raghaven, R. (2009). Pediatric to adult mental health service use of young people leaving the foster care system. *Journal of Adolescent Health, 44,* 7–13.

Plow, M. A., Mathiowetz, V., & Lowe, D. A. (2009). Comparing individualized rehabilitation to a group wellness intervention for persons with multiple sclerosis. *American Journal of Health Promotion, 24,* 23–26.

Rubin, A, & Babbie, E. (2007). *Essential research methods for social work.* Belmont, CA: Thompson Brooks/Cole.

Schwinn, T. M., Schinke, S. P., & Trent, D. N. (2010). Substance use among late adolescent urban youths: Mental health and gender influences. *Addictive Behaviors, 35,* 30–34.

Singleton, R., & Straits, B. (2005). *Approaches to social research.* New York: Oxford University Press.

Chapter 7

Bloom, M., Fischer, J., & Orme, J. (1999). *Evaluating practice: Guidelines for the accountable professional.* Boston: Allyn & Bacon.

Compton, B., Galaway, B., & Cournoyer, B. (2005). *Social work processes* (7th ed.). Pacific Grove, CA: Brooks Cole

Corcoran, K., & Fischer, J. (2000a). *Measures for clinical practice: A sourcebook. Volume 1: Couples, families, and children* (3rd ed.). New York: The Free Press.

Corcoran, K. & Fischer, J. (2000b). *Measures for clinical practice: A sourcebook. Volume 2: Adults* (3rd ed.). New York: The Free Press.

Hudson, W. (1982). *The clinical measurement package: A field manual.* Homewood, IL: The Dorsey Press.

Mattaini, M. A. (2010). Single-system studies. In B. A. Thyer (Ed.). *Handbook of social work research methods* (2nd ed., pp. 241–273). Thousand Oaks, CA: Sage Publications, Inc.

Weinbach, R. (2005). *Evaluating social work services and programs.* Boston: Allyn & Bacon.

Chapter 8

Anastas, J. W. (2004). Quality in qualitative evaluation: Issues and possible answers. *Research on Social Work Practice, 14,* 57–65.

Ayon, C. (2009). Shorter time lines, yet higher hurdles: Mexican families' access to child welfare mandated services. *Children and Youth Services Review, 31,* 609–616.

Beauvais, F., & Trimble, J. E. (1992). The role of the researcher in evaluating American-Indian alcohol and other drug abuse prevention programs. In OSAP, *Cultural competence for evaluators* (pp. 173–202).Washington, DC: U.S. Department of Health and Human Services.

Bergen, H. A., & Ezzy, D. (2009). Mass media and religious identity: A case study of young witches. *Journal of the Scientific Study of Religion, 48,* 501–514.

Blum, E., Heinonen, T., & White, J. (2010). Participatory action research studies. In B. Thyer (Ed.), *The handbook of social work research methods* (2nd ed., pp. 449–465). Thousand Oaks, CA: Sage Publications, Inc.

Brown, C. G., Weber, S., & Ali, S. (2008). Women's body talk: A feminist narrative approach. *Journal of Systemic Therapies, 27*(2), 92–104.

Butler, J. P. (1992). Of kindred minds: The ties that bind. In OSAP, *Cultural competence for evaluators* (pp. 23–54). Washington, DC: U.S. Department of Health and Human Services.

Dwairy, M., Achoui, M., Filus, A., Rezvannia, P., Casullo, M. M., & Vohra, N. (2010). Parenting, mental health, and culture: A fifth cross-cultural research on parenting and psychological adjustment of children. *Journal of Child and Family Studies, 19*, 36–41.

Gagne, P. (1992). Appalachian women: Violence and social control. *Journal of Contemporary Ethnography, 20*, 387–415.

Garcia, A. C., Standlee, A. I., Bechkoff, J., & Cui, Y. (2009). Ethnographic approaches to the internet and computer mediated communication. *Journal of Contemporary Ethnography, 38*, 52–84.

Goodson-Lawes, J. (1994). Ethnicity and poverty as research variables: Family studies with Mexican and Vietnamese newcomers. In E. Sherman & W. J. Reid (Eds.), *Qualitative research in social work* (pp. 21–31). New York: Columbia University Press.

Haight, W. L. (2002). *African American children at church: A sociocultural perspective.* Cambridge, England: Cambridge University Press.

Happell, B., Moxham, L., Reid-Searl, K., Dwyer, T., Kahl, J., Morris, J., & Wheatland, N. (2009). Promoting mental health care in a rural pediatric unit through participatory action research. *The Australian Journal of Rural Health, 17*, 155–160.

Harding, R., & Hamilton, P. (2009). Working girls: Abuse or choice in street-level sex work? A study of homeless women in Nottingham. *British Journal of Social Work, 39*, 1118–1137.

Harmon, V. (2010). Experiences of racism and the changing nature of White privilege among lone White mothers of mixed parentage children in the UK. *Ethnic and Racial Studies, 33*, 176–194.

Holosko, M. J. (2010. An overview of qualitative research methods. In B. Thyer (Ed.), *The handbook of social work research methods* (pp. 340–354). Thousand Oaks, CA: Sage Publication, Inc.

Kim, S., McLeod, J. H., & Shantzis, C. (1992). Cultural competence for evaluators working with Asian American communities: Some practical considerations. In OSAP, *Cultural competence for evaluators* (pp. 203–260). Washington, DC: U.S. Department of Health and Human Services.

Leenaars, A. A., Sayin, A. Candansayar, S., Leenaars, L., Akar, T., & Demirel, B. (2010). Suicide in different cultures: A thematic comparison of suicide notes from Turkey and the United States. *Journal of Cross-Cultural Psychology, 41*, 253–263.

Lipman, J. J. (2002). A qualitative analysis of women's relational and sexual functioning following date rape. *Dissertation Abstracts International: Section B: Sciences and Engineering, 63*, 1567.

Lowery, C. T. (2010). Ethnographic research methods. In B. Thyer (Ed.), *The handbook of social work research methods* (2nd ed., pp. 435–448). Thousand Oaks, CA: Sage Publications, Inc.

Malson, H., & Burns, M. (2009). *Critical feminist approaches to eating disorders.* New York: Routledge.

Marin, G., & Marin, B. (1991). *Research with Hispanic populations.* Newbury Park, CA: Sage Publications, Inc.

Reid, A. H. (2009). The garden of eves: Non-kin social support among low-income African American single mothers in a public housing community. *Dissertations Abstracts International: Section B: Sciences and Engineering, 70*, 3830.

Reinharz, S. (1992). *Feminist methods in social research.* New York: Oxford University Press.

Shek, D. T. L., Tang, V. M. Y., & Han, X. Y. (2005). Evaluation of evaluation studies using qualitative research Methods in the social work literature (1990–2003): Evidence that constitutes a wake-up call. *Research on Social Work Practice, 15*, 180–194.

Smith, V. (2009). Ethical and effective ethnographic research methods: A case study with Afghan refugees in California. *Journal of Empirical Research on Human Research Ethics, 4*, 59–72.

Takahashi, Y., Ushida, C., Miyaki, K., Sakai, M., Shimbo, T., & Nakayama, T. (2009). Potential benefits and harms of a peer support social network service on the internet for people with depressive tendencies: Qualitative content analysis and social network analysis. *Journal of Medical Internet Research, 11*, 1–14.

Taylor, L. (1998). Parents who lost an adult child to AIDS. In A. Godenzi (Ed.), *Abenteuer forschung* (pp. 189–258). Freiburg, Switzerland, University of Freiburg.

Trinidad, A. M. O. (2009). Toward kuleana (responsibility): A case study of a contextually grounded intervention for Native Hawaiian youth and young adults. *Aggression and Violent Behavior, 14*, 488–498.

Van de Vijver, F., & Leung, K. (1997). *Methods and data analysis for cross-cultural research.* Thousand Oaks, CA: Sage Publications, Inc.

Van der Velde, J., Williamson, D. L., & Ogilvie, L. D. (2009). Participatory action research: Practical strategies for actively engaging and maintaining participation in immigrant and refugee communities. *Qualitative Health Research, 19*, 1293–1302.

Weinbach, R. (1989). Sudden death and secret survivors: Helping those who grieve alone. *Social Work, 34*, 57–60.

Chapter 9

Cohen, J. (1988). *Statistical power analysis for the behavioral sciences* (2nd ed.). New York: Lawrence Erlbaum Associates.

Levy, P., & Lemeshow, S. (1999). *Sampling of populations: Methods and applications.* New York: Wiley-Interscience Publishing. Wiley Series in Survey Methodology.

Rosenthal, J. (2001). *Statistics and data interpretation for the helping professions.* Belmont, CA: Wadsworth/Thomson Learning.

Rubin, A., & Babbie, E. (2007). *Essential research methods for social work.* Belmont, CA: Thomson Brooks/Cole.

Thompson, S. (2002). *Sampling* (2nd ed.). New York: Wiley-Interscience Publishing.

Weinbach, R., & Grinnell, R., Jr. (2010). *Statistics for social workers* (8th ed.). Boston: Allyn & Bacon.

Chapter 10

Cervantes, R. C., Padilla, A. M., & Salgado de Snyder, N. (1991). The Hispanic Stress Inventory: A culturally relevant approach to psychosocial assessment. *Psychological Assessment, 3*, 438–447.

Constantino, G., Malgady, R. G., & Rogler, L. H. (1988). *TEMAS Tell-Me-a-Story.* Los Angeles, CA: Western Psychological Services.

Cuellar, I., Arnold, B., & Maldonado, R. (1995). Acculturation Rating Scale for Mexican Americans-II: A revision of the original ARSMA scale. *Hispanic Journal of Behavioral Sciences, 17*, 275–304.

Fischer, J., & Corcoran, K. (2007). *Measures for clinical practice and research* (4th ed.; 2 vols.). New York: Oxford University Press.

Gloria, A. M., & Robinson-Kurpius, S. E. (1996). The validation of the Cultural Congruity Scale and the University Environment Scale with Chicano/a students. *Hispanic Journal of Behavioral Sciences, 18*, 533–549.

Hudson, W. (1988). *CAS: The clinical assessment system.* Tallahassee, FL: WALMYR.

Neuman, W. L. (1997). *Social research methods: Qualitative and quantitative approaches* (3rd ed.). Boston: Allyn & Bacon.

Phinney, J.S. (1992). The Multigroup Ethnic Identity Measure. *Journal of Adolescent Research, 7*, 156–176.

Rubin, A., & Babbie, E. (2011). *Research methods for social work* (7th ed.). Belmont, CA: Brooks/Cole, Cengage Learning.

Chapter 11

Butler, J. P. (1992). Of kindred minds: The ties that bind. In OSAP, *Cultural competence for evaluators* (pp. 23–54). Washington, DC: U.S. Department of Health and Human Services.

Clark, M. M., & Bearman, P. (ongoing). *The September 11th, 2001 oral history narrative and memory project.* Columbia University Oral History Research Office. Retrieved from www.columbia.edu/cu/lweb/indiv/oral/sept11.html.

Hager, M.A., Wilson, S., Pollak, T.H., & Rooney, P.M. (2003). Response rates for mail surveys of nonprofit organizations: A review and empirical test. *Nonprofit and Voluntary Sector Quarterly, 32*, 252–267.

Hutson, R. A., & Kolbe, A. R. (2010). Survey studies. In B. Thyer (Ed.), *The handbook of social work research methods* (pp. 131–148). Thousand Oaks, CA: Sage Publications, Inc.

Logan, S. (2007). *In their own voices.* (*10 voices: Ten African American women who made a difference*). Columbia, SC: University of South Carolina College of Social Work.

Marin, G., & Marin, B. (1991). *Research with Hispanic populations.* Newbury Park, CA: Sage Publications, Inc.

Martin, R. (1995). *Oral history in social work: Research, assessment, and intervention.* Thousand Oaks, CA: Sage Publications, Inc.

McQueen, A. (2000, August 29). Students humiliated by hazing. *The State,* p. A1.

Mokuau, N., & Browne, C. (1994). Life themes of native Hawaiian female elders: Resources for cultural preservation. *Social Work, 39*, 43–49.

Paxson, M.C., Dillman, D.A., Tarnai, J. (1995). Improving response to business mail surveys. In B.G. Cox, D.A. Binder, B.N. Chinnappa, A. Christianson, M.J. Colledge, & P.S. Kott (Eds.), *Business survey methods* (pp. 303–315). New York: Wiley-Interscience.

Risley-Curtiss, C., Holley, L., & Wolf, S. (2006). The animal–human bond and ethnic diversity. *Social Work, 51,* 257–268.

Rubin, A., & Babie, E. R. (2011). *Research methods for social work* (7th ed.). Belmont, CA: Brooks/Cole Publishing.

Sales, E., Lichtenwalter, S., & Fevola, A. (2006). Secondary analysis in social work research education: Past, present, and future promise. *Journal of Social Work Education, 42*, 543–558.

Trei, L. (2006, September 27). Social science researcher to overhaul survey methodology with $2 million grant. *Stanford Education News.*

Chapter 12

Bogardus, E. S. (1947). Measurement of personal-group relations. *Sociometry, 10*, 306–311.

Fischer, J., & Corcoran, K. (2007). *Measures for clinical practice: A sourcebook* (4th ed.; 2 vols.). New York: Oxford University Press.

Miller, D. (1991). *Handbook of research and social measurement.* Newbury Park, CA: Sage Publications.

Nunnally, J., & Bernstein, I. (1994). *Psychometric theory.* New York: McGraw-Hill.

Westhuis, D., & Thyer, B. A. (1989). Development and validation of the *Clinical Anxiety Scale:* A rapid assessment instrument for empirical practice. *Educational and Psychological Measurement, 49*, 153–163.

Chapter 13

Auerbach, C. F., & Silverstein, L. B. (2003). *Qualitative data: An introduction to coding and analysis.* New York: New York University Press.

Bryman, A., & Cramer, D. (2005). *Quantitative data analysis with SPSS 12 and 13: A guide for social scientists.* New York: Routledge.

Cramer, D. (2007). *Quantitative data analysis with Minitab.* New York: Routledge.

Fielding, N., & Lee, R. (1998). *Computer analysis and qualitative research.* Thousand Oaks, CA: Sage Publications, Inc.

Gahan, C., & Hannibal, M. (1998). *Doing qualitative research using QSR NUD*IST.* Thousand Oaks, CA: Sage Publications, Inc.

Greasley, P. (2008). *Quantitative data analysis with SPSS: An introduction for health and social science.* New York: Open University Press.

Kuckartz, U. (2004). *An introduction to the computer analysis of qualitative data.* Thousand Oaks, CA: Sage Publications, Inc.

Marshall, C., & Rossman, G. B. (2011). *Designing qualitative research* (5th ed.). Thousand Oaks, CA: Sage Publications, Inc.

Norusis, M. (2003). *SPSS 12.0 Statistical procedures companion.* Englewood Cliffs, NJ: Prentice Hall.

Patton, M. (2001). *Qualitative research and evaluation methods.* Thousand Oaks, CA: Sage Publications.

Sudham, S. (1976). *Applied sampling.* New York: Academic Press.

Warren, C.A.B., & Karner, T.X. (2009). *Discovering qualitative methods: Field research, interviews, and analysis* (2nd ed.). New York: Oxford University Press.

Weinbach, R., & Grinnell, R., Jr. (2007). *Statistics for social workers.* Boston: Allyn & Bacon.

Weitzman, E. A., & Miles, M. B. (1995). *Computer programs for qualitative data analysis: A software sourcebook.* Thousand Oaks, CA: Sage Publications, Inc.

Chapter 14

American Psychological Association. (2009). *Publication manual of the American Psychological Association* (6th ed.). Washington, DC: Author.

Beebe, L. (1993). *Professional writing for the human services.* Washington, DC: NASW Press.

Houghton, P. M., & Houghton, T. J. (2009). *APA: The easy way!* (2nd ed.). Flint, MI: Baker College.

Louden-Gerber, G.M. (2009). A group forgiveness intervention for adult male homeless individuals: Effects on forgiveness, rumination, and social connectedness. *Dissertation Abstracts International Section A: Humanities and Social Sciences, 69,* 4640.

NASW Press. (2009). *An author's guide to social work journals* (5th ed.). Washington, DC: NASW Press.

Pyrczak, F., & Bruce, R. (2007). *Writing research reports.* Glendale, CA: Pyrczak Publishing.

Rossiter, J. (2009). *The APA pocket handbook: Rules for format and documentation.* London: Daryl Willcox Publishing Company.

Szuchman, L. T., & Thomlison, B. (2010). *Writing with style: APA style for social work* (4th ed.). Belmont, CA: Brooks/Cole.

Thyer, B. A. (2008). *Preparing research articles.* New York: Oxford University Press.

Photo Credits

Chapter 1:
Feng Yu/istockphoto, p. 1; Kevin Russ/istockphoto, p. 13

Chapter 2:
Sean Locke/istockphoto, p. 28; Alina555/istockphoto, p. 37

Chapter 3:
Bryan Myhr/istockphoto, p. 54; Jason Stitt/istockphoto, p. 69

Chapter 4:
Christopher Futcher/istockphoto, p. 73; Paul Hart/istockphoto, p. 86

Chapter 5:
Ahmad Hamoudah/istockphoto, p. 100; Jeanell Norvell/istockphoto, p. 111

Chapter 6:
Atno Ydur/istockphoto, p. 119; Juanmonino/istockphoto, p. 129

Chapter 7:
Alex Raths/istockphoto, p. 147; Yarinca/istockphoto, p. 163

Chapter 8:
Lisafx/istockphoto, p. 176; izusek/istockphoto, p. 189

Chapter 9:
CE Futcher/istockphoto, 193; wdstock/istockphoto, 207

Chapter 10:
Digicanon/istockphoto, p. 214; Jodi Jacobson/istockphoto, 224

Chapter 11:
Tomm L/istockphoto, p. 237; sdominick/istockphoto, p. 263

Chapter 12:
Kasayizgi/istockphoto, p. 268; stevecoleccs/istockphoto, p. 289

Chapter 13:
Cimmerian/istockphoto, p. 292; Goldmund/istockphoto, 304

Chapter 14:
Shironosov/istockphoto, p. 309; pixdeluxe/istockphoto, p. 316

Index

MySocialWorkLab will help you develop the skills you'll need as a professional social worker.

Features include:

- **NEW! Hundreds of assessment questions**—multiple choice, case vignette scenarios and reflective essay—to help you monitor your progress in mastering the skills you will need as a social worker. And, they are written in a similar format as you will find on the licensing exam.

- Complete **eText** with audio files and **chapter tests**

- **Numerous videos** of real scenarios that you are likely to encounter as a social worker.

- **75 case studies** to help you apply theory to practice

- A **Gradebook** that allows you to monitor your progress on all assessment questions on the site

- **MySearchLab**—a collection of tools that help you master research assignments and papers

- And much more!

If your text did not come packaged with MySocialWorkLab, you can purchase access at: www.MySocialWorkLab.com

A workbook that helps you master the skills you will need to be successful in your courses . . . and beyond.

Containing many questions written in a similar format as on the licensing exam, **Connecting Core Competencies: A Workbook for Social Work Students** includes 300+ assessment questions.

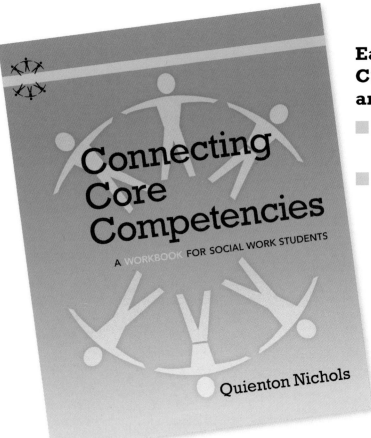

Each chapter covers one of CSWE's 10 core competencies and includes:

- A detailed explanation of the competency
- Assessment questions that help you master the skills in the competency with multiple choice, short case vignette, and reflective essay questions.

Students: If your text did not come bundled with this printed workbook, you can purchase it at:
www.mypearsonstore.com